McCulloch of Ohio

McCulloch of Ohio
For the Republic

by Mark Bernstein

Crown Equipment Corporation
2014

Published by Crown Equipment Corporation, New Bremen, Ohio

ISBN 978-0-692-20436-8

Library of Congress Control Number 2014938641

printed in Korea by Graphics International

jacket design: David Battle

text formatting, editing: Jane Baker

Photo Credits

From the Ohio Congressional Archives, Ohio State University:
front cover; page 5 (newspaper clipping); page 6, top, crowd scene;
page 7, top, the picketers.
All others are from the McCulloch family

to William Chappelle and Charles Greenberg

Contents

Acknowledgments

The author's task was both brightened and eased by members of the McCulloch family, the congressman's daughters, Nancy McCulloch and Ann Carver and son-in-law David Carver, who were generous with their memories, their reflections, and their wit. Much information was drawn from archives. Principal of these was the Ohio Congressional Archives at Ohio State University in Columbus, which houses the William M. McCulloch Papers and whose archivist Jeffrey Thomas was never at a loss for an answer or short on aid. Much material on William McCulloch's career in the Ohio legislature is from the Ohio Historical Society, with the always competent assistance of head archivist Thomas Reider and his staff. My thanks also go to Alan Miller, president of *Gongwer*, for providing access to the files of that legislative newsletter. Microfilm copies of the *Florida Times-Union* were available from the Library of Congress. Among individuals, Mary Kay Mabe, as on earlier projects, was proficient and precise in tracking down records of McCulloch's legislature career, newspaper clippings, and the like. Guy Stallman of Holmes County, Ohio, provided the writer with a driving tour of Congressman McCulloch's birthplace and environs. Yvonne Johnson, a genealogist in Jacksonville, Florida, truly startled the author by ascertaining where William McCulloch lived and worked during his time in that city. James Oda, Piqua librarian and historian, provided much engaging material about Piqua and its congressman. Barbara Whalen, the surviving author of that unmatched text on the 1964 Civil Rights Act, *The Longest Debate*, supplied background information and the important urging that I track down Robert Kimball, who proved invaluable. As the reader will learn, Kimball was at the core of the negotiations that produced the contents of the 1964 Civil Rights Act and was an observer/participant in many related events. He supplied all manner of fact, detail, and texture, offered advice on portions of the manuscript and general encouragement to its author. Most encouragement and the most intelligent soundingboard came, as it has before, from Susan Drake Swift.

CHAPTER 1

Mr. Marshall to Piqua

Not until David Carver's father-in-law asked him to pick up Burke Marshall at the Dayton, Ohio, airport did Carver realize that his fairly recently acquired relative was a man of considerable consequence. The request came in the fading days of June 1963. Burke Marshall was then assistant U.S. attorney general for civil rights, among the best of the very bright, very determined Ivy Leaguers with whom Attorney General Robert Kennedy had staffed his Department of Justice.

Carver's father-in-law, from whom the request originated, was William Moore McCulloch. McCulloch was, first, a long-time resident of Piqua, Ohio; second, the nine-term Republican congressman from Ohio's Fourth Congressional District; and third and foremost, the ranking Republican member of the House Judiciary Committee. President John Kennedy was then about to release his administration's proposals on civil rights, easily the most emotive issue of the day. These proposals would start their legislative journey in the Judiciary Committee. Marshall had been dispatched to Ohio—his first time in the state—to ask McCulloch to refrain from public comment on the Kennedy civil rights package until he and administration representatives had had the chance to sit down to discuss them in detail.

Unbeknownst to Marshall, McCulloch had an agenda of his own. His first move was to suggest to his son-in-law that it would be helpful if the visiting Justice Department official had to "cool his heels" for a few hours before meeting with the congressman. With Marshall safely seated in Carver's Chevy Impala, Carver told him that his father-in-law was busy addressing a luncheon meeting of the Piqua Rotarians. Marshall and McCulloch could meet at two o'clock. In the meanwhile, Carver suggested they lunch at the local country club whose restaurant looked out over the golf course.

Carver described Marshall as "a perfect gentleman." Nonetheless, somewhat intimidated by his high-ranking, highly polished guest, Carver did his stuttering best to make small talk over lunch. Lunch ended before two, so Carver gave the visitor a driving tour of Piqua. At one point, Marshall spotted a hardware store and, asking Carver to pull over, said, "I have to buy some nails." Marshall got out, entered the store, and soon emerged with a small brown bag of finishing nails, whose intended use Carver never learned. That errand completed, Carver dropped his charge on the north side of the Piqua National Bank, whose second floor housed the offices of McCulloch, Felger, Fite & Gutmann.

By one author's description, "The Congressman's office was a pleasant place overlooking the town square. The room belonged to a man of refined but spartan tastes; wood paneling, well-worn law books, comfortable leather chairs, and wall plaques that honored him for one reason or another." McCulloch was not physically impressive. At five foot seven, he had receding once-red hair and a thin moustache. Characteristically, he was dressed in gray pants and a blue blazer, with a sharpened No. 2 yellow pencil in his vest pocket. His voice was soft, and his face bore an expression of private bemusement.

Outwardly, Marshall and McCulloch were opposites. Marshall was eastern, pedigreed, a graduate of the exclusive Phillips-Exeter Academy in New Hampshire, and a holder of both undergraduate and law degrees from Yale University. McCulloch was midwestern, born and raised in a town too small to appear on most maps, and an alumnus of the College of Wooster and the Ohio State University School of Law. A long-time Washington correspondent, Andrew Glass, suggested that despite their differing backgrounds, the two had important characteristics in common: "Both were lawyers, reticent by nature. Both were always looking at how to get to 'Yes.' Pragmatic; morally honest; interested in results." Both, he added, believed that most things in life were achieved by the simple act of putting one foot in front of the other.

McCulloch, as noted, was the ranking Republican member of the House Judiciary Committee. GOP congressional policy at this time was that the ranking member of any committee was the party's lead spokesperson on matters that fell within that committee's jurisdiction, as civil rights fell within Judiciary. While no explanation for the number ever emerged, the general thinking in Washington was that, where civil rights legislation was concerned, sixty House Republicans would support whatever position McCulloch took.

In conversation, McCulloch was far likelier to be the listener than the speaker. Once conversational pleasantries were accomplished with Burke Marshall, however, McCulloch took the lead. He noted that in 1957 and 1960, the House of Representatives had passed strong civil rights bills. Each had been greatly watered down in the Senate to avoid provoking a filibuster by southern senators, which it was feared would kill the bills entirely. Both bills, McCulloch noted, had passed the House with overwhelming Republican support. For many rural Republicans, civil rights was a tough vote to cast. Generally, they had no great number of African-American constituents or white constituents who placed civil rights high on their list of concerns. As much as anything, Republican votes for civil rights were "conscience votes," casting out a lingering sense that they were members of the Party of Lincoln. McCulloch suggested to Marshall that House Republicans, himself included, had twice been led up the hill only to be tossed to the Dixie-accented lions on the Senate side. McCulloch had no interest in this happening again.

In his assessment of administrative intentions, McCulloch was entirely correct. As Deputy Attorney General Nicholas Katzenbach later acknowledged, both the Kennedy administration and the stronger civil rights advocates in Congress did indeed intend such a course: they would load up a civil rights bill in the House, and then trade it down in the Senate in exchange for whatever they could get.

McCulloch, however, told Marshall his own support for the Kennedy civil rights package turned on two conditions. First, nothing in the House version of the bill would be altered in the Senate without McCulloch's express approval. Second, should the bill pass, President Kennedy would give political credit to both parties. If the Senate passed a version different from that approved by the House, then by standard procedure a joint House-Senate conference committee would attempt to iron out the differences. Should this happen, McCulloch said, he would withdraw his own support from the bill. Likely sixty Republicans would follow McCulloch's lead and do likewise. Given that no support could be expected from the southern Democrats in Congress, no civil rights bill could pass the House without substantial Republican support. In short, McCulloch was threatening to kill the bill.

Marshall may or may not have grasped McCulloch's underlying perspective. Some civil rights supporters regarded the acts of 1957 and 1960 to be definite, if small, steps forward. McCulloch did not consider these acts to be half a loaf; rather, he thought they barely qualified as a crust. His view was that any civil rights bill whose provisions did not prompt a Senate filibuster was not really worth passing. It was time, he felt, not to avoid a filibuster, but to provoke one. And, having provoked one, to break it.

McCulloch's approach had only one problem. At the time he stated his position, no one in the Kennedy administration—indeed, virtually no one in political Washington—believed that a southern filibuster of a civil rights bill could be broken.

CHAPTER 2

An Ohio Farm

In the late nineteenth century, James McCulloch would stand each day on the porch of his farmstead to await delivery of the Cleveland *Plain Dealer*. McCulloch was the only resident of Holmesville, Ohio, to receive the newspaper, published seventy-five largely flat miles to the north. In the words of one local historian, he was "an individual interested in things of the world."

In that interest, James McCulloch may have been influenced by his father, George McCulloch. George was among the township's first inhabitants, believed to be the first male settler born in the Holmesville area. His own father, Hugh McCulloch, reached the area in 1811, cleared a patch of land, and planted a crop of rye. George McCulloch was in his maturity when the question of slavery started to nudge the nation toward disunion and war. Personally, he was an anti-slavery man who in the mid-1850s led his family into the Republican Party, from which it never strayed.

By the mid-1850s, Holmes County claimed 20,000 inhabitants, most of whom were farmers, with a sprinkling of craftsmen who forged and joined the tools farmers required. The local soils were varied, good for hay, oats, and corn, much of it fed to cattle or dairy cows. The land was peaceful; the times were not. Holmesville was one of the paths that made up the interlocking routes of the of the Underground Railroad, which ran to near Millersburg, the county seat, then five miles to Holmesville, and another dozen to Wooster. One Holmes County farmer, Ebenezer Bigham, is said to have aided 200 slaves in making their escape in the two decades preceding the Civil War. On another occasion, twenty escaped slaves were making a brief layover at the Hutchinson farm northeast of Holmesville when word came that slave hunters were en route. Departure was rapid. When the pursuers arrived, the Hutchinsons tried to slow them down with an offer of breakfast. Offer refused, the family insisted the slave hunters must wait so that their sudden departure did not interrupt the reading of the morning psalm. To this, the pursuers could only decently accede; the family trotted out a psalm 119 verses in length and read it in full while the slaves made good their escape. Such work was not without its risks: Wilbur Siebert's *Mysteries of Ohio Underground Railroads* reports that those aiding runaways could be fined $1,000 and be jailed for six months.

Risk was not lessened by the fact that, in Holmes County, Republicans who opposed slavery were outnumbered by Democrats who were prepared to ignore or to tacitly support it. Democrats found their voice in the *Holmes County Farmer*. As stated by one source, "During the Civil War, editorials revealed an overall lack of support for the Union cause in the county. To the many French, German, and Swiss immigrants, the war reminded them of the enforced military service, governmental repression, and violent European nationalism of the early nineteenth century that they had come to America to escape." The case for "Lincoln and Liberty" was made by the *Holmes County Republican*, founded in 1856. In his book on his hometown, David Stallman wrote that according to one source, the rival papers "engaged in ferocious political rancor" throughout the Civil War. The book *Mennonites, Amish, and the American Civil War* reports:

The more extreme language came from the *Farmer*, which pressed the Midwestern Democratic line of Ohio party leader Clement L. Vallandigham, denouncing Lincoln's handling of the war and using vicious racial slurs and blatantly anti-African American editorializing against abolitionists. When only one person in German Township and Walnut Creek Township dared vote Republican in the fall of 1862, the *Farmer* dismissed the first as illiterate and the other as "an abolition preacher."

James McCulloch—the third generation to live in the township and the son of the man "interested in things of the world"—was likewise a farmer, with perhaps 150 solid acres on which to plant a family. In 1887, he married Ida Moore, a local girl. They built a fair-sized, one-and-one-half story, wood-frame house on Vermillion Street, a short mile due north of Holmesville. The farmhouse was heated by an old-fashioned wood-burning stove. In that house, the couple raised five children: four daughters—Mildred, Elva, Stella, and Helen—who unabashedly doted on the family's only son, William M. McCulloch, born November 24, 1901. Much later, William McCulloch's elder daughter, Nancy, came across a family photo and noted, "Daddy was the fair-haired child; he was really little sitting on the floor. He had four sisters; they worshipped the ground he walked on." His younger daughter, Ann, recalled, "My father's father kept a farm that was immaculate; never any fallen trees. My father absorbed that." Playing up the family's Republican roots, James McCulloch claimed that William's middle name was McKinley, the recently assassinated Ohio-born president. Ida would correct her husband: their sole son's middle name was her maiden name, Moore.

Holmesville was one of the hundreds of dots one can count on a map of the Buckeye State. The town was laid out by Peter Painter in 1854. The railroad reached town in 1895 when the Baltimore and Ohio built a branch line; a two-room high school was completed in 1896 at a cost of $2,767; sidewalks were added in 1904. Law and order in Holmesville kept up with the times. On May 23, 1908, a local court fined Robert Flack because he "did unlawfully fail, neglect and refuse to remove manure and other filth from the alley in the area of his residence for more than 24 hours after being directed to do so." On August 24, 1912, Virgil Sterling was fined one dollar plus costs for driving a horse through town "unlawfully, willfully, carelessly and in a dangerous manner." Two years later, on September 14, 1914, Clyde C. Ballaugh was fined a dollar because "between the hours of sunset and sunrise" he drove "a motor vehicle of the Ford Type without displaying any rear red light or white light" on said motor vehicle. The following year, Holmesville got electricity.

The town had a snippet of industry. A local sawmill produced blanks which, shipped to Kentucky, emerged as "Louisville Slugger" baseball bats. The town boasted three saloons, two restaurants, a hotel, one physician (Dr. Edgar Cole), five teamsters, three carpenters, two blacksmiths, a wagon maker, a grain and feed dealer, two painters and decorators, a stone mason, a watch repair shop, one baker, one meat market, a shoe repair shop, and one "tonsorial artist." Characteristic of Ohio's small towns, Holmesville was Protestant, chiefly Presbyterian and Methodist. Uncharacteristically, for many years the two denominations shared the same Sunday service: Presbyterians sat on the right, Methodists on the left. After two years, the minister would be replaced by one of the competing faith.

When William McCulloch was born in 1901 and in the dozen years thereafter, the family farm knew the limits of the times. There was, of course, no gasoline tractor, or electric anything, nor were there yet hybrid seed, reliable weather forecasts, crop insurance, or price supports. Cows were milked before dawn. Corn was husked in December fields by chapped hands. Wood was split and carried to the stove. One Ohio farmboy, a contemporary of McCulloch, outlined the two hours of chores he did each morning before heading to school: Pigs to be slopped. Eggs to be collected. Hoeing and weeding. Asked which task had been his favorite, his face went blank as he answered, "Why, none of them."

At a time when most adults had perhaps five years of formal schooling, William McCulloch pursued his studies through high school graduation in the local schools. McCulloch graduated shy of his eighteenth birthday with the class of 1918, whose thirty-five members provide a sense of the school's scale.

Small towns have a pull and a security that can be difficult to break. The three eldest McCulloch daughters remained in or near Holmesville. Elva married Clarence Zehnder, Stella married D. J. Hoffman, and Mildred, known as Mim, taught school briefly. She then married an auctioneer named Lecky with whom she ran a good-sized grocery on the north end of town, just where the hill leading down from the family farm met the village. The youngest, Helen, was the only one to leave the area. She married a man named David McCabe and became a nurse in Coshocton, Ohio.

Bill McCulloch never lost his affinity for the farm. In the 1930s, he and his elder daughter would go out and walk the farm, sit on the gravestones, and talk to the animals. McCulloch was stamped by his farm upbringing. Physically, he grew up wiry. At age eighteen his bare 110 pounds made him look if anything shorter than his five-foot seven-inch frame. Farm life provided discipline, and the uncertainties that accompanied each year's crops left him with a deep distaste for debt. And for waste. Through his adult life, he was something of a hoarder—of paper clips, rubber bands, pencils—and somewhat tight with a dollar.

Still, he was son of James McCulloch, who waited daily on the Cleveland *Plain Dealer* out of an interest in the world that lay beyond the cornrow. Of the McCulloch children, William was the only one who would seek the larger world. His first step—actually, a large one, for someone who had only rarely set foot outside Holmes County—was to enroll in the College of Wooster. The school, located in Wooster, Ohio, was all of twelve miles north of the home in which he had been raised. His transition from farm boy to college man was not complete, however: when he arrived for classes, he still wore short trousers.

CHAPTER 3

An Ohio Education

William McCulloch was never particularly given to explaining himself or his actions. His reason, he said, was that if he spoke about doing something, he sometimes imagined he had already done it. This reticence was true in both his public and private lives. Later, when he was serving in Congress, his daughters both reported that he never discussed at dinner what had happened that day on Capitol Hill. Of more personal matters, he never told his daughters why he had chosen to become a lawyer or to pursue public life. Due to this, the facts of McCulloch's education fall somewhat thin on the ground.

The bare bones are that William McCulloch enrolled in the College of Wooster in fall 1920. When McCulloch entered, the institution was both reputable and improving. Entrance requirements had been raised: only those graduating in the top two-thirds of a "first-class" high school were accepted. (Indeed, one student in attendance during McCulloch's years—Earl M. Donbar—was later named a Rhodes Scholar.) Higher grading standards had been established. The college had received a $250,000 challenge grant from the Rockefeller General Education Board, an enormously influential body that aimed to strengthen institutions that had potential, while letting weaker ones fall as they may. The school had a well-laid-out campus of fourteen buildings, a faculty of forty-two, and a football team that struck terror in its opponents. Indeed, no visiting squad crossed the Wooster goal line from 1916 to 1921; the following year—McCulloch's second—Wooster outscored opponents 177-3, recording eight straight shutouts before yielding a field goal in the year's final contest.

McCulloch spent two years at the school. Between those years, he worked on a Holmes County farm to help with tuition. The one hundred dollars a month he received for his services was a high figure for the time and likely a tribute to his industriousness. McCulloch entered with a freshman class of 316, fully two-fifths of the school's enrollment of 710.

Preceding classes had been diminished by U.S. participation in the First World War.

The war marked a cultural turning point. Prior to the conflict, those of German descent—including a fair contingent of the Wooster enrollment—felt considerable allegiance to the fatherland. As war beckoned, that allegiance was set aside. Before U.S. entry, a group of boys broke into the German language classroom, took down the portrait of Kaiser Wilhelm II, and beheaded it. Next, the German Department was closed. Following U. S. entry to the war in April 1917, 207 staff and students enlisted in the military. Post-war, the institution found virtue in its small size. Waldo H. Small, an alumnus writing in the *Wooster Quarterly*, urged that Wooster not grow beyond 800 students: "Our country needs at the present more colleges content to remain small . . . eager to increase the *quality* of human product that goes forth from their halls."

McCulloch declared a major in political science. This was the likeliest preparation for law school if that was already his intention. It was also the major that would bring him into contact with the school's most esteemed faculty member, Professor William Estabrook Chancellor, who headed the Political Science Department. Chancellor, who held an 1894 degree from the Harvard University School of Law, was among the sprinkling of Wooster faculty with credentials from name institutions. He had served as superintendent of schools of Washington D.C., and had written forty books—half were on school teaching and administration; half were biographies of American presidents or other prominent public figures. However, several months after McCulloch arrived at Wooster, Chancellor was engaged in a controversy, racial in nature, which drew unwanted national attention to the college.

Undertaking a research trip, Chancellor stopped in Marion, Ohio, home of 1920 Republican presidential nominee Warren Gamaliel Harding. There, he encountered the longstanding local rumor that Harding's ancestry was partly African American. Chancellor embraced the story. Indeed, he embroidered it to the unlikely conclusion that Harding's candidacy was a first step toward African American domination of the country. Chancellor published his views, with the intention of dissuading "white Americans" from voting for Harding. Soon, thousands of pamphlets restating his premise in somewhat less academic terms began circulating. A quarter-million were mailed from San Francisco alone. The circulars cited Chancellor as the author and his post at the College of Wooster as his credential. Though Chancellor foreswore all association with the matter, the College of Wooster Board of Trustees decided that discretion was the better part of academic freedom. Chancellor was dismissed on October 29, 1920, just four days before Americans provided Harding with a landslide election over Democratic nominee James Cox.

Judging by the faces in the yearbook, the College of Wooster was an all-white institution during McCulloch's years there. Apparently, this was not by policy. An African American, Clarence Allen, graduated with the class of 1892. A campus publication noted that other black students had attended, though few. Black America was occasionally acknowledged during McCulloch's time on campus. The school's Congressional Club invited a speaker on "the price, the purpose, the path and the power of true greatness" as exemplified by the lives of "Two Washingtons"—George Washington and Booker T. Washington, president of the all-black Tuskegee Institute and America's most prominent African American. On May 3, 1922, the school hosted a concert by the Jubilee Singers, a chorale of black students from Lincoln Ridge School in Kentucky, founded when Kentucky outlawed interracial education. A college history reports that the town of Wooster had a "Negro colony [that] was small, self-respecting and respected. Though most of the Negroes lived in the south end of town where they had their own Baptist church and their own minister, a few families lived uptown near the college; nobody had called their presence there in question." The history writer was perhaps at some pains to suggest, "Whatever were Mr. Chancellor's prejudices they were not shared by the college community."

Besides an untouchable football team, Wooster had the characteristic array of student activities—a book club; a literary society; a newspaper; a leadership club; a student senate; physics, math and science clubs; and an organization for future ministers. Plus, it had a debate team, which argued such questions as whether "it would be wise for the U.S. Congress to provide a commission with the power to price and to distribute any article concerning which, in their judgment, there is profiteering." McCulloch likely took little part in extracurricular activities, as he commuted the dozen miles to the family farm to save the added expenses of campus room and board. Still, he did not go unnoticed by his peers. The school yearbook pictured each student along with some distinguishing phrase. Thus, Helen Hutchings was "sweet and smiling." Helen Koppert was "curls." J. Craig McClelland was "the wild Irishman." Albert Kurz was "a real Cavalier." And so on. The description of William M. McCulloch, however, was "Shades of Socrates," suggesting that in his brief stay at the institution McCulloch had demonstrated a notable intellect.

Ohio State School of Law

In the 1920s, the Ohio State University School of Law offered a five-year program leading to a Bachelor of Law degree. That, plus passage of the bar exam, was all the state required of someone wishing to hang out a shingle and practice the trade. In fall 1922, William McCulloch—"having completed two full years at a school of recognized standing"—was admitted to the School of Law with third-year standing. As with other new students, he spent his first few days being examined physically, tested mentally, and submitting to the registrar an intended course of study for the first term. The school had mainstream aims:

The purpose of the College of Law is to impart an accurate knowledge of the principles of the law. To illustrate the application of these principles to the practical affairs of life and to furnish such legal training as will fit students for practice in any part of the country; to teach students both to know and to apply the law.

With its 237,000 inhabitants, Columbus dwarfed any previous place McCulloch had lived. The campus itself lay four miles north-northwest of the Ohio State Capitol, in whose House of Representatives McCulloch later served six terms. While not yet the behemoth it is today, Ohio State University (OSU) was a substantial place. In November 1924, OSU's enrollment of 10,547 made it the seventh largest university in the country. The school was in the midst of a building boom, with eighteen new structures completed in the previous three years. Far and away the most important was the new Ohio Stadium, home of the Buckeyes football team, with its seating for 66,210. Football at Ohio State being what it was, and is, two-thirds of the $1.7 million needed to complete the structure had been raised by voluntary contributions.

When McCulloch arrived the law school enrolled several hundred students and had a teaching staff of seven. Administrative and classroom space and a 22,000-book library were located on OSU's main campus in Page Hall, named for an attorney alumnus who in the 1890s had bequeathed $250,000 to the institution. Even allowing for inflation, OSU was a considerably less expensive proposition at that time than today. Tuition was $105 a year. Beyond that, the school estimated room at $15 a week, board at $7, plus $40 a year for books, all of which with incidental expenses added up to $645 a year. During his final two years, McCulloch lived off campus in the Gamma Eta Gamma fraternity, a national organization for those intending to become lawyers. McCulloch and about thirty fraternity mates lived in a substantial brick house at 187 East Twelfth Street, across North High Street from the main campus.

At least to some extent, McCulloch mixed and mingled. The campus Tertulia Council promoted and coordinated the activities of student clubs. When the Southern Club was established, McCulloch and a fellow student named W. G. Bischoff were its original representatives. By his final year, McCulloch was a member of the Men's Panhellenic Council, which governed campus fraternities. On January 7, 1925, following a report on the recent National Inter-Fraternity Council's convention in New York, the Council voted to "forbid all favors at 'frat' parties." The favors were incidental gifts bestowed on the young women in attendance. The sadly discovered fact was that "most favors find their way to girls' dresser drawers, or similar places, to be forgotten until accidentally found."

Further, "the only reason a great many fraternities gave favors at dances was they believed they could not rate huge socially unless they did." Thirty-eight of the forty-one fraternities present voted for the change. The student newspaper added, "The penalty to be inflicted upon fraternities violating the new ruling and a committee to investigate all violations will be decided upon later." That same meeting ended on a high note for McCulloch. The Panhellenic Council's president declared it time to revise the body's constitution. Responsibility for this task devolved on the council vice-president, Robert S. Watts, while the task of actually doing the work devolved on William M. McCulloch.

Five months later, William McCulloch received his Bachelor of Law degree.

CHAPTER 4

Jacksonville

Diploma in hand, William McCulloch retraced his steps to Holmesville, Ohio. There, he spent the 1925–1926 school year teaching at the small high school from which he had graduated. Whether he was marking time or making plans is unknown. It is known that, a thousand miles to the south, the century's great land rush was unfolding in a manner that would soon fold William McCulloch into its story.

On September 28, 1925—just about the time schoolteacher William McCulloch's classes were settling into a routine—Charles Ponzi arrived in Jacksonville, Florida. His arrival came after an early release from a five-year federal prison sentence for bilking a great many investors of $20 million through a pyramid scheme known to this day as a Ponzi. Jacksonville, whose residents had gone unfleeced in the matter, was prepared to let bygones be bygones. The *Jacksonville Journal* described Ponzi not as a convicted felon, but as "the financial wizard" who had come to the Sunshine State to undertake land development. The newspaper added, "His purpose in coming to Florida, he maintains, is to repay his creditors before he takes one cent of profit for himself." As the saying goes, if you believe that, then there is swampland in Florida you might want to buy. As events soon demonstrated, the swampland existed. And, further, that swampland was being sold under false pretenses by none other than Ponzi, who suffered the indignity of further arrest.

If Jacksonville was credulous of Ponzi's motives, it may be because what was going on in Jacksonville and Florida was itself incredible—the great Florida land boom of the mid-1920s was in full alluring bloom. And, as is the case with bubbles before they burst, a seemingly great number of people were making great deals of money without any apparent effort on their part or much skepticism elsewhere. In November 1925, *The New York Times* subheaded a full-page promotion of the phenomenon "A New Season's Rush to the State is Under Way; the Land Deals Continue, Frenzied as Ever, and Prices are Still Going Up—Some Amazing Tales of Speculators Who Play Parts in the Big Boom."

The Florida Times-Union, published in Jacksonville, almost daily carried bright display ads on the newest commercial and residential developments. One, Venice—on Florida's Gulf Coast and boasting a future casino, tarpon club, golf course, yacht basin, esplanade, imposing railway station, business blocks, and an extensive system of wide boulevards—actually came into being. Many did not. McIntosh, Florida, billed as an alluring vacationland that would attract the lucky by the thousands, did not reach a population of 453 until 2012. As during the great housing boom of 2006 to 2008, few cautionary words were spoken. One Florida real estate expert did urge potential buyers at least to *look* at the land they planned to purchase before signing a deed. Prices, however, continued to soar. The developers of Davis Shores claimed a land sale of $18.7 million in a single day, adding that many who had bought lots at $4,000 a few weeks earlier were now refusing to part with them at $20,000.

Jacksonville, though at the other end of the state from the boom, prospered nonetheless as the gateway to the state, as Florida's leading banking and insurance center, and from the freighter traffic moving in and out of its deepwater port. Growth quickly healed the scars of the city's Great Fire of 1901, which turned 145 blocks, including most of the city center, to ash. In the next dozen years, 13,000 buildings were constructed. Jacksonville spread out and up, with a continuing contest over who could claim the city's tallest structure. In 1909, the 135-foot-high, ten-story Atlantic Place surpassed the 82-foot Dyle Upchurch Building to claim the prize. In 1912, it was eclipsed by the eleven-story Florida Life Building, which enjoyed only a one-year reign before completion the following year of the 180-foot, fifteen-story Heard National Bank Building.

By 1925, the city had nearly quadrupled its 1900 population of 28,429. Both commercial construction and bank clearings doubled from the year before: the former from $719,000 in 1924 to $1.43 million in 1925; the latter, from $7.31 million in 1924 to $14.76 million the following year. Seemingly, everybody was getting in on the act: the Jacksonville Post Office recorded a 51 percent jump in receipts, the highest in the nation. *The Florida Times-Union* promised the best was yet to come. One typical editorial stated: "No matter how 'good' Florida towns and cities and communities are, there is not one that can be called to mind that is satisfied with its state of goodness, but is pressing on, with every intent and purpose, to improve on whatever has already been accomplished. That, it can be said with all of truth, is the prevailing Florida spirit."

An Ohio Boy Heads South

A little less than a year after Charles Ponzi descended on Jacksonville a new resident of considerably less notoriety arrived. He was William Moore McCulloch. There is no certainty as to why McCulloch chose the 850-mile relocation almost exactly due south from Holmesville to Jacksonville. Perhaps, Holmesville was simply a place from which he—at twenty-five, an ambitious young man—needed to escape. Perhaps, as someone who may never have ventured outside the Buckeye State, McCulloch had decided it was time to see something of the world, in particular, one of the world's livelier parts. Whether he saw himself as a potential speculator is doubtful. As a public servant, McCulloch developed a reputation as something of a tightwad: "I am generous," he once said on the floor of Congress, "in all things but money." Still, reluctance to spend money is not the same as hesitancy about making it, so it is not beyond belief that William McCulloch came to Jacksonville in hopes of making his fortune.

His start was modest enough. McCulloch found employment with the law firm of McCollum & Howell as an abstractor, whose task is to draw up and certify brief histories of the ownership of a piece of real estate. Partners Oscar O. McCollum and Charles C. Howell shared quarters in the Graham Building, which, located at 108 West Forsyth Street, was a 180-foot structure that until recently had been the city's tallest building. McCulloch found lodgings with Charles and Mina Shearer at 122 Gilmore; his landlord worked as superintendent of the local Arnold Printing Company. McCulloch's lodgings were less than two miles from his place of employment; likely, he reached work by streetcar.

William McCulloch's time in Jacksonville marked a crucial turning point in his life. It gave him a perspective on life in the South rare among northerners—one carried with him thereafter and, not least, to Congress. Accused by one southern congressman during a 1957 debate as being just one more Yankee ignorant of southern ways, McCulloch had the pleasure of responding, "I lived in one of the great Southern states for approximately four years after I graduated from Ohio State University. And in that great Southern state I made the first money with which I paid the debt that I incurred in going to my state university."

McCulloch's years in the South were revelatory. Prior to arriving in Jacksonville, William McCulloch had only minimal contact with African Americans—Holmesville was all white; the College of Wooster apparently likewise; and McCulloch's law school class at Ohio State University was all-white and all-male. Crucially, however, a dozen sources—family members, colleagues, staff, and journalists—report that McCulloch told them that the period he spent in Florida and the racial intolerance he encountered there fixed him for life as an adamant civil rights liberal.

Here, a literary analogy: Rudyard Kipling asked, "What can he know of England, who only England knows?" The point is that it is difficult to gain perspective on something when one has no point of comparison. There is no argument that Ohio was without racism; but to white Ohioans, such racism was generally just part of how things were. Florida, rather rudely, provided McCulloch with a contrast.

One aspect of McCulloch's education in southern ways would have come to him as a lawyer witnessing the inequities with which laws were enforced. There was, for example, the case of one Charles Brantley. As reported in *The Florida Times-Union*, Brantley was found guilty of stealing $17 from W. H. Rogers; $9 and a watch from Lottie Hunter; a watch, chain, and $1.99 from Elmer Purdy; and a watch, chain, locket, and $6.15 from James Stewart. For these offenses—committed, admittedly, at gunpoint—criminal court judge James Peeler sentenced Brantley to sixty-one years in prison.

In truth, racism is less an event than something carried in the air one breathes. It is carried in a statement by an Ohio woman, describing the social realities of her youth: "In those days, people could just give you a look that said you didn't belong there." Racism, wrote the historian John Hope Franklin, himself a black man, was the "obsession to maintain a government, an economy, an arrangement of the sexes, a relationship of the races, and a social system that had never existed . . . except in the fertile imagination of those who would not confront either the reality that existed or the change that would bring them closer to reality." And like the air one breathed, it went largely unnoticed by those who held to it. As author Jason Sokol wrote, "If they did notice it [segregation], it was in the way they noticed water flowing from a tap or hot weather in the summertime—it was unremarkable."

While Jacksonville drew in thousands, occasionally it drove one off. Most notable, perhaps, was James Weldon Johnson, an African American of compelling talents, born in the city in 1871. A poet, he wrote "Lift Every Voice," which was for some decades considered the "Negro national anthem." A supporter of Theodore Roosevelt, he was rewarded with posts as U.S. consul in Venezuela and Nicaragua. A longtime official of the National Association for the Advancement of Colored People (NAACP), he was the first African American to head that organization. More pertinently, Johnson wrote a novel, *The Autobiography of an Ex-Colored Man*, published a decade before McCulloch reached Jacksonville and partly set in that city.

The book's narrator, though not from Jacksonville, is favorably impressed upon arriving in the city. He notices, "The streets were sandy, but were well-shaded by fine oak trees and far preferable to the clay roads of Atlanta. One or two public squares with green grass and trees gave the city a touch of freshness." Johnson's broader purpose was to explain the racial realities of Jacksonville. These were complicated, first, by the presence of a substantial number of Cubans, many of whom worked at cigar making—an occupation not segregated—and who enjoyed a social status somewhere between whites and blacks. Second, Johnson noted the white horror regarding miscegenation, but added, "Yet, when I was in

Jacksonville, I knew several prominent families there with large colored branches, which went by the same name and were known and acknowledged as blood relatives. And what is more, there seemed to exist between these black brothers and sisters and uncles and aunts a decidedly family feeling." Primarily, however, he was struck by the volume of energy expended by both whites and blacks to avoid transgressing the subtleties of the color line.

It is a struggle; for though the black man fights passively, he nevertheless fights; and his passive resistance is more effective at present than active resistance could possibly be. He bears the fury of the storm as does the willowtree.

It is a struggle; for though the white man of the South may be too proud to admit it, he is, nevertheless, using in the contest his best energies; he is devoting to it the greater part of this endeavor.

He noted that when either blacks or whites gathered in a group, the conversation within an hour was dominated by the "race question." Thus, he concluded, "the South today stands panting and almost breathless from its exertions." But Johnson found a saving grace in those southerners who were often so graceless to his people.

And yet in this respect how perplexing is southern character; for, in opposition to the above, it may be said that the claim of the southern whites that they love the Negro better than the northern whites do, is in a manner true. Northern white people love the Negro in a sort of abstract way, as a race; through a sense of justice, charity and philanthropy, they will liberally assist in his elevation. . . . Yet, generally speaking they have no particular liking for individuals of the race. Southern white people despise the Negro as a race, and will do nothing to aid in his elevation as such, but for certain individuals they have a strong affection.

Nonetheless, Johnson reported how white Jacksonville divided all colored people into three classes. The first were "the desperate"—men, say, who worked in turpentine camps: "These men conform to the requirements of civilization much as a trained lion with low muttered growls goes through his stunts under the crack of the trainer's whip." The second were all those connected to the white world through some form of domestic service—cooking, cleaning, gardening, waiting tables, and other tasks. The third consisted of independent craftsmen, tradesmen, and a sprinkling of professionals—roughly middle class in outlook if not in income. White Jacksonville feared the first, patronized and at times protected the second, and regarded the third as aspiring above their station.

The local press reinforced white fear. Virtually all references to black persons made in *The Florida Times-Union* were associated with crime or violence. Thus, Alex Scarlett, eighteen, is arrested for allegedly having "assaulted a white woman and beat her nearly unconscious." A "negro truck driver" is reported to have fled the scene after running over a seven-year-old boy, who the account reported was not expected to live. A night watchman was struck repeatedly in the head by "a negro armed with a pitchfork." A "negro desperado" shot down a local grocer whose death, following the attack, was "momentarily expected." A white boy, fifteen, was reported as near death after having been shot in a gang fight between white and black youths. All of these were reported in a single month. Further, the *Times-Union* noted that those named had a high propensity for confessing their crimes soon after they were in the hands of the police. The newspaper did not speculate on how such confessions were obtained.

The Hard South

One can speculate with some accuracy what McCulloch may have read or observed of race relations in Jacksonville's Duval County. Jacksonville, it should be noted, was rather more ethnically diverse, more prosperous, and more "forward looking" than many parts of the state. Jacksonville, in a sense, was one of the three Floridas then in existence. The second was the state's southern tip, distracted by the frenzied acquisition of land. Between the two lay a third Florida—a land of endless orange groves and unquestioned white supremacy.

In this third Florida, orange groves combined with timbering to create a labor-intensive economy whose labor was primarily that of blacks employed on such terms as pleased those who employed them. Temperatures and humidity were often high; pay was always low. On occasion, a worker might object to the pay, or object to being required to work on a Sunday after the normal six-day week. Such a worker was often arrested on some pretext, found guilty without benefit of counsel, and fined an amount that by necessity drove him back to picking oranges. (As to the means of southern justice, FBI director J. Edgar Hoover later testified that mistreatment of blacks in police custody in the South was commonplace, noting that in one county "it was seldom that a black man or woman was incarcerated who was not given a severe beating, which started off with a pistol whipping and ended with a rubber hose.")

The orange grove owners had a vested interest in maintaining their underpaid workforce. Generally, they and those with whom they allied exercised an authority that protected their workers from the region's more violent impulses. But not always. Blacks who accepted the subservience of the orange grove were usually left undisturbed by the surrounding white population. But if a black man was alleged to have committed the murder of a white, or—worse—the rape of a white woman, his chances of surviving until trial were not good. Not that the trials were of much use, in any case. In court, the simple word of a southern white woman, unsubstantiated by any evidence, was sufficient to send a black to the state's electric chair. There were, of course, worse fates. Between 1882 and 1930, 266 lynchings of black people occurred in Florida, the most of any single state.

The worst year may have been 1923. In the decade after the Civil War, some recently freed slaves chose to establish all-black towns, rather than live on the margins of white ones. Such communities were the focus of continuing suspicion among the whites who surrounded them. One such settlement was Rosewood, a small town 125 miles southwest of Jacksonville on Florida's Gulf Coast. In late January 1923—while William McCulloch was a law student in Columbus, Ohio—a black man was lynched in Florida for the alleged rape of a white woman. When blacks in Rosewood organized for the defense, several hundred whites began hunting down every black person in the vicinity. Estimates on the number lynched between February 4 and February 7, 1923, range from forty to one hundred.

Thurgood Marshall, head of the NAACP Legal Defense Fund and arguably America's finest courtroom attorney, spent years riding segregated railway cars through the South as counsel for black defendants. He was no stranger to lynching. The image that most stuck in Marshall's mind, Gilbert King wrote in *Devil in the Grove*, was not the photograph of the bullet-ridden body hanging from the limb of a Florida pine tree. "It was the virtually angelic faces of the white children, all of them dressed in their Sunday clothes, as they posed, grinning and smiling, in a semicircle around the dangling corpse." Marshall later only barely escaped lynching himself. In 1948, in Columbia, Tennessee—shortly after McCulloch had entered Congress—Marshall managed the almost unbelievable achievement of securing "not guilty" verdicts from all-white juries for all twenty-five black men charged in a series of related trials. A lynching of Marshall was planned in response to this outrage; he avoided that fate only by a ruse that allowed the future associate justice of the Supreme Court to slip out of town.

William McCulloch was not a man given to confiding. That a rural Ohio conservative Republican was his party's congressional leader on civil rights was cause for more than occasional comment and query. McCulloch never explained himself beyond saying that he had once practiced law in Jacksonville.

In 1927, however, McCulloch had his own career to pursue. Roughly a year into his stay in Jacksonville, he was hired as an attorney by the local firm of Fleming, Hamilton, Diver, Lichliter & Fleming. Geographically, this was a small step—a move of merely one block east and one block north from the 11 East Forsythe offices of McCollum & Howell to the 112 West Adams address of his new employer. It was, however, doubly a move up. McCulloch's new employer occupied offices in the Barnett Bank

Building, opened in February 1927 as the city's new tallest structure, at 224 feet. Moreover, his new employer was probably the most prestigious law firm in the city, with a client base of moneyed individuals and large corporations. One of the latter was the Seaboard Air Line Railway, the state's largest railroad, which initiated a $10 million expansion in 1926.

The firm's prestige traced to its variety of Flemings. The youngest, C. Seton Fleming, served as president of the Jacksonville Bar Association in 1915–1916, having previously been its treasurer for five years. His older brother, Francis P. Fleming Jr., served on the association's executive board. Both were the sons of Francis Philip Fleming Sr., who was the model of the southern aristocrat. Francis Sr. was born in Jacksonville and raised in antebellum grace on the St. John's River plantation "Hibernia." He served in the Civil War; one of his brothers died the definitive southern death, in Pickett's Charge at Gettysburg. Post-war, Fleming practiced law, married the daughter of a Florida Supreme Court judge, and prospered. In 1888, he was elected the fifteenth governor of Florida. In his four years in office, Fleming pushed back many of the gains black Floridians had made during Reconstruction. He enacted literacy tests and poll taxes to restrict voting rights. Governor Fleming also removed the state's only black judge from the bench, allegedly for having performed an interracial marriage. The law firm McCulloch joined did not so much advocate white supremacy as assume it.

Shortly after securing his new position, McCulloch returned to Ohio to make good on a long-held intention. William Moore McCulloch and Mabel Harris had known each other since childhood in Holmes County, when—by mutual account—Bill had chased Mabel across the playground at school. By their daughters' accounts, the minute the pair met, "She thought he was the one." Mabel Harris was strong-willed, poised, politically astute, and literate, particularly fond of Shakespeare, Benjamin Franklin, Charles Dickens, and Jane Austen. At a time when few women pursued higher education, she attended Ohio Wesleyan University, withdrew for a time due to illness, and then re-enrolled in Miami [of Ohio] University, west of Dayton. She was favored at Miami with an outstanding Shakespeare professor, with whose family she traveled to the Stratford Shakespeare Festival in Ontario. While she disliked math, she was a skilled bridge player, frequently entering tournaments. Crossing campus one day, she ran into her history professor who asked when she might be returning to class. Mabel replied, "When the bridge tournament is over." At Miami, she shared a ground-floor dorm room with her sister. Understanding the agendas of their classmates, the pair left their window unlocked and open so that any erring student could sneak back into the building post-curfew.

"Caution" was one of William McCulloch's favorite words; indeed, an "excess of caution" was a commonly invoked phrase. On at least this occasion, he threw caution to the wind, however. Borrowing the black Packard owned by his future father-in-law, William and Mabel eloped to Covington, Kentucky, where they were wed on October 17, 1927. Their marriage was in future years invariably described as close, a circumstance probably aided by the fact that McCulloch brought his wife coffee in bed every morning. The newlyweds were soon in Jacksonville, where they set up house in the Frances Court Apartments, No. 8, at 2545 Oak Street. The neighborhood was more than reputable. The apartments, of recent design, were the work of Leeroy Sheftall, one of the city's best-known architects.

Probably the Florida bubble had popped its cork even before the McCullochs had popped the cork on their wedding champagne. The signal event was the great Florida hurricane of September 1926. The storm crossed Miami and much of southern Florida, leaving at least 373 dead and damages estimated at $166 million, perhaps $3 billion in 2013 dollars. It was about that time that a series of smaller banks—unregulated and unrealistic in their lending practices—began to go under. Laws, winked at during the heat of the boom, were eventually enforced. The state controller was indicted for malpractice related to bank failures; forty-two individuals were indicted for mail fraud in connection with the sale of building lots. Larger banks resorted to emergency measures: on March 9, 1927, Miami institutions rushed $2 million in cash by automobile to two Palm Beach banks to prevent defaults.

The state promoted a brave front. On May 8, 1927, *The New York Times* reported, "Florida has never been in better business condition than at present, said B. P. Owen, Jr., manager of the Jacksonville Chamber of Commerce, yesterday. Mr. Owen had come to New York to confer with Florida investors." Owen added, "The work of reconstruction following the hurricane has long been completed and the state is forging ahead along constructive, sound lines, building at the rate of $1,000,000 a day." The hurricane, he argued, had been a positive boon to the state, as it had "served to clear Florida of the speculator and speculation."

But putting the air back into the bubble is no easier than putting the toothpaste back into the tube. As Jacksonville's leading law firm, Fleming, Hamilton, Diver, Lichliter & Fleming had resources to draw upon. But eventually, an outgoing tide lowers all boats. Even the most reputable must trim their sails. So, likely in late 1928, the Flemings *et al* decided they could reduce their expenses by dispensing with the further services of William M. McCulloch. For the McCullochs, the economic outlook in Florida was dismal. There is a final point; indeed, more of a speculation. Prior to his dismissal by Fleming, Hamilton, Diver, Lichliter & Fleming, it appears that William McCulloch had never known failure. Nonetheless, that dismissal prompted McCulloch's departure from a circumstance in which he was likely to remain something of an outsider.

CHAPTER 5

Piqua

The McCullochs returned to Ohio to seek a new livelihood. Means were soon found. Mabel McCulloch's father, Joseph Edward Harris, co-owned a veneering business in Dayton. He had a well-established customer in Piqua, Ohio, thirty miles to the north. Harris queried this customer about what prospects Piqua might offer his son-in-law. As it happened, Piqua attorney George Berry had recently lost his partner and was looking for someone to share the load. Berry interviewed and hired McCulloch. The only question that survives from that interview is Berry's asking about McCulloch's religious predilections. McCulloch allowed that he was a Methodist. Berry advised him to explore Presbyterianism. He, Berry, was already a member of Piqua's leading Methodist church. Having a Presbyterian in the firm, Berry explained, would broaden the range of clients. The McCullochs soon after became and for the rest of their lives remained members of Piqua's Westminster United Presbyterian Church. At the time, Piqua had perhaps half a dozen law firms, none more than three lawyers deep. In terms of status, all operated at some disadvantage to lawyers in nearby Troy. While with 16,000 people, Piqua had double the population of Troy, the latter had been founded in 1807 six months earlier than Piqua. Consequently, Troy had claimed the county seat and, important from a lawyer's point of view, the county courthouse.

Piqua did manage to snare the federal and state land office. The settlement soon boasted a hotel and multiple taverns, the former to house and the latter to liquefy those who came to town to claim or negotiate the sale of land. Those who do not know it often think of Indiana-fringed western Ohio as a place of much corn, many hogs, and not much else. Actually, Piqua was a canal town, a major stop on the Miami-Erie Canal, then the dominant north-south route of travelers and trade in western Ohio. Canal towns are river towns in miniature. They are places where merchants hang out their signs, where travelers tarry, where hotels and liveries find a reliable trade, and where men cross paths and pass on the news from farther away. In 1835, the town gained its first brewery; its first black businessman, Robert Smith, a barber; and its first newspaper, the *Western Courier and Piqua Enquirer*. Piqua milled the corn and wheat grown on the flat lands and packed the hogs fattened on that grain. In the ten years after 1847, Piqua exported 2.7 million pounds of pork, much of it in the quarter-million barrels the town produced.

The canal also accounted for the presence of nearby Rossville, a community of "Randolph slaves." These were among the 360 former slaves manumitted upon the death of long-time Virginia Congressman John Randolph, who left funds for their transport north; they had settled at various points along the canal. In fact, when Civil War came, blacks were recruited from the Piqua area to fill out two all-black regiments in the Massachusetts Volunteer Infantry.

Piqua was at the center of the country's flaxseed growing region. Not, perhaps, a glamour crop, flaxseed has a multitude of uses. Its seed, crushed for linseed oil, has dozens of industrial applications and gives its name to linoleum. Its fiber is used for paper and cloth. At one time, Piqua had thirteen flaxseed mills. At the turn of the century, these in turn gave rise to the French Oil Mill Machinery Company, which built the presses used to extract the oil. The town diversified to include the Hartzell Company, which produced walnut veneers; the Wood Shovel and Tool Company; and various textile mills that came to specialize in men's underwear—Piqua Hosiery, Union Underwear, Superior Underwear, Atlas Underwear, and Imperial Underwear. Many textile workers were women; consequently Piqua had an uncharacteristic proportion of two-earner families, which accounted for its relative prosperity. In 1903, Mays Opera House—one of the Miami Valley's premiere venues—opened on North Wayne Street. Over the years, it played host to Houdini, John Philip Sousa, and endless rounds of political orators.

Almost all those orators were Republicans. Piqua was a place where being a Democrat was not so much uncommon as simply abnormal. Actually, the most abnormal thing that happened was the election of Frank Hamilton, a Socialist, as Piqua mayor in a four-way race in 1917. Things did not thereafter fare well for Hamilton. During the First World War he was arrested under the Sedition Act for telling one gathering that the Liberty Bonds sold to support the war effort were not a good investment for the working man. Actually, they weren't. Hamilton was hand-cuffed and trundled off before a federal judge in Dayton, who tossed the case as ridiculous.

Piqua had its local hero: Johnny Weissmuller, winner of five Olympic gold medals, who gave swimming lessons at the town's pool and supplemented his income as a swimwear model for the Piqua Hosiery Company. One day, Hollywood called, and the rest of the story was the long yodeling screech of the film world's best-known Tarzan.

When George Berry took William McCulloch into his law practice, the firm's office was on the north side of the Piqua National Bank building, where the firm of McCulloch, Felger, Fite & Gutmann remains to this day. The bank sat on North Main Street, opposite the Orr-Statler Block, the downtown's dominant building, built in 1891 and used largely as a hotel. By one report, the hotel relocated the entrance to its bar to a basement corner, just as Prohibition was about to strike. Consumption of intoxicants continued uninterrupted. It was a lively spot. By a second report, the hotel was where men from Dayton would come for a bit of privacy with what one local referred to as "their insignificant other."

McCulloch himself was a homebody. The home was a large, white, Victorian, wooden structure, sitting at 710 Caldwell Street, five walkable blocks from McCulloch's office. On May 17, 1931, Mabel McCulloch gave birth to a daughter, Nancy. That birth came three months after the passing of William McCulloch's mother, Ida Moore McCulloch, who died on February 19 at home just north of Holmesville, following an illness of several weeks. Reporting the news, *The Holmes County Farmer's Hub* said, "Mrs. McCulloch was well known in the community in which she lived, and served." McCulloch received many notes of condolence. One, from his law partner George Berry, noted the loss, but added, "You have something to be thankful for, in that your mother lived this long and you have the pleasure of enjoying her, and she enjoying you."

The birth of a child, the death of a parent—these are milestones in one's life. In the life of William Moore McCulloch, they may have suggested that time was passing.

CHAPTER 6

Depression Era Legislator

William Moore McCulloch usually sought certainty before he spoke, wrote, or voted. In later political life, he commonly queried a staff member, "Are you sure?" Often, he announced a decision with the particularly wordy introduction, "Out of an abundance of caution." Once sure, however, he was not averse to risk. By 1932, William McCulloch had reached age thirty; he had lived in Piqua for barely three years, during which time he worked as the junior member of a two-man law firm. He was father to a toddler daughter. He was undisturbed by wealth or fame. Therefore, in the words of the *Ohio State Journal*, when McCulloch announced his candidacy for state representative of Miami County, it was a step taken "somewhat audaciously."

In doing so, McCulloch was moving against convention. Prior to the Second World War, a seat in the Ohio state legislature was typically the capstone of a career, the reward for a decade spent as the mayor of someplace small followed by several terms as a commissioner for the county in which that small place was located. Politics was decidedly local. A state house district might contain 20,000 or fewer voters. Local longevity helped build the familiarity with voters that, along with a reassuring touch of gray at the temples, encouraged election.

McCulloch lacked such tenure, such familiarity, and his red hair was neither gray nor receding. From the start, however, he had the important backing of the county's most widely circulated newspaper, the *Piqua Daily Call*, which listed McCulloch's qualifications for office:

Miami county citizens have every right to be proud of the Republican candidate for State Representative in the person of William M. McCulloch. Mr. McCulloch has intelligence; he is the right age to give hard work to the job; his integrity is unquestioned and he will go to the legislature with no strings tied to him.

The paper praised McCulloch's keen mind, poise, and temperament. What is notable about the endorsement is that it suggests McCulloch's capacity to impress those who were not beholden to him and had little stake in his advance. Days before the vote, McCulloch ran an ad in that same newspaper, which modestly stated his case:

He was born and reared on a farm; taught school; attended Wooster College for two years; worked his way through the Law College of Ohio State University; has been practicing law for more than seven years, and is the junior partner in the firm of Berry & McCulloch, attorneys-at-law, Piqua. He is married and has one daughter.

As a candidate, McCulloch had the crucial advantage of standing as the nominee of the county's dominant party. After what the local press termed "a hard fight," McCulloch defeated an active effort by Democrat Gainor Jennings of West Milton, 11,779 to 9,587. At year's end, McCulloch drove the seventy-two miles to the statehouse in Columbus, taking his oath of office on January 2, 1933. (McCulloch, throughout his decade in the legislature, never sought lodgings in Columbus, but always returned to Piqua to spend evenings with his family.)

Three circumstances framed the legislative life McCulloch entered.

The first was the physical setting. The statehouse was one of the great rabbit warrens of its day. The building itself was well proportioned—184 feet wide and 304 feet long. The House chamber measured 55 by 82 feet, with a gallery that ran its entire length. In later years, McCulloch's younger daughter, Ann, perched in the front row, would occasionally spit towards members who lacked her approval. More broadly, the Ohio Statehouse was a tribute to Virginia Woolf's statement about the importance of "a room with a view." Or even without a view. Everybody who considered himself somebody wanted an office to call his own. Eventually, the building's 53 originally generous rooms were sub-divided into 317 odd-sized compartments. In one case, three closets were combined and promoted to the rank of office. James Thurber, a one-time Columbus newsman, said that it was "almost impossible to find the governor's office, or any other, unless you have been accustomed for years to the monumental maze of corridors and rooms. Even the largest rooms seem to have been tucked away in great, cool, unexpected corners by an architect with an elephantine sense of humor." Legislators had no offices. Their desks, however, were arranged in a semi-circle that left gaps between each seat. Legislators stuffed these gaps with pending bills, reports, and personal correspondence.

The second was political complexion. Ohio was Republican to the core, and influentially so. Indeed, between 1869 and 1923, an Ohio-born Republican occupied the White House over half the time. Republican strength mirrored Democratic weakness. In most industrial states, the Democratic Party rallied around a large and partisan city—Chicago in Illinois, Detroit in Michigan, Philadelphia in Pennsylvania. Ohio had no dominant city. The Democratic organizations native to Cleveland, Columbus, Youngstown, Dayton, Toledo, and elsewhere were more inclined to feud with each other than to fight the opposition. The Democrats had a history of driving off supporters. In 1896, the "free silver" presidential candidacy of William Jennings Bryan offended economic conservatives. During the First World War, Democratic attacks on their patriotism drove off German-Americans voters. And in 1928, the nomination of Catholic Al Smith of New York for president so panicked small-town Ohio with the prospect of papal rule that Smith lost Ohio by a persuasive 1,627,526 to 864,210.

The Republicans, in contrast, besides controlling much of Ohio's wealth and many of its newspapers, benefited from a local obscurity known as the Hanna Amendment. Passed in 1902, this clause in the state constitution mandated that every Ohio county must have at least one state representative. Eighty-eight seats therefore went one-by-one to Ohio's eighty-eight counties. Only the fifty remaining seats were distributed based on population. The upshot was a legislature dominated by rural, generally conservative, representatives. Political scientist David Gold calculated that in the 1930s, "Sixty-four counties with an aggregate population of 1,781,000 could outvote the 11 largest counties, with 3,921,000, by 64-28."

The third circumstance—indeed, the imperative one—was that William McCulloch began his political career in Columbus just as the nation was sliding into economic despair. The 1932 election that brought Franklin Roosevelt to the White House delivered an uncharacteristic Democratic majority to the state legislature. Uncertainty ruled. Addressing the newly convened General Assembly, Ohio Secretary of State Clarence J. Brown stated, "You are meeting in a time of change and flux. Our skies have been clouded and the range of our vision reduced. Perhaps no man or woman can well predict the future."

Evidence was at hand. On January 12, 1933, *The New York Times* reported that 86,000 Ohio schoolteachers were going unpaid. On January 27, farmers in Wood County prevented the foreclosure of a farm by "removing" a finance company bidder from the vicinity of the auction platform. Events outran those elected to direct them. On February 25, second-term Ohio Democratic Governor George White announced, "There will be no Bank Holiday in Ohio." Notwithstanding, the following day the Dayton City Commission declared a three-day bank holiday. The day thereafter, banks in Cleveland, Akron, and Youngstown placed restrictions on the withdrawal of customer funds.

In crisis, comfort lies in routine. By legislative rule, lawmakers having bills they wish to have considered are wise to submit them by mid-February. Thereafter, introduction is possible only by unanimous consent of the body. As in any session, many of those offered in 1933 were trifling: a bill to alter the season for squirrel hunting; a bill to impose a tax on the sale of malt extract. A few were ahead of their time, like the

proposal to mandate that strip-mined land must be recovered and forest-
ed. McCulloch's earliest legislative proposals were also minor, and local.
He introduced bills to amend the method of electing Piqua's municipal
court judge; to ensure that every school district had its own superintendent; and to recalculate the rental Piqua paid on the land the city leased
along the Miami-Erie Canal. McCulloch's proposed revision of Piqua's
judicial election passed both houses and was signed into law in May—his
first legislative success.

Still, with one-half-million Ohioans out of work and the state government's deficit yawning, larger steps were needed. On February 7, *The
Washington Post* reported:

Both Ohio and Indiana are facing identical situations of "emergency revenue" legislation.
Both governors in their addresses to the assemblies have told the lawmaking bodies that
governmental expenses must be reduced, yet both have reluctantly admitted that something must be done to meet emergencies. This, of course, means new taxes, or further cuts
in budgets. Necessity for poor relief animates the situation in Ohio.

Actions, however, lacked urgency. While a bill to enact a general sales
tax was introduced on February 8, it was given little chance of passage.
Two weeks later, Representative Rogers of Belmont urged formation of a
commission to study the consequences of shortening the workweek. Even
with unemployment over 20 percent, many industrial and commercial
establishments continued to operate on a six-day week and a ten-hour or
longer day. The legislature approved the study—over McCulloch's "No"
vote—but allowed two years for the report to be prepared.

The pending collapse of banking system, however, was not readily
postponed. On February 28, *The New York Times* reported:

In the space of 38 minutes, the Ohio Legislature tonight passed two emergency banking
laws aimed at breaking the financial jam caused when fifty banks in the state restricted or
stopped withdrawal of deposits. The two laws clothed the state Superintendent of Banks
with drastic powers to control withdrawals of deposits and to cut red tape in the liquida-
tion and reopening of closed banks.

Both bills carried easily, both with McCulloch's support. Ohio banks
were swift to take advantage of the law. By the following day, 200 financial institutions were avoiding runs on the bank by limiting the amount
any single depositor could withdraw. On the revenue side, nothing very
burdensome was enacted; on April 7, the legislature legalized pari-mutuel
betting in Ohio, with a share of the take to come to the state's coffers.

Complicating the crises was the inability of Ohio's Democratic state
government, desperately short of funds, to collaborate with the new
Democratic administration in Washington, the only likely source of such
funds. In June, Governor George White requested $4 million in emer-
gency relief. In mid-July Harry Hopkins, director of the Federal Relief

Administration, responded that no funds would be forthcoming until the state "made further efforts to help its own people" by matching federal funds dollar-for-dollar. Hopkins, in correspondence with White, tartly noted that the Ohio legislature had been fully aware of this requirement when it had adjourned without taking any action.

In August, Governor White called the legislature back into session. Speaking to a joint session of the General Assembly, White noted that the legislature had rejected his call for a sales tax. It had rejected his proposal for a combined sales and income tax. Instead, it had passed incidental taxes on beer caps, cosmetics, and movie admissions. Governor White stressed, "We are considering, and must still consider, not the relief needs of some future time, but the present and immediate emergency of the current year." He offered five alternatives for raising revenues, including submission of a bond issue solely for relief. He closed, "If the Ohio legislature sees fit to accept any one of my five revenue-raising proposals, or to enact an adequate measure of its own, I feel confident that the federal relief administration will advance sufficient funds to meet the needs through September."

No major action followed. Political conflict in Ohio had at its heart the conflict between the small-town worldview of the typically conservative majority and the needs of the state's urban centers, notably Cleveland. In this, McCulloch—with the horror of debt common to those raised in the economically insecure fields of early-twentieth-century family farming—generally sided with the former. Far better that others tighten their belts than that the sober members of the legislature loosen their purse strings.

The Ohio city hardest hit by the Depression was Cleveland. Called into special session in March 1934, the legislature was unmoved by Cleveland's plight. On March 23, 1934, *The New York Times* reported from Ohio the headline that the House: "Rejects City Bond Aid Bill: Mayor Says Cleveland Must Curtail its Services and Continue to Default."

The Ohio House of Representatives by a vote of 53 to 40 today rejected the conference committee report on the bond refunder bill, designed to aid financially distressed cities.

The fight for the measure started in Cleveland last month when Mayor Harry L. Davis and Finance Director Louis C. West found that the city's sinking fund had been invested in municipal bonds which, being below par could not be sold to pay maturities of other bonds. A default resulted.

McCulloch, somewhat suspicious of financial machinations and never particularly friendly to welfare, voted "No" on the measure. In consequence of the vote, *The Times* added, municipal park workers faced dismissal; garbage collectors would be the next to go, with layoffs of police and firefighters to remain a last resort.

By November 1934, with a quarter-million families on Ohio's relief rolls, outgoing Governor White made one final appeal to the legislature. He told a joint session, "The 90th General Assembly has on a number of occasions approached but not decided the taxation question. That problem has been and is now the paramount state issue." Wisely, perhaps, Governor White chose November 20, 1934, to make his appeal. The date fell after the fall elections; legislators could approve new taxes secure in the knowledge they would not face the wrath of voters for another two years.

Perhaps the most financially strained institutions were public schools, traditionally supported by local property taxes. With tens of thousands of mortgages in default, income for public schools dropped drastically. Legislators were told that come January 1, 1935, 100,000 Ohio school-children would be dismissed from class by districts that had no funds to pay their teachers, to purchase coal to fire their furnaces, or to buy gasoline to run their buses. Perhaps because of the governor's timing, action ensued. Within days, a bill authorizing a comprehensive 3 percent state sales tax was introduced. It quickly passed the House. William Mc-Culloch—always more willing to spend on education than on any other public service—voted with the three-fourths majority. Passed by the State Senate and signed into law by Governor White, the tax took effect on January 1, 1935. In its first year, the tax raised $47.8 million, of which $16.8 million went to local schools, with the rest primarily directed to poor relief, pensions, and local government expenses.

The 1935–1936 Biennium

The fortunes of McCulloch's Republican Party—low after the Roosevelt victory of 1932—dwindled further with the 1934 off-year election. Nationally, Democrats elected 322 congressmen, the highest total any party had yet achieved. In Columbus, McCulloch found his party outnumbered by nearly three-to-one. Even in normally Republican Miami County, Ohio, sixteen of nineteen Republican nominees went down to defeat. McCulloch was one of the three survivors. Indeed, against the Democratic tide he defeated Democratic challenger E. L. Russell by an easy 9,994 to 6,841—increasing his 1932 margin of victory of 10 percent to 18 percent.

Several factors played in McCulloch's favor. He retained the support of the *Piqua Daily Call*, which informed its readers that "in William Mc-Culloch this county has a state representative who is honest, efficient and intelligent. He made a splendid record in his first term in the state assembly and is recognized as one of the leaders in the House of Representatives." In the legislature, McCulloch was neither an orator nor a frequent speaker, but he had two appreciated qualities: he spoke to the point, and, point made, stopped. Further, he was acquiring a reputation for that trait politicians value most—if, indeed, they do not always practice it. Namely, that when he gave his word, that word was kept. Indeed, through his long political career, nothing distressed him so much as the realization that he had been lied to, or lied about. His rising standing in Ohio was affirmed by the new legislature when on February 7, 1935, he—though a Republican—was named chairman of the House Judiciary Committee.

Given an activist president and huge Democratic majorities in both Washington and Columbus, the next few years might have been a high-point of progressive reform in Ohio. This did not happen. For Ohio, McCulloch's return to office mattered less than that the Democratic landslide landed Martin Luther Davey in the governor's chair. Davey was a five-time former congressman and president of the Davey Tree Expert Company, a major enterprise with headquarters in Kent, Ohio. The new governor had a talent for acquiring enemies. The week after his inaugural, *Gongwer*, the state legislative newsletter, observed, "Gov. George White passed out today with a chuckle and a snort and Gov. Martin Luther Davey came in with a gurgle and a goddam. When Martin Luther indulges in one of his bursts of profanity, it is like your dear old grandmother putting aside her clay pipe and lighting up a cigarette. What I mean is, it startles."

Trouble soon settled in. On March 18, 1935—barely nine weeks after his inauguration—*The Washington Post* reported that Davey "faced the possibility today of losing his job through impeachment." Federal relief administrator Harry Hopkins cited "incontrovertible evidence" of chicanery in Ohio's relief efforts. Davey obtained a warrant alleging "criminal libel" on Hopkins's part. Hopkins was not the last to question Davey's honesty. Though the governor acquired the nickname of "the grafting tree surgeon," nothing very serious was proven. At heart, the problem was that while Davey was a Democrat, he was wholly out of sympathy with the New Deal, whose programs he regarded as an infringement of states' rights. Complicating matters, of course, was that Ohio was desperately in need of money and that the only likely source of those funds was the Roosevelt Administration, which Davey opposed.

Davey had a flair for needless conflict. When officials at Ohio State University expressed doubts that the state's leading university had sufficient funds to open for the fall 1935 term, Davey—to whom apparently nothing was sacred—replied that so many members of the Ohio State Buckeye football team had been placed on the state payroll that the university could hardly lack for funds.

Given the bickering, it would be surprising if the General Assembly accomplished much of consequence. Surprisingly, it did. On February 20, 1935, House Bill 466, an aid to education measure, was dropped into the hopper:

For the purpose of creating a public school fund in the state treasury and providing for the distribution thereof, with a view to providing a thorough and efficient system of common schools throughout the state, promoting economy and efficiency in the operation thereof, and providing for the equalization of educational opportunities.

When the measure came to a vote in the House, McCulloch voted in its favor. *The New York Times* reported, "Revolution in public school financing has struck Ohio, and its outcome is due within the two or three weeks remaining before recess of the Ohio Legislature. The House has passed a long-debated 'foundation' bill to allot $48 million a year to carrying weak town and county schools." McCulloch voted with the 87-16 majority to adopt the Senate amendments to the bill, and then voted with a nearly unanimous House, 115-7, on the final bill.

Overall, McCulloch's voting record was fairly consistent. It reflected the small, individualistic, and self-reliant world from which he had come. Following this, he was deeply skeptical of relief measures, particularly any that would create long-term debt, and generally unsympathetic to any collectivist action, labor unions included. At the same time, the farmer's son who was the first in his family to attend college was a consistent supporter of education. Along with the school foundation bill described above, McCulloch voted for a bill requiring provision of free textbooks to all elementary, junior, and senior high school pupils. The bill passed by a 73-23 margin, suggesting that most of McCulloch's fellow Republicans were in opposition. His farming background manifested in other ways. In the age-old contest between the chicken and the fox, he sided unreservedly with the chicken, casting his Yea vote in favor of establishing open season on foxes, a bill that passed the House by 92-27.

In the 1935 session, McCulloch had the satisfaction of seeing various bills he sponsored passed into law. His House Bill 437, which allowed voters to change the terms of certain debts, went to the governor for signature on May 31, 1935. Two more McCulloch-sponsored measures—House Bill 511, relating to jury service in small counties, and House Bill 160, limiting to $100 the annual compensation of cemetery trustees—were signed into law on June 3, 1935. One measure espoused by McCulloch failed passage, a proposed 3 percent sales tax on certain automobile sales.

Despite the partisan disadvantage he faced, William McCulloch's political fortunes continued to thrive. In November 1935, Republican Minority Leader Myron B. Gessaman sought and secured the post of Columbus mayor. No special session was in the offing. Nonetheless, with Gessaman's departure, the thirty-some GOP representatives informally designated McCulloch as the party's leader in the lower house. At the time, he had served in that body just three years.

William McCulloch was typical of those with whom he served. At the time, nearly half the members were farmers; perhaps a third were lawyers. McCulloch had some claim to being both. The 138-member House contained no African Americans and just three female members, who in 1938 formed the National Order of Women Legislators. The most significant was Anne F. O'Neil of Summit County, who served nine terms between 1933 and 1954. As mentioned earlier, the legislature was shifting from being the capstone of a career to being its starting point. McCulloch was one case in point. A second was the young man appointed House journal clerk in 1935. This was James A. Rhodes, of whom more would be heard in the future.

The 1937–1938 Biennium

The national election of 1936 was the Democratic Party's greatest triumph. In the Electoral College, Franklin Roosevelt swamped GOP nominee Alfred Landon of Kansas by a convincing 523-8 margin. In Congress, Democrats claimed 333 congressmen, another new record. And in Columbus, the Republican contingent led by William McCulloch had only thirty-three members. Again, McCulloch weathered the electoral storm, though by a reduced majority, gaining victory by a margin of 12,405 to 11,048. The unwavering support of the *Piqua Call* probably helped. That journal reported, "Seldom in the history of the Ohio legislature has a young member of that body made as splendid a record or risen as rapidly to leadership as has William M. McCulloch, the efficient and hard-working representative from Miami County."

McCulloch—splendid, efficient, and hard-working though he may have been—was a realist. When the legislature voted to elect a Speaker, he came out on the short end of a 101-32 tally to Democrat Frank Uribe of Cuyahoga County. Leading a party outnumbered three-to-one in the state assembly, he said, "About all we can hope to do is to build a constructive record with which the party can go before the people in the next election." Fortunately for McCulloch, life was providing other satisfactions. On February 9, 1937, Mabel McCulloch gave birth to the couple's second child, also a daughter, named Ann.

Complicating matters in Columbus was that the Roosevelt landslide had dragged Martin Luther Davey back to the governor's mansion for a second term. Davey presented little to the newly elected legislature. He had, he said, "two fervent hopes. One is that the business of this session can be completed within three or four months. The second is that no new taxes will be necessary." Between a Democratic governor with no grand ambitions and an almost powerless minority, the 1937 session was uneventful. When it adjourned in late June, *The Washington Post* on June 27, 1937, reported the comment of the closer to home Cleveland *Plain Dealer:*

The assembly which veteran Columbus observers called the "do-nothingist" legislature of the last quarter century reached the theoretical end of its regular session in perfect character—doing nothing.

The record of this session's bungling presents an impressive argument for those who favor a one-chamber legislature. If ever there was a hopelessly balky legislative team, it is the Senate and House of Ohio's 92nd General Assembly.

A considerable portion of the problem was Governor Davey, who on January 3, 1938, opened the legislature's next session with an hour-long harangue on the slings and arrows of outrageous legislators. His administration, he claimed, had been "subjected to the worst and most pernicious torrent of abuse" in state history. Particularly, he said, from the State Senate. Here, he named Senator Byrne, who Davey claimed had offered to support him in exchange for the presidency of Kent State University; Senator Campbell, who was the "puppet" of the Hanna Coal Company; Senator Seidner, who had lobbied for an entirely unmerited pardon; and Senator Lipcher, who suffered from "very loose public morals." All of whom were members of Davey's own party.

Through it all, McCulloch managed to keep his dignity and, with perhaps somewhat greater effort, his temper. His performance as minority leader was widely praised. In the *Ohio State Journal*, Karl B. Pauly described McCulloch as "the spark that drove the Republican minority, small though it was, in compact form against the Democratic regime. He was a strategist of no mean ability." Pauly added, "The House sometimes sees in the Republican leader the flash of temper which is generally associated with red hair, particularly in these days when members of his party find so much to be indignant about in affairs of government."

CHAPTER 7

Mr. Speaker

William McCulloch's standing in Columbus was rising; his position as state representative from Miami County was secure. For his 1938 campaign, he reported his expenditures as "zero." This expenditure equaled that of the opposing candidate, as no such person came forth. At thirty-seven, McCulloch had completed his apprenticeship. He had not sponsored principal legislation, but he was mastering the more significant task of managing men. Further advance awaited opportunity.

Opportunity came with an abrupt reversal of the nation's economic fortunes. After four years of New Deal recovery, the economy sputtered in mid-1937: unemployment jumped from 14.3 to 19.0 percent; manufacturing production dropped by 37 percent. Economists, then and since, argued over causes. Voters, more prosaic, reached a straightforward conclusion: it was time for a change. In Columbus, change was substantial. The 92nd General Assembly, which met in 1937–1938, had but thirty-three Republican members. When the 93rd General Assembly convened, the GOP contingent numbered an even one hundred.

When these five-score Republicans caucused following the election, their first act was a unanimous vote to nominate William Moore Mc-Culloch to be Speaker of the House. When the legislature convened in January 1939, McCulloch was easily elected to that post by a 98-30 margin over Democrat Michael Feighan. The Speaker-elect told the House that his "speech making days were over." McCulloch did offer a few words on how he planned to execute his new responsibilities: "I believe members that have served with me will understand that I never intended to be arbitrary but there are two things I do wish all members to understand. My policy, to do those things best suited for all the people of the state and for our party. My purpose, to be the servant of all members of the House and never their master." Not long thereafter, Piqua honored its own with a dinner at the Piqua Country Club. The evening featured a midwestern dinner of baked ham, *au gratin* potatoes, and Parker House rolls, with music by Tommy Collins and his Accordion. The ceremonial high point was the presentation of a tasseled gavel, hand-made and handed over by the Piqua Fish and Game Protective Association.

As speaker, McCulloch would be a chief lieutenant to Ohio's new governor, Republican John Bricker. While not as flamboyant or ethically flexible as his predecessor, Bricker easily matched Martin Davey as a conservative and as an antagonist to centralized government from Washington. In his outgoing remarks, Davey stressed, "Once a state accepts federal money, it no longer controls its own affairs, but immediately becomes the victim of the theories or caprice of the federal bureau." In his inaugural address a week later on January 9, 1939, Bricker called for restoring "common honesty" to state government and achieving "stringent economies no matter how distasteful." He made good on that pledge: 1,047 jobs in the highway and liquor departments were axed within weeks; 2,000 more layoffs followed in the ensuing months. In Bricker's first biennium as governor, he and the Republican-controlled legislature managed to reduce Ohio's Depression-strapped $43 million general fund budget by $3 million. And he fully shared his predecessor's antagonism to the federal government and the New Deal:

The world has seen many people giving up opportunity and liberty for false promises of temporary security . . . New forms of government in the world, Communism and Fascism, are founded upon the use of stark unbridled power. . . . Even in this country we have seen a marked tendency toward centralization of political power. . . . The election last November indicates a trend—nationwide in scope—away from undue centralization of power in Washington, accompanied as it has been by reckless public spending.

Bricker pledged, "We shall defend, with all the ability we possess against the abuse of Federal power when it means the destruction of local self-government within its proper sphere."

As Speaker, McCulloch soon demonstrated that he was up to the job. On January 12, 1939—during what was only the legislature's second week—*Gongwer* reported:

McCulloch has gotten off to a good start. He is not arbitrary. He is fair to all the members and leans a little backward when the Democratic members desire a little extra time and stray from strict parliamentary procedure. He has always said that his desire is to be the servant of the House and not its master. If he continues in this course he will undoubtedly emerge as one of the outstanding Speakers of General Assembly.

While McCulloch did not share Bricker's view that the New Deal verged on totalitarianism, he did share his governor's emphasis on economic government. On February 5, one statehouse paper reported, "House Speaker McCulloch and Senate Majority Leader J. Harry McGregor scored a rare personal triumph last week in the Senate Taxation Committee." The committee, yielding to the importuning from its urban representatives, had agreed to delete from a pending relief bill the requirement that state relief funds must be matched by the cities that were to receive them. As reported, "McCulloch and his majority leader actually read the riot act to the taxation committee. They told the members that a relief bill requiring no matching would have no chance of passage in the rural-dominated House of Representatives." The committee compliantly reversed itself.

A month later, the House Judiciary Committee came close to endorsing a labor-backed bill that would restrict the power of Ohio courts to issue injunctions to halt or limit strikes. The actual vote was 7 to 7; and while the tie meant the measure had failed, the closeness made reversal possible. Following the vote, McCulloch personally intervened to urge the committee to hold hearings on a substitute Republican bill that would reaffirm the court's injunctive powers. He noted that the current state GOP platform stated, "The Republican party believes the courts ought not to issue an injunction against either party in a labor dispute." Organized labor protested the move. Thomas J. Donnelly, secretary of the Ohio State Federation of Labor, said McCulloch's substitute "would not prevent injustices now prevailing in courts of equity and would provide no proper and desirable remedy of law to labor." McCulloch was proceeding from safe ground. The tie vote had occurred because three Republican representatives had been absent from the committee meeting at which that vote had occurred. McCulloch lined up the missing trio, and their votes sent McCulloch's version to the full House, which enacted it. Commenting on this chain of events, the newspaper noted that McCulloch had placed "the Republican leadership in direct opposition to the leaders of organized labor."

Throughout his career, McCulloch maintained that he would not ask others to undertake any task he avoided himself. During his later service in the U.S. Congress, McCulloch joined his office staff in the Saturday chore of stamping his return address on the stacks of *Congressional Record* reprints he mailed to constituents. Given the variety of claims on a congressman's attention, it was an activity one staff member termed "an absolute total waste of his time." McCulloch, perhaps, imagined it as an act of reciprocal loyalty. In May 1939, the House considered a bill to lower the percentage of votes required to approve any local property tax, provided that tax was dedicated to poor relief. The measure was particularly unpopular with rural conservatives. A vote in its favor was "considered the same as a politician signing his death warrant." However, the *Piqua Daily Call* reported, "Had the bill been defeated, the Bricker relief program would have been shattered." The bill passed. As Speaker, McCulloch normally voted only in the event of ties. In this event, he directed the clerk to call out his own name. McCulloch's "Aye" vote clarified that he stood with those who had taken an unpopular stance.

He handled the House with a firm hand. During one session,

Speaker McCulloch busted two gavels in attempts to bring an unruly House to order. He succeeded with a third gavel—the ceremonial one bestowed on him by the Piqua Fish and Game Protective Association. That task achieved, McCulloch admonished the assembly: "The Chair trusts that it will not again become necessary to remind the members that they are representatives of the state of Ohio." When the House adjourned in late May 1939, United Press statehouse correspondent Richard A. Blackburn reported, "For more than five months, McCulloch, a slight, wiry Scotsman with a guardsman moustache, labored mightily with the gavel and a sharp tongue while cannily steering the Bricker administration's legislative program through to successful passage." Blackburn added, "As speaker of the House, he is known for his fairness and for his fiery temper which always is noticeable to his colleagues because of the red hair which accentuates his taut, white face."

The General Assembly did not reconvene during 1939. Governor Bricker declined to call the body back into session, despite continuing pressure from Cleveland officials that the state act to aid the city, which was once again in dire straits. Bricker blamed the Roosevelt administration. In 1938, he noted, Cleveland's allocation of jobs through the federal Works Progress Administration (WPA) was 74,000. The following year, that total was cut to 30,000—a reduction Bricker called political payback for Ohio's heavy support of Republicans in the 1938 election. Narrowly speaking, Cleveland's case was weakened by the fact that the city had ceased to make matching contributions to relief funds. In this, McCulloch supported Governor Bricker, praising him for resisting the pressure for a special session, adding, "The time to resume relief payments by local subdivisions is here."

Privation trumped principle. In mid-November, 65,000 relief recipients in Cleveland were placed on "short rations." On December 7, *The Washington Post* quoted Cleveland's health director, who said that medical authorities "feared the results in the immediate future. If you have undernourished or starved people you haven't good health; you may expect a toll to be exacted later."

In truth, Bricker was in something of a bind. The *Cleveland News* reported that Governor Bricker's "proudest achievement as governor is his record for economy. To the extent to which he yields to Cleveland, he reduces his state savings. To the extent that he refuses to help Cleveland, he lends ammunition to the Democrats." For the moment, the governor would not budge. When, Bricker said, the Federal government had matched Ohio's efforts at economizing, then he would be interested in their advice on "how to run our state." By December 12, 1939, however, sufficient funds were scraped up to return those on reduced rations to full relief.

Robert A. Taft, newly elected to the U. S. Senate, offered an assessment that spread the blame around. Taft was thoroughly conservative, but as a Cincinnati native he knew somewhat more about municipal realities than did the average rural representative. The problem, he said, "lies with the rural legislators, and with the lack of understanding in the cities themselves of the necessity of some action [to match relief]." National columnist Clayton Fritchey found a more focused target. He "blamed Depression-era problems in Ohio cities on rural legislators who controlled the General Assembly and could not or would not comprehend the extent of suffering in the cities." McCulloch, as ever, saw virtue in economy. During his first term as Speaker, he noted with satisfaction, the costs of operating the Ohio House of Representatives were reduced by 25 percent from the previous biennium.

Second Term: 1941–1942

For William McCulloch, the 1940 election brought a double triumph. His bid for a fifth term was unopposed, though he did draw 15,931 complementary votes in his Miami County district. While Franklin Roosevelt carried the Buckeye state by 150,000 votes, John W. Bricker was reelected governor—crushing the comeback attempt of Martin Davey by a margin of more than 350,000 votes. Davey received no help from FDR, who refused to allow the unpredictable Democrat to ride on the presidential campaign train as it crossed Ohio.

By tradition the Speaker of the Ohio House of Representatives served a single term. When, however, Republicans caucused after the 1940 election, *Gongwer* reported, "There was no question in the minds of the caucus members as to who would be selected." McCulloch was the unanimous choice. Elaborating on the selection, the *Ohio State Journal* reported, "The [outgoing] Legislature won wide acclaim for the expeditious manner in which it has transacted its business, for its economy, for the almost complete absence of political bickering, and the shortness of its session." That periodical added, "McCulloch's ability, his impartiality, and the businesslike manner in which he presided over sessions of the current House were recognized and admitted not only by the members of his own party, [but also] by his Democratic colleagues."

McCulloch's election came when the legislature met on January 6, 1941. The formal vote was seventy-seven for McCulloch, fifty-seven for Democratic representative H. L. Mason of Wyandot County. With the formal party-line vote concluded, Mason moved to make the tabulation unanimous. Ohio Supreme Court Justice E. S. Matthias then administered the oath of office. Speaker McCulloch's remarks were characteristically brief. He described himself as "deeply appreciative" of the honor received, adding that his purpose would be "to fairly and impartially preside over the deliberations of this representative body; to jealously guard, and, if necessary, to aggressively assert, the rights of one of the co-ordinate branches of state government."

Governor Bricker was equally inclined to assert the rights of a different branch of Ohio government; namely, his own. He continued to preach economy. In his January 15, 1941, State of the State address to the General Assembly, he took pride in announcing that he had replaced the general fund deficit inherited in 1939 with a $6 million surplus. Money in the bank was meant to stay there; Bricker was adamant that no portion of the surplus would go as relief aid to Ohio's cities. Indeed, his legislative agenda was small—what Ohio needed, he believed, was frugality and honest administration. During his re-election bid, Bricker had told voters that "not one single charge of misconduct" had been made against his administration. "Today state employees are doing their work better because they are free. There are no forced assessments. There is no spying, no secret check-up, and no forced political activity." Speaker McCulloch was in general agreement. In his own campaign, he had pledged that no new or higher taxes would be levied. It would, he believed, be necessary to continue the present taxes on public utilities, on cigarettes, and on liquid fuels.

While that final levy—on liquid fuels, chiefly gasoline—had the endorsement of the governor, it was highly unpopular with the public. Here, for a second time, McCulloch showed his willingness to stand by those casting an unpopular vote. As the *Ohio Republican News* reported on April 3, 1941:

A few days ago, for the second time during his terms as presiding officer of the House, Speaker McCulloch requested that the clerk call his name so that his vote on a highly controversial question might be recorded. The bill before the House was the bill to re-enact the liquid fuel tax. It was an administration measure, and had been opposed vigorously by some interests.

When the roll was completed, the bill had 73 votes—three more than enough for passage. The reading clerk, acting under previous instructions, called the Speaker's name and he voted "Yea" to make the total affirmative 74. Explaining his action, McCulloch said, "The Republican majority members have been very loyal. I voted for this bill to show them that I am not asking them to vote for any measure for which I don't want to go on record myself."

With the purse strings drawn tight in Columbus, the legislature had a relatively brief and uneventful season. Writing in the *Ohio State Journal* of May 19, 1941, political correspondent Karl B. Pauly identified only limited areas of contention. One was the continuing dispute over what share of the state's general revenue should be directed to local government. A second was the need to resolve the disputed result of a state representative election, which the Republican majority resolved in favor of the Republican aspirant. The third was the formal banning of the Communist Party from the state elections ballot, a step a number of states took that year. The fourth was what Pauly termed "the long-drawn-out devious struggle over the mine safety code."

Mining was a continued target of reform in Ohio, likely because no area of the state's economic life so needed reform. In 1933, legislation that would require strip-mined land to be repaired by those who had carted off the coal failed to make it out of committee. In 1937, legislation that would require miners to be certified by an examining board as physically fit before being allowed to work underground also failed to come to a vote. The issue returned to the legislative forefront with each fresh mining disaster. On March 16, 1940, a late-morning explosion ripped through the Hanna Coal Company No. 10 Mine at Willow Grove, Ohio, killing seventy-two. On November 29, thirty-one Ohio miners died at the Nelms Mine in Cadiz, Ohio. The hazard of the work was not in question: nationally, thirty miners were killed each year for every 10,000 employed in the trade. But in 1940—a year in which Ohio produced 49 million tons of coal, 9 percent of the nation's total—the mine owners continued to hold the upper hand, a hand that could reach into deeper pockets.

Further Ambitions

William McCulloch's success as speaker prompted speculation as to what he might do next. United Press correspondent Richard A. Blackburn suggested that McCulloch wished to serve as Ohio's attorney general. Blackburn added, "But it is probably a safe bet that he will not run for it so long as the incumbent, Thomas J. Herbert, wants to keep the job." McCulloch's security in his current position might in part be traced to a rather simple cause, namely, his continued refusal to reside in the state capital and his continuing the seventy-two-mile commute from Piqua to the Statehouse. Familiarity famously breeds contempt. Likely, McCulloch's decision to be a homebody—to read bedtime stories rather than rub elbows—helped to secure the sense of authority he held over the House.

For a politician, residence in Columbus did little to add to one's stature. Once away from the legislative floor, politics in Columbus revolved around the downtown Neil House. In 1923, President Warren Harding—a former Ohio Statehouse politician—said the Neil House "might fairly have been called the real Capitol of Ohio. On its floor, I first saw and felt the pulsing movement of the political throng." When the General Assembly was in session, fully one-third of its members took lodgings in the hotel. Waking, they could easily find their way to their legislative desks through the tunnel that ran under High Street, conveniently connecting the hotel with the Statehouse on the other side of the street. A legislator could complete an entire session without ever risking light of day. Evenings, the generously sized bar in the Neil House was the focus of political discussion. Of no lesser importance, it was a place where a legislator could eat and drink at the expense of a lobbyist; or play poker with a lobbyist who had no serious intention of taking his money; or meet women who found the legislator rather more attractive than he had previously led himself to believe. One muckraking journalist, Walter L. Liggett, painted a lurid picture of corruption in Columbus, with "public utility lobbyists wining and dining staunch Anti-Saloon League followers and throwing parties where 'wild women' do their stuff" with "as many as a dozen female 'entertainers' dancing in the nude."

Nude dancing aside, the 1941 session drew high marks, particularly from the more conservative newspapers. Following adjournment, the *Ohio State Journal* of May 19, 1941 reported:

Another Ohio legislative session has come and gone, one which was not only the shortest in years, but also one of the best. . . . The longer the session, the stronger the pressure of lobby groups and the more prevalent the ancient practice of back scratching and log rolling. . . .

Mr. Bricker has reason for feeling gratified over his second-term session . . . . He owes thanks to the Senate and House leadership, the Republicans having a bare majority in the Senate and a slim majority in the House—the leadership so conducting itself as not to create insurgents in their own ranks and usually, on the other hand, gaining and holding the support of some of the Democrats.

The writer noted that the biennial budget was balanced without new taxes, "a feat which is exceptional" in New Deal America. Nonetheless, no essential state service had been "handicapped." Extensive improvements in the state's physical plant had been promised. Aid to the aged increased. The inherited school debt was substantially reduced. These accomplishments were not trivial. They were, however, accomplishments likely to be associated with unruffled years of peace.

CHAPTER 8

War and Thereafter

Politically, the November 1942 election changed little in Ohio. Once again, John Bricker was returned to the governor's mansion, receiving over 60 percent of the vote. Once again, William McCulloch ran unopposed in securing his sixth term as state representative from Miami County. And, when the newly elected Ohio House convened on January 4, 1943, William McCulloch was elected to an unprecedented third term as Speaker by a convincing 108 to 23 margin.

The difference, of course, is that when the 1942 election occurred, America was at war—and had been for nearly a year. A few days after the November election, American troops landed in North Africa, their first step to freeing Europe. Of greater consequence, a week later Soviet armies launched the great counteroffensive at Stalingrad that would destroy the German Sixth Army, arguably the turning point of war on the Eastern Front.

War dramatically shifted the balance of power between state and federal government. In the 1930s, Martin Luther Davey and John Bricker had been thorns in the side of President Roosevelt and his New Deal. With war, what state governors and legislatures might want suddenly mattered a great deal less than what the president and the Department of Defense wanted from Washington. Industrial directives issued by the federal government took precedence over the plans and formal prerogatives of industry. War did what nearly a decade of New Deal activity had failed to accomplish; it put Ohio in full harmony with the federal government and got the state's industry up and humming.

In his opening address to the General Assembly, Governor Bricker called attention to the state's role in the war effort: "Ohio today is an outstanding state in war production. Over one million men and women are employed in over two thousand Ohio war plants. A quarter of a million more employees will be needed in the next few months." One source reported that between 1940 and 1943, Ohio coal production rose by 82 percent; employment in basic industry rose from 754,886 to 1,268,685;

nearly $18 billion in defense contracts were received during the war; industrial wages rose 65 percent. In war as in peace, Bricker pushed the need for economy. Bricker's biographer, Richard O. Davies, wrote, "He repeatedly preached the importance of a large surplus as a necessary hedge against possible wartime economic restrictions." The state was hardly threatened with insolvency. On January 14, state treasurer Don H. Bright reported a year-end balance of over $111.5 million, the consequence of four years of strict fiscal discipline.

With initiative focused on Washington, with a "waste not, want not" governor in Columbus, little of significance emerged from the legislature. By mid-February, legislators had introduced the measures they sought. Anna S. O'Neill (D-Summit County) presented a resolution to lower the voting age to eighteen. Other bills were introduced to encourage the propagation of pheasants, to declare central standard to be the legal time in Ohio for the duration of the war only, and to abolish taxes on prescription drugs. One further motion offered the sympathy of the chamber to its Speaker. On February 18, 1943, McCulloch's father, James H. McCulloch, died in Holmesville four days after his eighty-eighth birthday. The House resolution marking that death read in part, "James McCulloch had been a lifelong resident of Holmes County, [and] a successful farmer, [who] having been born, lived all his life, and passed away on his own farm in Holmes County." The statement added that the Speaker's father "was a lifelong Republican and a political and civic leader of Holmes County for many years." A nine-member legislative delegation attended the funeral. Burial was at Prairie Township Cemetery, a quarter-mile north of the home in which William McCulloch had been born.

The war provided its heroes. Pleasing, doubtless, to McCulloch was that the celebrated air ace, Dominic Gentile, was a Piqua native, educated in the local schools. Gentile was an experienced private pilot when, in July 1941, he attempted to enlist in the pre-war Army Air Corps. He was rejected because he lacked the two years of college education then required of pilots. Undeterred, Gentile enrolled in the Canadian Royal Air Force, becoming one of the few Americans to see combat prior to Pearl Harbor. With U.S. entry to the war, he was accepted into the Army Air Corps. All told, he shot down twenty-two German aircraft. British Prime Minister Winston Churchill publicly referred to Gentile and his wingman, Captain John T. Godfrey, as "Damon and Pythias," who in Greek mythology symbolized loyalty and friendship.

The Second World War was the country's "great mingling." Prior to that conflict, most Americans lived rather isolated lives—in Irish or German or Jewish urban neighborhoods, in New England fishing villages, Appalachian coal mining towns, and amidst the endless plains of grain that covered the nation's midsection. Pre-war, many young men reached adulthood having met few if any persons not from their own ethnic neighborhood. The Second World War, by pulling twelve million men and women from their previous abodes, brought the nation face-to-face with itself for the first time. But not entirely. One group—10 percent of the country's populace—remained largely apart, that group being African-Americans.

Incidental notice was taken. On February 10, 1943, Ohio state representative David D. Turpeau offered a resolution "commending the Negro race" for its "unswerving loyalty and devotion to the American ideals of life" and "loyalty to the Stars and Stripes upon every emergency and field of battle in defense of our country." The resolution marked the celebration of National Negro History Week.

William McCulloch's own district verged on lily white, with a black population only 1.8 percent of Miami County's 52,000 residents. The most famous of these by far were the Mills Brothers—John, Herbert, Harry, and Donald, Piqua natives who would eventually sell fifty million records. As teenagers, they entered an amateur contest at Mays Opera House in Piqua. When Harry Mills realized he had left his kazoo at home, he imitated the sound of a trumpet. Soon, each brother undertook instrumental imitations of his own, a style distinctively associated with the group. In 1928, Cincinnati's major radio station, WLW, began airing the group. Two years later, CBS president William S. Paley brought them to a national audience. In 1934, they were the first African Americans to perform for the British royal family.

In the 1930s, their parents divorced. Subsequently, their mother married a man who had worked as a janitor. John, Herbert, Harry, and Donald decided to buy the couple a large home on Piqua's upscale Park Avenue Hill. A local historian said that had Piqua's most famous African Americans tried to purchase a home in that neighborhood for themselves, objections might have been few. But to install a black janitor in the city's main street of white privilege did not pass muster. The sale was blocked. Thereafter, the Mills Brothers gave their place of origin as Bellefontaine, an Ohio town some forty miles away.

There were lesser-known black residents of Piqua, among them Emerson and Viola Clemens. He was born in 1904 and she in 1908; she was seventeen when they married in 1925. The Clemenses were workers. Rejected for employment at a local factory because of his race, Emerson became a chauffeur and a barber in a private home. He then worked in Piqua Memorial Hospital, where he brought his seven-year-old, Colleen, ice cream following her tonsillectomy. Colleen, the third of four daughters, recalled her mother as somewhat more aggressive. They went to Dayton to hear Marian Anderson. When Langston Hughes came to Piqua, he stayed across the street from the Clemenses because no hotel in town would admit the famed black poet. Emerson Clemens was also a cook, his wife sewed and baked, and the couple did private catering for the affluent families on Piqua's Park Avenue Hill—the street that had barred the Mills Brothers' mother and stepfather. Those who lived on the Hill had lawyers; often enough, their lawyer was William McCulloch, and it was probably at an event catered by the Clemenses that McCulloch made their acquaintance.

William McCulloch was one of the few whites in Piqua to take notice of the town's black population. By the 1940s, he was a regular visitor at the Clemenses' home at 1008 Cam Street, a once one-story home to which Emerson Clemens added electricity and rebuilt as a one-and-a-half-story dwelling of wood and brick. The front door opened onto the living room, with a big double window and two large upholstered chairs. William McCulloch sat in one of those chairs and, in his soft voice, pursued a question with the Clemenses. That question, which no white person had previously posed, was what was it like to be black in Piqua, Ohio?

Colleen Clemens McMurray recalled, "Mr. McCulloch would visit in the daytime. I remember him sitting in the corner with his legs crossed. He would ask about us. He would ask, for instance, was my mother treated with respect when she went to the library?" He wanted to learn, she said, the difference between "the law" and "the rules." Colleen McMurray added that whatever the law might say, the "rule" was "we could not go into any restaurant or hotel or the swimming pool." Churches, tennis courts, golf course, and skating rinks were all segregated. The local movie theatre limited black patrons to the back three rows. When McCulloch visited, Colleen McMurray recalled, he never seemed pressed for time: "He was a listener; a gentleman with whom my parents were not afraid to share their thoughts. He did not have that pretentious attitude the people who owned the factories and the banks had. I viewed him as a listener and a friend." Years later, when Colleen McMurray was clearing out her parents' house, she discovered several hundred copies of the *Congressional Record* that McCulloch had forwarded to them through the years.

Enlistment

William McCulloch rarely confided in anyone except his wife, Mabel. It is difficult, therefore, to determine how he felt about this war and himself. In 1943, he was forty-one, three years beyond the upper limit of those eligible for the draft. McCulloch had a smattering of military experience; he had served as a lieutenant with Piqua's Ohio National Guard unit. However, his position as Speaker of the Ohio House was likely of greater consequence than any he would obtain in uniform. That being the case, he could readily and reasonably have decided his duty lay in Columbus. A long-time family friend, however, observed that McCulloch "did what he thought was right in his Calvinist way." And in that Calvinist way, William McCulloch enlisted in the U.S. Army. He supplied a letter of reference from Edward S. Matthias, for twenty-five years a justice on the Ohio Supreme Court, and sought a commission.

Whatever McCulloch's motives, *The Cincinnati Enquirer* was quick to jump to the politics of the matter. Unless a special session was held in 1944, and none was expected, there would be no need to replace McCulloch as Speaker. He would hold that title, *in absentia*. The newspaper added, "McCulloch is to have a captain's commission and friends are only sorry that it is not higher." McCulloch came to share this view himself. He soon learned that a captain's rank afforded him considerably less responsibility than he was used to handling. During training, he wrote a friend, "I am of the opinion that my civilian experience is almost wholly lost or not understood." For the moment, *The Enquirer* was quick to give McCulloch a fulsome sendoff: "It can be said of McCulloch that he heard the still small voice of conscience far more often than he heard expediency, 'good of the party,' or other subtle appeals. And so men and women respect him and respect him deeply."

On December 3, 1943, McCulloch received a Western Union telegram instructing him to report to Patterson Field, near Dayton, for his pre-induction physical. There, physicians declared his eyesight good; his hearing, nose and throat normal; his blood pressure low (114/70); his X-ray clean, and his mouth short four teeth. He weighed 143 pounds, having gained thirty pounds since leaving Holmesville for the College of Wooster. McCulloch was "recommended for extended active duty." On Christmas night, McCulloch went to the Dayton railway station, where his family bundled him onto a train, which his daughter Ann recalls grew ever smaller as it disappeared down the track of her father's next undertaking.

McCulloch served with the First European Civil Affairs Division, a newly designated military unit charged with providing civil administration to sections of France and Germany once they were liberated by the Allies. Its members were older, largely in their forties. McCulloch's training began at Ft. Custer, Michigan. This major base, fourteen miles northeast of Kalamazoo, eventually provided basic training to 300,000 soldiers. Several days after arriving, McCulloch wrote home, "We really swung into a full day today. Up at six o'clock and classes straight thru to 5:30 except 45 minutes for noon mess" and a two-mile march. Napoleon famously asserted that an army marched on its stomach, and McCulloch's stomach found nothing of which to complain. "The food is of high quality and well-cooked. I had two T-bone steaks, celery, salad, peas, potatoes, peaches and coffee for evening mess." The following day, he wrote he was studying for the unit's first exam, on "The Legal Aspects of Military Government."

McCulloch was in uniform slightly less than two years. The seven hundred letters he wrote home worked out almost exactly to one a day.

His daughter Ann, after a later reading of those letters, commented, "I noticed not only did he talk about his job. He talked about missing my mother; but he really showed how much connected to politics in Columbus he still was and how some of the people he served with in Columbus as Speaker came through. Things to do with the furnace; what to do with the checks he sent home; how our education was getting on. He was very concerned with that." McCulloch wrote in a tiny script to accommodate the size of the standard G.I. letter. McCulloch was not the only Ohio legislator in uniform. By 1944, six representatives, including the minority floor leader and the majority whip, were in military service.

On February 1, 1944, McCulloch and others assigned to civil affairs were transferred to the U.S. Army depot at Camp Reynolds in Greeneville, Pennsylvania, just over the Ohio line an hour south of Lake Erie. Ten days later—on Lincoln's Birthday—McCulloch boarded a troopship that sailed in convoy for Britain, arriving, by nice symmetry, ten days later on Washington's Birthday. McCulloch's unit went into barracks in a former girls' school in Shrivenham, a thoroughly unremarkable Berkshire village of fewer than six hundred residents. Howard Wesley Johnson, a fellow Civil Affairs officer and future president of MIT, wrote that the school "had served as housing for several military units in the years before we had arrived, and the buildings showed it." Shrivenham also showed that while no one doubted that liberated territories would have to be administered, not many in high positions considered that work a top priority. The site offered room, classroom, and training space for 1,000 men at a time. On close inspection, Shrivenham proved to be sorely wanting in the amenities expected by officers, particularly field grade officers, of whom there would be a substantial number. All officers, lieutenant colonels and below, would have to be billeted sixteen to a room. They would have to do their own cleaning and sweeping, and some rooms would have to double as classrooms in the daytime. The officers would be required to carry knives, forks, and cups to the dining hall, where they would eat off compartmented metal trays, which they would have to wash themselves.

Five weeks after arriving, McCulloch managed a weekend pass and went off to see London—Westminster Abbey, Buckingham Palace, and a performance by Alfred Lunt and Lynn Fontanne in *There Shall Be No Night*. Visiting Parliament, he reported home that he was "treated royally"—allowed to handle the Golden Mace that is the symbol of parliamentary authority. He attended a session of Parliament, where Prime Minister Winston Churchill crossed swords with the left-leaning aristocrat, Lady Nancy Astor. (McCulloch was not present for the pair's most famous exchange. When Lady Astor declared that if Churchill was her husband she would give him poison, Churchill replied, "And if you were my wife, I'd take it.")

In one letter home, McCulloch described the two dozen men serving in his unit. These included by some coincidence Earl M. Donbar, the College of Wooster student named a Rhodes Scholar. Others included a college graduate who worked for Indiana Bell, a lawyer and magazine writer from Nebraska, past members of the Arkansas and Arizona state legislatures, a specialist in economics and a specialist in agriculture "who headed some Indian school," and others. McCulloch added, perhaps unhappily, "All but three or four were New Dealers." The range of occupations reflected the range of tasks for which Civil Affairs would be responsible in newly occupied territory: government administration; public safety, health, and welfare; utilities and communications; transportation; salvage; commerce; agriculture; law; and finance and supply.

For reasons generally attributable to the uncertainty that is war, the program at Shrivenham was not well organized. The original plan was that each unit would study up on the particular sites in France and Germany that they would eventually administer. This specificity was dropped when higher authority deemed it a security risk. Author Earl Ziemke wrote in the Army Historical Series volume *The U.S. Army in the Occupation of Germany*, "To the student officers, the courses at Shrivenham seemed most of the time to be an elaborate effort to generate mass boredom while at the same time assaulting individual self-esteem and possibly physical well-being as well."

McCulloch, if disgruntled, never referred to it in his letters home. He urged Mabel to tell their daughters "they have a very proud father with all those A's and Hundreds." Further, he expressed the hope that Mabel McCulloch had attended the Republican Federation Convention to help maintain contacts in party circles. In late April, McCulloch was somewhat surprised to learn that he had been supplanted as Speaker of the Ohio House. The somewhat garbled explanation he received was that a special legislative session had been called for 1944; various newspapers argued that any legislation passed in the absence of a Speaker might lack authority. McCulloch's post was taken by an acting Speaker, William H. Deddens (R-Hamilton County). Shortly thereafter on May 3, McCulloch wrote Mabel of a visit he had paid to Coventry, one of the areas most devastated by the German bombing: "I'm not sorry that I went and would like to tell you all about the visit, but [due to censorship] obviously I can't."

At Shrivenham, the clouds lifted on May 9, 1944. In part this was literal; the day was the first of the season to feel like spring. In larger part, however, it was because Shrivenham played host to an inspection visit of the Supreme Allied Commander General Dwight Eisenhower. Following a "more or less well-executed and enthusiastic parade," Eisenhower gathered the unit in for an informal talk. Eisenhower stressed that while the task of Civil Affairs was broadly humanitarian, it was essential to victory.

Perhaps most welcome was his closing, which acknowledged the group's sense of being sidetracked:

Now a word about what you are doing here. . . . For some time you have been in reserve. You're probably getting bored, some of you. You are a little tired of idleness, particularly when some of you were extraordinarily busy men in civilian life, and you gave up many things—made many sacrifices—and you are getting damned tired of not being used usefully in view of your sacrifices. Your time is coming, so don't worry.

The actual date for the invasion of France was a secret known to few, not including McCulloch. On June 3, 1944, he wrote, "If the children wish to buy me something else, they could get me a couple of khaki colored neckties. Good ones are unobtainable over here." Three days later, France was invaded, and the neckties presumably forgotten. McCulloch heard the invasion announcement with his fellows in their barracks. Soon thereafter he wrote Mabel, "A few moments ago His Majesty the King completed his broadcast to the Empire and the U.S. There was quite an audience in the barracks as there are few radios on the post. The message was in quite a religious vein, wasn't it?" Somewhat anticlimactically, McCulloch added, "When the broadcast was complete I repaired to the laundry room and completed my weekly washing."

On July 1, McCulloch's unit sailed to France. "Our trip was wholly uneventful and very pleasant. The sea was as smooth as a mill pond." Landing in France, he added, "We were greeted by both youth and old as we drove along, with smiles and with the Churchill victory salute." Units of the First European Civil Affairs Division were assigned a variety of tasks and locales. McCulloch could hardly complain of his own posting in the Sixteenth Arrondissement of Paris. McCulloch's unit reached the French capital on August 26, 1944, seven days after the last German troops had retreated from the city. McCulloch and his forty-man unit were quartered at 62 Avenue Henri Martin, which, as gossip had it, had been commandeered by the German general during the occupation. Unlike bomb-cratered and threadbare London, Paris was relatively unscathed by the war. McCulloch assessed his unit's two-story billet, which included an upright Louis Cartier piano and a steel safe. He declared the paint, roofs, walls, and floors to be good; the windows fair; the water supply and sewage poor; and the refrigerator "worthless." He noted that the walls were covered with tapestries; a double French window faces the lawn, with lovely old bookcases to either side of the windows. On the whole, not bad for wartime.

McCulloch had a list of responsibilities long and largely bureaucratic. One primary assignment was to arrange billeting for Allied personnel traveling through the French capital. Paris was not entirely unpleasant. On November 18, 1944, McCulloch wrote his wife, "We had a theatre party last night. *Folies Bergère*. The girls were pretty, the costumes, when they were dressed, were beautiful and the stage settings were novel and varied. Again I wished that you had been along."

His former duties as an attorney reached across the Atlantic. On April 6, 1945, he received a letter from Miami County Probate Court Judge Carl Felger regarding "the still unsettled estate of Eliza Boal Orr." About $900,000 was at issue, and the case had become far and away the most complicated before the court. As McCulloch had been the original representative of one of the litigants, Judge Felger wrote, "I trust you may work out some solution to his difficult problem." Apparently, it did not occur to the Miami County judge that McCulloch was otherwise occupied.

On April 15, for example, his commanding officer asked him to lead a memorial service for President Franklin Roosevelt, who had died three days previously. McCulloch was rather taken aback by the request; he was neither a great fan of FDR, nor did he regard himself as a compelling public speaker. He wrote to Mabel, "I really sweat for an hour or two, but at the appointed hour I had about a four minute tribute organized. Outside of calling a paragraph from Lincoln's second inaugural address a paragraph from the Gettysburg address I made no major mistakes. I offered no prayer, simply saying that the American people and, therefore, the American military personnel of all faiths and all creeds, and the entire group would therefore arise for a minute of silent prayer."

Soon thereafter, McCulloch undertook two trips outside Paris—a three-day assignment in Limoges, France, followed closely by five days' service with the military government in Belgium and along the German-French border. The latter assignment began May 7, 1945—the day before German surrender—and covered 1,700 miles through Liege, Nancy, Metz, Verdun, and Essen. Writing home, McCulloch stated, "Hardly a building was undamaged and from 50 to 85 or 90 percent were piles of rubble. In Essen, the Krupp plant was a mass of broken, twisted and torn girders in every position." He added several observations of note:

The Germans . . . cast furtive glances at us but when we looked directly at them they almost always turned away. In the small towns and villages where there had been no damage or destruction, German children were everywhere. I have never seen so many. Yes, it appears that Hitler was breeding cannon fodder for another war. The children appeared to be unusually well fed and well clothed.

Nancy McCulloch recalls learning the news of the German surrender when the mother of the neighborhood friend with whom she was playing in the yard came to tell them of the announcement. In Piqua, there were spontaneous parades, speeches, and band shows. With peace at hand, CBS war correspondent Eric Sevareid wrote that in America, the end of the war would probably be greeted with fireworks and boisterous parades. In Europe, the men who had fought it were more likely to react with silence. They were, he said, so very tired of the noises of war. McCulloch's reaction, written to Mabel, was similar: "War, to me, will always be damage, waste and despair."

His work in Paris continued. On July 26, 1945, he wrote, "The pressure is really on for us to complete our work and get out. I am at the billet this morning, however, pulling out of our warehouse the rations for a trainload of Dutch who are returning home early tomorrow morning." Pressure was reaching him from another direction. An acquaintance from Piqua wrote that he had paid a call on McCulloch's old law office: "Mr. Berry is simply swamped with work and there seems to be no letup in the amount of work your office is trying to turn out." Was there any way for McCulloch to go on inactive status, return to Piqua, and shoulder the burden at the law firm? The letter closed, "Bill, they need you."

Back in Piqua, events were moving that presaged McCulloch's future. In 1944, a local chapter of the NAACP was formed in town. The local bus station operated a segregated lunch counter. Shortly after the German surrender, Emerson and Viola Clemens, their daughter Colleen, and a scattering of others entered the lunch counter, took seats, and sought service. The counter's operators, Joe and Cleo Terry, informed the group that they did not serve blacks. Colleen recalled, "I heard someone say, 'We need to call the police.'" One demonstrator asked why no blacks could be served. Joe Terry dropped a shoulder, thought a bit, said "Okay," and was soon making sandwiches for those on hand. Soon thereafter, a similar group decided to challenge the requirement that blacks sit only in the back rows of the town's movie theatre. In Colleen McMurray's recollection, "We went in and sat everywhere. They stopped the movie. Finally, a white man in the back said, 'These people have done nothing wrong.'" He reminded the other patrons that two of Piqua's black families had lost sons in the war. He added, "They should be allowed to sit wherever they want." And they did. Desegregation would not always be so smoothly achieved.

William McCulloch felt the same urgent desire to get home that was all but universal among those in the nation's military. On September 6, 1945—five days after the formal Japanese surrender—he informed his headquarters that the law firm of which he was a partner "has a large number of suits pending and ready for trial, which were commenced and personally handled by me prior to my entry into the Army. . . . My only partner is over 70 years of age and cannot continue to carry the burden alone. The good will steadily built up over a period of more than 20 years is being steadily reduced by reason of this inability to dispose of the legal matters entrusted to me."

No reply arrived. However, the following day McCulloch was directed to surrender his military property to military authorities. This included one M1911 pistol (No. 873692); three ammunition clips, a pistol belt and pistol holder; canteen, cup, and canteen cover; first aid packet; meat can, knife, fork, and spoon. Still uncertain of his status, on October 20, McCulloch wrote his congressman, Robert F. Jones, seeking clarification: "I might add that I have donned civilian garb and have begun preparation for final disposal of the Orr Felt & Blanket Co. and other cases that have been pending so long."

McCulloch was formally separated from the military on November 24, 1945, at the Indiantown Gap Military Reservation in Pennsylvania. He made his way back to Piqua, where his daughter Ann was a third-grade student at Spring Street Elementary at the corner of Spring and Ash. Ann's teacher, Mary Wheeler, was also her godmother. "My teacher sent me into the cloakroom, and there my father was." McCulloch then managed a ride to his home at 710 Caldwell. Nancy, the elder daughter, was in the front yard raking leaves when the car pulled up to the curb and her long-missing father emerged.

By Christmas 1945, William McCulloch had settled back into Piqua with Mabel, Nancy, and Ann. McCulloch returned to the offices of Berry & McCulloch on the second floor of the Piqua National Bank, tackling a backlog of cases. He remained in that office and with that law firm for the next three decades. McCulloch always regarded his legal practice as his principal source of support. The war he had served in marked millions of his fellow servicemen with an expanded sense of aspiration. It was not likely that small town legal work would long remain the limit of William McCulloch's ambition.

CHAPTER 9

Junior Congressman

On September 5, 1947, President Harry Truman appointed Congressman Robert F. Jones to the Federal Communications Commission. Jones, as it happened, was the office holder whose intercession McCulloch had sought to speed his discharge from the service. Congressman Jones was from Lima, Ohio, which—like Piqua—was in Ohio's Fourth Congressional District. McCulloch's local congressional seat would fall vacant. Shortly after Truman's intention to appoint Jones was announced, McCulloch decided he would re-enter public life and run for Congress.

McCulloch's war service, added to his legislative Speakership, made him a very attractive candidate—so much so that he was soon endorsed by Ohio U.S. Senators Robert Taft and John Bricker. McCulloch drew only minor opposition in the August 7, 1947, special primary election. That opposition came from G. Dewey Fetter, chairman of the Allen County Republican Party. Fetter's principal objection was that the party appeared to be giving McCulloch a free ride. Actually, not quite. When McCulloch went to former Congressman Jones to learn the "big names" McCulloch should cultivate in the district, the recent legislator refused to help, a fact that rankled McCulloch for years thereafter.

McCulloch's campaign style was set early on. Years later, he told a junior member of his law firm, "Always run scared." For McCulloch, that generally meant attending each of his district's seven county fairs, where he would discuss milk yields with farmers, wages rates with retailers, and foreign policy with whoever was interested. McCulloch would set up a tent on the fair's midway, inside of which one of his daughters, Nancy or Ann, wrote down on file cards the names of the interested. Beyond that, McCulloch worked the service club circuit, speaking to innumerable gatherings of Elks, Lions, and other beasts. As an added note, from earlier legislative campaigns, he dug up and donned a battered brown felt hat that he wore for luck. Indeed, he was wearing that hat the evening he handily defeated J. Dewey Fetter by a vote of 10,120 to 4,159.

McCulloch carried Miami County by a remarkable victory, 4,708 to 173. The Democratic primary was much closer: Joseph E. Quartman of Lima edged State Representative Roy E. Harmony of Sidney by fewer than fifty votes, 2,923 to 2,879, with New Bremen, Ohio, mayor Reuben Dickman collecting 1,918.

In the general election that followed, McCulloch's campaigning was personal and inexpensive. Nothing cost less or paid off better than newspaper endorsements. A typical one, from the *Stillwater Valley News,* ran:

> We feel that with McCulloch's wide experience, and with his reaching the upper group in most every endeavor he had tried, showing a strong intellectual mind as well as a strong sense of patriotism in his country's hour of need, that Bill McCulloch would make this district a good representative in Congress.

McCulloch's most compelling asset was that the Fourth District was reliably Republican. Democrat Quartman ran an aggressive race. McCulloch's margin of victory was solid if unspectacular, 41,677 to 34,464. Actually, the solid aspect of McCulloch's victory came in his home, Miami County. This, he carried by 12,031 to 5,175, thus providing all but 357 votes of his 7,213-vote margin.

William McCulloch was one of eight mid-term congressmen sworn into office on November 17, 1947. His swearing in was hardly the day's top story. That morning, President Harry S. Truman had addressed a special joint session of Congress. Truman pressed for passage of his emergency aid bill for Italy, Austria, and France and discussed the post-war inflation, which was spiraling at an alarming pace. The Congress that Truman addressed was the most Republican since before the New Deal: its 246 Republican members held an easy advantage over the 188 Democrats. It was the assemblage that President Truman would famously pillory in the 1948 national election as the "Do Nothing" Congress—though in truth it may have been less a matter of the Congress doing nothing than of it doing a great deal Truman did not like.

For McCulloch, reaching Congress was something akin to "old home week." Four of his fellow Republicans had served under him in the Ohio legislature, including Representative Harry McGregor of West Lafayette, Ohio, who had been McCulloch's closest ally in the General Assembly. McCulloch's initial remarks to the press were duly modest: "I am a private in the rear rank and will take any assignment given me." Thirty days later, in an offhand move of considerable consequence, McCulloch was appointed to the Judiciary Committee, the body from which he would exercise national leadership on civil rights.

For William and Mabel McCulloch, the final months of 1947 were rather like those of any couple relocating to a new city due to a change in employment. *The Washington Post* reported, "The sandy-mustached McCulloch newly elected to Congress hesitated to urge his wife and the two school-age daughters to make the move from their comfortable establishment in their home town until Washington housing conditions present a more promising picture." That journal added, "Known as a 'collecting couple,' Mabel Harris McCulloch and her WWII veteran husband have filled their home with interesting objects of art. Antiques are the delectation of 'the missus,' while Congressman McCulloch goes in for collecting good-luck elephants." While hunting for a residence, the McCullochs stayed at the fashionable Carlton Hotel, at Sixteenth and K Streets, four blocks north of the White House. With a residence rented at the Westchester Apartments, a decidedly upscale complex located at 4000 Cathedral Avenue, NW., the couple's two daughters, Nancy, then seventeen, and Ann, ten, joined their parents as 1948 opened.

The Education of a Congressman

It is said that children should be seen but not heard. In practice, children are not as adept at practicing this precept as are junior congressmen, who generally keep a low and quiet profile. Still, even a review of Congressman McCulloch's first few months in office indicate the patterns he would follow for a quarter-century.

First, he was an opponent of what he regarded as federal overreach. He voted against establishing a peacetime draft as a "drastic proposal" that intruded on personal liberty. (The full House did not share McCulloch's view, ratifying the measure by a 283 to 130 vote.) He opposed Truman's efforts to expand the size and range of the federal purse. Indeed, McCulloch commented that his single point of agreement with President Truman was "that certain controls are instruments of the police state." Along with this, McCulloch favored regionalism over federalism. When on April 14, 1948, he delivered his maiden address to the House floor, he talked of the success of the Miami Conservancy District in providing the Ohio region that included his district with a quarter-century of effective flood protection. His central point was that the district's six major dams had been financed entirely by those Miami Valley residents who benefitted from their existence.

Second, he stayed close to his district. The June 19, 1948, issue of the *Congressional Record* listed the schedule of meetings he would hold with constituents in each of the seven county seats in his district. Anyone with a question to pose, a bone to pick, or advice to give was welcome to the congressman's ear. Of one such visit, the *Lima News* reported that McCulloch had met with fifty Allen County constituents in Lima Courtroom No. 1 in eight hours, an effort that included advising a young man as to whether he should marry his sweetheart who was on a visitor's visa from Sweden. "Congressman McCulloch listened to the young man's story for more than 15 minutes and then promised to assist in any way he could."

McCulloch had a sense of the practical. The demobilization of twelve million servicemen, many of whom wed in the year or two following their discharge, created an enormous housing shortage. The bottleneck to that shortage was that the economy, transitioning out of war production, was not yet producing building materials in quantities sufficient to meet the demand. That—combined with his general antipathy to government actions where he felt private industry would suffice—prompted McCulloch's voting against public housing, which would among other things increase the demand for the building supplies then in short supply. He likewise voted against the displaced persons act, as this, he thought, would add further to the existing housing shortage. His views on civil rights, however, were closer to those of President Truman, with McCulloch arguing that all federal and state statutes in this realm should be "implemented" to ensure that both the spirit and the letter of basic rights are guaranteed.

A poll reported in the *Ohio Republican News* underscored how conservative McCulloch's Fourth District was. Respondents wanted to reduce federal income taxes and reduce federal spending by margins of 77 percent to 19, and 77 percent to 18. The Taft-Hartley Act, generally regarded as strongly anti-labor, gained the approval of 75 percent of those polled. Three-quarters opposed economic controls; two-thirds supported increased military expenditures; an equal number opposed increasing the admission of refugees. A narrow margin supported better pay for government employees, but there was an even split on the Marshall Plan, the Truman Administration's program of major financial aid to post-war Europe.

Like virtually everyone in American politics, McCulloch expected Republican Governor Thomas E. Dewey to score an easy triumph over incumbent Harry Truman in the 1948 election. From the campaign trail in Waynesfield, Ohio, the *Stillwater Valley News* reported, McCulloch defended the Eightieth Congress for its work in eliminating the "Red Menace in both high and low places." Once Dewey was inaugurated, McCulloch told the audience, the federal government would start shedding employees at the 500 to 600 daily rate that Truman had been adding them.

This was standard Republican fare, 1948. However, speaking in Allen County two weeks before the voting, McCulloch framed his candidacy in words rarely heard from an aspirant from either party, words that redefined the terms in which he saw his relationship to his constituents. He stated, simply, that he did not believe it was his task to see that the Fourth District's plate be turned upward when the goodies were being ladled out. Contrarily, and straightforwardly, McCulloch declared, "If you expect to measure your congressman's ability by what he can get from Congress, I would rather not be returned. . . . There is always a day of reckoning in the spending of government money and that day is now here. There just isn't enough money to go around for everything we might want to do."

More startling, he meant it. In later debate on the House Floor, a Georgia congressman complained of the quantity of time taken up by special requests from congressmen wishing to aid and comfort their districts. McCulloch secured the floor and tartly asked the Georgia congressman to name the occasion upon which he, McCulloch, had sought special favors for his district. The Georgia congressman confessed he had not paid sufficient attention to McCulloch's doings to answer. Sealing off any doubt, McCulloch added, "I would like to advise the gentleman from Georgia as well as other members of the committee that the member from the Fourth District has not appeared before any committee or any subcommittee requesting authorization for his district in Ohio."

Harry Truman's 1948 victory was less a "miracle comeback" than the consequence of journalistic groupthink. Franklin Roosevelt secured his fourth term in wartime 1944 by 3.6 million votes. Four years later, Truman—despite losing one million largely Democratic votes on the left to Progressive candidate Henry Wallace and one million largely Democratic votes on the right to States Rights candidate Strom Thurmond—was re-elected by 2.2 million votes. The more accurate story of 1948 was that the press traded back and forth its unexamined assumptions until it had polished them with the ring of truth.

That said, Truman's victory was a considerable surprise to many. The Democratic triumph came not only at the presidential level, but also in Congress, where Truman's party added 75 seats to obtain a 263 to 171 majority. The upset changed nothing in Ohio's Fourth District, where McCulloch increased his previous year's victory margin from 9 to 12 percent in defeating Democrat Earl Ludwig of Lima by a 57,330 to 45,575 margin.

The congressman's family was well settled in Washington. At the time, most wives went to Washington with their husbands. In those less partisan days, the McCullochs found it easy to establish a social life. Mabel McCulloch told one reporter, "Some of the friends who had served with Bill were there in Washington and we became busy immediately, both socially and otherwise."

Mabel McCulloch's main social engagement was with the Congressional Club, a Congressionally-chartered association of the spouses of members of Congress. The club had standing: among other activities, it held alternate year receptions for the president and for the entire Supreme Court and annually hosted the incumbent First Lady. These events generally were held in the upscale Shoreham Hotel. It was in Washington a less partisan time than it is today and members routinely had friendships that crossed party lines. Conviviality may have been aided by the club's inviolable rule against talking shop. Mabel McCulloch told one reporter,

"I learned my most important political lesson early. A wife never discusses her husband's work with anyone." Of her mother, Mabel's elder daughter, Nancy, observed, "My mother's real career was my father's career. She was the one person he trusted most."

Daughter Nancy, then seventeen, enrolled in the Holton-Arms private school, a well-established Washington undertaking then located at 2125 S Street, NW, where she excelled in history, particularly British. For fifth and sixth grades, daughter Ann began the school year in Piqua, and she then transferred to Holton-Arms after Congress convened in early January. As the private school in Washington set rather higher standards than the public school in Piqua, the McCullochs decided to educate their younger daughter in Washington full time. Ann recalls that the school had a chauffeur who picked up day students who did not board at the school, "So we rode to school in a limo with a driver wearing a cap." Barely a year after arriving in Washington, Nancy McCulloch was named one of the forty-nine contenders for the crown of Cherry Blossom Queen. She confided an ambition to the newspapers. She hoped to take to the stage: "I'll try for summer stock this year—if my parents will let me. Maybe I can convince them I'm not too young."

Mabel McCulloch went on antique hunts. Later, in 1956, Senator John Kennedy sold his Hickory Hill estate in Virginia to Robert and Ethel Kennedy. Thereafter, Mabel McCulloch and Ethel Kennedy frequently shopped together for antiques. At one early point, Mabel was informed that a set of Dubach cabinets she owned were of doubtful authenticity. She decided to make a clean slate of things—emptying the apartment of every antique. When William McCulloch arrived home, nothing was left of the furnishings except their bed and his desk.

McCulloch was somewhat ambivalent about Washington. Holmesville, Ohio—his birthplace and a spot frequently visited over the summer—was a place he loved. As noted, his father-in-law, Joseph Edward Harris, ran a veneering business. One year, Harris had four shotguns specially made with burl walnut stocks. He kept one, gave one to his son, and gave the remaining pair to his sons-in-law, McCulloch included. Each Thanksgiving, the foursome would hunt pheasant and rabbit.

From her own visits to Holmesville, Nancy McCulloch recalls, "The town only had 300 people. You had to go to the post office to pick up your mail. It was an excuse to get some exercise. We went every summer, from the time I was old enough to be alone until I was maybe 14. As child, he and I would go for walks. I'd go swinging on the grapevines; the most exciting thing I could do. We'd pick watercress." She remembers Holmesville as a place where she believed in Santa Claus, where she learned to love cows, and where—because of their diet—the township's numerous Amish "smelled of sour milk."

For Ann, however, Piqua was home. The family house at 710

Caldwell Street was a stately Victorian wooden frame structure, whose high ceilings brought some relief from summer heat and whose curving banister gave Ann something to slide down. The family always had a live-in housekeeper, including four successive daughters of a local dairy farmer, whose farm the full family visited on their regular Sunday afternoon car rides into the gently-rolling country surrounding Piqua. The home was fronted by a large yard in which Ann and the neighborhood's complement of children would play "Spy," a game of uncertain rules that involved dividing into teams and tracking down anybody lying low in the alley that split the block. For Ann, Piqua meant occasional shopping sprees to Rike-Kumler, Dayton's leading department store, a visit to a nearby dress shop, and dinner at a leading restaurant, the King Cole.

The congressman came home to Piqua most weekends and when Congress was not in session, and he lived in the city those months that followed adjournment. Customarily when in Piqua, McCulloch each morning walked the five blocks from his home to his second-floor law office at the Piqua National Bank in the city's downtown square—about the only exercise he ever took, though he did use the stairway rather than the elevator. He was a creature of some habits. Each mid-day McCulloch walked the several blocks to the local Elks club at the corner of Ash and Williams for lunch topped off with his favorite dessert, pumpkin pie doused with turkey gravy.

Both McCulloch daughters recall their mother as an outstanding cook who learned to make standard midwestern fare—fried chicken, corn on the cob, "the world's best" cherry pie, and Christmas cookies. Mabel McCulloch did the shopping, bought the vegetables last, and in her kitchen, dinner was served the moment the corn on the cob was done.

For the McCullochs, the best place to shop in Piqua was Ulbrich's market on South Wayne Street. Mabel went there regularly. William struck up an acquaintance with Ulbrich's butcher. Before heading back to Washington, he stopped at the store for a stack of fresh-carved steaks. If he was driving, the steaks would be frozen and packed in ice. If he was flying, he simply slipped them into his briefcase. In either case, McCulloch believed the only way to prepare a steak was to fry it in a large skillet.

If McCulloch was ferrying steaks back to Washington—or just about any other time—he "drove like a bat out of hell." One time in eastern Ohio a local policeman caught up with him and told McCulloch to drive back to the previous town to settle his ticket. McCulloch refused. He pulled his congressional license plates out from under his seat and told the patrolman that a member en route to Congress could not have his travel interrupted. The officer in question, finding himself constitutionally one-upped, was in no good humor when McCulloch drove off. McCulloch set somewhat higher standards for others. His son-in-law, David Carver, recalls picking the congressman up at the Dayton airport, and then turning on the radio as they drove off. McCulloch said, "I would like to suggest that you not listen to the radio, but that you attend to your business when you drive." There were always standards. McCulloch generally drove Chevys, though not necessarily the latest model. Later, when Carver was working in Washington, D.C. for Ford, he suggested his father-in law take advantage of an offer from the automaker that amounted to a half-priced Lincoln for any member of Congress. McCulloch declined, saying, "And when Rob Barkley [senior Ford representative in Washington] wants me to do something, what do I do?"

Holmesville, the place of his birth and upbringing, remained a strong influence on McCulloch—in terms of hard work and a commitment to thrift characteristic of those brought up on turn-of-the-century farms. He was particularly frugal with the public dollar. Addressing Congress on May 24, 1949, he spoke of it being far easier to expand expenditures when times were lush than to retract them when times were lean.

In times of prosperity, the careless spenders justify on the grounds that the people can well afford taxes and larger and larger Federal expenditures. In times of inflation or recession or depression, the careless spenders justify their action on the grounds that huge expenditures and deficit financing result in a lasting stimulant for business. In good times and in bad times, their program is to tax and spend, tax and spend. The fiscal year ending June 30, 1949 will be the most prosperous in our history. Unbelievable as it may seem, we will end the fiscal year with a deficit.

On August 25, 1949, McCulloch—who would argue for the rights of any not fully able to defend them—took to the House floor to argue that any person thought "insane" should not be institutionalized without a formal hearing.

On January 18, 1950, McCulloch announced his candidacy for re-election. McCulloch said that he would "continue to advocate economy and efficiency in government and would vigorously oppose further interference of federal government in purely state and local affairs." By the time the election came, Americans were fighting in Korea. On June 25, 1950, North Korean troops poured over the border with South Korea; initially, South Korea's resistance was feeble. In the Pusan Perimeter, South Korean and American forces held on to barely one-tenth of the land originally part of South Korea. McCulloch offered a home truth. Conditions in Korea, he told one Piqua audience, were "not good." Among other things, he told a Rotary Club audience in Troy, the morale of the enlisted man was "not nearly as good as those of the fighting men" of the First and Second World Wars. This, he attributed to their uncertainty over why this war was being fought. McCulloch also had bad news for the home front. The money needed to fight the war would have to come out of the standard of living of the average American, who would also face strong wage and price controls. He told one September audience, "If you hire [elect] me, I'm going to vote to lay heavy taxes on your backs. No one deserves to remain in public office unless he has the courage to tell people the facts, even when they hurt."

Telling the voters that, if elected, he would tax them was one thing. A second, and equally uncommon thing, was McCulloch's assertion in his campaign that Americans had gone soft on themselves. Speaking before a group of spouses of physicians and dentists at the Troy Country Club, McCulloch said, "Because too many of us haven't assumed our responsibilities to government, the government has been taken over by those who want to make the people's choices for them." The Republican candidate for re-election continued, "The result has been the loss of freedom. If the present administration is given encouragement at the polls, it will further curtail our right to choose by socializing medicine and housing." McCulloch had similar words when he spoke in Piqua at the dedication of the Miami Valley Bridge: "America's progress in the development of matters scientific and material has not been matched by its spiritual and moral enhancement."

His views—individualist; Constitutionalist; anti-Communist—were where the Fourth District's mainstream lived. On November 7, 1950, McCulloch was re-elected by two-to-one, gaining 65,749 votes to the 32,565 garnered by Democratic candidate Carleton Carl Reiser of Celina, Ohio. This victory came, the *Piqua Daily Call* editorialized, despite the fact that "long before the election, the Piqua Republican told his constituents that he would have to vote for higher taxes to finance our defense program. He told them he would have to vote to cut all non-defense spending."

McCulloch was firmly anti-collectivist, and in international matters, McCulloch saw little reason for fine distinctions. In December 1950, Congress voted 225 to 142 to approve $38 million in aid to Yugoslavia, at the time thought to be taking a stance somewhat independent of the Soviet Union. McCulloch voted "No," and explained his vote by saying that a Communist was still a Communist.

However one plans one's life, the unexpected occurs. In June 1951— six months after McCulloch's re-election—the major league baseball owners gathered to select a new commissioner. Discussion whittled the field down to three finalists, one of whom was Ohio's Democratic Governor Frank J. Lausche, a one-time semi-pro infielder. Lausche's major booster was P. K. Wrigley, owner of the Chicago Cubs. Newspaper speculation ensued as to who was bested suited to serve as Ohio's governor should Lausche leave Columbus for friendlier confines. The *Troy Daily News* reported that Republican Senator John Bricker termed McCulloch "a likely prospect." The *Lima News* stated, "McCulloch has been mentioned as a possible gubernatorial choice if the post is made vacant by the election of Gov. Frank J. Lausche as baseball commissioner." In the end, the question did not matter, as the owners selected National League president Ford Frick as the new commissioner. Nonetheless, the frequency with which McCulloch's name was mentioned as a prospective Ohio governor was a testament to the rising regard in which he was held.

On January 15, 1952, Ohio Fourth District Republicans caucused at the Hotel Wagner in Sidney. Unsurprisingly, they endorsed William McCulloch for reelection to Congress, John Bricker for reelection to the United States Senate, and Robert A. Taft to be Republican standard bearer for president that November.

McCulloch's Political Hero

As fortune would have it, William McCulloch and Robert A. Taft had just missed crossing paths in the Ohio State Legislature. The 1932 election that first brought McCulloch to Columbus handed Taft, who was seeking reelection to the state Senate, the only defeat of his career. Taft was a conservative intellectual committed to the rights of individuals against the many. For example, he led Republicans even though he did not share their advocacy of Prohibition or their preference for mandatory Bible readings in school. His person and views merit attention, as he was clearly the American political figure William McCulloch most admired and by whom he was most influenced.

No American family—not the Kennedys; not the Adamses—was as rooted in the nation's politics as the Tafts of Cincinnati. The family was Republican from the start and from the heart. Alphonso Taft, who arrived in Cincinnati from Vermont in 1838, was an Ohio delegate to the 1856 Republican National Convention, the first the party held. The family was abolitionist. Taft traveled to a national anti-slavery convention to hear Frederick Douglass, the runaway slave and eloquent champion of black freedom. Alphonso Taft served later as secretary of war under President Ulysses S. Grant, then as attorney general, and finally as ambassador to Austria-Hungary.

His son, William Howard Taft, had perhaps the most impressive political resume in American history: he served as solicitor general, secretary of war to the rather truculent president, Theodore Roosevelt; as president from 1909–1913; and in 1921 was appointed chief justice of the United States. His enormous appetite for work was matched by his enormous appetite—indeed, when elected president in 1908, he weighed more in pounds (325) than he had received in electoral votes (321), an outcome unlikely to be matched.

The Taft who mattered to McCulloch was of the third political generation, Robert Alphonso Taft. Serving in the U.S. Senate from 1939 to 1953, Bob Taft was so unquestionably the leader of the GOP minority that he was widely referred to as "Mr. Republican." Harry Truman, who rarely if ever agreed with Taft, nonetheless called him "a high-class man . . . honest, intelligent and extremely capable." Taft had been first in his undergraduate class at Yale University, first in his class at Yale's law school, and when he took the Ohio bar exam, he produced the highest score yet registered.

Taft and McCulloch shared personal traits. Neither had the flash or charisma that eases a politician's rise. Neither had much hair. Both delivered speeches more literate and logical than compelling. Taft was admired for his ordinariness, shy and rumpled; he did not enjoy the push and shove of politics or the humor that can be the occupation's saving grace. In a profession in which expediency is often the better part of valor, Taft was blunt. Once asked by a reporter what Americans could do about the then-high cost of meat, he famously replied, "Eat less."

Politically, two traits of Taft's midwestern Republicanism were predictable. First, he was opposed to the centralizing tendencies of the New Deal and to virtually all the works of its creator, Franklin Roosevelt. Underscoring this point, Taft stated, "If democracy is to be preserved, we must have more local self-government instead of less. The more government is removed from the people, the less interest they take in it . . . and the more likely it is to become unresponsive and tyrannical."

McCulloch often expressed a similar attitude. Once on the floor of the House, he questioned a fellow member, Charles Wesley Vursell (R-Illinois) about how many individuals worked in the Office of Price Administration (OPA) just to deal with shoes and leather. McCulloch believed it time the federal government stopped regulating commodity prices. Congressman Vursell said he did not know, but the entire OPA employed 12,600. McCulloch asked, "Might I conclude from what the gentleman has said that this is just another example of the Federal bureaucracy being given a grant of power and then refusing to relinquish it after the cause of its use no longer exists?" Congressman Vursell responded, "I fear you may be right." Second, Taft leaned toward isolationism. Following the First World War, future president Herbert Hoover—placed in charge of emergency food relief in war-ravaged Europe—invited Taft to serve as an administrative assistant to the relief effort. The experience, wrote a biographer, left Taft "a disillusioned skeptic" about internationalism as a philosophy and foreigners as people. In the months before the United States entered the Second World War, Senator Taft opposed Lend-Lease and other forms of aid to Britain, including the arming of U.S merchant ships and the instituting of a military draft. Later, when publishing magnate Henry Luce announced the advent of "the American century," Taft was appalled:

It is based on the theory that we know better what is good for the world than the world itself. It assumes that we are always right and that anyone who disagrees with us is wrong.

It reminds me of the idealism of the bureaucrats in Washington who want to regulate the lives of every American along the lines that the bureaucrats think best for them. . . . Other people simply do not like to be dominated and we [will] be in the same position of suppressing rebellions by force in which the British found themselves during the 19th century.

McCulloch's views were similar: Once the post-war Marshall Plan had completed the task of aid to Europe, McCulloch invariably voted against foreign aid. He was skeptical of foreign trade, believing it a bad deal for Americans if the country traded with countries that paid lower wages.

One trait perhaps less to be expected—Taft was a firm supporter of civil rights. This was in part family tradition. Nearly a century earlier, his grandfather had heard Frederick Douglas speak and had helped the newly founded Republicans draw the line that said slavery would go no further than it already had. In *The Fifties*, David Halberstam described Taft as a consistent civil rights supporter. He voted to establish a Fair Employment Practices Commission in 1948, to abolish the poll tax, and to enact a federal anti-lynching law. Further, he voted for a bill to require the Ku Klux Klan to file its membership lists with the FBI.

Taft's objective, however, was the presidency. He actively sought the Republican nomination in 1940, 1948, and 1952. His likeliest chance came on his final attempt. In 1952, Taft campaigned in forty-one states, giving 524 speeches. The nomination was all but his. The "all but" was the uncertainty surrounding General Dwight D. Eisenhower, the commander of D-Day. Was he interested in politics? Was he a Republican? On April 12, 1952, Eisenhower answered both questions by seeking a leave of absence from the military to seek the Republican nomination.

The contest underscored the gap between the Republican Party's midwestern conservatives and its eastern moderates. Taft won primaries in Wisconsin, Illinois, Ohio, and Nebraska. Eisenhower was victorious in New Hampshire, New Jersey, Pennsylvania, and Massachusetts. Still, Taft's odds looked good. A pre-convention poll by the Associated Press gave him 458 delegates—a total that included Congressman William McCulloch—to Eisenhower's 402, with 607 needed to nominate. In the convention's maneuvering, Taft lost out to Eisenhower's popularity and the infighting skill of Thomas E. Dewey, himself a twice-defeated nominee and leader of the eastern Republicans. Eisenhower's first ballot lead of 595 to Taft's 500 quickly turned into the needed majority as delegates jumped onto the winning bandwagon.

Congressman to Korea

A month later, William McCulloch was one of the four members of the Judiciary Committee picked to spend three weeks touring military facilities in Japan, Korea, and Formosa. Upon his return, McCulloch described the war-ravaged country for his constituents. In Seoul, the capital, conditions were "terrible with everything battered and the filth is terrible." He noted that many children were without clothes; he praised the work of helicopter crews in evacuating the wounded; noted that the Turks and Colombians were "terrific fighters." The weather, he said, was unbearably hot and humid, with 250,000 refugees in Pusan, filthy water, and young teenagers working for sixty cents a day. Again, McCulloch delivered words hardly likely to curry favor with taxpayers. If, he told repeated audiences, he was re-elected in 1952, he would support an immediate income tax increase to pay the costs of defending South Korea. The Fourth District swallowed McCulloch's stiff medicine; he gained his fourth term in office by the easy margin of 92,302 to 42,835, the largest margin in the district's history. Indeed, in his home, Miami County, he outpolled Dwight Eisenhower—a landslide winner nationally—by a 20,436 to 19,575 margin.

Unbeknownst to all—unbeknownst, for that matter, to the aspirant himself—Senator Robert Taft was a dying man. Cancer, not yet discovered, had metastasized. Diagnosed, he declined quickly, dying July 31, 1953, barely six months after the date at which he had hoped to take office. William McCulloch took to the floor to offer this tribute:

We have lost a great and good man. Few men in the history of America have measured up to Robert A. Taft. Although the highest gift in the power of the American people was denied him, he became even greater in such denial. Without rancor and without resentment, he gave his great ability to his President and to his country. Like Lincoln, his life ended far too soon.

Five years later, when portraits were unveiled of the five individuals selected by the Senate as the greatest members to serve therein, Robert Taft stood with Henry Clay, Daniel Webster, Robert Calhoun, and Robert La Follette. As a further show of fealty, McCulloch took a lead in getting the monument to Robert Taft established on the Senate side of the Capitol grounds.

So it was rather heady talk when on August 29, 1953, the Dayton *Journal Herald* reported that local GOP county chairmen "have begun talking up Rep. William M. McCulloch" as the man best fitted to succeed Mr. Republican. The newspaper noted, "McCulloch's voting record has been compared favorably with that of Senator Taft." A second paper on December 12, 1953, reported that there was a "rather widespread belief among those who know Mr. McCulloch best that no man in public or private life in this state is better qualified to fill the immense void left by the death of Senator Taft." However, the publication added, it could be that McCulloch, along with Seventh District Republican Congressman Clarence Brown, might see more value in accruing seniority in the House than in joining the upper branch as a junior member.

Faced with the Korean Emergency, McCulloch had flat-out told his constituents that higher taxes were needed. He was not, however, a believer in a large standing army. He was a believer in government economy. With the Korean Armistice signed, McCulloch told the Sidney, Ohio, Junior Chamber of Commerce that only two government fields offered the opportunity for "sizeable savings": defense and foreign aid.

Through these years, McCulloch was routinely re-elected. In 1954, he defeated Forrest Blankenship of Covington, Ohio, by a 67,564 to 33,445 vote. Two years later, he gained his sixth term defeating Lima, Ohio, attorney Ortha Barr by a new district record, 93,607 to 42,416. He remained attentive to constituent concerns. He helped a Lewisburg man achieve victory in a fifty-two-year-long effort to have his mailbox moved 1,056 feet so that it was properly located in front of his house. McCulloch's office estimated the half-century of misplacement had required the postal patron to travel 6,250 miles to collect his mail. As a member of the Judiciary Committee, he sought and secured passage of a bill that reunited a Chinese couple. The bill provided U.S. citizenship to the wife, who had been living in Toronto, Canada, where her husband, an American citizen, was studying medicine. In time, McCulloch took on civic responsibilities in Piqua. In 1954, he was appointed to the Board of Directors of Piqua's Third Savings and Loan. The board's president told McCulloch, "While the financial remuneration received is not large, we feel that you, too, will derive much satisfaction in furthering the aims of the [Third] Savings and Loan." McCulloch did so, from this and other civic pursuits. His daughter Nancy commented, "My father felt he belonged to Piqua." In June 1955, the McCulloch's daughter Ann, then eighteen, graduated cum laude from Holton-Arms, where she received the Scribe Award as editor-in-chief of the school yearbook. Ann opted to attend Denison College, to the deep annoyance of the school's headmistress, who had wanted Ann to attend her own alma mater, Vassar.

Through the mid-1950s, McCulloch's major legislative work related to small business. In 1953, Republican minority leader, Representative Joseph Martin, appointed McCulloch to a committee to investigate the subject. The committee was formed when a study showed that one hundred large concerns were receiving 62 percent of defense contracts, with small businesses rarely applying or being considered. One purpose of the committee was to redress this imbalance.

He noted that small companies had a limited number of capital sources; that fluctuating earnings made taxes in their "good years" more severe; that most small businesses were intensely competitive; that more limited administrative staffs made regulations more burdensome on small business. Given these points, he said, "The essential thing which we believe is that the administration and the Congress of the United States must recognize is the absolute necessity for an adjustment of the tax

burden of the small business and small farmer." In a later context, Mc-
Culloch explained further: "There has been an alarming concentration
of economic power in some fields which is contrary to the healthy growth
of industry."

In March 1957, McCulloch told the House:

We in Congress can no longer sit by and watch big business with its vast financial resources take the lion's share of the government's production and service contracts, some
95 percent of research and development contracts, or develop new products and take
over existing smaller companies to dominate new and established civilian markets. We are
at least partially responsible for this dilemma, and we must find a solution. I personally
believe that at least a partial answer lies in tax relief for small business.

Shortly, McCulloch and other Republicans introduced pertinent legislation. This would allow small firms to accelerate depreciation on used
property; permit firms with fewer than ten stockholders to be treated as
partnerships or proprietorships for tax purchases; allow closely held firms
to extend estate tax payments over a decade; and give investors in small
firms more liberal treatment of losses in such firms.

The House did not respond immediately to the McCulloch-sponsored proposals. Both houses of Congress were by this time embroiled
in what would be the central issue of American domestic politics for the
ensuing decade—civil rights.

CHAPTER 10

First Step on Race

In *An American Dilemma*, his landmark 1944 study of race in America, Swedish sociologist Gunnar Myrdal states that the question of race was "something difficult to settle and equally difficult to leave alone." Myrdal believed that, compared to Europeans, Americans were moralistic and morally conscious, that the typical American was likely to be "a believer in and a defender of the faith in humanity" who thought it important to carry out his or her ideals in daily life. Myrdal noted this approvingly. He wrote that he counted himself as among those who regarded these qualities as "the glory of the nation, its youthful strength, perhaps the salvation of mankind." The dilemma—to which he would devote more than 1,400 pages—was how individual Americans reconciled these beliefs with the clearly unequal status of the nation's black population.

To a great majority of white Americans the Negro problem has distinctly negative connotations. . . . The very presence of the Negro in America . . . represents to the ordinary white man in the North as well as in the South an anomaly in the very structure of American society. To many, this takes on the proportion of a menace—biological, economic, social, cultural, and, at times, political. This anxiety may be mingled with a feeling of individual and collective guilt. A few see the problem as a challenge to statesmanship. To all it is a trouble.

Most white Americans, he noted, suppressed any awareness that their attitude toward race constituted a fault in their moral integrity. Rather, he wrote, they intermingled such thoughts "together with all of the confusion, the ambiguity and inconsistency, which lurk in the basement of men's soul." It was just such ambiguity that, as described earlier by author James Weldon Johnson, dominated discussion in Jacksonville. But as both Johnson and Myrdal note, this very discussion created a mental strain, unease, a moral struggle. Myrdal then offered a fundamental truth: "The moral struggle goes on within people and not merely between them." That is, the conflict over race that dominated mid-twentieth-century

American public life was not simply a struggle between those who sought change and those who resisted it. It was also a fight that occurred within each individual, bringing at various times to the fore what was best and worst in each.

It is not the intention of this book to give a full history of the American civil rights movement, its pain and its glory. The present volume is a biography of an Ohio congressman, William Moore McCulloch, who—as the story told here will demonstrate—played a singularly important role in the legislation that the civil rights movement sought and secured. However, to tell the story of William McCulloch, it is necessary to present something of the broader context so that his contribution takes a balanced place within the whole.

There is no identifiable point at which history places its finger across the unscrolling passage of time and says, here, this was the start of the American civil rights movement. Or, if there is such a time, it occurred in 1619 when the first complement of twenty Africans was sold into slavery in Jamestown, Virginia. Once slavery was introduced onto the continent, only two possibilities existed: either it would continue, or it would end. The Civil War that brought an end to the nation's "peculiar institution" posed another question: would those whose forebears had been brought to America in shackles achieve the full rights of citizenship?

But if the inception of the post-World War Two civil rights movement cannot be fixed in time, events that advanced it can be identified. The first, broadly, was the previously mentioned "great mingling" that war brought about. Millions of black Americans had been uprooted by that conflict, either to serve in the nation's military or to work for hitherto unimagined wages in the war industries that fed that conflict. Post-war, many African Americans who had had that experience were less willing to go gently back into the subservience that had characterized their earlier existence. In the popular arena, that cause was advanced on April 15, 1947, when Jackie Robinson took the field for the Brooklyn Dodgers, the first African American to be part of "the national pastime." Quickly, he became the most-talked-about black man in America.

The effort was advanced within the nation's legal framework by a remarkable group of lawyers gathered around the NAACP's Legal Defense Fund and the person of Thurgood Marshall. In the 1944 ruling in *Smith v. Allwright*, the U. S. Supreme Court declared unconstitutional the all-white primary in Texas. This was huge—since Texas then had no Republican Party to speak of, gaining the Democratic nomination was tantamount to election. Earlier courts had held that, as the Democratic Party was a private organization, it could set whatever rules it wished—including the rule that excluded blacks from voting in the only state election that actually mattered. In 1946, the California State Supreme Court ruled that blacks could not be excluded from union membership in any work place that made membership a condition of employment. In 1948, the Supreme Court ruled in *Shelly v. Kramer* that racially restrictive property covenants had no constitutional standing. And, most important, in the 1954 decision in *Brown v. the Topeka [Kansas] Board of Education*, the High Court overturned nearly sixty years of settled law to declare that segregation in public facilities was unconstitutional.

The effort advanced through violence, as in the August 1955 abduction, torture, and murder of Emmett Till, a fourteen-year-old Chicago youth who, while visiting relatives in Mississippi, was alleged to have flirted with a white girl. Unlike earlier occasions, when the families of those lynched quietly buried their dead and hoped no further harm would come, Till's family insisted on a public funeral in Chicago, an open-casket funeral so that the brutally slain young man was shown to the world.

The effort advanced through non-violence. Most famously, it coursed forward on December 1, 1955, when Rosa Parks, a domestic worker in Birmingham, Alabama, refused when directed to move to the back seats the local transit company reserved for black passengers. She refused, she later said, because she was tired. She was also arrested. Her arrest sparked a fifteen-month boycott by local African Americans of the segregated city bus lines, a boycott that drew as a leader the then twenty-six-year-old minister, the Rev. Martin Luther King, Jr. On June 5, 1956, the federal district court declared the operation of segregated public transportation to be unconstitutional, a decision the Supreme Court upheld the following November.

The effort, often overlooked, would also be advanced through technologies. One was television, which brought to many in the South, black and white, images of a world of which many had known little. True, while these images included impossibly well-mannered children and implacably steel-eyed gunmen, television advertising presented a world that was far more affluent than that of many southern whites and almost all southern blacks. And from these images, aspirations arose. The second technology, somewhat later in influence, was air conditioning. Whatever one might say of the North, its winters were cold. When technology found a way to cool and to dehumidify the South, northerners began to move to the region. Those moving south were not necessarily racially enlightened, but they in any case had not grown up socialized in the caste system of the South and therefore did not draw their identities from allegiance to its ways.

The Battle in Congress

All of the above recounts actions occurring outside the halls of Congress. But it was within those halls that the legislative battle for civil rights was fought. Therefore, it is important to consider the institution of Congress itself and those who found their battlefield there.

Much has been written about how congressional southerners fought a grimly determined battle against civil rights. Less attention has been paid to why they fought so hard. A northern or western member represented a mix of constituents with varying interests—teachers, union members, retirees, small businessmen, and others. In the common ways of politics, a member weighed and balanced those varied interests against both his own beliefs and the likely influence each group might have on his re-election. Some things were not done: no representative of Wisconsin ever said a word against cheese. But while elsewhere a congressman's agenda was varied, in the South only one matter had true consequence: white voters were committed to continued segregation. A southern representative might cast a liberal vote on hospital construction or social security, but a vote in favor of school integration would likely be the last he ever cast. Heavily outnumbered as the South was in both Senate and House, the region took recourse in a number of weapons that could be used in defense of its peculiar social arrangements.

The foremost advantages flowed from the seniority rule. As for all practical purposes there was no Republican Party in the South, Democrats elected tended to enjoy lengthy tenures. Committees were invariably chaired by the member with the most years of service. In consequence, chairmanships were disproportionately held by southern representatives. And committee chairman had enormous power. They determined whether and when the committee would meet, what it would discuss, and who would be allowed to speak. On February 28, 1956, due to the death of another senator, Democrat James Eastland of Mississippi—perhaps the Senate's least apologetic segregationist—became chair of the Judiciary Committee, through which all civil rights legislations moved or failed to move. Eastland was only fifty-one, so it was entirely plausible he would sit at the gates to justice for a quarter-century. With only moderate hyperbole, the NAACP's chief lobbyist, Clarence Mitchell, said of Eastland's ascension, "A mad dog is loose in the streets of justice." Long tenures had a second advantage. Congress proceeds according to rules—a great many rules, some quite remarkably arcane, and all sacrosanct. Commonly, southerners, due to their long tenures, had a better understanding of the rules than their northern counterparts. By contrast, historian J. W. Anderson wrote: "Senate liberals had almost a tradition of disdain for the rules," viewing them perhaps as so many tricks of the devil.

In the House, southern conservatives could draw the line at the Rules Committee. This committee was responsible for determining when each proposed piece of legislation would reach the floor for debate, how many hours of debate would occur, and how debate time would be apportioned between interested members. Rules Committee Chairman Howard ("Judge") Smith of Virginia was deeply persuaded no civil rights bill had any real need to advance to the full House floor for debate. Smith, deeply versed in the arcana of legislative procedure, generally got his way. On one occasion, he cancelled a committee hearing on civil rights because, he said, he needed to return to his estate to investigate a recent barn fire. Of this move, House Speaker Sam Rayburn commented, "I knew Howard Smith would do most anything to block a civil rights bill, but I never suspected he would resort to arson." In the Senate, the strongest weapon was that body's tradition of unlimited debate. Unlike in the House, in the Senate, discussion of a given matter need never end or come to a vote.

The Congress, having a rule for everything, also had a rule for overcoming that rule. While Chairman Smith could bottle up a bill in the House Rules Committee, a procedure known as a Discharge Petition could force its release to the full House. Such a petition needed to carry the signatures of 218 congressmen. In the previous two decades, 198 attempts to use this procedure had been undertaken. Only a single bill—the 1938 Wages and Hours Act—had actually become law as a consequence. Likewise, the Senate's treasured prerogative of unlimited debate could be ended if two-thirds of senators voted to close discussion. This procedure was known as enacting cloture. Cloture had been sought on civil rights bills eleven times, without success.

There is a point of some irony. The South lagged behind the rest of the country in all phases of development. A young person of talent in that region had fewer options in business, finance, academia, or elsewhere than did his or her counterpart in the North. In consequence, a greater portion of the talent of the South sought careers in politics. The irony is that the same could be said of southern blacks. They, precluded from becoming leaders in almost every field of endeavor, gravitated to the ministry, providing the wholly remarkable array of individuals who later clustered around the Southern Christian Leadership Conference and like bodies.

The sparks that began the twelve-year congressional battle over civil rights came in the summer of 1955. One, as noted, was the murder of Emmett Till. The second was the murders, likewise in Mississippi, of two African Americans working to register black voters. Local authorities saw nothing particularly illegal about either act. The federal government was widely called upon to intervene. Such calls were a particular frustration to Herbert Brownell, attorney general of the United States. Brownell was the member of President Eisenhower's cabinet most committed to civil rights; as a member of the New York State legislature in the 1930s, he was a very early sponsor of equal employment opportunity laws. In 1955, Brownell was constrained by a simple fact. Murder was not a federal crime; the Mississippi deaths fell wholly outside his jurisdiction. Until that time, the Eisenhower Administration's record on civil rights had been limited to a series of executive orders. Following the Supreme

Court's *Brown* decision, Eisenhower ordered the integration of schools in the District of Columbia. In his 1956 State of the Union Address—delivered six months after Till's murder—Eisenhower cited as racial progress the elimination of discrimination in the award of federal contracts; the increased number of promotions of blacks within the Armed Forces; and some decline in racial barriers in public accommodations. The president added, "It is disturbing that in some localities allegations persist that Negro citizens are being deprived of their right to vote and are likewise being subjected to unwarranted economic pressures." The president spoke with considerable understatement. As contemporary figures showed, of the 1,800 voting-age African Americans in Georgia's Baker County, none was registered; of 1,500 in Lincoln County, three could vote; of the 1,300 in Miller County, six could exercise the franchise. Eisenhower announced, however, that he would soon introduce legislation to protect voting rights. Attorney General Brownell then oversaw the drafting of a bill with four main provisions:

• First, create a Civil Rights Commission to gather information about racial discrimination in voting, hiring, and other areas;

• Second, create a Civil Rights Division within the Department of Justice with enforcing laws related to discrimination as its sole focus;

• Third, authorize the attorney general to seek court injunctions to protect voting rights and school desegregation efforts and to end discrimination in public accommodations;

• Fourth, authorize the attorney general to seek court actions—including injunctions and charges of contempt—against individuals denying or interfering with an individual's right to vote in federal elections.

President Eisenhower, however, was not prepared to proceed at Brownell's pace. In early April, he decided he would support only the first two points. The internal debate delayed the measure's introduction to April 9, 1956. Congressman Kenneth Keating (R-New York), the ranking member on the Judiciary Committee and a civil rights liberal, secured from Brownell the text of Part III and Part IV. He then added these as amendment to the administration bill. J. W. Anderson commented, "In his astonishingly bold tactic, Brownell had deliberately jeopardized his own office to get this set of powerful bills introduced; it appeared that he had, as a Cabinet member, overstepped the line that divided initiative from insubordination." The four-part bill reached the Senate on April 24. Nonetheless, the piecemeal way in which the bill reached the House prompted many members to question whether Eisenhower was committed to the latter two titles—as, indeed, he was not. In May, political columnist Joseph Alsop wrote, "If the Eisenhower Administration had had the faintest serious desire to pass a civil rights bill, the bill would have been introduced at the beginning of the session and pushed with maximum power thereafter."

Since 1956 was an election year, more than the usual amount of politics was involved. Eisenhower's team, Vice-President Richard Nixon and Attorney General Herbert Brownell, hoped that election-year resistance to civil rights by southern Democrats would break that party's hold on the black vote in the North. If northern blacks switched allegiance, the Republicans might become the majority party. To strengthen the Republican case, President Eisenhower in October reversed himself and endorsed the entire Brownell program. In consequence, Eisenhower gained the endorsement of two of the three sitting black congressmen, including Harlem's influential Adam Clayton Powell. Powell defected when Democratic nominee Adlai Stevenson refused to support Powell's efforts to withhold federal school construction funds from states that were not moving toward desegregation. The key Democratic player was Senate Majority Leader Lyndon Johnson. Johnson, as one close to him reported, was not seeking the presidency, he "was slavering" for it. Johnson knew that to gain his party's nomination (presumably in 1960) he would have to shed the label of "Southern Democrat." That goal might be reached if he shepherded through Congress the first civil rights bill to pass since 1875. From Johnson's perspective, however, that passage needed to be delayed until 1957. Any fight over civil rights in 1956 would divide the Democratic Party in an election year and leave Johnson with enemies on both sides of the fight.

Congressional conservatives stalled. At the Rules Committee, Chairman Smith traded territory for time. Not until June 14 did his committee vote to debate the measure. The 6-to-4 vote to move the measure to the House floor turned on the "Aye" cast by Representative Clarence Brown (R-Ohio), whose Seventh District neighbored McCulloch's and who was similarly an advocate of civil rights. Following floor debate, a vote was set for July 23. The House passed the bill by a comfortable 279 to 126 margin. Of more consequence was that passage came on the final Tuesday of the scheduled congressional session. The bill reached the Senate barely in time to be dropped down the black hole that was James Eastland's Senate Judiciary Committee.

To a curious extent, both sides got what they wanted. In 1956, Eisenhower—easily gaining re-election—raised his share of the black vote from 21 to 38 percent; in fact, in Adam Clayton Powell's Harlem District, Eisenhower raised his 1952 vote of 17 percent to 34 percent. Less surprising was the result from Ohio's Fourth District. There, William McCulloch, attending his customary seven county fairs, coasted to a sixth term.

1957

Beyond voting in support of civil rights, William McCulloch had played little public role in the House floor debate of the issue. In 1957, however, he stepped into the limelight. In his 1957 State of the Union address, Eisenhower endorsed passage of the full four-part bill from the previous year. The following day, January 21, 1957, Attorney General Brownell resubmitted the measure to Congress. *TIME* magazine predicted that by the session's end, "The tiny band of southerners who over the years have combined seniority and archaic rules to strangle legislation that displeased them will have suffered a momentous defeat."

For the moment, the auguries were favorable. The 1956 election produced a 49 to 47 Democratic Senate, with Lyndon Johnson as majority leader. Clarence Mitchell's biographer reported, "Johnson's office quietly let it be known that a civil rights bill would be passed in the next session of Congress. He told southerners in no uncertain terms that they had better drop their customary 'cornpone and pot liquor' arguments and address themselves to the merits of the issue." Senator Thomas Hennings (D-Missouri), whose three-member judiciary subcommittee had jurisdiction over civil rights, announced that his subcommittee would not need to hold hearings on the matter. Its members, all of whom supported the bill, considered themselves sufficiently well informed from the previous year's hearings. Important allies were stepping forth. The AFL-CIO issued a strong statement saying it "endorses without reservation" the pending civil rights bill.

Only unwisely would one underestimate southern opposition. Following the 1954 *Brown* school desegregation decision, Mississippi governor James Coleman led the fight to pass a state constitutional amendment mandating that any Mississippi school faced with integration would be closed. Coleman stated, "If the U.S. Supreme Court were to order one [school] integrated they would just be closed up and those who sought to have it integrated would be like Samson who pulled the temple down upon his head." In 1956, after the Eisenhower Administration's first introduction of its civil rights package, the fourteen-term congressman William Colmer (D-Mississippi) denounced the proposal in terms that today are somewhat difficult to believe ever passed as acceptable in Congress:

[Black] progress has been accomplished under the leadership of his white friends, chiefly his Southern white brother. We in the South are proud of this progress, and we hope for its orderly continuation. But it must be realized that it is impossible by legislative enactment or judicial decree to place overnight a race of people, who until a few generations ago were unenlightened human beings, running wild in the jungles of Africa, on an equal plane with another race of people who for thousands of years have enjoyed the benefits of civilization, education, culture and Christianity.

With that bill before Congress, southerners went into their traditional stall. Senator Hennings had announced that his three-member subcommittee was prepared to move immediately. That subcommittee, of course, was a creature of the full Senate Judiciary Committee. Exercising his prerogative, Judiciary Chairman James Eastland appointed four additional members to the subcommittee, thus creating a segregationist majority. He added that the new members would require ample time to familiarize themselves with the issues.

In the House, similar stalling occurred. Not until April 1, 1957, did the House Judiciary Committee report out the bill. The Rules Committee began hearings on May 2. On May 21, the committee voted 8 to 4 to send the bill to the House floor. By this time, the early optimism regarding passage had begun to fade. On May 23, *The New York Times* reported, "The prospects [for civil rights] in the Senate are, to put it mildly, gloomy."

In the House, floor debate began June 5. Those speaking for the South raised two objections that carried some substance beyond simple racism. The first was that the bill was a power grab by the attorney general, who would be granted unprecedented powers, including the power to initiate school integration. Indeed, in both Senate and House, southern congressmen repeated the accusation that, shorn of its pretense, the bill was nothing but a pretext for forcing school integration on the South. The second objection was that a person held in contempt for violating a court injunction would be deprived of trial by jury. Indeed, the first week of House floor debate was devoted largely to this issue.

Speaking to the House on June 10, Frank Ellis Smith (D-Mississippi) began by asserting his region's innocence. The bill, he said, had been written "with the stated intent of eliminating wrongs which are alleged to take place in southern states. The exhaustive hearings before the committees in both the House and the Senate have proved this indictment of whole people to be insupportable. . . ." Worse, the pending bill involved "many specific encroachments upon liberty," the most serious being "the denial of the right of trial by jury to those charged with violations of the act." That right—the individual's right to confront and cross-examine witnesses—was, Smith said, "part of the inviolate heritage of American citizens." Worst of all, he added, was that any violation of the right to a jury trial "will serve as a precedent for the denial of similar freedoms of all Americans throughout the country."

McCulloch took up the response. First, he argued, no precedent was involved. It was already established practice that a judge who had the power to issue an injunction against an individual could do so without having that injunction ratified by a jury. Turning rhetorical, he asked was he not correct in asserting that under the Taft-Hartley Act, when a "defendant was ordered to do something, which he did not do, and then was cited for contempt of court, that the person would not be entitled to a trial by jury." Hearing no answer, McCulloch "at the risk of repetition" asserted that when the United States government secured an injunction, "a person cited for contempt is *not* entitled to a trial by jury."

To this, Congressman Robert Ashmore (D-South Carolina) conceded: "Correct, sir."

South Carolina congressman Mendel Rivers was not so ready to concede the point. He called attention to six northern states that permitted jury trials when injunctions involved labor disputes. McCulloch responded, "I want to say that even in South Carolina, the home state of my good friend, I am advised there is no provision for trial by jury and you cannot have a trial by jury if the person is cited for contempt for violating the decree of a court of equity." This, Congressman Rivers dismissed as irrelevant:

We are not talking about the law of South Carolina. We are talking about a law that you would want to put on the books here to let a federal judge try him, a federal judge who is looking for promotion to the federal court of appeals and from there is looking for promotion to the United States Supreme Court. . . . We want to let a man be tried by a jury of his peers before you incarcerate him in that jail where you have the judge and jury and the man with the key to the jail.

Mississippi Congressman Colmer spoke near the truth of the matter when he said, "When all is said and done . . . the fact remains that this bill was drawn purposely to avoid a jury trial, was it not?" Sidestepping that thought, Congressman Clare Hoffman (R-Michigan) argued that the entire provision was unnecessary because a U.S. attorney already had the power to seek a grand jury indictment if voter discrimination was suspected. Hoffman added, "The answer that a southern jury would not convict if the facts justified a conviction is not sound—it is an indictment of a whole section." Underlying the exchange was the assumption—rarely spoken aloud—that a jury of southern whites would never take the side of a black individual against a white official.

House southerners advanced one weakening amendment after another, all of them beaten down. On June 17, Congressman Hoffman moved to eliminate both the proposed U.S. Civil Rights Commission and the funds for a civil rights division within the Justice Department. The first, he asserted, would be inclined to undertake "persecutions." The second represented an unnecessary expense. McCulloch replied that the Civil Rights Commission was charged with discovering whether racial discrimination in voting existed. If the commission found no such discrimination, "it will have served a useful and necessary purpose." If, however, it did find discrimination, "all the world will know about it" and the nation can proceed better informed on its remedy. Regarding the cost of creating a civil rights division within the Justice Department, he stated that as member of the Judiciary Committee he believed most House members agreed that, relative even to its existing responsibilities, the Justice Department was understaffed.

McCulloch did succeed in having one amendment attached to the bill. Reflecting his concern with due process, the amendment stated that if a person charged with criminal contempt "does not have the funds with which to procure his own counsel the Federal judge is obliged to assign him counsel."

Late in the twelve-day House debate, McCulloch attempted to establish some common ground. It was here that he referred to his having practiced law for some years in "one of the great Southern states." He carried no ill will for anyone:

I hope that we can all be tolerant down through the years so by education, by understanding, by determined gradualism, and that by following the golden mean, we may achieve the goal that every person in this country who is qualified to vote may exercise the right.

In the meanwhile, however, "I am opposed to any amendment" that would permit jury trials for persons cited with contempt of court for violating a court injunction. He had no desire, he said, to see federal troops used to enforce the law. However, "I do think we should move forward with the trend of the times, as they are evidencing themselves all over the world." McCulloch's statement of his hopes was curiously in line with that advanced by Gunnar Myrdal: "The American Negro problem is a problem in the heart of the American." The Swedish observer added, "The moral struggle goes on within people and not merely between them." McCulloch, whether he had ever read Myrdal or not, shared his view that the conflict over race that dominated mid-twentieth-century American public life was not simply a struggle between those who sought change and those who resisted it. On June 18, 1957, the House put H. R. 6127 to the vote. For all that had been said, the bill was little changed from the form in which it had been proposed the previous January:

• Part I created the U.S. Civil Rights Commission, empowered to investigate voter discrimination, study the status of equal protection, and submit findings and a report to the president within two years.

• Part II authorized hiring an assistant attorney general to head the new civil rights division of the Department of Justice.

• Part III gave the attorney general the right to file injunctions against persons who violated the Equal Protection Clause of the 14th Amendment.

• Part IV gave the attorney general the power to obtain relief in cases of voting rights violations in either federal or state elections.

The bill passed easily, by a 286 to 126 margin. Republicans favored the measure by 168 to 19. Democrats did so by 118 to 107, with virtually all the "Nay" votes coming from southern Democrats. There had never been any doubt that the House would pass a civil rights bill. Doubt was the province of the U.S. Senate. On July 2, 1957, Georgia Democrat Richard Russell attacked the proposed bill in a speech of considerable length and greater impact. It was a speech, the NAACP's Clarence

Mitchell ruefully admitted, that showed "why this normally urbane man was such a highly respected master strategist."

Russell gained drama for his remarks by requesting—for what was, he said, the first time in his lengthy Senate tenure—that all comments or questions be held until he had completed his remarks. He began with the simple assertion that northerners were animated by "conscious hate" of the South. He dismissed the notion that voting rights were the issue. Voting rights, he asserted, were merely "a smoke screen to obscure the unlimited grant of powers to the attorney general of the United States to govern by injunction and federal bayonet." In substance, he said, the bill was "cunningly designed" to "bring to bear the whole might of the Federal Government, including the Armed Forces, if necessary, to force the white people of the South at the point of a federal bayonet to conform to . . . a commingling of the races throughout the social order of the South."

He spoke, he said, with "great sadness. If Congress is driven to pass this bill in its present form, it will cause unspeakable confusion, bitterness, and bloodshed in a great section of our common country. If it is proposed to move against the South in this manner, the concentration camps may as well be prepared now, because there will not be enough jails to hold the people of the South who will oppose the use of raw federal power forcibly to commingle white and Negro children in the same schools and places of public entertainment." He noted that segregation had been the law of the South for a century and was "the only system the present generation has ever known." And yet that system was to be "overturned in the twinkling of an eye," not because the Congress had at length debated the matter and reached the conclusion that such was the best path to take, but simply because the Supreme Court, in *Brown v. Topeka*, struck down "long-established law."

The strategy behind Russell's remarks was to stress what he asserted would be the vast expansion of federal power under the proposed law. It was an argument that carried weight with midwestern conservatives and moderates, traditionally opposed to the expansion of federal authority. Under the weight of Russell's words, the civil rights alliance began to fracture.

With the Democratic Party itself split into North and South, Majority Leader Lyndon Johnson decided the time had become to play both ends against the middle. To northerners, he argued that passage of any civil rights law after eighty years of federal inaction constituted a victory, one that ensured future victories as well. With something less than charm, he said, "Once you break the virginity, it'll be easier next time." To southern senators, he argued that allowing a "weak" bill to pass was better than initiating a filibuster to prevent it. Any filibuster would make the South look obdurate and gain it onus for holding up all other business.

As this juncture, President Eisenhower signaled retreat. On July 3, 1957—the day after Senator Russell spoke—President Eisenhower announced that he regarded Part III (public accommodations) as negotiable. This was widely viewed as a willingness on his part to see the provision dropped. To the NAACP's Clarence Mitchell, Part III was crucial. He termed it the "the restraining hand" the federal government would place on "the shoulder of any state, city or local official who would arrest and intimidate a colored person for exercising a constitutional right." Still, with the administration backing away from its own proposal, the Senate on July 24 voted 52 to 38 to excise the section from the bill.

Civil rights forces also broadly lost on Part IV, the issue of jury trials. As the matter was resolved, "if a federal judge tried to hold someone in contempt of court for disobeying a federal order to enforce the law, that person was entitled to a jury trial *if a significant penalty were involved*." A highly bendable phrase. Thus amended, the civil rights bill passed the Senate by a 72 to 18 margin. All forty-three Republicans voted for the measure. All votes against came from southern Democrats.

Because the House and Senate versions varied, the House could accept the Senate amendments or seek a conference committee to resolve differences that gave every evidence of being irresolvable. Congressman Richard Bolling (D-Missouri) felt civil rights supporters faced a Hobson's choice—a choice in which no good option is given: "It seemed apparent that civil rights forces would do no better next year. It seemed that the civil rights advocates outside Congress faced a decision whether to accept any bill, however short of their high-powered desires, or accept an issue steeped in partisanship." Various black leaders, challenging Johnson, argued that the bill as passed was worse than no bill at all. Among others, labor leader A. Philip Randolph and Jackie Robinson urged Eisenhower not to sign. Roy Wilkins, head of the NAACP, believed he could have organized opposition sufficient to prompt a veto. President Eisenhower, however, signed the measure into law on September 9, 1957.

What had the two-year fight produced? Viewed retrospectively, creation of the U.S. Civil Rights Commission proved highly important. The act created a six-member commission, headed by John A. Hannah, president of Michigan State College (later University) and charged with investigating allegations of discrimination with respect to voting. The commission was charged with studying the status of, and federal laws pertaining to, equal protection. All federal agencies were directed to cooperate with the commission, which was to submit a final report within two years. Second, creation of the Civil Rights Division within the Department of Justice carried something more than symbolic value by establishing a federal body with no other task than civil rights enforcement.

The greatly weakened Part IV proved all but useless. In the words of Robert Caro, Johnson's most assiduous biographer, local election officials, certain they would still be tried by friendly juries, were "emboldened to continue discriminatory election practices." Further, there was a "lack of will within the administration to enforce" Part IV. When, for example, the Eisenhower Administration filed a voter discrimination suit in Georgia's Terrell County, a local judge ordered election officials to withhold the records and authorized creation of a special police force to enforce that order.

Lyndon Johnson, according to confidante George Reedy, thought a great victory had been won. "He felt that if you could get something through, it would no longer be a question of yes or no, but of how much." Caro wrote, "The Civil Rights Act of 1957 was more than half a loaf, a lot more. It was hope."

Senator Richard Russell likewise claimed victory: "The fact that we were able to confine the Federal invasion to the field of voting and keep the withering hand of the Federal Government out of our schools and social order is to me the sweetest victory in my twenty-five years in the U.S. Senate."

Back in Piqua

As noted, Congressman McCulloch returned to his home and law firm in Piqua almost every weekend that Congress was in session. That May, he met one Saturday with his law partners, Carl Felger and Robert Fite, to interview a prospective fourth member of the firm, Paul Gutmann, a recent graduate of the Ohio State University School of Law. Gutmann was about to leave for military training and was hopeful of having a position lined up before departing. He was, he recalled, "absolutely in awe of McCulloch," who was the first congressman he had ever met. McCulloch, he added, was soft spoken, "but when he spoke no one interrupted. He did not have a commanding voice. He spoke on point." The point—to McCulloch, Felger, and Fite—was to learn if Paul Gutmann's intentions were honorable. What was his family like? Did he see Piqua as a stepping-stone, or did he intend to move there permanently? Those were half the questions. Then Gutmann's fiancée, Rosemary Doerr, hosted a dinner for all four couples. Mabel McCulloch asked Paul Gutmann his opinion of Christopher Robin of the Winnie the Pooh books. Gutmann replied he had never heard of him. The three existing partners agreed that Paul's answers were what they were seeking; further, all had been enamored with Rosemary. With all tests passed, Gutmann was informed, "You're hired." Mabel McCulloch went out and bought the Gutmann and his fiancée a complete set of Winnie the Pooh, saying they would want them when they had children.

Legislatively, McCulloch continued to serve on the Select Committee on Small Business. McCulloch's general view was, "there has been an alarming concentration of economic power in some fields which is contrary to the healthy growth of industry." Even before final action came on civil rights, McCulloch had joined with a half-dozen other congressmen to introduce a series of bills favorable to small business. Their general aim was to create economic circumstances more favorable to small business. These, the Dayton *Journal Herald* reported, included provisions to accelerate depreciation on used property; allow corporations with fewer than ten stockholders to be treated for tax purposes as partnerships or proprietorships; allow family-owned companies to extend their payment of estate taxes over a decade; and give investors in small firms more tax-liberal treatment of losses. The following month, Congress enacted a five-part small business bill that included three measures originally put forth by McCulloch: speedier depreciation; elongated estate tax payment; and more liberal tax treatment of losses.

One congressional responsibility that McCulloch shared with his peers he took with exceptional care. That was the annual appointment of young men from the Fourth Congressional District to the nation's service academies. He met with each candidate personally. He preferred, his daughter Nancy McCulloch reported, to choose young men who were not enamored of any particular girl back home – he wanted them to look ahead; not to moon over who they had lost. Some years, he would host a Christmas dinner at the Piqua Country Club for the young men he had selected and the parents who had raised them. A June 16, 1958, photo in the *Piqua Daily Call* shows McCulloch at the Naval Academy in Annapolis, Maryland, grouped with nine of his young appointees.

Beyond that, McCulloch returned to the more mundane aspects of this job. He traveled to Versailles, Ohio, to crown Ms. Karen Earhart as "Miss Chick of 1958" at the seventh annual Poultry Day Festival, attended by 15,000. In September, he reported on his recent votes to the Troy Rotary Club. He had voted against a labor reform bill as insufficient. He had opposed reciprocal trade agreements as unfair to American firms that paid higher wages than were paid by its trading partners. He had opposed statehood for Alaska because its 75,000 residents were too few in number and too dependent in practice on federal subsidies for their well-being. He had opposed "pork barrel" legislation on flood control. He noted that the citizens of the Miami Valley had through the Miami Conservancy District "paid for their own flood protection and now, through this new law, they are paying for that of others throughout the nation." Finally, he confessed to voting to raise the national debt limit to $288 billion because, as a practical matter, "there was no alternative."

His financial stringency continued to bring him favorable press. Ralph Holsinger of the Dayton *Journal Herald* noted, "Few congressmen have voted consistently to cut the cost of government as have Representatives Paul F. Schenck (R–Dayton), Clarence J. Brown (R-Blanchester), and William M. McCulloch (R-Piqua)." McCulloch continued to receive an almost entirely favorable press, particularly in his hometown paper, the *Piqua Daily Call,* which editorialized:

Some of the dignity radiates from the man himself. Easily spotted in a crowd, he is clean cut through and through, always immaculately groomed, and has a firm carriage that spells confidence. His crisp diction suggests that he may once have been an English professor. McCulloch, who has been known to blush right through his neatly-trimmed mustache when given an unexpected compliment, is strictly business from head to toe.

The most important news came from out of state. In August 1958, Congressman Kenneth Keating (D-NY) defeated New York District Attorney Frank Hogan for the Democratic senatorial nomination. Win or lose, Keating would vacate his post as the ranking Republican on the House Judiciary Committee. McCulloch would therefore become ranking member on the Judiciary Committee, provided Fourth District voters returned him to office in the 1958 election. For the first time, McCulloch's opponent was a woman, a Lima, Ohio, schoolteacher named Marjorie Conrad Struma. While his margin declined somewhat from previous years, McCulloch was easily returned to office by a vote of 73,332 to 46,832.

CHAPTER 11

Four Perspectives

When Congress reconvened in January 1959, the recently reelected William McCulloch took up the task of ranking member of the House Judiciary Committee, a position he held for better than the next dozen years. Throughout that time, the committee chairmanship was held by Brooklyn Democrat Emanuel Celler, with whom McCulloch enjoyed a generally congenial relationship. As ranking member, McCulloch would regard himself as the upholder of what he considered the civil rights tradition of the "Party of Lincoln." McCulloch would also be influenced by persons outside of Congress. Most particularly, where civil rights were concerned, McCulloch would place his trust in Clarence Mitchell, the long-time chief Washington lobbyist of the NAACP. McCulloch, Celler, and Mitchell were, in civil rights, advocates of sufficient prominence that their views deserve further explication. Obviously, civil rights had its opponents—a fact that calls for comments from the white southerners often viewed as the target of civil rights legislation.

Emanuel Celler

In the House of Representatives, not all committee chairmen were conservatives. One of them, Judiciary Chairman Emanuel Celler of Brooklyn, was among the most liberal members of the House. First elected to Congress in 1922, he had been accumulating seniority since that date. He obtained chairmanship of the House Judiciary Committee in 1949, during William McCulloch's first full term in Congress. Except for the two years, 1953–1954, when Republicans controlled the House, Celler served as Judiciary chairman until 1972.

His committee's general areas of responsibility were crime, antitrust, immigration, copyright, and civil rights. Immigration was not yet a hot issue; civil rights was never anything but.

Born in May 1888, Celler led a life that was both thoroughly American and thoroughly different from the likewise American life of William

McCulloch. His four grandparents were all immigrants, from Germany. His maternal grandparents met when the ship carrying them to Ellis Island in New York's harbor foundered. To save herself, Lena Grab-felder leapt overboard. To save Lena, or so he imagined, fellow passenger Adolph Mueller jumped next. Thus introduced, they courted and married with the agreement that they would raise their children in her Jewish religion rather than his Catholicism. In time, they had a grandson named Emanuel Celler. Like McCulloch, Celler was the favored child in a large family—though McCulloch was never required to play the violin.

At twenty-four, Celler graduated from Columbia Law School, passed the bar exam, and married Stella Baar. A decade later, Celler ran for Congress in what had been a Republican district. The district was largely first- and second-generation immigrants, Jewish, Italian, and German, along with a fair sprinkling of African Americans, whose forebears had arrived earlier and less willingly. Celler built his own political organization and won a 3,111-vote victory. He excelled at personal contacts; he excelled at constituent services; he spoke well and frequently, in and out of his district, before live and broadcast audiences. In time, he became the only person many in Brooklyn could imagine as their congressman.

In Congress, he was associated with issues. He opposed restrictions on immigration. He supported civil rights. In 1926, when A. Philip Randolph, head of the all-black Pullman Porters' Union, wanted Congress to undertake a study of racial issues, he brought the proposal to Celler for introduction. In 1949, Celler was chief House sponsor of President Truman's extensive civil rights proposals. Celler was a long-term supporter of antitrust legislation and lead House sponsor of the 1951 effort that strengthened the Clayton Antitrust Act. He was a passionate Zionist and supporter of Jewish causes. He lobbied, without success, to raise immigration quotas and open the door to European Jewry, before, during, and after the Holocaust. Later, he was an outspoken critic of the ways and whys of Senator Joseph McCarthy in his "hunt" for Communists. Speaking to the 1952 Democratic convention, Celler said:

Deliberately and calculatedly, McCarthyism has set before itself the task of undermining the faith of the people in their Government. It has undertaken to sow suspicion everywhere, to set friend against friend and brother against brother. It deals in coercion and in intimidation, tying the hands of citizens and officials with the fear of the smear attack.

In all of this, Celler—rather like McCulloch—had the advantage of representing a one-party district. A tree may grow in Brooklyn, but Republicans did not take root there. Celler thrived on New York City. He lived for a good many years on Prospect Park West, one of Brooklyn's finest avenues; attended the Metropolitan Opera on Saturday nights; the theatre regularly; and rubbed elbows with just about anyone who was interested in rubbing elbows back. In his own life, Celler liked stability, and enjoyed a long and secure marriage. In 1928, he hired Mary Daugherty as his legal secretary in his New York office; she worked with him through and past his departure from Congress in 1973. In 1941, he hired a woman named Bess Dick as a clerk; she remained thirty years, serving effectively as chief of staff.

And Celler liked the stability of being a member of Congress, though not all in Congress returned that liking. Massachusetts Congressman Tip O'Neill—a future Speaker of the House—called Celler "an arrogant old man." Congressman John Rankin of Mississippi said, "I know of no man who in my opinion has done the Jews in this country more harm than the Gentleman from New York." In fairness, however, some may question whether the well-being of American Jews was a matter of any personal importance to the Mississippi congressman. Celler drew more substantial criticism, for example, from David Berman, author of a book on the 1960 Civil Rights Act:

While making a reputation as a fighter for civil rights, Celler, like many liberals in Congress, continued to bask in the friendship of his southern colleagues. In common with other Democrats who possessed seniority and held positions of power, he had a close relationship with the party leadership. He enjoyed an unusually high degree of acceptance because, although he spoke for liberal principles, he conscientiously avoided straining party unity.

That judgment may have been harsh. Celler, in his dealings with his fellow committee members, was attentive to their political needs. When, for example, a junior congressman strongly urged the appointment of an important constituent to a judgeship, Celler—as committee counsel Thomas Mooney recalled—responded, "We aren't going to give you that judge, but we'll make sure he knows no one could have put on a better fight than you." Celler's neutrality had its limits. He had good hearing only in his right ear, so committee Republicans always sat to his left. Nancy McCulloch, the congressman's daughter, said that in time her father and Celler "were friends, but not close friends." On August 25, 1960, after the Civil Rights bill had cleared the House, Celler wrote to McCulloch, "You and I have performed wonders working as a team. . . . I hope it will continue for many years to come whether it be you or I who occupies the chairmanship of our Committee." Of course, in offering these generous remarks, Celler was probably aware the chances of the Republicans regaining control of the House verged on nil.

Clarence Mitchell

In October 1933, Clarence Mitchell—twenty-two-year-old cub reporter for the *Baltimore Afro-American*—traveled to Maryland's Eastern Shore to report on the recent lynching of George Armwood, a black man "generally recognized as feeble-minded." Armwood had also been twenty-two years old. His body was still on display. Mitchell wrote in part, "A cursory glance revealed that one ear was missing and his tongue between his clenched teeth, gave evidence of his great agony before death." Curiously, Armwood had been lynched by proxy. A second black man, Euell Lee, had been sentenced to death for the murders of a farming couple and their two daughters. Uncommonly lengthy appeals delayed Lee's arrival at his moment of judgment. Losing patience, a mob decided to lynch Armwood as a surrogate. Perhaps oddest of all, Mitchell—a black man—passed through the scene of the crime with its lingering observers in the rather innocent belief that his press pass from an obscure Baltimore black newspaper was all the protection he required.

Thurgood Marshall, the famed civil rights lawyer, referred to his and Mitchell's shared hometown as "upsouth Baltimore." Maryland had been a slave state. When in 1861 the first Union troops moved through Baltimore en route to securing the federal government in Washington, D.C., a pro-secession mob attacked. In 1911, Baltimore passed an ordinance that made it a crime for any black person—or, more exactly, any black person not a servant—to move into any block that had a white majority. Baltimore, simply, was mean. Mitchell later stated, "The system of justice in Baltimore was at its worst at the police station level. Blacks were herded into such stations if they happened to be walking by when there was lineup. Hundreds were arrested on 'suspicion' and held for days without bail. It was awfully easy to get arrested for nothing."

Mitchell's family struggled economically. His father was a waiter at a Rennert Hotel. His mother kept house, took in occasional boarders, and bore ten children, of whom seven survived childhood. As is commonly the case for those who rise from straitened circumstances to lives of adult accomplishment, Mitchell's parents were determined people. Determined that their children would be educated. Determined that their children would not define themselves by the slings and arrows of racism. Mitchell was educated locally in grade school—one of his teachers was Thurgood Marshall's mother—and then attended Lincoln University in Pennsylvania and the University of Minnesota in St. Paul. After graduation, he became executive secretary of the local Urban League, his introduction to organized racial agitation. In Baltimore, the Mitchell family was a small army for racial progress. In 1938 Mitchell married Juanita Jackson, who became the first black female lawyer in the state. Mitchell's brother Parren was elected a Baltimore congressman, and several of Mitchell's children served in the state legislature.

Principally, Clarence Mitchell worked as chief Washington lobbyist of the NAACP, a post he held from 1940 until 1978. There was a small initial cause for optimism—for instance, the presidential order banning discrimination in munitions work during World War Two. Post-war, however, optimism faded with the defeat of a comprehensive series of civil rights measures advanced by President Truman. The cause appeared stymied. One casebook on American civil rights legislation states, "Amidst such turmoil, and under the tireless pressure of Clarence Mitchell, Jr., the director of the Washington bureau of the NAACP, Congress began to intervene." Mitchell, when on Capitol Hill, was commonly in the company of liberal lawyer Joseph Rauh, who commented:

Being Clarence's fellow traveler down the corridors of Congress for thirty years hasn't been so damn easy. First, the guy walks so fast and so far that I can't keep up with him. Around noon I get hungry and he doesn't eat; at about late afternoon I want a drink and he doesn't drink. Not only does he not rest, eat or drink, but you get called names just for sitting beside him the gallery.

Battle followed battle: the fight to prevent the resegregation of the armed forces; the fight to eliminate all-white barracks; the fight to withhold federal funding from all-white schools, and from segregated facilities at National Parks. And behind these fights were more fundamental rights; specifically, the right to vote and to attend an integrated school. There were measures of progress: the number of blacks registered to vote in the South increased from 200,000 in 1944 to 1.3 million in 1948. Hard work went into enrolling each of those voters. And there were greater numbers of defeats. To pick a single example, the House Education Committee voted 17–10 to reject Harlem Congressman Adam Clayton Powell's proposal that federal education aid be restricted to states that were moving to school integration. Throughout the South, blacks were kept from registering to vote by a combination of obscure technicalities, subjectively enforced, and the threat of physical or economic consequence. In Congress itself—particularly in the Senate—delay after delay was achieved largely by southern members who could pull obscure rules out of a hat faster than a magician could bring forth rabbits.

Through it all, Mitchell remained focused not on today's defeat but on tomorrow's possibilities, on the minor step that could be combined with other minor steps to produce a place to take a stand. One then-young congressional staffer recalled:

I remember Mr. Mitchell as an elegant, warm, tall, fit, gracious and engaging personality. He was always dressed impeccably, usually in a gray suit; he was soft spoken—clearly a gentleman with great intellect, personal poise and a wise, modulated command of the English language. I never saw him express frustration or discomfort, no matter the topic of the day. Mr. Mitchell was always asking us in the office to "call me Clarence." But he was such an impressive man that my 21-year-old self would always find myself responding, "Yes sir, Clarence" and then slipping back into calling him just "Sir" knowing that if I called him "Mr. Mitchell" he would just renew the invitation to "call me Clarence."

In terms of partisan politics, Mitchell was always a registered "independent." He believed black people had more to gain by being open to all comers than by tying themselves to any given party. Mitchell's own hopes for racial progress were to an extent revived with the re-election of Dwight Eisenhower in 1956. Eisenhower had received 38 percent of the black vote, the highest Republican total since 1932. As noted, Eisenhower's 1957 State of the Union message called for legislation to create a commission to investigate racial discrimination in voting and other steps. That proposal would begin its course in the House Judiciary Committee. As an "independent," Mitchell was inclined to take people as he saw them, not as he might have assumed them to be. For example, Mitchell's biographer writes, "Mitchell was impressed by [William] McCulloch, from Piqua, Ohio, because there were only a handful of blacks in his district. Despite this lack of political incentive, he had few equals in his consistent support for civil rights."

William McCulloch

One television anchorman is said to have described William McCulloch as resembling a "department store floorwalker." Those who knew the congressman did not consider this statement a putdown. After all, they pointed out, who has a better idea of what is going on in the store than the floorwalker? William McCulloch was short, slightly heavier with the years, sparing in speech, attentive in listening, cautious about reaching conclusions, and—when it came to civil rights for all Americans—a rock.

In part, his commitment was family tradition. As reported, his grandfather had early embraced the Republican Party *because* it strove to draw a line against slavery's spread. In part, his commitment reflected his sojourn in Jacksonville in the 1920s, which had shown him enough prejudice to last a lifetime. McCulloch lived in Piqua, Ohio—a town so overwhelmingly Republican that, as the town historian reported, to be a Democrat was simply "abnormal." But for McCulloch the Republicans were not simply the team to cheer for, they were the Party of Lincoln. As such, they carried the responsibility for furthering the cause of freedom and equality.

In 1968, McCulloch wrote an essay, "Man Was Born to be Free: Toward Fulfillment of the Dream," which was printed in the book *Republican Papers*, edited by then Michigan Congressman Melvin Laird. Though the essay precedes the narrative, it is presented at this point because it fairly presents the views McCulloch held at the time.

In his essay, McCulloch roots the dream of freedom in the country's founding documents. He opens with the Preamble to the Constitution, "We hold these truths to be self-evident, that all Men are created equal, that they are endowed by their Creator with certain unalienable Rights, that among these are Life, Liberty and the Pursuit of Happiness." He notes that the Northwest Ordinance—passed by the Continental Congress prior to the adoption of the Constitution—declared that in those territories (approximately the future Midwest), "There shall be neither slavery nor involuntary servitude in the said territory, otherwise than in the punishment of crimes, whereof the party shall have been duly convicted. . . ." These statements, McCulloch acknowledges, remained "merely words of unfilled promise"—despite the early efforts of Benjamin Franklin, Alexander Hamilton, and others to promote anti-slavery societies.

Action, McCulloch asserted, awaited the coming of the Republican Party. Founded in Jackson, Michigan, on July 6, 1854, the party elected its first president, Abraham Lincoln, six years later. In April 1862, the Republican-controlled Congress abolished slavery in the District of Columbia, the only portion of the nation over which the federal government enjoyed unfettered jurisdiction. On January 1, 1863, Lincoln issued the Emancipation Proclamation. On February 10, 1864, Illinois Republican Lyman Trumbull presented a constitutional amendment abolishing slavery—the measure passed the Senate, but failed in the House, where the 93 to 65 vote in favor fell short of the two-thirds required.

As 1865 opened, Southern defeat was apparent. Lincoln was compellingly anxious that a constitutional amendment banning slavery be adopted before the former Confederate states regained their vote in Congress. Lincoln could count on a unanimous vote from the 103 Republicans then sitting. This, however, would fall short of the two-thirds vote required. Passage, therefore, turned on at least a semblance of support from Democrats, whose party leadership had declared slavery's end to be "unwise, impolitic, cruel, and unworthy of the support of civilized people." As it happened, the vote would be by a "lame duck" Congress—the legislators chosen in November 1864 had not yet taken office. Lincoln focused his efforts—and a minor treasury of federal favors—on those Democrats who had lost their seats the previous November and were therefore less beholden to party discipline. In the end, sixteen of the eighty Democrat members voted to end slavery. The final vote—119 to 56—was three more than the two-thirds needed.

Southerners were in general simply unwilling to concede social and legal equality to the recently freed slaves. Laws known as "black codes" were widely enacted to restrict their exercise of the rights of citizenship. The Republican Congress responded with the far-reaching Civil Rights Bill of 1866, which said in part:

That all persons born in the United States . . . are hereby declared to be citizens of the United States, and such citizens, of every race and color, without regard to any previous condition of slavery or involuntary servitude . . . shall have the same rights, in every State and Territory in the United States. To make and enforce contracts, to sue, be parties, and give evidence, to inherit, purchase, lease, sell, hold and convey real and personal property, and to full and equal benefit of all laws and proceedings for the security of person and property as is enjoyed by white citizens, and shall be subject to like punishment, pains and penalties, and none other, any law, statute, ordinance, regulation, or custom to the contrary notwithstanding.

Two Republican-enacted amendments followed. The Fourteenth Amendment guaranteed equal protection under the law. The Fifteenth Amendment—proposed by Senators William Fessenden and James G. Blaine of Maine and John Howard of Michigan—asserted that "the right of citizens of the United States to vote shall not be denied or abridged by the United Sates or any state on account of race, color or previous condition of servitude."

In the South, federal law was widely flouted, particularly by the nightriders of the Ku Klux Klan. Republican congressional leadership responded with the Act of April 20, 1871, sponsored by Ohio Republican Congressman Samuel Shellabarger. Known as the Ku Klux Klan or Anti-Lynching Act, it forbade conspirators to go in disguise upon the public highway to deprive a person of his federal or constitutional rights.

In 1874, Senator Charles Sumner (R-Massachusetts) introduced a public accommodation law. Based on the Fourteenth Amendment rather than the Commerce Clause, it was intended to apply to forms of private discrimination. The bill passed on March 1, 1875. McCulloch wrote that in the twenty years since its founding, the Republican Party had achieved its first aim of limiting the spread of slavery. The first Republican president had led the nation through a war that resulted in slavery's abolition. Since then, the party had legislated for black Americans "a comprehensive program of civil rights covering every possible aspect of equality."

Here, McCulloch acknowledges, "The sudden revolution in the Negro status, which the Republican Party had championed had made the country weary." In 1883, he noted, the Supreme Court held that the 1875 public accommodations bill could not be supported by the Fourteenth Amendment, which merely prohibited discrimination by the states. The Panic of 1893 brought a strongly Democratic Congress to office. That Congress, McCulloch reported, "repealed no less than 39 provisions of the Republican Reconstruction program. Federal protection of Negro voting fights was completely abolished. The door to the polling booth was now closed to Negroes in the South." America's two-tier society was reinforced by the 1896 *Plessy v Ferguson* decision, in which the U.S. Supreme Court ruled that separate public accommodations for whites and blacks were not unconstitutional.

The question remains, why McCulloch wrote the essay. Clearly, personal belief was uppermost. Perhaps he was trying to set the partisan record straight. But it is likely, as well, that William McCulloch was trying to summon his fellow Republicans to that which he thought most admirable in their heritage.

The White South

There is, of course, another player in this drama. That player is the white southerner, the participant in events who enjoyed something akin to the home field advantage. For some years—before riots in Watts and Detroit and Newark, before school busing—it was the fashion in the North to think of the southern whites as poorly educated, poorly motivated, purely racist beings who were virtually beyond the call of reason or the lure of rhyme. Curiously, their story is least frequently told. The Southern perspective receives fair telling in Jason Sokol's *There Goes My Everything.* The book describes the response of the white South to the surging demand for civil rights. It was a land where, for no reason readily apparent to the white population, the poles were suddenly being reversed: the habits and traditions of a century were declared not only wrong, but inadmissible; indeed, a disgrace.

Thus, the words of Dr. James Shepard, founder, North Carolina Central University:

As you well know, the average white Southerner is a fairly decent citizen who wants to do the right things. He can be persuaded with reasonable arguments; he can be shamed through a fair appeal to his [conscience]; but he cannot be coerced into a course of action, however right. He is stubborn, proud and utterly allergic to threats.

A native Mississippian stated in 1935:

The white man of the Delta says to the world beyond his gates: I live with my family among an overwhelming mass of Negroes. . . . Nowhere do we receive them on terms of social equality. . . . Most of us have a deep and abiding affection for the Negro. Our paternalism is not designed to enslave him. It is in our blood. The Negroes of our plantations are both our partners and our wards.

Curiously, racism was the only integrated thing in the South, encompassing local government and police, schools, churches, and casual assumption. In Jackson, in 1963, the governing board of the Galloway Church— known as the "Cathedral of Mississippi Methodism"—voted 184 to 13 to maintain segregation. Thereafter, twenty-eight Methodist ministers publicly endorsed integration. Within a year, fewer than half were still in Mississippi.

There was very little negotiable turf between the two positions. The divide was enormous. Sokol relates the experience of Edgar Mouton, a Louisiana state senator, who said that he "never shook hands with a black person before I ran for office . . . the first time I shook hands it was a total traumatic thing." The divide was resistant. As late as 1971, the chapter head of a local Veterans of Foreign Wars outpost wrote in the *Yazoo Herald:*

To the many fine, colored people I can only say this: you are a part of our community, you have helped to raise our children, worked in our homes, but you have deserted us. . . . May I suggest that you return to the churches you have left, and kneel down and ask the Good Lord's help. Then ask your trouble makers to go somewhere else, to let you live as you know you must."

For even the more thoughtful, it was less a matter of justice than of feasibility. A Mississippi planter stated this well:

Up until thirty years ago there was almost a slave-landowner relationship. Then all of a sudden—at least it seemed sudden to us—we're told that the system we're living under [is] not only morally wrong but legally wrong and everybody has to change. . . . To expect a people raised and nurtured for one hundred years on a system they evidently didn't think was wrong and expect them to agree that the whole thing has been wrong and reverse themselves and change at once . . . that's asking too much of human nature.

And perhaps it was. But at the same time, it was asking too much of the human nature of African Americans to continue to live as second-class citizens in what was pleased to regard itself as a first-class country.

CHAPTER 12

McCulloch Steps Forth

One hot, humid summer day when all who could flee the city had done so, *Washington Post* columnist Joseph Alsop wrote, "In August 1959, the Congress can be expected to pass still another civil rights bill, moderate yet substantial like the last one." With two exceptions, Alsop was right: the bill did not pass until 1960 and, when it passed, it was not substantial.

On February 12, 1959—which, as the speaker noted, was the sesquicentennial of the birth of Abraham Lincoln—William McCulloch introduced the Eisenhower Administration's civil rights bill. McCulloch described it as a "moderate, practical, sound and, I believe, generally acceptable step forward." By section, it proposed:

• Title I made it a federal crime to interfere with any public official carrying out a desegregation order;

• Title II made it a federal crime to cross a state line to avoid prosecution for any act of bombing or arson;

• Title III required local election officials to preserve voting records for three years [there was a widespread practice to destroy voting records soon after an election so that they could not be used as evidence of possible wrongdoing];

• Title IV granted a two-year extension to the Commission on Civil Rights;

• Title V established a commission on equal job opportunity in government contracts;

• Title VI provided for the education of military children in the event that the local districts they attended closed for any reason;

• Title VII provided technical assistance to school districts seeking to comply with the *Brown* desegregation decision.

In the House, Emanuel Celler introduced a more far-reaching bill. He would add Part III of the 1957 bill (public accommodations); provide federal financial aid to school districts attempting to integrate their classrooms; and explicitly declare the Supreme Court's *Brown* decision as the law of the land.

On the Senate side, four bills were introduced. The broadest, put forward by Jacob Javits (R-New York), would add Part III of the original bill, along with the original undiluted wording of Part IV, empowering the attorney general to initiate court actions. Paul Douglas (D-Illinois) presented a bill that would add Part III and fund desegregation efforts. Acting for the administration, Everett Dirksen (R-Illinois) presented a bill identical to McCulloch's. And Majority Leader Lyndon Johnson anted up a bill that would create a community relations service to address issues related to civil rights.

The Eisenhower Administration, on whose behalf McCulloch was acting, was somewhat less enthusiastic about civil rights than was McCulloch himself. In his January 9 State of the Union address, Eisenhower barely mentioned civil rights. The chief administration spokesperson, Attorney General William Rogers, did bring out the international implications: "We must consider the image that racial discrimination presents to a largely nonwhite world. These nations have not committed themselves either to Western ideas of democracy or to Communism. But they are watching." But Rogers was unwilling to play any stronger card. He affirmed that the administration would not now support including Part III (public accommodations), which had been deleted from the 1957 act.

In presenting his bill, Congressman McCulloch had closed, mildly, "I am convinced that this bill is a sensible, middle course which Congress should look upon with favor." Not all members did. The bill prompted serious misgivings among the handful of black legislators. William Dawson (D-Chicago) thought much more aggressive government action was needed to protect the exercise of minority rights and safety. Dawson stated, "We cannot leave to the young child the burden of facing the mob, nor should the government leave the constitution to be carried on the shoulders of the poor and harassed individuals who seek only that which the constitution guarantees to them."

In 1959, House and Senate moved forward simultaneously on their respective bills. The House versions—McCulloch's bill (H.R. 4457) and Celler's bill (H.R. 3147)—began their journey in Subcommittee No. 5 of the House Judiciary Committee, chaired by Celler himself.

Subcommittee No. 5 held seventeen days of closed hearings on the measure. Since the subcommittee met in executive session with no minutes produced, one cannot learn the part McCulloch played in the proceedings. Those hearings produced a hybrid proposal: basically, the McCulloch bill with Celler's Part III (public accommodations) added. Noting the absence of southern members on the subcommittee, L. Mendel Rivers (D-South Carolina) fell somewhat short of understatement: "We have been 'hanged, drawn and quartered,' as Shakespeare would say, *in absentia*."

The Subcommittee No. 5 proposal then went to the full Judiciary

Committee. While the subcommittee had no southern members, the full committee had ten. On July 29, 1959, they made their presence known, as the full committee rejected the hybrid bill by an 18–13 margin. Compromise set in. Part III (public accommodations) was deleted. A proposal to give a presidential commission on job discrimination statutory rather than mere advisory authority was dropped. Funds for assisting in school desegregation were also dropped. McCulloch expressed his disappointment. In an August 6, 1959, interview with the *Piqua Daily Call*, McCulloch said he regretted that the proposal "raising the President's Committee on Government Contracts to commission status and authorizing grants to assist state and local educational agencies to effectuate desegregation" had been eliminated.

Author David Berman described Celler as loathe to strain party unity, and "first, last and always an organization man." However fair that characterization, Celler was convinced the full Judiciary Committee would never vote out a strong bill. He pushed the weakened measure along in hopes, he said, that once it reached the House floor strengthening amendments—in particular, Part III—might be added. The bill, now redesignated H.R. 8601, was not heading for the House floor, however. Its next stop was the Rules Committee, where Chairman Howard Smith (D-Virginia) was prepared to let it fester. As noted, a bill can be dislodged from the Rules Committee by a Discharge Petition signed by half the members of the House. Faced with a lack of alternatives, Celler initiated the rarely successful discharge procedure.

If the House was moving slowly, the Senate was not moving at all. There, the bill was assigned to the Judiciary Committee, where James Eastland (D-Mississippi), exercising his power as chairman, limited committee meetings to ninety minutes a week. At the start of each meeting, various senators would clamor to be recognized. Eastland would call on a fellow southerner, who could generally find something to talk about for an hour and a half. On one occasion, Olin Johnson (D-Mississippi) absorbed a month of Mondays with a talk that totaled six hours.

The 1959 session of Congress did have one useful coda. The 1957 Civil Rights Act established the U.S. Civil Rights Commission, charged with appraising the status of civil rights and to report its findings and recommendations to the federal government. The commission represented the first systematic federal effort since the Truman Administration to study race in America. A blue-ribbon panel was gathered, with John A. Hannah, president of Michigan State College (later University), as its chair, along with fellow members Father Theodore Hesburgh, president of Notre Dame; Robert Storey, dean of Southern Methodist University; the former governors of Virginia and Florida; and a labor department attorney. Given this composition, the commission could not easily be written off as anti-southern in intent.

Focusing on voter discrimination, the commission conducted extensive hearings in Georgia, Alabama, Mississippi, Louisiana, and Texas. On September 9, the commission released a 668-page report, which detailed wholesale racial discrimination. As just one example, the report listed sixteen southern counties in which blacks were a majority of the residents, yet not one single African American was registered to vote. There was a serious fly in the commission's ointment. The act creating it had granted the commission a two-year lifespan. That period was about to expire. In a small but significant victory for pro-civil rights forces, the 1959 Congress in its waning days appropriated $500,000 to continue the committee's work. Those funds were appropriated as a rider to the foreign aid bill. As evidence of the political realities of the day, the chief Senate sponsor of the foreign aid bill, William Fulbright (D-Arkansas), voted against the bill he had sponsored to avoid any association with the approval of funds for the Civil Rights Commission.

By mid-September, Senate majority and minority leaders, Lyndon Johnson and Everett Dirksen, acknowledged that matters were at an impasse. Lyndon Johnson took the Senate floor on September 15, 1959. Speaking in his most Delphic tones, Johnson stated, "I serve notice on all members that on or about 12 o'clock on February 15, 1960, I anticipate some Senator will rise in his place and make a motion with regard to the general civil rights question"—leaving no one entirely certain what the majority leader had up his lengthy sleeve.

A Personal Setback

Nineteen-sixty did not open well for William McCulloch. Congressman Richard M. Simpson (R-Pennsylvania) faced brain surgery expected to hospitalize him for several weeks. Simpson chaired the National Republican Congressional Committee, which gathered facts and funds for GOP congressional candidates. Simpson designated McCulloch to fill the post so long as Simpson was ailing. Simpson, however, never returned. A week after asking McCulloch to stand in, the Pennsylvania congressman died.

The post was more than honorary. On January 8, the *Piqua Call* reported, "Simpson's successor eventually will be chosen by a caucus of the committee's 34 members. Three or four congressmen are believed interested in the chairmanship, which is considered a stepping stone toward the position of floor leader."

McCulloch was one of those likely candidates. By one newspaper report, he wanted the post "openly and ardently." He was not, however, the first-round choice of House Minority Leader Charles Halleck. Here, again, the Republican Party's right-center split emerged. McCulloch was a midwestern conservative. Halleck sided with such party "easterners" as Thomas Dewey and Dwight Eisenhower. The Halleck faction saw in Mc-

Culloch what they considered a fatal flaw, given the task involved. One of the principal duties of the National Republican Congressional Committee was to raise funds. McCulloch, in fact, had little experience as a fundraiser; he never spent even $8,000 on a single campaign. Further, his general deference did not suggest he would be skilled at picking the pocket of some industrial prince, while leaving the victim smiling.

McCulloch very much wanted the position. He complained in the press, "a great deal of pressure has been put on my friends, on the members of the committee and on other members of the House to throw their support to other persons." Newspaper accounts described it as "an apparently close race." Then, on January 20, McCulloch suddenly withdrew his candidacy on behalf of Halleck's choice, Congressman William E. Miller (R-New York), who four years later stood as the Republicans' presidential candidate Barry Goldwater's vice-presidential nominee.

McCulloch attempted to put a good face on things: he issued a statement noting that, as midwesterners then held all House Republican leadership posts, it was wise to give the position to an easterner. In truth, McCulloch was deeply disappointed and somewhat concerned. It was the first serious setback since he had entered politics; virtually a public rebuke at the hands of his fellow Republicans, at that. It was not an auspicious opening to the New Year.

In the Congress

Within the week, however, William McCulloch was on to more important matters. During the 1959 session, his name rarely appeared in the *Congressional Record* in reference to civil rights, partly because much of the 1959 civil rights discussion occurred in closed session. In 1960, however, McCulloch took the lead as chief public spokesman for the administration's civil rights bill. As ranking member of the House Judiciary Committee, he assigned the floor speaking time reserved for Republican members. Beyond that, McCulloch advocated actions, answered questions, clarified discrepancies—addressing the House on over one hundred occasions in four months.

McCulloch began on January 28, when his office distributed one of his rare press releases. It announced that McCulloch had that day introduced "a bill to provide for court-appointed Federal voting referees to protect citizens who have been 'systematically and deliberately denied the right to vote because of race or color.'" He noted that the civil rights bill of 1959 had not emerged from committee until August 20, far too late to permit action by the Senate. He added with an uncharacteristic pugnaciousness, "We cannot afford a repetition of the delay which allowed this to happen. If meaningful civil rights bills are to reach the Floor this Session, I call upon my colleagues of the Majority to cease their tirade of empty words and political baloney. I call for deeds, not words."

Here, some framing is needed. The various civil rights bills put forward dealt with a range of issues. At their heart, however, was the question of voting rights for black Americans. The Eisenhower Administration and most northern congressman of both parties favored such rights, at least in some form or under some conditions. Three approaches stood out. First, while the Civil Rights Commission had no power to introduce legislation, it presented a voting rights plan as part of its September 1959 report to the president. The core of that plan read:

Any individual could submit to the President of the United States an affidavit alleging that he had been unable to register with state voting officials by reason of race, color or national origin. He would have to swear also that he believed himself qualified under state law. If the President received nine or more such complaints from a single county, he would refer them to the Civil Rights Commission for verification. After an investigation had weeded out any petitions that might be lacking in merit, the President would designate a federal officer or employee in the area to act as a temporary voting registrar.

On February 7, when President Eisenhower sent his initial civil rights plan to Congress, he favored a more moderate approach, known as the "referee plan." Advanced by Attorney General William Rogers, this called for the attorney general to seek injunctions against state or local actions that precluded a specific individual from voting. Further, if an injunction was obtained, a court would determine if some "pattern or practice" of discrimination existed. If it did, the attorney general would appoint a "referee" to register that voter. Local officials would have the opportunity to challenge the decision. However, no jury trial would be involved—an important point—it being assumed that no white jury would rule for a black plaintiff against white voting officials. The Department of Justice soon revised its plans. On February 19, Anthony Lewis reported in *The New York Times* that the new plan "says that Negroes shall appear before the referee alone, without opposing witnesses and without being subject to cross-examination by state officials. The draft also says that the Negro applicant should not have to do anything more to show his voting qualifications than a white person would."

On March 14, William McCulloch offered a plan that carried a significant extension of the administration's position. McCulloch sought to use the "referee plan" as a trigger. As quoted in the *Congressional Record,* "After the appointment of the voting referee, any person [resident in the same county] of the same color or race as those against whom the practice or discrimination exists shall have a right to make applications to the referee for an order of the court declaring him qualified to vote."

In short, once a pattern of discrimination had been established, other would-be voters of that county would not have to demonstrate that they had been personally discriminated against. Instead, they would be immediately registered. That edict would remain in force for twelve months. Further, McCulloch's proposal stipulated that voting rights would extend to both federal and local elections. This prevented states from precluding blacks from voting in state elections by the simple expedient of scheduling state elections on some other day. The central advantage of the McCulloch amendment was that it reduced the minimum number of legal actions required to one per county. McCulloch offered a concrete example, recounted in the March 16 edition of the *Congressional Record*. One Louisiana parish had stricken 1,350 black voters from the rolls on the same day. Under the Justice Department proposal, 1,350 separate "adversary proceedings" would be required to re-enroll these voters. Under McCulloch's proposal, only one would be needed.

At the same time, while McCulloch sought to broaden the impact of the "referee plan," he still preferred it to the "federal registrar" plan proposed by the Civil Rights Commission and advocated by most liberal civil rights advocates. Paraphrasing his comments in the *Congressional Record*, McCulloch offered two reasons for his position. First, he believed it was generally better for authority to be exercised by state and local, rather than federal, officials. Second, while he did not question that southern authorities had a substantial history of racial discrimination in voter registration, he believed that one ushered in a "new day" not by declaring local authority guilty, but by giving it the presumption of "innocence" until it showed that innocence was unmerited. Further, he was aware that the intrusion of federal authority into the South would rekindle that region's fear of "Reconstruction" and stymie rather than advance the cause of black voting. As he told the House:

At the same time, I am acutely aware of the delicate problems which will be created in the event there is an indiscriminate displacement of State authority by Federal authority in the field of voting qualifications. My awareness of this problem has prompted me to support the administration measure rather than the various proposals for establishing voting registrars, who would be federal officials and who would actually displace and supersede the existing State authority.

Civil rights advocates advanced various criticisms of each proposal. One substantial misgiving was that while the mills of the courts ground fine, they ground extremely slowly. As one legislator put it, the referee procedure, "because it presented virtually limitless opportunities for procrastination, would give scant help to the Negro." Another was the arguably inherent unfairness of asking a potential black voter to undertake a legal steeplechase that a potential white voter would never face. A further complication: even though the pro-civil-rights forces were made up of a coalition of Republicans and Democrats, it was not a coalition whose members were indifferent as to who ended up with the credit or the blame.

On the Senate Side

As the House parsed the various proposals, Majority Leader Lyndon Johnson was demonstrating that the rules of the Senate were marvelous to behold. As noted, when the 1959 session ground to a close, Johnson had predicted that come February 15, 1960, someone would rise on Senate floor and place a civil rights bill before that body.

When February 15, 1960, arrived, Johnson sought the Senate floor and asked unanimous consent to bring H.R. 8315 before that august body. Sadly, he said, the high school in Stella, Missouri, had burnt to the ground. Fortuitously, a nearby Army base, Fort Crowder, had a fine officers' club that was going unused. The bill in question would authorize leasing the unused officers' club to the school district that lacked a high school, until such time as a new one could be constructed. What could be less objectionable? Unanimous consent was granted.

Unlike in the House, the Senate is free to amend a bill in ways that have nothing to do with the bill itself. With the school leasing bill on the floor for discussion, Minority Leader Everett Dirksen rose to speak. He offered an amendment. The amendment he offered was to add to this exceedingly minor measure the entire Eisenhower Administration civil rights bill. Dirksen's amendment was adopted. And there was more. Johnson had made certain that the leasing bill had already received approval on the House side. This meant the amended version would never see the inside of the House Rules Committee, where Chairman Smith could apply his tactics of delay. On the Senate side, since the measure to aid the Stella, Missouri, schools (as amended) was already on the Senate floor, it would not fall under the jurisdiction of James Eastland's Senate Judiciary Committee, where previous civil rights bills went to abandon all hope.

It took only minutes for southern senators to figure out they had been snookered. One opponent of the bill, J. William Fulbright (D-Arkansas), stated that it was "high time our northern brothers ceased to treat the South as a conquered territory and conquered people." Immediately, southerners announced plans to launch a filibuster. Johnson, at his most courtly, said he had no objection. The southerners could hold the floor as long as they wished, provided, of course, that they spoke uninterrupted for twenty-four hours a day, seven days a week.

On the House Side

Whatever Lyndon Johnson's machinations in the Senate, the various House proposals still had to find their way through the House Rules Committee. Slowly, the discharge petition initiated by Congressman Celler gained leverage. When 210 of the 219 required signatures were obtained,

House Minority Leader Charles Halleck urged Rules Committee Republicans to vote to send the bill to the floor. This the committee did by a 7-4 margin, with only four southern Democrats in opposition. With the bills on the floor, the House reconstituted as a Committee of the Whole. It was the task of Speaker Sam Rayburn to designate the congressman who would chair the Committee of the Whole. The next step was curious. Rayburn was widely believed to support voting rights for blacks. Nonetheless, he chose Francis Walker (D-Pennsylvania) as chair. Walker, as a long-time member, had some claim by seniority. He was, however, more generally known as the chairman of the House Un-American Activities Committee, a body routinely inclined to regard civil rights agitators as Communists.

On March 10, McCulloch took the House floor "to speak in support of and to explain, as best I can, H.R. 8601, a bill to enforce certain basic constitutional rights, and for other purposes." The congressman from Ohio's Fourth District took forty-five minutes to present without interruption a five-thousand-word explanation of the bill before the House. He quoted President Eisenhower, "The United States had a vital stake in striving wisely to achieve the goal of full equality under law for all people. On several occasions I have stated that progress toward this goal depends not on laws alone but on building a better understanding." President Eisenhower's sentiment was one McCulloch broadly shared. By this point, the bill consisted of five titles:

• Title I would make the willful obstruction of court orders in school-desegregation cases a crime;

• Title II would make it a federal offense to cross any state line in an effort to avoid prosecution for bombing or burning any building;

• Title III would require that voting records be preserved for three years and that courts have the jurisdiction to direct that these records be made available;

• Title IV rendered the Civil Rights Commission a permanent body;

• Title V ordered that in the event that military children attending public schools were unable to do so because their school closed to avoid desegregation, they would be educated at the expense of the federal government.

McCulloch told the House that he regarded himself as almost the perfect spokesmen for the bill:

Mr. Chairman, I am in an enviable position in this matter, and I say this without sarcasm and without any interference whatsoever. I am not a candidate for President. I am not a candidate for Vice-President. I am not a candidate for the U.S. Senate or for any state office. Furthermore, Mr. Chairman, it is probably a fact that 98 percent of the people of the Fourth Congressional District of Ohio are native-born white. I advocate this legislation because I think it is in the best interests of the nation.

And he was quick in the bill's defense. When one member rose to suggest the proposed bill would unduly burden the federal courts, McCulloch responded: "That this legislation might raise the workload of the federal courts need not be a matter of concern because, should it do so, the Judiciary Committee would stand ready to create more judgeships." To this, strong civil rights advocate Congressman John Lindsay (R-New York) quickly noted that the landmark *Brown* desegregation decision had also created work for the federal courts. Would the questioner prefer segregation to continue simply to save the federal courts a few dollars?

This was the moment that Celler, in particular, had been waiting for—the chance to offer amendments to strengthen the bill. First, he offered an amendment to end racial discrimination in federal contracting. A voice from the floor objected, asserting that Celler's amendment was not germane to the matter before the House and therefore out of order. The chairman sustained the objection. Celler was flabbergasted. He responded:

We see, therefore, that in each title of this legislation the main purpose is enforcement of constitutional rights. That is the fundamental purpose of the bill and that is the fundamental purpose of the amendment. It is clear, therefore, that there is a definite relationship between the subject matter proposed in the bill and that proposed in this amendment.

McCulloch rose immediately in Celler's support:

With regard to the question of germaneness, I concur with the statement of the distinguished Chairman of the Committee of the Judiciary. I repeat what I stated at the beginning, that the pending bill is one that deals with fundamental constitutional civil rights. In my opinion, the point of order should be overruled.

Placed to a vote, the House upheld the chair's ruling. Celler and McCulloch were decisively defeated—157 to 67.

Celler then moved an amendment to make financial aid available to school districts that were attempting to integrate. Once again, a voice called out "not germane." And though once again McCulloch immediately rallied to the defense of his Judiciary Committee chairman, the amendment was ruled out of order. Celler then attempted to add Part III to the bill; again, ruled not germane. As was Celler's final attempt—to abolish the poll tax. This series of votes left Celler and McCulloch absolutely beside themselves, though, in truth, their side was not the winning one.

The ensuing debate moved some to eloquence. Warren Magnuson (D-Michigan) stated:

We all have known for a long time that the Negro in the United States is treated as a second-class citizen. We know that his company is shunned. We know that he is denied the same educational opportunities that the rest of us enjoy. We know that the color of his skin is an automatic handicap to his seeking and obtaining job opportunities equal to his ability and training. . . . We know that the subtle, silent hand of racial discrimination surrounds him at every turn, blocks his natural human desire to enjoy life, liberty and the pursuit of happiness.

Events moved the normally prosaic McCulloch to poetry.

One of my good friends . . . has recently said that he was discouraged that he felt badly that someone, perhaps the author of . . . the McCulloch bill, had the effrontery to do something that has never been done before. In answer to that statement I would like to use, if I can remember them, the words of a famous bard of old, who said: "New actions teach new duties. Time makes ancient customs uncouth."

(McCulloch was actually slightly misquoting the words of English poet James Russell Lowell, who, having lived from 1819 to 1891, might not strictly qualify as a "bard of old." The actual quote is, "New occasions teach new duties. Time makes ancient good uncouth.")

Southern congressmen were moved by neither poetry nor prose, advancing opposition that fell into five rhetorical categories. The first was that there was really no problem needing solution. A Louisiana Democrat asserted:

[Following Reconstruction], we were able to devise a system wherein two races of mankind could live peacefully and with mutual respect. It is a system of "separate but equal" opportunities and facilities, allowing each race to work out its own destiny within its own people, allowing, at the same time, each race to preserve its racial integrity. The Negro has benefited from the mutually agreeable system. He has grown in with the South. In terms of point of origin, he actually has grown faster than other races.

The second was that all problems were the doings of outsiders. Congressman Elijah Forrester (D-Georgia) stated:

This Civil Rights issue has been built up by fat and rich malcontents who have received far more from this Government than they ever gave in return and by do-gooders, unscrupulous politicians and Communists, as it demonstrated by the Communist platform of 1928.

The third was that northerners were simply ignorant of southern ways. As Congressman William Winstead (D-Mississippi) said:

If I did not know any more about the racial relationship that exists in the Southern States than I read in *The Washington Post* and other northern publications and have seen on television and what I hear on radio, I would get the impression that every elected official of the State of Mississippi deserves to be electrocuted.

The fourth was that the bill was simply a low, shameless hustle to attract black votes. As Hugh Alexander (D-North Carolina) said, "The liberal Democrats are vying with the Republican administration to see who can out do the other in the hope that they will reap the harvest of the minority vote this fall."

The fifth was more direct: pass this bill and blood will run in the streets. Mendel Rivers (D-South Carolina) was unabashed on this point: "It won't be long now before the official slaughter of the white people of the South begins."

The southerners were still able to show their northern counterparts that they knew how to shuffle and deal. With McCulloch's amendment on the floor, John Lindsay (R-New York) offered an amendment to the McCulloch amendment, which was adopted. Next, Robert Kastenmeier (D-Wisconsin) offered an amendment to extend the Civil Rights Commission, and to broaden presidential discretion in determining if a voting referee was needed. The Kastenmeier amendment was a substitute for the Lindsay amendment of the McCulloch amendment. Somewhat surprisingly, a number of southern congressmen supported Kastenmeier's amendment, which was approved 152–128. The next step was to make the Kastenmeier amendment part of the Lindsay amendment. As one newspaper put it, "the rare combination [of northerners and southerners] held together again," with Kastenmeier's amendment added to Lindsay's by a margin of 179–116. The final step was to vote on the Kastenmeier amendment itself—that is, to adopt the strongest version of the twice-amended amendment. At this point, the southern congressmen who had cast "Yea" votes on the first two steps switched sides, defeating the Kastenmeier measure by a 170–143 margin.

Writing in *The New York Times*, Russell Baker noted that this left the bill without any provision whatsoever on advancing black voting rights. McCulloch reacted quickly. He could not resubmit his own amendment, as it had been voted down. So he crossed several sentences out of his previous offering, which technically made it a new amendment. When southerners objected to this procedure, Vice-President Richard Nixon, presiding, ruled in McCulloch's favor, telling the southerners their objection was out of order. The House then voted to accept McCulloch's amendment of his previous amendment, thereby restoring the voter rights provision to the bill. He and other rights supporters breathed more easily. Too easily, perhaps, as the South was being more attentive than the North. At one point, the House came within three votes—137 to 134—of adopting an amendment that would limit the voting rights to federal elections only. State and local elections could have continued as before.

Parliamentary maneuvers aside, it was always clear that a majority of representatives favored some action. Back at the rostrum, Speaker Rayburn called for a vote on all amendments that had been accepted by the Committee as a whole. All were adopted. McCulloch, underscoring the point, sought a separate vote on the voting referee provision. On March 23, a formal roll call vote approved the plan McCulloch had advocated by a 295–124 margin. The partisan split was 172 Democrats and 123 Republicans in favor; 100 Democrats and 24 Republicans against. The final vote on the full bill was even more lopsided, 311–109. The finished measure contained:

- Criminal penalties for obstruction of court orders in school desegregation cases;
- Criminal penalties for flight from one state to another in order to avoid prosecution for destroying any building;
- A requirement that state officials retain federal election records for two years and make them available to the Attorney General;
- A provision for federally subsidized education for children of military personnel in areas where local schools closed to avoid desegregation; and
- The voting referee plan.

A major victor in all of this was William Moore McCulloch. Two months earlier, McCulloch had been cast aside by his fellow Republicans for a high party post because, as the *Washington Evening Star* put it, "he was perhaps a bit too plodding, too conservative or too legalistic for an aggressive fund-raising assignment." His star was now again in the ascendant, given bipartisan praise for his handling of the civil rights legislation. That newspaper continued, "Congressional Republicans and most Southern as well as Northern and Western Democrats acclaimed his firmness and fairness, especially in battling for the voting rights provision." Speaking for himself, McCulloch said, "The Southern opponents do not agree with me on the legislation, but I feel they know I want to be fair."

Praise was his closer to home. On March 27, 1960 *The Columbus Dispatch* said McCulloch had "turned the trick by outstanding leadership in steering through the House, in a bitter 10-day dispute, the civil rights bill, with new voting rights protection for minority groups, and sending it to the Senate in such shape that that body may accept it." The newspaper particularly praised McCulloch for managing inclusion of the administration's voting referee plan. It continued:

McCulloch is not a forceful orator, nor is he eloquent in the political speech—making sense of the world. But every time he spoke in the House—and there were many times that he did so during the 10-day struggle—members stopped and listened to what he said, a courtesy they did not extend to every speaker.

By the time praise landed on McCulloch, the great filibuster in the Senate had ended, having lasted only sixteen days. At that point, civil rights advocates moved—against the advice of Lyndon Johnson—to invoke cloture, the two-thirds vote that would cut off debate. Their failure was embarrassing: needing 64 votes to silence the South, they received only 42. In his history of the 1960 Civil Rights Act, David Berman records that an effort to attach Part III to the bill drew only 34 votes in its favor; further, when Senator Jacob Javits (R-New York) proposed creating a permanent Commission on Equal Job Opportunity, the measure died 48 to 38.

Senator Joseph Clark (D-Pennsylvania) acknowledged the extent of defeat. "Surely in this battle on the Senate floor the roles of Grant and Lee at Appomattox have been reversed. The eighteen implacable defenders [southern senators] of the way of life of the Old South are entitled to congratulations from those of us they have so disastrously defeated." With that done, little remained for the Senate except to pass the emasculated bill; this it did on April 8, 1960, by a 71–18 margin. Subsequently, the House accepted the Senate amendments and President Eisenhower signed the bill into law on May 6, 1960.

Emanuel Celler, perhaps attempting to seize self-respect from the jaws of defeat, said blacks should be aware that although the measure passed was small, "sometimes a small key can open a large door." More bluntly, NAACP lead attorney Thurgood Marshall said the 1960 Civil Rights Act "isn't worth the paper it's written on."

That same day, May 8, 1960, the *Lima News*, a newspaper in McCulloch's home district, added a restrained coda of its own.

Finally, after months of bitter debate, a law has been enacted that may bring about the first time equal voting rights for all Americans regardless of race.

But we suspect that there's a little shame in the hearts of many of us that it was necessary in 1960 to enact a law to carry out one of the basic principles of our American system of government.

Settling Out of Court

Between September 9, 1960—when Dwight Eisenhower signed the 1960 Civil Rights Act into law—and July 2, 1964, when Lyndon Johnson signed the Civil Rights Act of 1964, not a single measure related to civil rights was enacted by the Congress of the United States. Yet these forty-six months were not a pause; they were a period of steadily growing activity and tension, rather like the rising humidity and ominous sense that precede a midwestern cloudburst. While, again, this book is not a history of the civil rights movement, a summary of what occurred in those years is necessary to an understanding of the role William McCulloch played and the steps he took when it finally became Congress's time to act.

One most important first step occurred prior to the 1960 signing. On February 1, 1960, four undergraduates from the North Carolina Agricultural and Technical State University in Greensboro, North Carolina, entered a downtown Woolworth's and took seats at the lunch counter. Their names were Joseph McNeil, Franklin McCain, Ezell Blair, Jr., and David Richmond. They had no expectation of being served, as they were black. Instead, they sat—largely ignored and doubtless increasingly hungry—until closing time. On the second day, the number sitting in at Woolworth's rose to twenty. On the third day, sixty. On the fourth day, three hundred. The event lit up the South like a meteor in the night, with similar actions in Nashville, Jackson, Richmond, and elsewhere. And the action brought results: on July 25, 1960, Woolworth's desegregated every one of its stores in the country.

A split was opening on the black side of the equation. Increasingly, African Americans who were younger and less deferential rejected the step-by-step pursuit of rights taken with no small measure of success through the federal courts by some truly excellent attorneys. The most excellent, Thurgood Marshall, commented, "The young people are inpatient . . . and, if you mean, are the young people impatient with me, the young people are impatient with me."

But if the sit-ins clearly brought at least local results, it was also clear what was not working. Author Mark Stern writes, "The 1950's civil rights legislation had proved to be ineffective against an intractable South. Not a single black voter had been added to the voting lists by litigation carried out under the Eisenhower Justice Department." Nicholas Katzenbach— attorney general to both Presidents Kennedy and Johnson—concurred: "Legal suits . . . took a lot of manpower and a lot of time and [it was] very difficult to get results. . . . In fact, in my opinion, they never did get results until the 1965 Voting Rights Act was passed."

And many blacks, young and old alike, were growing impatient with the newly inaugurated John Kennedy. NAACP head Roger Wilkins, lobbyist Clarence Mitchell, and a handful of other black leaders believed Kennedy had reached the White House by pursuing a "southern strategy." Wilkins noted that in the book *Profiles in Courage*, the chapter on the impeachment of President Andrew Johnson reflected the southern view of Reconstruction. Further, at the 1956 Democratic convention—when nominee Adlai Stevenson threw the selection of the vice-presidential nominee over to delegates, Kennedy, though unsuccessful in securing the vice-presidential slot, received 250.5 of 332 southern votes on the convention's second ballot.

There were more palpable matters. The 1960 Democratic platform had pledged to broaden the powers of the Civil Rights Commission and make its charter permanent. The platform had also promised to end discrimination in federally assisted housing. When the decisions came down, the commission got no new powers and a mere two-year extension. The housing decree exempted existing structures and applied to only one-fifth of new construction. Further, Wilkins complained to an ally, "Not once were the responsible Negro leaders called in and told formally what the Administration planned to do." When such a meeting brokered by author James Baldwin was held, the invitees dumped their anger and antagonism on the president. For three hours. Scholar Kenneth Clark commented, "It became one of the most violent emotional verbal assaults . . . that I have ever witnessed before or since."

Stymied in Washington, civil rights proponents took to the streets.

Or, more accurately, to the buses. So-called "Freedom Riders"—blacks and whites in concert—took chartered buses into the lower South to test public accommodations. On May 14, 1961, one such bus was set on fire in Anniston, Alabama, with the knowledge and support of the local sheriff, Theophilus Eugene Conner, better known as "Bull." Six days later, a bus was attacked in Montgomery, Alabama. The federal government wanted peace. Robert Kennedy asked Martin Luther King to put a stop to the Freedom Rides. The thirty-three-year-old King had his own agenda. Again, according to Stern, King replied, "I am different from my father. I feel the need of being free now." Civil rights was becoming a mass movement, and a movement that often paid its dues in prison. In the summer of 1962, protests in 186 cities were accompanied by the arrests of over 15,000 African Americans.

Interestingly, William McCulloch, who was extraordinarily empathetic with the black plight in America, did not support civil disobedience as a tactic. He wrote to one campus minister, "I do remain of the strong opinion that planned and practiced civil disobedience is not in the best interests of the people in a Representative Republic. It makes such practitioners a judge without portfolio with responsibility to no one but himself or the mob."

The foregoing barely touches on the story of those years. But it and the preceding chapter suggest a pause for assessment. The first lesson one might draw was that the South had enormous procedural advantages. Southerner Howard Smith controlled the Rules Committee, whose power to sit on a given bill was almost unlimited. Southerner James Eastland chaired the crucial Senate Judiciary Committee. The general longer tenure of southern representatives was reflected in their generally greater mastery of the rules of Congress. And, as the final backstop stood the Senate's tradition of unlimited debate, the filibuster.

Second, and given this, for a civil rights bill to make headway it needed the very strong and very public support of the president. This, Dwight Eisenhower did not provide.

Third, the liberals who made up the bulk of civil rights supporters needed to look to their motives. As chronicler David M. Berman stated, liberals were "less interested in the dusty legislative process than in striking noble, popular postures." Berman addd that Majority Leader Lyndon Johnson believed "it was far easier to make liberals believe that progress against entrenched social and economic evils must of necessity be slow. . . . In the civil rights debate he concentrated far more on trimming the demands of the liberals than on prodding the southerners." There was a final point, not altogether lost on Ohio Fourth District Congressman William Moore McCulloch—in 1957 and 1960 the House of Representatives had passed civil rights legislation, only to see both bills vitiated in the Senate.

Surveying the scene, Walter Lippmann, the dean of American opinion columnists, wrote on May 28, 1962, "The cause of desegregation must cease to be a Negro movement, blessed by white politicians from Northern states. It must become a national movement to enforce national laws, led and directed by the Federal Government."

CHAPTER 13

The Battle Is Joined

The 1960 election brought John Kennedy narrowly to the White House and, with considerably less uncertainty, returned William Moore McCulloch for his seventh term in Congress. Kennedy's inauguration fell on Friday, January 20, 1961. In an event of more personal consequence for McCulloch, the following day his second daughter, Ann, was married to David Benson Carver at Piqua's Westminster Presbyterian Church. Carver was a graduate of Ohio Wesleyan University. Politics had played a small part in the timing of the wedding. When the engaged couple first approached the McCullochs to suggest the date for the event, the father of the would-be bride said it depended on the outcome of the 1960 election. If Republican Richard Nixon was elected, than Congressman McCulloch would have no end of competing inauguration weekend activities to attend.

Ann and David had met, indirectly, through her father's good offices. Having received his draft notice, and uncertain of what his options might be, David Carver called Congressman McCulloch at home to inquire. The congressman was elsewhere; Ann answered. First, she gave him the advice she thought her father would give: write his office a letter about the matter. Second, she advised him never to call her father at home after 6:30 p.m. The two continued talking. With some combination of boldness and lack of tact, David Carver said he was heading to Troy, Ohio, for a party that evening. His regular girlfriend was unavailable. Would Ann like to accompany him, sights mutually unseen? She would. She did. They spent the entire evening talking to each other and, at least according to David, Ann told her mother she had met the guy she was going to marry.

The courtship continued. David, by then in the military, was stationed at Ft. Lewis, Washington. He regularly telephoned Ann in the evening after he got off duty. This posed the only wrinkle in the courtship. The time in Piqua was three hours later than in Ft. Lewis; David's calls occasionally awakened the congressman, to the latter's annoyance.

In David Carver's telling, "It was assumed that I would need to ask Ann's father for permission." Mabel McCulloch and daughter Ann "cooked up a plan." Christmas 1960, they invited David over to help trim the tree. At one point, David and the congressman repaired to the kitchen for a drink. With William McCulloch, David noted, it was always one drink, never two.

Summoning himself, David said, "I would like to marry your daughter."

The congressman asked if David felt he could support her in the manner to which she was accustomed.

David replied, "Not right away, perhaps, but in a matter of time." David thinks his father-in-law had some doubts on the matter. If so, then what happened next did not help. Delighted with receiving his would-be father-in-law's blessing, David Carver drove home, head in the clouds, foot on the gas, red light unnoticed and police car nearby. The policeman carted David off to the pokey. As ill-chance would have it, he did not have on him the forty dollars to pay the fine. When he informed the police that he had just become engaged to the congressman's daughter, they allowed him to return to the McCulloch residence and borrow the money from the congressman to pay his fine. Carver commented drily: "I knew he disapproved of that."

The wedding followed soon thereafter. Congressman McCulloch wrote a friend that Mabel McCulloch had spent "most of January in Piqua preparing for a very important event, Ann's wedding." Of the wedding, a local paper reported, "Escorted by her father, who gave her in marriage, the bride wore a gown of *peau de soie* and Alencon lace, re-embroidered with pearls. She carried a single, long-stemmed white rose."

By the time of their marriage, Carver had completed his military service. He was now a trainee for the Ohio Seamless Tube Company, the Dayton, Ohio, branch of Copperweld Steel Company. From this period, he recalled, "When we got married one of my uncles asked if we would like some of the family silver or a French poodle. We got the poodle, a black dog named Samantha. Bill [McCulloch] lectured us: he said the dog would cost more than any children we might have. McCulloch's actual objection, Ann McCulloch later related, was that as a former farm boy he did not consider a poodle to be a dog. Nonetheless, in time the congressman grew fond of the canine and would insist on taking her for walks. "When we were back in Piqua, he would pull a chair up to next to his. He would not give Samantha food. He would give her the ice cubes from his martini." Invariably, it was a Tanqueray gin martini, on the generous side, and with an olive.

Back from Piqua following the wedding, McCulloch resumed his various tasks as congressman. His conservatism was undimmed. In 1959, for example, the liberal organization Americans for Democratic Action

(ADA) commended McCulloch for his vote in favor of statehood for Hawaii. So far as the ADA ratings were concerned, that vote was the only good thing McCulloch did all year. In 1954, the Congress of Industrial Organizations had listed McCulloch as one of the 104 congressmen who had voted "wrong" on the half-dozen issues critical to organized labor. Conversely, in 1961, the conservative group Americans for Constitutional Action presented its Distinguished Service Award to McCulloch.

In Congress, McCulloch was reappointed to the Select Committee to Conduct Studies and Investigations of the Problems of Small Business. He repeatedly urged the government to cut spending, telling Congress that "the time has therefore come to make the decision to balance the budget, painful as it may be . . . this is a debt-ridden country, and the resulting burden on the people is becoming intolerable." The country, he added, "faces $7 billion fiscal year deficit. If Congress implements even half of what is being proposed by President Kennedy, the deficit will grow to $10–18 billion." On an unrelated matter, he praised Associate Justice Potter Stewart for his dissent in the Supreme Court decision banning prayer in school, an issue that drew a huge volume of mail from McCulloch's constituents, virtually all of it pro-prayer. He noted Justice William Douglas's observation that American coinage had carried the phrase "In God We Trust" since 1865 and that the Pledge of Allegiance had included the words "under God" since 1954. McCulloch noted the irony that the ruling against school prayer had come from a court whose every session since 1800 had opened with the cry, "God bless the United States and this Honorable Court." In time, McCulloch changed his views on the appropriateness of prayer in school, but he never backed up an inch in his belief that the government could not make an honest being of itself without cutting spending.

McCulloch was now ranking member of the Judiciary Committee and most of his time was devoted to its requirements. A new administration meant a slew of appointments to the federal bench. He noted that when Eisenhower had become president, 84 percent of the sitting federal judges were Democratic appointees. Eisenhower had, McCulloch added, only partly redressed the balance. He believed the federal judiciary should be balanced; he called on Kennedy to make appointments accordingly. On May 4, speaking on the House floor on the pending judicial appointments bill, he said, "I realize that the pressures to reward the politically faithful with the passage of this bill will be more than any president in our history has been called upon to withstand." Moved, as he occasionally was, to poetry, McCulloch challenged the standing notion that to the victors belonged the spoils. "I am reminded of the statement of the bard of old, when he said: 'The old order changeth, yielding place to new; and God fulfills himself in many ways, lest one good custom should corrupt the world.'" McCulloch generally attributed his poetic comments to the "bard of old." In this case, he was quoting Alfred Lord Tennyson.

Judicial appointments were not only a partisan matter. They also set the two Houses of Congress against each other. As one-time Judiciary Committee staff attorney Thomas Mooney explained, the Senate always wanted to create more judgeships than the House wanted to pay for. For the Senate, which in 1961 hoped to appoint seventy new judges, a judge appointed was a friend for life. The House, regarding each new judge as only so much additional expense, wanted to reduce the new appointments to thirty-five. McCulloch, the Dayton *Journal Herald* reported, fought "the good fight" for the lower number, but lost. The matter was resolved in a closed-session meeting of members of both the House and Senate Judiciary Committees. In Mooney's recollection: "It was bourbon and branch water; they would all have a welcoming drink. Celler, who outranked almost everyone, would lead off. He would face up against [Senator James] Eastland, chairman of the Senate Judiciary Committee. Both men wore hearing aids. Eventually, Eastland would say, 'Manny, Manny, let's get down to the giving and the taking.'"

Washington in the 1960s

The Washington, D.C. in which this giving and taking occurred would hardly be recognizable to a visitor today. President Kennedy had aptly characterized the nation's capital as a "city of Southern efficiency and Northern charm." Focusing on the National Mall, in 1961 there was no East Wing to the National Gallery, no National Air & Space Museum, no Hirshhorn Museum, no African or Asian Museum, or Museum of the American Indian. Nor was there any memorial to those who served in the Second World War or in Korea, nor Maya Lin's stunning memorial to the dead of a Vietnam War that had barely claimed its first casualty. Slightly farther afield, there was no underground Metro and only a sprinkling of the hundreds of upscale restaurants today supported by the expense accounts of tens of thousands of lobbyists.

Social Washington was equally different—which is to say, unequal. Such prominent associations as the Cosmopolitan Club and the Metropolitan Club did not admit blacks as members. Journalist Andrew Glass moved to Washington, D.C. with his physician wife in 1962; they looked for housing in the in-town Capitol Hill neighborhood. Realtors, Glass reported, kept separate lists of homes to be shown to white persons and homes to be shown to black persons, and no home appeared on both lists. As Glass told the author, "It was such a time." It was a time in which dozens of nations in Africa were gaining independence and sending ambassadors and small staffs to Washington. Often, these diplomats' duties took them to the United Nations in Manhattan. It was a continuing source of Department of State anxiety that a black ambassador from some little-known country, en route to New York City by car, would be refused service in some restaurant along the way.

In the Eighty-Seventh Congress, McCulloch was active on a range of issues. He supported granting professional football a "very narrow" antitrust exception to allow the National Football League to sign a league-wide contract with the television networks, provided such broadcasts did not interfere with times routinely used for college games. (This action provided the legal basis for "Monday Night Football.") McCulloch opposed a move by Congressman Wright Pattman (D-Texas) to establish a moratorium on new non-profit organizations while their economic impact was studied. Pattman quoted President Truman's view that such organizations "are used as a cloak for business ventures," and quoted a *Washington Daily News* editorial that a partial survey of existing non-profits showed they enjoyed "revenue of $7 billion, all out of reach of federal taxation." McCulloch was an advocate of the voluntary impulse; many non-profits operated in his own district, and "the good that has resulted therefrom has been well-nigh incalculable." McCulloch pressed the case for better pay for Justice Department attorneys, saying, "We have trial lawyers in the Department of Justice who are participating in such cases as those against General Electric, Westinghouse, General Motors and others, and who are now receiving only $15,000 a year"—less, he indicated, than many corporate attorneys were paid for a single case.

With the close of Congress, McCulloch placed in the *Congressional Record* a list of his committee's major accomplishments:

• Public law 87-216, a prohibition on the interstate transmission of betting information;

• Public law 87-368, which made it a crime to cross a state line to avoid prosecution or testimony related to a felony;

• Public Law 87-369, which extended espionage laws to acts committed in foreign countries;

• Passage by the House (though not the Senate) of the Celler-McCulloch-Lindsay bill that addressed conflict of interest in government employment.

McCulloch closed by observing, "There was no consideration of civil rights legislation during the past session of Congress other than a bill to extend the life of the Civil Rights Commission." There was no such consideration because, among other things, the Kennedy Administration had not submitted a civil rights bill.

In his book *Calculating Visions*, Mark Stern wrote, "The decision to delay civil rights legislation specifically was taken before Kennedy took the oath of office." The accepted wisdom was that Kennedy did not want to place other objectives in jeopardy by stirring up the hornet's nest of race—southern hornets, in particular. Contributing to this was the fact that Kennedy had not yet made an emotional commitment to civil rights. One example: In 1959, Jackie Robinson—an authentic American hero and a member of the NAACP Board of Directors—was arrested in Greeneville, South Carolina, for declining to vacate the "whites only" section of the local airport. Later, Robinson explained to a sportswriter who had covered his playing days with the Brooklyn Dodgers why he, Robinson, had endorsed Richard Nixon. Robinson reported he had paid a call on then-Senator Kennedy to solicit the latter's views. According to Robinson, Kennedy stated that because Massachusetts had a small black population, he was not that conversant with its concerns. Robinson told the sportswriter that Kennedy, having served a dozen years in Congress, could have made the time to become conversant.

Race was a sore point with Kennedy. Leading Washington civil liberties attorney Joe Rauh commented, "He [Kennedy] was perfectly happy to be pressured on economic issues, but he was very unhappy to be pressured on civil rights." Kennedy believed that while positive steps could come by executive order or court challenge, legislation would achieve little. In truth, the achievements of previous civil rights legislation were not substantial. The passage of the 1957 and 1960 Civil Rights Acts had led to the registration of only 37,146 southern blacks, less than two percent of those potentially eligible. It is also true that court challenges did not achieve much. The first federal lawsuit to end segregation by a school district receiving federal financial aid was not filed until September 17, 1962, against the schools of Prince George County, Virginia.

In January 1962 *The New York Times* reported the president "has let it be known that he will put forward no major civil rights legislation" during the current year. Soon thereafter, the administration advanced a proposal to end the poll tax by a constitutional amendment. On March 15, Attorney General Robert Kennedy told Judiciary Committee Subcommittee No. 5, "The anti-poll tax measure and a bill to cut abuses of state literacy tests required for voting are of vital importance and should get swift action." McCulloch, a member of the subcommittee the attorney general was addressing, was unimpressed. The measures proposed, he said, "will not solve a majority of the problems that we have." McCulloch said he might support a constitutional amendment to end literacy testing. Extending his argument to the House floor, he quoted a 1961 report from the U.S. Civil Rights Commission:

With the possible exception of a deterrent effect of the poll tax—which does not appear generally to be discriminatory upon the basis of race or color—Negroes now appear to encounter no significant racially motivated impediments to voting in 4 of the 12 southern states—Arkansas, Oklahoma, Texas, and Virginia.

McCulloch added, "Do we really believe that abolition of the poll tax will, in fact, enfranchise many additional citizens who today are barred from voting? Of course not, because there are many subtle and clever devices that can be used to prevent a person from voting."

If there was little pressure from the administration to push civil rights, there was equally little push from the congressman's own constituents. Even in slack times, the average congressman receives considerable mail. During the 1961–1962 Congress, McCulloch received many letters on Communism (which the writers regarded as evil); gun control (regarded as almost as evil); postal service (generally regarded as inefficient); and taxes (invariably regarded as too high). Only a sprinkling of letters, however, concerned civil rights. Even these did not urge Congressman McCulloch to take any action. Eight residents of Lima and Elida, Ohio, wrote in to say, "Keep the Federal Government Out of [Mississippi's] State's Rights." A constituent from Covington wrote to inform Mr. McCulloch, "Before Eleanor Roosevelt entered the White House we never had one minute of trouble out of the colored people." A management consultant from Troy wrote at great length to inform his congressman that "Justice is largely rigged by consent in favor of the Negroes, their crimes are not like others, nor treated as such whether it be robberies or rapes."

Generally, Congressman McCulloch's responses to such letters were prompt if not always direct. To the management consultant quoted above:

Hundreds of thousands of pages have been written on these matters and the radio and television commentators have been spending hours and days and months in the aggregate discussing such problems. Therefore, I could not begin to answer, to alone discuss, the many questions you raise and the comment that you make.

Often, McCulloch extended an invitation to his correspondent. If they were hostile, he would invite them to drop by his booth at the next district open house he held in their vicinity. If they were friends, he would urge them to drop by his Washington office the next time they were in town, and then sweetened the offer by suggesting they lunch at the congressional dining room over a bowl of its famed bean soup.

When, however, "a loyal Negro citizen" and "student at Troy High School" wrote to criticize the effort to maintain segregation at the University of Mississippi, McCulloch's reply—dated just three days later than the original letter—agreed that events in Mississippi were "a sad commentary on our times." The student told McCulloch, "Negroes and all races should have the same educational rights!" and that she saw no solution beyond "prayer, understanding and love of all our fellow man." Nonetheless, McCulloch said he felt that the 1957 and 1960 Civil Rights Acts had brought more progress in the past decade than any time since the Civil War. Somewhat defensively, perhaps, he enclosed information on his own role in the passage of that legislation.

McCulloch Drafts a Bill

The next move was up to William McCulloch. As Adam Clymer of *The New York Times* observes, when people recall the events that led to passage of the 1964 Civil Rights Act, their attention falls on two sites—the "street" and the Senate. The street may be a shortcut reference to the popular agitation on behalf of the bill—the marches, the sit-ins, the March on Washington with its transcendent "I Have a Dream" speech—as well as the opposition to that agitation, the police dogs, and the murders. The Senate was scene of the longest filibuster in American history, seventy-three days in all, during which the number of senators prepared to cut off debate—invoke cloture—rose slowly, inexorably, and finally above the water line. But as Clymer points out, the 1964 Civil Rights Act itself—one of the landmarks of American law—was *written* in the House of Representatives. It was in the House, that is, that the actual content was determined. And, Clymer adds, "The bill that passed the House, except for the clause on women, which both Celler and McCulloch opposed, was McCulloch's bill." Written, that is, largely by William Moore McCulloch, the unprepossessing representative of Ohio's Fourth District. (In the Senate, Minority Leader Everett Dirksen introduced a number of changes—but all were minor, cosmetic, and undertaken to give wavering Republicans the belief that their Senate leader had given the bill a thorough going over before lending it his crucial support.)

McCulloch acted on January 31, 1963, when he—supported by nine fellow Republican congressmen—introduced H.R. 3139. The bill contained five provisions:

• First, the Civil Rights Commission would become a permanent body;

• Second, a seven-member Commission for Equality of Opportunity in Employment would be created to investigate allegations of job discrimination by any employer or labor union that did business with the federal government, with this commission authorized to cut off the flow of federal funds if discrimination was demonstrated;

• Third, the attorney general would be authorized to act on behalf of citizens who claimed that they were being denied access to a non-segregated school (a revival of the 1957 Civil Rights Act's deleted Part III);

• Fourth, provision of federal technical assistance to states desegregating their school systems; and,

• Fifth, that in those states that maintained literary tests for voters, completion of six grades of school would constitute the criterion for literacy.

As noted, nine other congressional Republicans had introduced identical bills. A further twenty-eight Republican representatives had offered their endorsement. As McCulloch was not loath to observe, theirs was the only rabbit in the race. McCulloch declared that the failure of the Kennedy Administration to press for comprehensive civil legislation was "one of the most serious shortcomings of the last [1961–1962] Congress."

On February 28, 1963, President Kennedy presented his first civil rights proposals. These focused on minor changes to voting rights laws, some financial support to school districts that were voluntarily desegregating, and an extension of the Civil Rights Commission. McCulloch was quick to criticize. That same day he told the House the administration was presenting ideas "not nearly as broad in scope" as he and over forty fellow Republicans had introduced the previous month. He charged that the administration was doing nothing about what McCulloch thought was probable vote fraud in Philadelphia, Detroit, and Chicago. He added:

I am further disturbed by the failure of the President to make recommendations to end conditions that exist in discrimination in employment by those who have authority in the labor movement in America. . . . The opportunity to get a job and earn one's bread by the sweat of one's brow is even more important and more basic than the right to help select public officers.

A junior Republican congressman and rising star, Manhattan's John Lindsay, added pointedly, "I wonder if poor Abe Lincoln is not turning in his grave a little bit as I read this sentence in the President's message: 'In the last two years more progress has been made in securing civil rights for Americans than in any comparable period in our history.'"

As the biographer of NAACP chief lobbyist Clarence Mitchell stated,

Rather than take the hint that the time was overdue for his leadership, Kennedy merely sought to deflect the increasing pressure by submitting to Congress on February 28 what was essentially another voting rights bill. The administration's initiatives were obviously very late and inadequate. Evidently deciding to run in 1964 on his record of unprecedented black appointments and aggressive executive action, he failed to use this opportunity to implement the exemplary 1960 Democratic platform, as civil rights forces were urging.

On March 14, Attorney General Robert Kennedy met with the Judiciary Committee, in the words of *The New York Times*, to warn it against "asking for the moon" and to argue that the administration's proposals had "the best chance of success." McCulloch noted that, for those states that maintained literacy tests for voters, the bill defined literacy as having had six years of schooling. He commented that eight million Americans lacked that level of education. Among the individuals who could not meet such a standard, he added drily, was Abraham Lincoln. Personally, he said he favored a constitutional amendment that would ban literacy tests altogether.

Meg Greenfield, then a widely read columnist for *The Washington Post*, commented, "I seemed to have the lineup of players just about absolutely wrong." With the Democratic Party heavily dependent on its southern wing, even the northern liberal Democrats who were most vociferous in their denunciations of Jim Crow were, she suggested, mainly posturing. For the moment, she recalled, "the principal force truly committed to taking immediate action against the kinds of crude racial repression still in place seemed to be, of all things, a bunch of Republicans, many of them unknown." She counted among them Senators Thomas Kuchel, Jacob Javits, and Clifford Case, but added that the most active organizers were "a few generally conservative Midwestern House members," notably Thomas Curtis of Missouri and William McCulloch of Ohio.

On May 8, 1963, William McCulloch addressed the House on behalf of H.R. 3139, the bill that carried the endorsement of nearly forty House Republicans. While asserting that "great progress has been made in the field of civil rights in the past decade . . . both material and psychological," he was well aware that the task had barely begun:

No one would suggest that the Negro receives equality of treatment. . . . Thousands of school districts remain segregated. Decent hotel and eating accommodations frequently lie hundreds of miles apart for the Negro traveler. Parks, playgrounds, and golf courses continue to lie off limits to Negroes whose tax monies go to support them.

McCulloch noted there were many sites of conflict—Little Rock, Arkansas; Oxford, Mississippi; Chicago, Illinois; Birmingham, Alabama; and others. These, he said, were "convincing proof that tension exists and resistance remains. But turmoil is [a] sign of birth as well as decay."

Here, then, is a comprehensive bill that seeks to advance the cause of civil rights in the United States. At the same time, however, it is a bill keyed to moderation. And the reason for moderation is obvious. We members of the Republican Party are honestly desirous of proposing legislation that stands a chance of enactment. Anyone, of course, can introduce grandiose legislative schemes. But reaching for the sky, rather than aiming for the possible, is a form of showmanship we don't wish to engage in. Reality is what we live by and accomplishment is what we seek. For only in compromise, moderation, and understanding are we able to fashion our society into a cohesive and durable structure.

The statement is almost pure McCulloch. He was one of the few persons in American politics with no capacity for showmanship. He had no abstract interest in being right, or feeling himself in the right. He had no belief that a perfect society, or even a greatly improved one, could be legislated into existence, unless the heart and mind kept up with—indeed, kept ahead of—the law.

The Street

In Dixie, things were moving with greater pace and urgency. A generation of young people, no longer satisfied with court victories, took more direct action. In Albany, Georgia, local officials arrested 1,100 protestors in the ten months ending in July 1962. A great unraveling was occurring. Despite a century of pretense, the understanding southern whites had held of southern blacks was false. Ralph McGill, long-time editor of the *Atlanta Constitution*, stated, "One of the persistent falsehoods . . . is the 'stereotype' of the Negro into the 'preacher,' the 'Amos and Andy,' 'Uncle Tom,' 'Boy,' 'Uncle,' 'Mammy.' Most Southerners do not know, or want to know, the facts of Negro development. . . . This is one reason why the students in their sit-ins . . . have produced such a revolutionary effect. They have fitted none of the stereotypes."

Jason Sokol relates this 1962 exchange between Zeke Matthews, sheriff of Terrell County, Georgia, and a crowd that included a fair number of blacks from that county:

> "Are any of you disturbed?"
> The reply was a muffled, "Yes."
> "Can you vote if you are qualified?"
> "No."
> "Do you need people to come down here and tell you what to do?"
> "Yes."
> "Haven't you been getting along well for a hundred years?'
> "No."

Sokol quotes writer Robert Penn Warren, "The white southerner has had a shock. . . . All at once . . . he has been confronted with the fact that what his cook or yard boy or tenant farmer had told him is not true." The response was a convoluted mix of reassessment, apprehension, denial—and an odd awakening of "memories" of Reconstruction when federal authority advanced black rights. Following from this, many white southerners vehemently objected to federal intervention, often to the point of violence. Recounting the efforts to enroll James Meredith at the University of Mississippi, Nicholas Katzenbach recalled:

> We arrived down there, and the marshals surrounded the building. Then some students began to gather around and jeered and catcalled and called nasty names and so forth and so on, flipped cigarettes at these Army trucks which we had used to transport things, threw bottles—it gradually accelerated—threw some rocks.

By the time Meredith was enrolled, five hundred U.S. Marshals, elements of the Second Infantry Division, National Guardsmen, and other units were brought in, full-scale rioting occurred, two were dead, twenty-five received gunshot wounds, and 160 were injured. Katzenbach invariably maintained his composure. During the University of Mississippi crisis, the U.S. Army Signal Corps system that tied Katzenbach back to the White House broke down. Later, the general commanding asked Katzenbach how he managed to stay in touch with the president. Katzenbach took a dime out of his pocket and said, "General, you put this into a pay phone and dial NA 8-1414, collect."

In May 1963, the Reverend Martin Luther King, Jr. announced he would make Birmingham the target of civil rights agitation. Soon, authorities had arrested 250—including Dr. King, who used his prison time to write his acclaimed "Letter from a Birmingham Jail." Northern civil rights leaders found the federal response wholly inadequate. Clarence Mitchell's biographer wrote: "Kennedy, responding to the Birmingham crisis, seemed almost to invite ridicule when he declared during his May 8 news conference that the federal government lacked authority to intervene and protect the rights of demonstrators" against physical assaults directed by Sheriff Eugene "Bull" Conner. He added: "Mitchell welcomed the challenge from Senators Javits and Keating and Congressmen Cellar, Lindsay, McCulloch, and Mathias that Kennedy could use existing laws to protect the demonstrators."

Celler declared it "barbaric" that local authorities had used police dogs and fire hoses against demonstrators. New York Republican Senator Keating said there was a "glaring gap in the legal arsenal of the Federal Government" if it could not act effectively to protect protesters.

On June 12, 1963, the first two black students were admitted to the University of Alabama after Governor George Wallace—who literally "stood in the schoolhouse door"—yielded to the federal authority. On June 19, Medgar Evers, the NAACP field secretary who shortly before had been slain in an ambush, was buried in Arlington National Cemetery in Virginia.

Here, analogy arises. In the 1850s, the Fugitive Slave Act mandated that all northern officials must aid in the return of runaway slaves. This act declared the North to be actively (as opposed to passively) complicit in slavery. It was one thing to tolerate an abusive neighbor; it was another to be required to return the victim to the abuser's hands. This act contributed greatly to the glacial shift in northern sentiment toward slavery that occurred during that decade. Journalist Andrew Glass noted white reactions in the early 1960s: "At this time, there was an outpouring of feeling. The widespread view was—segregation was one thing; but it was not right for segregation to be supported by state authority."

Early Maneuvering

On June 11, President John Kennedy—pegging his remarks to the crisis at the University of Alabama—delivered a 2,000-word address to the nation from the Oval Office on the subject of civil rights. He said in part:

The heart of the question is whether all Americans are to be afforded equal rights and equal opportunities, whether we are going to treat our fellow Americans as we want to be treated. If an American, because his skin is dark, cannot eat lunch in a restaurant open to the public, if he cannot send his children to the best public school available, if he cannot vote for the public officials who represent him, if, in short, he cannot enjoy the full and free life which all of us want, then who among us would be content to have the color of his skin changed and stand in his place? Who among us would then be content with the counsels of patience and delay?

He announced that he would seek legislation from Congress. He closed by asking the support of all citizens. On June 19, 1963, President John Kennedy sent a special message to Congress presenting his administration's revised proposals on civil rights.

• Title I enforced the constitutional right to vote in federal elections;
• Title II prohibited discrimination in places of public accommodation;
• Title III desegregated public schools and authorized assistance to solving problems related to desegregation;
• Title IV established a Community Relations Service to assist communities in solving racial disputes;
• Title V granted a four-year extension to the Civil Rights Commission;
• Title VI banned discrimination in programs that received federal financial support;
• Title VII granted the president to power to create a Commission on Equal Employment Opportunity.

Titled H.R. 7152, the bill was assigned to the House Judiciary Committee. On June 20, Committee Chairman Emanuel Celler routed the measure to Subcommittee No. 5. This subcommittee, its members hand-picked by Celler, was considerably more liberal than the full House Judiciary Committee. Indeed, the eleven-member subcommittee contained not a single southern congressman.

The ensuing twenty-two days of hearings began with Attorney General Robert Kennedy as first witness. For the Kennedy Administration, Attorney General Robert Kennedy was clearly the point man on civil rights. Personally, Robert Kennedy was not the easiest of persons with whom to deal; nor, at the time in Washington, a person widely liked. David Broder, for many years the dean of Washington political reporters, said that Kennedy had the unnerving habit, when asked a question, of sitting silently while withdrawing eye contact. Broder said he never knew whether Kennedy had not heard the question or whether he simply regarded it as too stupid to answer. In either case, Broder said, it was an effective bit of one-upmanship.

Robert Kennedy was capable of great charm, but he did not use his June 26, 1963, appearance before the Judiciary Committee to demonstrate it. Congressman George Meader (R-Michigan) asked what Kennedy thought of the public accommodations bill that two dozen Republicans, led by John Lindsay (D-New York), had introduced three weeks earlier. As it happened, the Lindsay proposal went rather further than what the administration was suggesting. Kennedy replied that a great many proposals were floating around, and he hardly had time to read all of them. Kennedy subsequently added that he had not read the McCulloch civil rights bill, introduced five months previously, prior to developing his own.

From this, many committee Republicans drew the conclusion that Kennedy believed a civil rights bill could pass without significant Republican support, a position they regarded as foolish. Further, they regarded Kennedy's manner—which Anthony Lewis was later to term in *The New York Times* as "unnecessarily insulting"—as foolish. Necessarily or not, Congressman Lindsay found Kennedy's dismissal of the major Republican proposals insulting. He challenged the attorney general, "The rumor is all over the cloakrooms and corridors of Capitol Hill that the administration has made a deal with the leadership to scuttle the [public] accommodations" portion of the bill in an effort to palliate the South. What Lindsay said was true—at least to the extent that such rumors *were* afloat. Kennedy's response was combative: "I don't think the President nor I have to defend our good faith in our efforts, here to you or really to anyone else." Turning to his legislative assistant, Robert Kimball, Lindsay asked, "Do you think I was too hard on him?" Kimball responded, "Well, maybe a little, but I can understand why you were."

Kimball would be eyewitness to and participant in many of the most crucial behind-the-scenes events. He had reached Washington, D.C. in the summer of 1961, working as an intern for New York Congressman John Lindsay. He returned to serve as Lindsay's legislative assistant until 1963, when he moved to the Republican Legislative Research Association (RLRA). The RLRA, which provided research and staff assistance to Republicans, consisted, pretty much, of Kimball and a part-time secretary. Kimball had been accepted into the Yale University School of Law's 1963 entering class. When he mentioned this to Congressman McCulloch, the latter suggested Kimball might wish to give the matter some further thought. Kimball recalled McCulloch saying, "You and I may never again work on anything as important as this. Think about that." Kimball thought, and decided to try to postpone his admission at Yale. He had some help. McCulloch called the admissions office on Kimball's behalf. So did Roy Wilkins, executive secretary of the NAACP. So did Hugh Scott, Republican senator from Pennsylvania. Kimball's admission was deferred by a law school admission's officer who must have wondered who in hell was this guy Kimball that he had so much pull with so many important people.

Following Kennedy's testimony, Chairman Celler attempted some fence mending, commenting on the importance of bipartisan support in past civil rights initiatives. Perhaps with that thought in mind,

Nicholas Katzenbach suggested the administration send an emissary to Piqua, Ohio, to establish diplomatic relations with the Judiciary Committee's ranking Republican, William McCulloch. The task fell to Burke Marshall, assistant U.S. attorney for civil rights. Briefly restating this book's introductory chapter, McCulloch informed Marshall that he and many fellow Republican congressmen had felt burned in 1957 and 1960. Twice, they had supported strong civil rights bills, only to see that strength bargained away by an administration anxious to avoid a filibuster in the Senate. McCulloch, as reported, set two conditions. First: no substantive changes would be made in a House-passed version unless he, McCulloch, passed on those changes. Second: in the event a civil rights bill was enacted into law, he wanted assurances that President Kennedy would give credit to both political parties. McCulloch's leverage was that if the Senate passed a weaker law, a joint House-Senate conference committee would ensue. At which point, McCulloch said, he would pull enough GOP votes to sink the measure.

When Burke Marshall returned to Washington to report on the conditions set forth by a small-town conservative Republican congressman, he was not received as the bearer of good tidings. In an oral history recorded years later, Nicholas Katzenbach acknowledged that McCulloch's suspicions were well founded. Katzenbach stated, "I think initially we thought in terms somewhat similar to the '57 and '60 tactics. I think Vice-President Johnson thought in terms of what can you give away as you move through. I think President Kennedy thought in these terms. All of us thought in these terms." In his memoirs, engagingly entitled *Some of It Was Fun*, Katzenbach commented that "however principled on McCulloch's part" the Ohio congressman's position might be, that position was "the initial monkey wrench" thrown into the works. McCulloch, Katzenbach said, "wanted an unequivocal assurance that [a trading down] would not occur. That was true from the first time he talked to us."

The Kennedy Administration knew that the question of trade-offs in the Senate was moot if McCulloch withdrew his support. Commonly (though it was never explained how the figure was determined) it was assumed that on civil rights sixty House Republicans would follow McCulloch's lead. Without those sixty votes, no bill would reach the Senate or emerge from a conference committee. This, Katzenbach continued, made it very clear that passage of a civil rights bill into law would require the administration to face down the Senate grandees: "At which point we began to think more seriously of cloture than we ever had before." House Judiciary Committee Chairman Emanuel Celler, briefed on the circumstances, was in accord.

Enthusiasm elsewhere was limited. The Democratic Study Group— a caucus of more than one hundred House liberals— wanted to take the same approach as in 1957 and 1960. Again, Katzenbach: "I remember a large meeting with some of the more responsible liberals in the House like Dick Bolling [D-Missouri], Jim O'Hara [D-Michigan] and Frank Thompson [D-New Jersey] all objecting to the way in which we were doing this. We explained that was the only way McCulloch would do it. And they said, 'It won't work.'" In Katzenbach's memoir, he wrote, "Finally, the most experienced and thoughtful of the Democrats, Richard Bolling of Missouri"—who initially disagreed with the McCulloch approach— "reluctantly acquiesced, sort of: 'If you really mean what you are saying and you are prepared to stick with it, then I don't think it's impossible that it could succeed.'"

At about this time, an assessment was made of the chances of invoking cloture in the Senate. As noted, this required sixty-seven votes. The assessment determined that the administration could count on fifty-one. Still, the Kennedy Administration decided to adopt the strategy put forth by the mild-mannered Mr. McCulloch. Katzenbach recalled, "Very early in the game, August [1963] perhaps, we decided that that was our strategy."

March on Washington

As quoted previously, columnist Walter Lippmann wrote in May 28, 1962, "The cause of desegregation must cease to be a Negro movement, blessed by white politicians from Northern states. It must become a national movement to enforce national laws, led and directed by the Federal Government."

And this it became. By the time the civil rights bill reached the Senate for debate, Congress found itself inundated by delegations of hundreds of clergymen of all faiths; representatives of organized labor; major business; typical citizens—all urging action as a moral imperative. The forerunner of this was the August 28, 1963, "March on Washington for Jobs and Freedom," an event that brought over 200,000 persons to the Reflecting Pool just east of the Lincoln Memorial, where they heard the soaring words of the Dr. Martin Luther King, Jr., "I Have a Dream" speech.

When the day was done, the crowd dispersed, the litter gathered, and the words of eloquence sung and spoken that day still warm in the ears of many, hardly anyone mentioned the fact that at the start, political Washington strongly opposed the "March on Washington for Jobs and Freedom." In *Calculating Visions*, Mark Stern wrote that President Kennedy "was very concerned about proposals for a black march on Washington. Rumors abounded that the March leaders planned to stage sit-ins and generally disrupt life in the capital." Kennedy announced on July 17—six weeks before the date of the March on Washington—that having "looked into this matter with a good deal of care, we have no evidence that any of the leaders of the civil rights movement are Communists."

Actually, there were other fears. One was that an undisciplined mass of hundreds of thousands would descend on the city, wreaking chaos in their path, and, perhaps, fatally undermining support for the cause for which they marched. Anticipating this, one Capitol Hill staffer reported, his roommate left town for the weekend. As did others. One ranking Department of Justice figure was assigned to spend the day in an underground office of the Pentagon to assist in organizing whatever countermeasures would be needed if events got out of hand. The second fear—more commonly held among members of Congress—was that the march was an attempt to bully action from a body that was fiercely proud of its prerogatives. Congressman William McCulloch fell into this category, stating on August 24, "They are not going to bluff me. Doctors, lawyers, everybody could start marching and there would be no end to it."

The March on Washington was a replica of one never held. In 1942, A. Philip Randolph, founding president of the all-black Brotherhood of Sleeping Car Porters, informed President Franklin Roosevelt that he would lead tens of thousands to march on Washington unless Roosevelt signed an executive decree banning discrimination in war industries. Roosevelt signed. In the waning days of 1962, Randolph revived the idea for a march. As matters progressed, the event drew in more and more participating groups, with thirty civil rights, religious, and labor leaders meeting at the Roosevelt Hotel in New York. Katzenbach later wrote, "While the administration was in no position to oppose the march, we were quite worried about it."

The worry proved ungrounded. Writing in *The New York Times*, Russell Baker caught the mood of the day: "For the most part they came silently during the night and the early morning. . . . Instead of the emotional horde of angry militants that many had expected, they gave this city a day of music, strange silences and good feeling in the streets."

The huge crowd—which included such luminaries as James Baldwin, Harry Belafonte, Paul Newman, Charlton Heston, Marlon Brando, Burt Lancaster, Sidney Poitier, and such singers as Mahalia Jackson, Marian Anderson, Bob Dylan, Joan Baez, and Peter, Paul, and Mary—came, heard, cheered, roused themselves for the struggle ahead, and departed. Not a single arrest occurred. In the aftermath, the general view in official Washington was that the march had not swayed the vote of a single congressman or senator. It had done two things of greater importance. First, it impressed the civil rights movement with its own strength, competence, and breadth of support. Second, it impressed the American public— many of whom had been more than a bit leery of the prospect. And what impressed the public about the march was that it was so American.

The peacefulness of the march contrasted with the continuing reports of violence in the South. The event most compelling of public opinion was the September 15, 1963, bombing of the Sixteenth Street Baptist Church in Birmingham, Alabama—an act that killed four young girls, one of whom was a childhood friend of future Secretary of State Condoleezza Rice. As such stories showed just how far southerners were prepared to go to protect white supremacy, the nation experienced a groundswell. Or perhaps more accurately, an earthquake. Earthquakes travel along fault lines. This earthquake spread variously, but one track led to Washington, D.C., where the House Judiciary Committee was writing a civil rights bill. And the energy of that earthquake reached Room 346 of the Longworth House Office Building, where it found a great deal of fault.

And one man in particular, committee chairman Emanuel Celler, felt this earthquake approach and reacted with a certain tremor. Celler was by this time seventy-five years old. He had served in Congress for forty-one years and had chaired the Judiciary Committee since 1949 (except for 1953–1954, when the GOP briefly controlled the House). A few observers thought he had lost a step or two. Charles and Barbara Whalen write that many people "believed Celler was losing his touch, a victim of the generation gap . . . not noticing the changes that were taking place on Capitol Hill, not grasping the restlessness among junior members who wanted greater participation in the decision making process."

Celler became the focal point of pressure, sustained and increasing pressure, from his long-time constituencies, black, white, union, and others, to strengthen the bill just then being written by Celler's Subcommittee No. 5. That pressure might be typified, perhaps, by the exchange between United Auto Workers President Walter Reuther, a supporter of a stronger bill, and Attorney General Nicholas Katzenbach, an exchange that ended with Reuther dismissing Katzenbach as an out-of-touch academic.

Days later, Katzenbach left for a trip to Latin American in the belief that everything was moving smoothly enough. When he returned, he learned that all hell had broken loose. Katzenbach explained the cause: "Well, Manny [Celler] was pressured by all the people he respected and from where he's had support throughout the years and he was at that point perfectly persuaded it was perfectly all right for the subcommittee to report [an amended] bill out and that it would be straightened out in the full committee." Congressman Richard Bolling (D-Missouri) wrote: "Despite seniority based on forty years' service, intellect, and his committee position, Celler often finds himself [in] the awkward position of a chairman who presides over, but does not command, a majority of his committee." Others said, less charitably, "Manny caved."

What he caved to was a series of "strengthening amendments" to the bill:

• First, authorizing the attorney general to file suit against any alleged breach of anyone's constitutional right anywhere in the country;

• Second, expanding the definition of public accommodations to any enterprise that operated under government "authorization, permission, or license";

• Third, launching immediate federally directed voter registration drives in any county in which fewer than 15 percent of African-Americans were voting.

Additional amendments authorized the attorney general to initiate school desegregation cases; to extend voting rights to state and local elections; to empower the federal government to file suit in any undertaking that used federal funds; and more. Author Mark Stern wrote, "Despite an earlier pledge to McCulloch and the Republicans that he would back a circumscribed public-accommodations section, Celler now backed an extension of this section to include every form of business—even private schools, law firms and medical associations." Syndicated columnists Rowland Evans and Robert Novak wrote that such civil rights advocates as Clarence Mitchell, Joe Rauh, Andrew Biemiller, Walter Fauntroy, Arnold Aronson, and others "stomped Manny" in favor of a stronger bill.

Celler defended his action by saying that the new clauses were for "trading purposes" in the full committee or on the House floor. This approach, Charles and Barbara Whalen wrote, "would allow Celler to score points with his constituencies; to maintain his friendships with conservatives [by giving them some victories] and [would] result in 'a decent civil rights measure.'" Apparently unnoticed by Celler, his actions ran counter to the pledge John Kennedy had given William McCulloch as the price of the latter's support.

The amended bill, however, thrilled two groups—strong advocates of civil rights and strong advocates of states' rights. The latter were southern conservatives deeply persuaded that no bill carrying the "strengthening" amendments would ever pass the House of Representatives, let alone the Senate. And so, regarding them as a poison pill, they voted for all the strengthening amendments. The view that the "strengthened" bill was not passable was shared by John and Robert Kennedy, by Nicholas Katzenbach, and an Ohio congressman, William McCulloch. McCulloch told the press the pending amendments were "so severe they threaten passage of the civil rights legislation, not only in the Senate but even in the House. I am opposed to these unbelievably severe powers that would cover every business in Ohio that carries goods and services to the public." Less publicly, McCulloch described the amendments as "a pile of garbage." Not all Republican representatives shared McCulloch's view. Of these, the most influential was John Lindsay of Manhattan, among the most passionate of civil rights advocates in Congress.

Congressman Richard Bolling (D-Missouri) agreed with McCulloch, "The subcommittee strengthened the Administration's measure to the point where President Kennedy and many strategically placed pro-civil rights House Members judged that the strengthened measure could not be passed on the floor even if it managed to escape the ambush the conservative House Rules Committee would certainly lay." The Republicans—McCulloch and Minority Leader Charles Halleck (R-Indiana) chief amongst them—were furious at the Hobson's choice they were being handed. Either they supported the amendments—thus, creating a bill they believed would never become law—or they opposed them, thus becoming the guys who watered down a bill the civil rights leaders wanted. Nonetheless, on October 2, 1963, Subcommittee No. 5 approved the amendments, recommending their passage to the full committee.

The following year, in June of 1964—when passage of the bill was assured—*New York Times* reporter Anthony Lewis wrote, "Nearly everyone by now has forgotten the chaos and bitterness into which the civil rights legislation had fallen last autumn. It seemed then that only a miracle could save it from suffocation at the hands of its own supporters." That moment was now, and while that moment did not bring forth a miracle, what it brought forth did suffice.

On October 8, the full House Judiciary Committee opened its hearing on the Subcommittee No. 5 amendments. By this time, the Republican moderates had hit the wall. Not only did the original bill need to be restored, but the Democrats had to take the lead in that restoration. In this, McCulloch and company had the backing of the Kennedy Administration. It was time for Celler to back down. Feeling himself cornered, Celler tried to outsource the unpleasantries. One individual close to the negotiations says Celler ducked his responsibility; as committee chair, he should have taken it upon himself to present the "weakening" amendment, thus making his position clear. Instead, he passed the task to Representative Roland V. Libonati (D-Illinois). Libonati, as a long-term, low-profile member whose only constituent of consequence was Chicago Mayor Richard J. Daley, was considered safe from any backlash from civil rights groups. As instructed, Representative Libonati presented a motion to the full Judiciary Committee to reject the Subcommittee No. 5 amendments.

With Libonati's motion pending, Attorney General Robert Kennedy met in closed session with the Judiciary Committee on October 15 and 16. Kennedy, Nicholas Katzenbach later wrote, "had the unpleasant task of testifying against provisions that the civil rights leaders wanted and many of which, but for the political need for Republican support, he [Kennedy] favored." Most reports from the closed session have Kennedy saying that no attorney general should have or should wish to have the authority to intervene at his own discretion on behalf of any citizen, complaining of anything, anywhere. It was misplacing a power that was in any case too broad to use. By other accounts, Kennedy's testimony was considerably less definitive.

Reports of Kennedy's testimony left civil rights leaders furious. Clarence Mitchell's biographer wrote that the NAACP lobbyist was "fit to be tied." Mitchell later said there was "no reason for this type of sellout." Bayard Rustin said to Martin Luther King, Jr., "There are few, if any, who claim the administration is putting its full weight behind these measures." The committee's strongest liberals likewise felt betrayed. They had believed the administration would accept strong versions on public accommodations and on equal employment opportunity if these received endorsement from the full House Judiciary Committee. As late as October 18, *The New York Times* reported Congressman Lindsay saying the Subcommittee No. 5 amendments would be retained: he believed seven of the fourteen Judiciary Committee Republicans would support them, enough to ensure passage.

Suddenly, the man on the hot seat was Congressman Libonati. He was being leaned on by Chicago's redoubtable Mayor Richard Daley to vote against adopting of the "strengthening" amendments. At the same time, Chicago's powerful black congressman, William Dawson, was predicting a dire fate for Libonati if he chose this moment to fold. Libonati carried a curious distinction in Congress: he was all but universally thought to be a ranking member of organized crime. As such, he may have felt he knew a set up when he saw one. Celler, appearing in a television interview, announced his continued support for the strong bill. Republican researcher Robert Kimball suggests that Celler acted out of a combined desire to placate his liberal supporters and the thought that no one would actually watch the show.

Libonati, however, was watching. And now, he saw things differently:

So then I'm sitting down . . . and I'm watching television and who do I see on the television but my chairman. And he's telling 'em up there in his district that he's for a strong bill, and that he doesn't have anything to do with any motion to cut the bill down. So when I hear that, I says to myself, "Lib, where are we at here, anyway?" And I think if you're going to get some Republican votes anyway, and if the chairman says he doesn't want to have anything to do with my motion, then certain representations that were made to me [are] out of the window.

When the full Judiciary Committee met on Tuesday, October 22, Roland Libonati, believing he was about to become the fall guy, startled everyone in the room by withdrawing his motion. Immediately, Arch Moore (D-West Virginia) moved for the adoption of the "strengthening" Subcommittee No.5 report. Here, literally, things were saved by the bell. House committee meetings must end by noon, when the full House convenes. Moore's motion came just as the clock struck 12:00 p.m. No vote occurred. Robert Kimball believes that, given the tenor of the room, had Moore's motion come five minutes sooner, the "strengthened" bill would have passed.

On the evening of Wednesday, October 23, a number of the principals met at the White House. The Republicans, notably Minority Leader Charles Halleck and William McCulloch, were a shade to the right of livid. As authors Charles and Barbara Whalen recount, McCulloch said, "Certainly I can't vote for the bill that came out of subcommittee." Halleck added, "Goddammit, Mr. President. Our principal trouble over there has been the conviction that Manny's subcommittee blew this thing up to beat hell, that the whole purpose of that was to put the Republicans in the position of emasculating the bill." To which McCulloch added, "And can I interrupt there, Charlie. And that I had been taken for a ride."

Earlier, pro-civil rights Congressman Clarence Brown (R-Ohio) had stopped by Congressman John Lindsay's office only to encounter Robert Kimball. To Kimball, Brown said with some passion: "We cannot cut it back; the Republicans must not cut it back; we will be the villains." This was fairly obvious, and made clear McCulloch and Halleck's insistence that the weakening amendments have equal Democratic and Republican support. President Kennedy was himself angry at Celler and the leading civil rights groups for overplaying their hand. Again, quoting the Whalens: "President Kennedy pointed out that the support of Clarence Mitchell was of much less importance than the support of William McCulloch: 'Can Clarence Mitchell and the [civil rights groups] deliver three Republicans on the Rules Committee and sixty Republicans on the House floor?'" This, McCulloch could. The meeting broke up with the general understanding that some compromise was needed and with the general hope that such compromise would prove possible.

Easier, of course, said than done. The full committee had thirty-five members; the ten southerners among them would vote for every amendment they believed would make the bill impassable. A number of the committee's most liberal members—Democrat and Republican both—would join them, out of either principle or politics. McCulloch and others, effectively in the center, remained committed to the original strategy and to the bill that strategy had produced. With ten southern votes certain for passage of the Subcommittee No. 5 amendments, defeating that draft would require securing the votes of eighteen of the remaining twenty-five committee members.

In 1919, in the wake of "the Troubles" that darkened Ireland following the First World War, poet William Butler Yeats wrote: "Things fall apart; the center cannot hold; Mere anarchy is loosed upon the world." The question now before the Judiciary Committee was: would the center hold? Robert Kennedy and Nicholas Katzenbach lobbied committee Democrats for "moderate" votes. Republican minority leader Charles Halleck and others pressured committee Republicans. The key exchange, though, was that between McCulloch and Lindsay, one of the Republican advocates of the stronger bill. Complicating matters at this point was that neither, for differing reasons, particularly trusted the Kennedy Administration. McCulloch was still smarting from an earlier denial by Robert Kennedy that a particular conversation between the two had ever occurred. One McCulloch staff member said, "This got him upset; he said to me, 'The Attorney General effectively called me a liar.'" From that point on, McCulloch had an office staff member listen in on any call to or from Kennedy. Lindsay assistant Robert Kimball thought, "The whole thing would fall through because we couldn't fully trust the Administration." The McCulloch bill, H.R. 3139, had made the U.S. Civil Rights Commission a permanent body; the administration bill called only for an extension. Kimball commented, "We had been screwed on the Civil Rights Commission. They broke their agreement." Kimball believed, "the Administration was perfectly willing to throw overboard anybody they didn't need."

Outwardly, Lindsay and McCulloch had little in common. Lindsay was two decades McCulloch's junior. Expensively educated and blessed with what Norman Mailer termed "stricken eagle good looks," he was eight inches taller than his mild, gracious, and immoderately determined fellow Republican. Fortunately, if the two men had their doubts about Kennedy, they had developed some regard for each other. Kimball commented, "My impression was that the two men really liked each other. McCulloch was fond of Lindsay and vice versa; each was impressed by the other's good qualities. As the battle had gone on, they became closer personally. Lindsay was impressed by how far McCulloch had come; McCulloch was impressed by how reasonable Lindsay was being. They were two people who wanted to agree with each other and reach an agreement."

On Friday, October 25, McCulloch made an initial approach to Lindsay. He asked Judiciary Committee minority staff counsel William Copenhaver to sound out Robert Kimball's views on John Lindsay's state of mind. Kimball replied that he doubted Lindsay would go along with anything. "Not that we don't want a bill," said Robert Kimball. "Lindsay simply doesn't trust the administration to keep any kind of commitment." Joseph Alsop, writing in *The Washington Post*, stated, "The vital civil rights bill is directly imperiled by the sorriest display to date of the endemic disease of American liberalism: which is the Liberals' fatal fondness for empty, competitive posturing."

Early on Saturday morning, Robert Kimball found McCulloch who, characteristically, was already in his office. McCulloch reported that he had spoken to Lindsay by phone; the Manhattan congressman set up a Sunday meeting in McCulloch's office. Joined by Copenhaver and Kimball, they moved rapidly through the pending bill, title by title. Disputed points were fairly easily resolved. The Whalens note: "And throughout, Kimball played devil's advocate, voicing arguments that were sure to be raised by the civil rights people like Joe Rauh and Clarence Mitchell." When the gap between the Ohioan and the New Yorker was finally closed, the next step was to join with the administration and finish forging a new project.

Nicholas Katzenbach, Burke Marshall, William Copenhaver, and Robert Kimball had already gathered at the Congressional Hotel when William McCulloch arrived. He was furious. He and other Republicans were being trashed in the press. From McCulloch's perspective, Minority Leader Charles Halleck and a handful of others were pulling the president's bacon from the fire, and the fat spitting from the pan was landing on them. With that, McCulloch departed and the others went to work. Most of the differences between the McCulloch-Lindsay "consensus" and the other two bills—the original administration bill and the House Judiciary Committee offering—were resolved in favor of the former.

One matter intruded, in a way that offered a victory for those seeking a stronger bill but without it being a defeat for McCulloch. The matter turned on the question of the Fair Employment Practices Commission (FEPC). Conceptually, the proposal went back to the package of civil rights measures introduced by President Harry Truman. Depending on the iteration, FEPC would be a federal body that, at minimum, would monitor employment discrimination and, at maximum, could sue racially discriminatory employers in federal court. During the early stages of planning the bill, civil rights advocates—including Attorney General Nicholas Katzenbach—regarded FEPC as prospectively the bill's most important component, but the one it would be most difficult to pass. Here, labor organizations joined civil rights groups to generate pressure for a strong FEPC. Andrew Biemiller, chief lobbyist for the AFL-CIO, stated, "There is no FEPC in the package. Probably the one piece of legislation most required in America today is FEPC." UAW president Walter Reuther was another strong advocate. And advocacy reached beyond the labor-civil rights alliance. House Speaker John McCormack said he would not support a bill that did not include the FEPC section. Debate continued, but without resolution.

Now, action came. As it happened, some years earlier three Republican members of the House Labor and Education Committee—Robert Griffin of Michigan, Charles Goodell of New York, and Albert Quie of Minnesota—had drafted wording for an FEPC to include in a bill that had failed passage. The wording was not particularly strong. Now, Congressman Frank Thompson [D-New Jersey] made an out-of-the-blue proposal that this language—which, as it had been written by Republicans, would be hard for them to disavow—be added to the civil rights bill. Nicholas Katzenbach welcomed the suggestion, later commenting that Thompson "was one of the people who, while he did not do very much except at particular times, was a very good observer and advisor on this process." Katzenbach approached McCulloch, who found himself somewhat painted into the corner by the proposal. But he did not oppose adding the FEPC wording.

President Kennedy now took a lead role. He and his brother, the attorney general, met with the non-southern members of the judiciary committee and "made earnest and emotional pleas for their vote against the subcommittee's bill and for the compromise bill." They met with mixed success. Soon thereafter, Kennedy asked Katzenbach to telephone McCulloch and go over the proposed legislation, title by title, to ensure that they were in full agreement. Among other things, McCulloch told Katzenbach that while Minority Leader Halleck supported all other portions of the bill, he was not committed to FEPC. Remarkably, Katzenbach assured the president that FEPC had Halleck's blessing.

For the moment, that was a problem to be addressed later. The immediate problem, from McCulloch's perspective, was that unless Congressman Moore's motion to adopt the Subcommittee #5 amendments was defeated, no civil rights bill would pass that session of Congress. Sometime during the night of Monday/Tuesday (October 28–29), Robert Kimball received a telephone call from William Higgs, a staff member with the Student Nonviolent Coordinating Committee, which, like everyone else, was counting votes. Higgs told Kimball, "It could go either way, by one or two votes."

The full House Judiciary Committee met Tuesday, October 29. Congressman Moore's motion was the prime order of business. With ten Democrats and nine Republicans (including Lindsay) voting against the motion, the "center held" by a vote of 19 to 15. Next, the compromise bill—that is, the draft negotiated between McCulloch and Lindsay, with the FEPC clause added—was offered as a substitute to the existing bill. That amendment carried, 20 to 14. Finally, the Judiciary Committee voted on the bill as amended, passing it by 23 to 11. That the non-southern members of the Judiciary Committee favored passage by 23 to 1 suggests the level of consensus achieved.

Congressman Libonati, for reasons unknown, defied Chicago Mayor Daley and voted for Moore's motion. Word soon reached Libonati that Mayor Daley had decided that the Congressman's services were no longer required. Later, Libonati bemoaned the injustice of it all to *New York Times* reporter Adam Clymer, telling that journalist, "After 30 years of fine service, I make one little mistake and now I'm going to lose my job."

CHAPTER 14

The Battle Is Won

There are days that all Americans of a particular age remember. December 7, 1941. September 11, 2001. And November 22, 1963, when President John Fitzgerald Kennedy was slain by an assassin as he rode in a motorcade in Dallas, Texas. Much of the nation spent the next three days slumped in front of a television that never once brought news that the event, indeed, had not actually happened. Congressman McCulloch had not been close to President Kennedy; in fact, he had not long before been sharply critical of what he saw as Kennedy's slow action on civil rights. McCulloch, however, an aide recalled, was deeply saddened by Kennedy's death: "He just thought it was a terrible thing to happen to our country and government."

In his first joint address to Congress, newly inaugurated President Lyndon Johnson stated, "No memorial oration or eulogy could more eloquently honor President Kennedy's memory than the earliest passage of the civil rights bill for which he fought so long. We have talked long enough in this country about equal rights. We have talked for one hundred years or more. It is time now to write the next chapter, and to write it in the book of laws." Johnson's principal biographer, Robert Caro, asserts that the Kennedy Administration was insufficiently aware that the South had already declared passive war on the civil rights bill. Such war took the form of delay—delay in just about every committee that had a southerner as its chair, which is to say more than half the committees of Congress. The intention was to create a legislative logjam, so that increasingly civil rights supporters would have to choose between getting action on bills that mattered to their districts (and their reelections) and the civil rights bill itself. No one, however—perhaps no one ever—knew the Congress of the United States as well as Lyndon Johnson.

By the time President Johnson spoke, the civil rights bill was mired in the House Rules Committee which, chaired by Howard Smith (D-Virginia), was where much liberal legislation was allowed to abandon all hope. The rules committee could be forced to disgorge a bill onto the

House floor by a Discharge Petition. If 218 members of the 435-member House signed such a statement, the bill in question moved forward. Discharge petitions were historically unlikely to succeed, in part because any congressman who signed such a petition had the option of subsequently removing his name, should he or she have thought better of it, or received a better offer or a plausible political threat.

Nonetheless, seeing few alternatives, civil rights advocates initiated the discharge process. In this, they acted without the initial support of either Congressman William McCulloch or Republican Minority Leader Charles Halleck. Both men thought the step was coercive and therefore at odds with the spirit of the House. McCulloch termed the effort "very damaging to the bipartisan nature of the civil rights legislation." Still, the petition slowly gathered signatures. By December 1, 172 members had signed their names. At this point, it was leaked to the press that relatively few of those signatures had come from Republicans. With that news public, Republicans signatures began to accumulate.

Congressman Clarence J. Brown (R-Ohio), whose Seventh District lay immediately east of McCulloch's, was himself a strong civil rights supporter. He took pride in the fact that numerous routes of the Underground Railroad passed through his district. He and McCulloch were the two Ohio congressmen called out for praise by NAACP lobbyist Clarence Mitchell. Of greater immediate consequence, Brown was a member of the Rules Committee.

On December 4, 1963, Congressman Brown confronted Chairman Smith with certain harsh realities. The discharge petition was nearing the number that would take the matter out of Smith's hands. Brown did not have to point out the embarrassment this would cause the eighty-one-year-old Smith, now in his thirty-third year in Congress. The only alternative would be for Smith to allow the Rules Committee to vote on whether to send the civil rights bill to the House floor. By one account, Smith said, "I know something about the facts of life around here, and I know that many members want this bill considered. They could take it away from me, and they can do it any minute they want to." After considering Brown's comments for a fortnight, he decided he could read the handwriting on the wall. Congressman Smith announced that the House Rules Committee would take up the matter of the civil rights bill once Congress returned from the holidays, on January 9, 1964, and that he would limit discussion to nine days.

On January 9, 1964—promptly, as promised—Congressman Howard Smith gaveled into session the House Rules Committee, to consider H.R. 7152, the civil rights bill. Lindsay aide Robert Kimball and Judiciary Committee minority staff counsel Bill Copenhaver sat through the nine days of hearings that ensued. Kimball wrote down every question Smith posed to witnesses, noting the topics to which the chairman returned and what seemed to be the focus of his attack—"scouting him," so to speak—to allow for better preparation. In Kimball's words, "I spent hours watching Smith just to see how he operated; he knew I was following him and he knew who I was. He never attacked me personally."

Kimball recalled of Smith, "He was tremendously gifted, both generally and at playing the system. He pretended to be a country boy but he was very sharp, 81 years old. He was the leader, but a little reluctant. He felt the younger men should be carrying on this fight. He was a bit wistful: 'You guys are going to have to run over us.' He knew that something would pass the House." Kimball had seen Smith take on House Speaker Sam Rayburn during the hearings on the 1961 foreign aid bill, and not even Rayburn—one of the strongest Speakers in House history—was Smith's match. Kimball commented, "He was a natural leader because he seemed wise about the process."

The hearings were not without amusement. Opening day, Chairman Smith complained to witness Emanuel Celler that the proposed bill "stretched the commerce clause beyond all intention of the Constitution." Celler replied that the Commerce Clause had been the basis of many federal regulations, including, for example, the Mann Act. (The Mann Act makes it a crime to transport a woman over a state line for "immoral purposes.") Smith blandly replied that he was "not familiar" with that particular statute. Did Celler have any first-hand knowledge of it he cared to impart? More seriously, Smith noted that under the proposed law, if a white barber worked in a hotel, he would be required to cut the hair of a black person, but if that same white barber operated an independent establishment, he would not be. One way or the other, Smith observed, this appeared discriminatory.

William McCulloch testified on the hearing's second day. Asked why he had been given time before the committee, the Ohio congressman replied it was "because of my receding red hair." McCulloch began with a formal presentation on the bill. He described the bill as "comprehensive in scope but moderate in application." He said that a sincere effort had been made to eliminate any provision that would unfairly invade the prerogatives of any person or thing. Further, each of the bill's provisions was wrapped in judicial safeguards to keep its application appropriately honed. He then added:

There is a considerable agitation for civil rights legislation from certain quarters on the grounds that unless legislation is enacted there will be rioting in the streets, heightened racial unrest, and the further shedding of blood. This kind of activity is, in my mind, improper behavior and could do much to retard the enactment of effective civil rights legislation.

No people can gain liberty and equality through storm troop or anarchistic methods. Legislation under threat is basically not legislation at all. In the long run, behavior of this type will lead to a total undermining of society where equality and civil rights will mean nothing.

McCulloch said he believed "in the effective separation of powers and in a workable federal system." Within that system, the national government was charged with the responsibility to see that all citizens were treated equally. He did not believe in federal usurpation of local powers. However, "when [state] authorities fail to shoulder their obligations, and only stress their rights, it is the duty of the Congress to correct that wrong." McCulloch continued, "No one would suggest that the Negro receives equality of treatment and equality of opportunity in many fields today." He therefore urged that the Rules Committee move the legislation forward to the floor of the House for action.

McCulloch then returned to the barbershop issue raised by Chairman Smith. He referenced a recent case in his home state in which a black man, refused service by an independent white barber, brought suit under a nearly century-old state anti-discrimination law. This prompted from Smith the rejoinder: "They do strange things in Ohio." *The New York Times* article continued:

Mr. McCulloch waited for dramatic effect, smiled at the Chairman and quoted from [James Russell] Lowell's "The Present Crisis":

"New occasions teach new duties,
time makes ancient good uncouth;
They must upward still and onward,
who would keep abreast of truth."

The Times added, "Under the somewhat aggressive questioning of Mr. Smith, the Ohioan never lost his aplomb. His replies were soft spoken but not deferential." Regarding public accommodations generally, Congressman McCulloch observed that "for hundreds of years the Anglo-Saxon common law had required an innkeeper to serve every customer who could pay and whose person and behavior were seemly."

Of greater weight, McCulloch said, his "head was still bloody from 1957" when he had pushed hard in the House for a tough civil rights bill only to see it bargained away in the Senate. He repeated his warning: if the House passed a version later watered down by the Senate, he would withdraw his support.

Chairman Smith held the hearings to the allotted nine days. Thirty-three witnesses appeared. All appropriate procedures were followed. Pretty much, decorum ruled. On January 30, 1964, the Rules Committee voted H.R. 7152 out to the House floor by an 11 to 4 margin, with only southern Democrats in opposition. Sitting through all nine days of open committee hearings were Robert Kimball and William Copenhaver, the former now with the Republican Legislative Research Association, the latter an attorney for the Republican minority on the judiciary committee. Both had helped write the version of the civil rights bill now under review. Kimball said, "The key guys to watch were Ed Willis [D-Louisiana] and the chairman, Smith." Kimball and Copenhaver prepared answers for McCulloch and Lindsay to use in response to questions that might be raised during floor debate. Both discovered that the "Judge" focused on Titles I and II and very little else. The attack would come at these points. Kimball concluded: "If they were unable to make any headway against I and II, the rest of the battle would be a formality."

Full debate began in the House on January 31. "Judge" Smith, as events were to prove, had other cards to play—and other sleeves from which to snatch them. As one of the floor managers for the bill, William McCulloch had responsibility for assigning one-quarter of the time allotted for the bill. Floor debate continued until February 10, during which time McCulloch addressed the full House well over one hundred times. That debate opened with a series of almost ritualistic denials on the part of southerners that anything was amiss in Dixie—save, perhaps, the federal government's wrongheaded determination to intrude. It was opening day, so to speak, and Congressman Albert Watson (D-South Carolina) threw that pitch out first:

Let me say that notwithstanding the accusations which have been made in other places that we of the Southland have put these people of the Negro race under subjugation, that we have treated them wrongly, that we are hatemongers. May I just remind you, Mr. Chairman, that over the past 100 years we have been the true friends of the Negro race.

The following day, Congressman McCulloch addressed the House intermittently but at aggregate length. He began by reading into the record "additional views" on civil rights prepared by himself and half a dozen other congressmen, including John Lindsay (R-New York). The statement ran to 20,000 words and detailed racial discrimination in voting and in hiring; the limited progress in school desegregation, and kindred matters, and how the pending legislation would address each. His oral testimony covered the waterfront, with considerable give and take. Congressman Howard Smith asked if McCulloch knew anything about the provenance of H.R. 980, added to the proposal so that Native Americans would fall under the same protections of the law. McCulloch replied, "I admit the parentage of this well-written and effective amendment, and will defend it whenever there is time available."

Perhaps the first substantive move came several days later; not surprisingly, it came from Congressman Howard Smith. Smith moved that three words—"or in part"—be struck from the definition of which elections would be subject to the bill should it become law. The longer phrase from which these words were expunged was "held solely or in part" to elect federal officials. In short, the amendment would permit state and local elections to be held any day of the year; as such, they would not be subject to federal voting rights protections. McCulloch immediately challenged the statement, asserting that the proposed amendment "aims at the very heart of the effectiveness "of the voting rights section of the bill. Smith's amendment was defeated.

McCulloch was open to some amendments. Along with Emanuel Celler, he accepted an amendment offered by fellow House Judiciary Committee member Richard Poff (D-Virginia) that would provide reasonable legal fees to recompense persons sued by the federal government, provided the court found the individual guilty of no wrongdoing. McCulloch estimated the annual cost of this at $15 million, a figure that he—"Scot though I am"—thought reasonable to protect innocent persons from being punished by having to pay legal expenses. Surprisingly, perhaps, the House rejected the motion by a 156 to 131 vote.

Some watering down occurred. Celler agreed to accept a change in the tenure of the U.S. Civil Rights Commission: it would not become a permanent body; instead, it would receive a four-year extension. This was the occasion of some unspoken antagonism. Lindsay aide Robert Kimball said that in accepting this amendment, Celler had simply gone back on his word. McCulloch reportedly shared that view, but went along to avoid breaking ranks.

McCulloch was less tolerant of an amendment offered by Congressman George Meader (R-Michigan) that would largely weaken the public accommodations section of the bill. Responding, McCulloch noted that Congressman Meader hailed from Ann Arbor, "home of a great university and great football team." Suppose that team scheduled a game in Florida; many fans might make the trip down to see it. Suppose, he added, "a Negro family was traveling with them and could not get service in Ft. Lauderdale, Florida, what could be done? There [are] just no teeth in this amendment, and it should be defeated." And it was defeated, by a vote of 153 to 68.

These were mild matters. Several days later, the legislative fat was clearly in the fire. The flames were fanned by Congressman Oren Harris (D-Arkansas). Harris noted that the bill, as it stood, would cut off federal support to anybody who used federal funds in a discriminatory manner. He proposed substituting for this the considerably milder language used in the original version of the Kennedy bill introduced the previous year. Kennedy had been ambivalent on the issue: funding cutoffs would have the effect of punishing individuals served by the program in question, even though they had themselves done nothing discriminatory. The original language had been that no law authorizing federal assistance "shall be interpreted as requiring that such assistance shall be furnished in circumstances under which individuals participating in or benefitting from the program are discriminated against." The original Kennedy language also lacked judicial review of decisions. The Harris amendment was quickly seconded by Hale Boggs (D-Louisiana), a high-ranking congressman known to be close to President Lyndon Johnson. *The New York*

Times reported, "The House was immediately in an uproar. Mr. Boggs' speech made the Republicans suspicious that a deal was afoot, possibly with White House backing. There was great hurrying and scurrying. Mr. Celler left the chamber. So did the Republican floor manager, Mr. Mc-Culloch." Civil rights advocates leapt to the conclusion that a side agreement was being made to weaken the bill.

Mabel McCulloch, as she commonly did, was attending the session, seated in the House gallery with Roy Wilkins, executive director of the NAACP. Congressman McCulloch returned to the floor. *The New York Times* reported that McCulloch returned with "his face white." Mrs. Mc-Culloch saw things chromatically differently. "Look!" she whispered to Wilkins, "Bill's face is red. He's mad!" McCulloch took the microphone and in what *The Times* termed "a voice of barely controlled anger" said that if this amendment were adopted, "I regret to say my individual support of the legislation will come to an end." The shock of those words brought the House to silence. And, perhaps, to its senses. The amendment was crushed—206 to 80—with every single Republican supporting McCulloch. Representative Clifford Case (R-New Jersey) said that McCulloch had "singlehandedly, I believe it is fair to say, stopped the weakening Harris amendment in the House. [His] stating that if that amendment were to pass—and it looked at that time as if the leadership on the floor was about to accept it—he would find it impossible to further support the bill."

Congressman Smith had one further card to play. On February 8, he rose to offer a two-word amendment. He noted that on pages 68, 69, 70, and 71, the bill banned discrimination due to race, color, or religion. At each of these points, Smith urged that the words "or sex" be added. Smith argued that his amendment "will help an important minority." He noted that as the general population contained more women than men, some women of necessity supported themselves. That being the case, they had a reasonable expectation that the federal government ensure they receive equal pay for equal work. Interpretations of Smith's actions varied. Many civil rights supporters believed that it was a monkey wrench tossed into the works at the last moment. Nicholas Katzenbach, for one, believed the amendment could lead to the defeat of the entire bill. Both McCulloch and Celler rose to speak against it. Others, including some close to Smith, said the action was at least partially sincere, as Smith—whatever his views on racial matters—had been a general advocate of women's rights. In either case, the legislative dam was opened. Five Democratic congresswomen—all civil rights supporters—spoke in turn in favor of Smith's amendment. And to the anxiety of many civil rights supporters, the amendment was adopted by a 168 to 133 vote.

The House vote came on February 10, 1964. The outcome was not then in doubt. The broadest civil rights bill in ninety years was approved by a 290 to 130 vote. Richard Bolling (D-Missouri), a younger Democrat who had played an effective behind-the-scenes role, described that vote as "deceptive."

The bill did not have an easy passage. It required vast labors on the part of the pro-civil rights members of the House, members of the White House staff, the Attorney General and his principal assistant, the numerous legislative agents of the labor movement, various civil rights organizations and religious groups to keep the bill from being gutted in the amendment stage.

Looking back nearly half a century later, Adam Clymer of *The New York Times* noted a matter of first importance: "The bill that passed the House, except for the clause on women, was McCulloch's bill." Political scientist Geoffrey Kabaservice quoted *Washington Post* columnist Meg Greenfield on the various pressures McCulloch had faced. From liberals, who wanted a bill stronger than the full Congress would stomach. From some Republicans, who hoped to create a bill so objectionable that it would fail and rob Lyndon Johnson of an election-year triumph. Greenfield, Kabaservice wrote, "was struck by how much more McCulloch had paid for his efforts than had all those congressmen from districts where, unlike his, it was to their political advantage to support the bill and who, having acquiesced in no action for all that time, were now sighing, 'At last!' and pretending it was their handiwork."

And, with that accomplished, William McCulloch went home to have a celebratory drink with his wife, Mabel.

Senate Filibuster

With House passage in hand, the civil rights bill moved to the Senate and its inevitable filibuster. As noted, the Senate's tradition of unlimited debate could be set aside only if two-thirds of the members of the Senate voted to end debate, a step known as invoking cloture. Once invoked, each senator has a single hour for additional comments. Proponents of one measure or another had sought to invoke cloture twenty-seven times since 1917; on five occasions, they had been successful. Speaking in Baltimore on January 17, 1964, Minnesota Senator Hubert Humphrey—floor manager for the civil rights bill—said that cloture would come only as passage of the bill had been achieved in the House—that is, through bipartisan support. He estimated that twenty-five Republican votes would be required to those expected from Democrats to cut off debate.

On February 26, the Senate passed the administration's tax package. With that task done, civil rights moved to center stage. Pro-civil rights strategy turned on an acknowledged circumstance: the *sine qua non* for Republican support in the Senate was Republican minority leader Everett Dirksen. Nicholas Katzenbach said, "As Congressman McCulloch had been the key in the House, so Senator Dirksen was in the Senate. Burke Marshall and I went to work with Dirksen and his legislative assistant."

Actually—and unnoticed at the time—the pro-civil rights forces had several years earlier won an important victory. Though opposition to cloture was strongly associated with southern senators resisting civil rights legislation, a number of non-southern senators also held that unlimited debate meant unlimited debate; under no circumstances would they vote to invoke cloture. In 1962, a small group of senators launched a filibuster against a bill to turn authority for operating communications satellites (COMSAT) over to private interests. Opposition was led by Wayne Morse (D-Oregon), whose twenty-two-hour, twenty-six-minute speech to the Senate against the bill tried the patience of that body. On August 14, 1962, the Senate invoked cloture—with the support of some northern and western senators who had previously opposed cloture on general principle. When the civil rights bill arrived, they found themselves deprived of the argument that they would never vote for cloture.

Underscoring the pledge made to McCulloch, Humphrey on March 3 told reporters that the administration was committed to the House version of the bill. A few days later, Humphrey added, "If it takes until September to pass the House bill, it's perfectly all right with us. We'll be there."

On March 16, Richard Russell, Democrat of Georgia and the acknowledged leader of southern opposition, proposed with a straight face a $1.5 billion plan to redistribute the nation's black population even across the fifty states. The following day, the Senate voted 67 to 17 to move the bill forward for consideration on the floor. With that, the filibuster began. Nicholas Katzenbach, discussing strategy, stated:

Once a filibuster commences, perhaps the hardest part of managing the forces against it is to be sure that whenever there is a call for a quorum, fifty-one senators can be rounded up. That means they must be somewhere on the premises, whatever the day of the week and the hour of the day—not easy when a filibuster may go on for a long time.

Civil Rights and the Senate filibuster were the nation's lead story. At the *New York Herald Tribune*, publisher "Jock" Whitney declared that his paper would run a page one story on civil rights every day. Other media gave similar attention. On March 18, 1964, CBS Reports broadcast "Filibuster: Birth Struggle of a Law," hosted by Eric Sevareid. Interviewees included William McCulloch, perhaps not the most telegenic of men. The show broadly summarized high points of the previous year, including the Judiciary Committee fight over the Subcommittee #5 amendments. McCulloch's lone contribution was to emphasize the importance of having the full Judiciary Committee vote out a bill that could gain passage. The major roles went to Robert Kennedy, Hubert Humphrey, Strom Thurmond, and Howard Smith. Perhaps the oddest comment came from one southern senator, who in an exchange with Senator Humphrey asserted that requiring a masseuse to provide service to a person of another race constituted "involuntary servitude." The real legislative work, of course, went on outside the camera's eye.

McCulloch and other strong civil rights congressmen, such as John Lindsay and Charles Mathias, met routinely in McCulloch's office, Room 1020 of the Longworth House Office Building, working to support Senate passage. Mabel McCulloch, the congressman's wife, was a frequent visitor. She was, as ever, her husband's confidante and sounding board, with quick ideas about people and events. Often, the McCullochs would lunch in the congressional dining hall—on some occasions, with office manager Vera Page as a guest, and on all occasions, with the dining room's bean soup the congressman's favored item.

By this time, another youngster had joined McCulloch's office staff. He was Joseph Metz, a graduate student in political science at the Catholic University of America in Washington. Seeking some practical experience, Metz applied for a job at McCulloch's congressional office in the Longworth Building. He chatted with the congressman; a week later he was hired. Vera Page, McCulloch's long-term office manager, told Metz that he had been hired because he had worn a blue suit and "had a nice demeanor." One of Metz's tasks was to answer the office phone. On one occasion, he was met by the voice of Hubert Humphrey who, saying simply, "Keep up the good work," rang off. On another occasion, President Johnson called for McCulloch, who, as it happened, was in the bathroom. Metz told the president the congressman was temporarily unavailable. Johnson replied equably, "Go to the men's room door and tell Bill to get off the pot and come talk to his President." Met did so.

Metz offers a second recollection from that time.

I went to a Judiciary Committee meeting with him. We were in the elevator of the old Cannon building, which had a black elevator operator. A group of people got on; citizens; all black, like a family. When we got on the elevator they saw him and they all sort of bowed with big smiles on their faces—"Oh, thank you, Mr. McCulloch." It was a beautiful picture and he was pleased. He was not demonstrative. Not much emotion about anything. But you could tell he was pleased.

Having been a co-floor manager of the bill in the House, McCulloch had expert standing on the bill. Almost daily—if not multiple times a day—senators or their aides would seek him out for clarifications of the bill's contents and arguments to use on its behalf. Characteristically, McCulloch was the receiver of these calls, not the initiator. McCulloch's role did not sit well with all senators. As *The Longest Debate* reports, "To some, annoyed with McCulloch's insistence that there be no substantive changes in the bill without his approval, McCulloch became known as the czar of the Senate. 'We must go to him on bended knee with an amendment and say to him, "Will you accept this?" charged Joe Clark (D-Pennsylvania). 'If he says no, we dare not make the change.'"

Opposition came from outside Congress as well. In early April, an organization called the Coordinating Committee for Fundamental American Freedoms ran inserts in several hundred newspapers nationwide, attacking the pending bill as a massive power-grab on the part of the federal government. As journalist Andrew Glass pointed out, the civil rights bill—in dictating rules for public accommodation and private employment—ran counter to the deeply held sentiment best expressed as "a man's home is his castle." The argument that the bill was a major intrusion into the private lives of the citizenry found resonance. Some midwestern and Rocky Mountain senators reported that their mail was running 10 to 1 against approval.

William McCulloch was, for once, concerned. On April 20, 1964, he attacked the Coordinating Committee's position on the House floor. His 2,000-word statement, reprinted in part in *The Washington Post* on April 26, stressed what the bill would *not* do. It would not force racial balancing in schools. It would not tell teachers what to teach. It would not tell anyone to whom they could or could not sell their house. It would not tell banks how to lend. It would not tell farmers how to run their farms. However, it would tell the owners of hotels, restaurants, gasoline stations, and places of entertainment that they must "serve all customers who are well behaved and able to pay."

Unlike the 1957 and 1960 civil rights bills, this one was carried forth on the wave of public opinion, both organized and spontaneous. The organized side included thousands of clergymen of all denominations lobbying on Capitol Hill. Hundreds of representatives of organized labor, which got relatively little credit for its efforts, made their support clear to senators in states rich in the votes of union members. Withal, the tide began to turn again. Reversing earlier results, Michigan senator Philip Hart reported receiving 204 letters in support of the bill and only 90 opposed in a single April week's mail.

Dirksen—ostentatiously wooed by Hubert Humphrey—remained the key. At one point, James Farmer, head of the Congress of Racial Equality (CORE), threatened to send pickets to Dirksen's Senate office. Dirksen, with typical grandiloquence, took the Senate floor to reply: "When the day comes that picketing, distress, duress and coercion can push me from the rock of conviction, that is the day, Mr. President, that I shall gather up my toga and walk out of here and say that my usefulness in the Senate has come to an end."

On May 11, the filibuster reached its fifty-fifth day, equaling the longest in history. Four days later, pro-civil rights forces ran their totals and determined they had fifty-five committed votes for cloture, a dozen shy of the number needed. That number increased thereafter, not daily, but regularly. The tide turned further. The Whalens report that in May, New York Senator Kenneth Keating received 31,762 letters in favor of the bill, only 1,292 opposed.

On May 26, Senators Dirksen and Humphrey and Attorney General Kennedy held a news conference announcing they had reached a settlement. As *New York Times* reporter Adam Clymer noted, "Dirksen demanded and got a good many cosmetic changes." Their purpose—besides aggrandizing Dirksen—was to suggest to his more conservative brethren that he had given the bill a thorough shaking down and found it suitable. Perhaps more accurately, one observer suggested that Dirksen sold conservative Republicans on a strong bill by insisting that it was a weak one. Soon thereafter, the Senate adjourned while the Republican National Convention was held in San Francisco, where it nominated Barry Goldwater for president.

By June 8, there were sixty-four votes counted for cloture and another twelve—including California's bed-ridden Clair Engle—considered possible. The pro-civil rights forces gained over half of that "doubtful dozen." On June 10, the Senate voted 71 to 29—four votes more than required—to cut off debate. In a scene of some drama, Engle, dying of brain cancer, was carried into the Senate chamber to cast his vote. Democrats favored the measure 44 to 27; Republicans, by 23 to 6. On June 19, the bill received its formal passage, 73 to 21.

The House of Representatives approved the Senate version by a vote of 289 to 126 on July 2, 1964. President Lyndon Johnson signed the bill into law later that same day in the East Room of the White House. *The New York Times* reported, "The air of grand occasion hung over the chamber from the moment that Chaplain Bernard Braskamp began his prayer with the quotation from Leviticus: 'Proclaim liberty throughout the land upon all inhabitants thereof.'" In his speech to the nation upon signing, President Johnson, among other things, said of the act:

> It does not restrict the freedom of any American, so long as he respects the rights of others.
>
> It does not give special treatment to any citizen.
>
> It does say the only limit to a man's hope for happiness, and for the future of his children, shall be his own ability.
>
> It does say that those who are equal before God shall now also be equal in the polling booths, in the classrooms, in the factories, and in hotels, restaurants, movie theaters, and other places that provide service to the public.
>
> I am taking steps to implement the law under my constitutional obligation to "take care that the laws are faithfully executed."

President Johnson called on all Americans to show each other the respect they would themselves expect. Among the six Senate Republicans voting against passage was Republican nominee Goldwater. In his book *Rule and Ruin*, on the eclipse of moderate Republicanism, Geoffrey Kabaservice wrote:

Goldwater and his legal advisors, William Rehnquist and Robert Bork, were narrowly correct in pointing out that the Civil Rights Act would entail an expansion of federal power to regulate private enterprise that was not contemplated by the Founding Fathers. But only the sophistry of doctrinaire conservative ideology could produce the conclusion that the cause of freedom was best served by maintenance of the South's apartheid system.

Everett Dirksen, for one, was appalled by Goldwater's vote. Before it was cast, the Republican minority leader took his party's nominee aside to say: "You just can't do that. You can't do that to yourself. You can't do that to the party." But Goldwater could, and did, and in so doing robbed the most important single piece of domestic legislation in the twentieth century of much of its bipartisan aura. Kabaservice comments further:

A number of political scientists and historians have concluded that by the early 1960s, America's two major parties had "essentially switched positions on civil rights issues," with the Democrats embracing racial liberalism and the Republican Party espousing the cause of racial conservatism. This interpretation greatly exaggerates the spread of the new conservatism in the GOP at the time and ignores the genuine Republican civil rights idealism that influenced Midwestern stalwarts like McCulloch, Dirksen and [Clarence] Brown. These scholars are thus unable to understand why Republicans overwhelmingly supported the Civil Rights Act of 1964, or even to explain how the bill passed at all.

Perhaps the best explanation was put forward by Republican Minority Leader Charles Halleck, who complained that the nation's press corps "couldn't understand that once in a while a guy does something because it's right. I had a few experiences. I had a black driver. We used to go down to Warm Springs, Virginia, to see friends. We'd stop at a little bit of a restaurant. I'd go in and ask if he could go in with the Hallecks. They said no but they would be glad to serve him in the car. The goddamned thing just didn't look right to me."

Following passage, McCulloch restated his core position. Life was not changed by laws alone, but by how persons chose to live within the law: "How do you tear hatred and suspicion out of the heart of a man? No statutory law can completely end discrimination. Intelligent work and vigilance by members of all races will be required for many years before discrimination completely disappears."

In his speech accompanying the signing, President Johnson said he would take steps to see that the law was faithfully executed. In truth, federal officials had no very clear idea of what opposition the passage of the law might prompt in the South. The clear and present power of the federal government in the person of Nicholas Katzenbach backed by the U.S. Marshals Service was sufficient to move Alabama Governor George Wallace from his position blocking entry to the University of

Alabama. But no number of federal marshals was sufficient to override the passive resistance if thousands of southern restaurants, gas stations, hotels, movie theatres, and other places of public accommodation simply declined to abide by the act. There was, indeed, in Washington considerable apprehension on this point.

So far as public accommodations were concerned, that apprehension was soon quieted. In *Calculating Visions*, Mark Stern writes, "There was widespread, immediate compliance with the law across much of the South." Step away from the enclosed world of Washington and read an account from the nation's heartland, published the day after passage in William McCulloch's hometown newspaper, *The Piqua Daily Call.* That paper's lead story ran under the headline "Negroes Find New Law Valid Most Places But Some in South Refuse to Accept It". More specifically, the *Call* reported:

> In Albany, Georgia, the scene of racial violence in recent years, seven restaurants that catered to whites only admitted Negroes for the first time Thursday night. Negroes also found no resistance in entering another troubled southern city, Savannah, Georgia.
>
> In Jacksonville, a white waitress in the serving line of Morrison's cafeteria greeted Negroes Robert Ingram and Prince McIntosh with the dignity that [President] Johnson asked to be shown to all races.

Acquiescence was not universal. In Kansas City, a barbershop refused to cut the hair of a thirteen-year-old black teenager. The *Call* reported, "Negroes moved into the barbershop and filled the chair. Today, according to hotel spokespersons, the barbershop will be open to all."

Some obeyed the law reluctantly. The Georgia Restaurant Association issued a statement, "We have no alternative" but to go along with the law.

And some decided to go down fighting. "In Charlottesville, Virginia, Buddy Glover closed his restaurant for the first time in twenty-seven years: 'I quit. It's going to be a financial loss, but dollars and cents can't take the place of principles.'"

In general, the public accommodations section of the Civil Rights Act was accepted with a calmness that many found both pleasing and surprising. Less pleasant was the continued opposition to black voting and to school integration. These questions remained, for the Congress, and for William McCulloch.

By the time the filibuster was broken and the Civil Rights Act signed, McCulloch's role in the matter was slipping from public awareness. Therefore, it may have particularly pleased him to receive the plaudits of another group whose contribution has historically been somewhat overlooked—that group being organized labor; specifically, the AFL-CIO.

On July 7, 1964, James B. Carey, the labor organization's secretary-

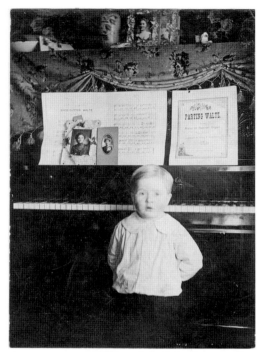

A very young William McCulloch, standing
before a piano he never learned to play.

McCulloch as an adoleccent. His outfit
shows his family's relative affluence and
his face reflects his serious purpose.

William McCulloch poses with the three dozen other members of his high school graduating class in Holmesville, Ohio. McCulloch is readily identified; he is the person just left of the tallest individual in the back row.

While a law student at Ohio State University, William McCulloch was a member of Gamma Eta Gamma, the fraternity founded to house future lawyers of America. McCulloch stands at the left end of the second row from the back.

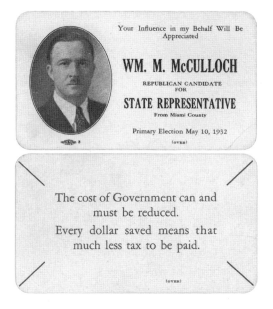

Your Influence in my Behalf Will Be
Appreciated

WM. M. McCULLOCH

REPUBLICAN CANDIDATE
FOR

STATE REPRESENTATIVE

From Miami County

Primary Election May 10, 1932

(OVER)

The cost of Government can and
must be reduced.

Every dollar saved means that
much less tax to be paid.

(OVER)

In his first campaign—the 1932 Republican primary for state representative
from Miami County—McCulloch pushed his views on economy in government.
In four decades in politics he never changed his view.

McCulloch was 37 when first elected Speaker of the Ohio House of Representatives. He served a then unprecedented three terms. One journalist wrote: "As
speaker of the House, he is known for his fairness and for his fiery temper which
always is noticeable to his colleagues because of the red hair which accentuates
his taut, white face."

William McCulloch as a young Congressman. In his 1948 campaign, he told prospective constituents not to expect him to bring any goodies home from Washington. In 1950, he announced his intention to support higher taxes to pay for the Korean War. Despite such honesty, he never lost an election.

Mabel McCulloch collected antiques. Her husband collected elephants, though generally they were of the figurine variety and stored in a corner cabinet.

Two architects of the Civil Rights Bill, Rep. Emanuel Celler (D. N.Y.) and Rep. William M. McCulloch (R. O.) congratulate each other after the bill's passage. (UPI Facsimile)

Rights Bill Author

Rep. McCulloch Given Ovation

By ROBERT CRATER
Citizen-Journal Staff Writer

WASHINGTON — Veteran Republican U.S. Rep. William M. McCulloch of Piqua, O., headed back home Friday after receiving a rare honor from the House of Representatives—a standing ovation.

The spontaneous acclaim from GOP and Democratic members alike came just before the House, by a vote of 289 to 126, passed the historic Civil Rights Bill and sent it to the White House for President Johnson's signature into law.

IT WAS McCulloch who, as ranking GOP member of the House Judiciary Committee, played the leading role in writing a bill acceptable to a majority of both houses of Congress.

The House tribute, seldom accorded with such warmth, came after McCulloch reminded it was time for members to vote their conscience on civil rights.

ONLY ONE OF Ohio's 24 representatives, Rep. John Ashbrook (R. Johnstown), voted against passage. He is co-founder of the original Draft Goldwater Committee, and he voted with the Arizona senator against the bill.

Several other Ohio Republicans, notably Reps. Samuel L. Devine of Columbus and Donald Clancy of Cincinnati, felt considerable pressure from some constituents who wanted them to vote against the bill. The others were subpected to antagonism in varying degrees.

Arms across the divide. Judiciary Committee Chairman Emanuel Celler and William McCulloch, the committee's ranking Republican, embrace following passage of the 1964 Civil Rights Act. The headline announces the rare standing ovation McCulloch received on that occasion.

At the formal signing of the 1964 Civil Rights Act, William McCulloch sits near the left end of the front row, strategically placed between Lady Bird Johnson and Robert Kennedy, not the warmest of mutual admirers. To Robert Kennedy's left are the two Senate leaders who eventually broke the filibuster, Republican Minority Leader Everett Dirksen and Minnesota Senator Hubert Humphrey.

A more casual moment: McCulloch, Lady Bird and President Johnson, and Mabel McCulloch at the White House.

Advocay of civil rights was hardly universal, and all who took to the picket lines did not do so in support. Here, McCulloch is picketed for supporting the issue.

In this 1965 photograph, McCulloch confers with former President Dwight Eisenhower and House Republican leader Gerald Ford. McCulloch was a great admirer of both Gerald and Betty Ford. McCulloch, however, had strongly preferred Ohio Senator Robert Taft to Eisenhower as the party's 1952 nominee.

President Lyndon Johnson hands Congressman McCulloch the pen with which he is signing the 1965 Voting Rights Act. Senator Hubert Humphrey stands behind McCulloch's left shoulder. Above Johnson is House Speaker John Mc-Cormack; to McCormack's left is Judiciary Chairman Emanuel Celler.

With the Capitol Done in the background, Congressman McCulloch poses with his two daughters, Ann [on the viewer's left] and Nancy,

The McCullochs gather in the Congressman's Rayburn Building office. Left to right are Mabel McCulloch (holding her daughter Ann's family's current poodle), Ann's daughter Elizabeth staffinf the phone; Nancy McCulloch; the Congressman, and younger daughter, Ann.

The McCullochs—victims, their daughters agreed, of love at first sight—formally dressed for an evening out.

Congressman McCulloch confers with NAACP chief lobbyists Clarence Mitchell (left) and Massachusetts Senator Edward Brooke, with whom McCulloch served on the President's Commission on Civil Disorders.

NATIONAL ASSOCIATION FOR THE ADVANCEMENT OF COLORED PEOPLE
WASHINGTON BUREAU
CONGRESSIONAL BUILDING
422 FIRST STREET, S.E.
WASHINGTON, D. C. 20003

202-544-5694

June 8, 1971

Honorable William McCulloch
United States House of Representatives
Washington, D. C.

Dear Bill:

A few days ago Aaron Henry of Clarksdale, Mississippi, said that
nearly two hundred Negroes will be seeking office in the forthcoming elections. We have had and continue to have some problems
with the Justice Department in getting full enforcement of the
1965 Voting Rights Act, but even with such impediments, the
law continues to have a magnificent effect in the places where
it is so badly needed.

I often think of how you have so stoutly defended human rights
and how your courage has made it possible to have a national
bi-partisan commitment to civil rights in Congress. Because of
your long personal contributions to the effort to protect the
right to vote, each one of the candidates mentioned by Aaron
Henry is a member of the party of human decency in which you
hold one of the highest positions of trust. The same can be
said about all of the other bills for which you have worked
to get through Congress.

I hope that your health continues to improve and that I shall
soon have an opportunity to greet you in person.

Always with appreciation,

Clarence Mitchell
Director
Washington Bureau

CMM/ewh

The announcement of McCulloch's retirement drew this
warm praise from Clarence Mitchell.

As the city turns gray with winter, Congressman Mc-Culloch takes in the view of the Capitol Dome from his congressional office.

WILLIAM MOORE McCULLOCH
CAPT
US ARMY
WORLD WAR II
NOV 24 1901
FEB 22 1980

McCulloch learned in the mid-1960s that he would be buried at Arlington National Cemetery, a fact of which he was humbly proud.

treasurer, presented a plaque to McCulloch, introducing that act with these words: "It is not often, we concede, that organized labor pays tribute to a Republican Party leader, but we do so enthusiastically because it was Representative McCulloch's fine work that insured passage of the bill."

CHAPTER 15

Reapportionment

On June 15, 1964—with final passage and signing of the landmark Civil Rights Act more than a fortnight away—the Supreme Court ruled in the case of *Wesberry v. Sanders* that the then common practice by which a state could apportion one branch of its legislature on a basis other than population was unconstitutional. The ruling, which brought enormous repercussions for state government, was colloquially referred to as the "One man; One vote" decision. Writing for the majority, Chief Justice Earl Warren stated, "Legislatures represent people, not trees or acres. Legislators are elected by voters, not farms or cities or economic interests." The congressman from Ohio's Fourth District, William Moore McCulloch, disagreed with Warren's thinking, disagreed with his decision, and took immediate action to have it reversed.

On June 24, nine days after the court handed down its 6–3 decision, William McCulloch took to the floor of the House to propose a constitutional amendment that, in substance, would overturn that ruling. His proposed twenty-fifth amendment read as follows:

ARTICLE XXV:

Section 1: Nothing in the Constitution of the United States shall prohibit a State, having a bicameral legislature, from apportioning the membership of one house of its legislature on factors other than population, if the citizens of the State shall have the opportunity to vote upon the apportionment.

Section 2: This article shall be inoperative unless it shall have been ratified as an amendment to the Constitution by the legislature of three-fourths of the several states within seven years from the date of its submission to the States of the Congress.

McCulloch's first section contained a crucially important hedge. One central charge against apportionment based on anything other than population was that those who benefited from a "malapportioned" legislature were hardly likely to vote their advantages out of existence. Anthony Lewis, writing in *The New York Times*, quoted as pertinent the observation of H. L. Mencken, who "said in the 1920s that rural over-weighing in legislatures was too absurd to last, but he has not been proven right yet. A major reason is that the bias, once built in, is almost impossible to remove by political means because the politicians will not vote themselves out of office."

McCulloch was clear—"factors other than population" were legitimate only if the apportioning scheme was approved by a statewide referendum. McCulloch was motivated in part by the fact that Colorado, in a recent referendum that had drawn a high turnout, had by a 305,700 to 172,725 vote approved a districting plan that was weighted in favor of certain geographically large but thinly populated counties. In his ruling, Warren had dismissed this referendum as "without federal Constitutional significance."

On the other (and more numerous) hand, liberals—who in previous months had bestowed considerable praise on McCulloch for his fight for civil rights—were at a loss to explain why he had wandered from the road of equality down some apparently recidivist path. Opponents were quick to point to two things. First, as things stood, state apportionment routinely favored conservative rural districts over populist urban ones, which in practical politics meant Republicans were favored over Democrats. This was undeniably the case. Second, opponents pointed to particularly egregious examples of disproportionate representation. In California, in theory, 10.7 percent of voters could elect a majority of the state senate. On August 9, *The Washington Post* reported that, in Georgia, which had not redistricted since 1901, Fulton County—encompassing the city of Atlanta—with 556,326 residents returned three representatives to the state legislature; Echols County's 1,876 citizens returned one. *The Post* went on to suggest the pending impact of the High Court's decision: "It would affect such legislative decisions as who gets California's limited water resources and how much of the pork barrel goes to Hawaii's neighboring islands. And it could mean the end of the line for some powerful figures in state political circles if their districts were expanded to include other incumbents."

McCulloch viewed this as beside the point. All of the disparities cited would continue to exist only if a majority of the voters of a given state wished them to do so. Beyond that, McCulloch's proposal rested on several of his core beliefs about politics and the public good.

First, he shared with other conservatives the view that the Supreme Court, under Earl Warren, had reconstituted itself as a kind of "supra-legislature," reaching decisions it thought politically correct and then finding some ways to hang them on the "equal protection" clause of the Fourteenth Amendment. This particularly annoyed McCulloch—he championed the Fourteenth Amendment as directed specifically against racial discrimination, not at any inequality someone might wish to define. In addressing the House on June 15, 1964, McCulloch stated:

It has appeared to a rapidly increasing number of thoughtful citizens that the Supreme Court has begun in recent years to exceed its proper authority and usurp powers that long have been held to belong to the States or to other branches of the Federal Government. Without doubt, these most immediate decisions of the Court proceed the farthest along the wayward path and do the most harm to the longtime concept of States rights.

Calling on the views of a more illustrious citizen, McCulloch quoted Abraham Lincoln:

The candid citizen must confess that if the policy of the Government upon vital questions affecting the whole people is to be irrevocably fixed by decisions of the Supreme Court, the instant they are made in ordinary litigation between parties in personal actions the people will have ceased to be their own rulers, having to that extent practically resigned their Government into the hands of that eminent tribunal.

Second, McCulloch believed, rightly or not, that most of the nation's voting fraud occurred in its largest cities. A strictly population-based system would lead, he believed, to the over-representation of city voters because a number of those on the voting list—though doubtless fine persons in other ways—had some years earlier suffered the misfortune of being dead, a misfortune that did not, however, prevent them from voting. Following from this, McCulloch believed that a purely population-based system would stick rural voters with the bill for the salaries of people placed on city payrolls by their office-holding brothers-in-law. Third—and more fundamentally—McCulloch simply took issue with Chief Justice Warren's statement "Legislatures represent people, not trees or acres." The distinction between Warren and McCulloch was that Warren viewed society as an aggregation of individuals, each of whom was a freestanding entity whose chief right was equal treatment. McCulloch viewed society as a constantly interacting web of entities to which those individuals belonged, everything from religious denominations, to occupations, to civic associations, and many others, including physical geographies. People who lived in mountains had different interests from people who lived on the plains. Some of the coherence of society, McCulloch held, came from the fact that land was divided into townships; townships became counties, counties became states. People in any individual township or county had interests they did not share with their neighbors. A strictly population-based system was antagonistic to what McCulloch saw as part of an organic society.

There was also a possible additional reason why McCulloch disagreed with the Supreme Court ruling: quite likely, McCulloch was among those Republicans who believed that machine politics and voter fraud in Illinois and Texas had deprived Richard Nixon of the White House in 1960.

McCulloch's position received immediate editorial support—though, admittedly, not from any particularly large newspaper. The Salina, Kansas, *Journal* wrote on June 16, "the opportunities for graft and other forms of corruption when the state is controlled by a few big machines will be enormous, and you can count upon the machine legislators to take advantage of it." The following day, the Dodge City, Kansas, *Globe* praised the dissent of Justice Potter Stewart, who wrote, "This pronouncement finds no support in the words of the Constitution, in any prior decision of this court or in the 175-year political history of the federal union." Following that point, the *Indianapolis Star* stated, "The [Supreme] Court deals with people as with a sack of marbles. They are to be rolled out on a table top and divided into equal piles." Indiana's *Richmond News Leader* commented, "Constituencies are not formed of so many warm bodies; they are formed of ideas; of ambitions, of vital groups. Common sense demands as well that certain facts of geography must be given some respect."

All but simultaneously, Senate minority leader Everett Dirksen introduced legislation to delay the High Court ruling until the various state legislatures were able to vote on McCulloch's proposed amendment, assuming, of course, that the amendment was approved by Congress.

In Congress, McCulloch's major opponent was the man who in previous months had been his closest ally, Judiciary Committee Chairman Emanuel Celler. Celler was adamantly opposed, saying McCulloch's proposal "could wind up rendering the Court a nullity, destroying our republican system of government." And with Celler controlling a majority of the Judiciary Committee, McCulloch's constitutional amendment appeared to be dead.

Then, once again, a southern congressman pulled an obscure rule out of the hat. On August 14, William Tuck, a Democrat from Virginia and a former governor of that state, cited a ruling, associated with a man named McCardle, that had lain unused and apparently unnoticed since 1869. The rule had come from a pro-civil rights majority that was seeking some expedient way of bypassing a House committee then in unfriendly hands. As Congressman Tuck explained matters, the ruling allowed McCulloch's constitutional proposal to bypass the Judiciary Committee and move directly into the friendlier embrace of the Committee on Rules. *The New York Times* reported, "Word got out early, and at 10 a.m. the [Rules Committee] chamber was jammed. [Chairman] Smith lighted his cigar, looked out from under his craggy brows at Mr. Tuck at the other end of the oval table, and brought down his gavel."

Congressman Tuck asserted that the recent Supreme Court decisions had "usurped the right of the sovereign states to conduct their domestic affairs." Celler complained bitterly that the measure had been kidnapped from his committee. He continued his complaint for some length, thus affording Congressman Smith the delicious pleasure of accusing Congressman Celler of engaging in a filibuster. In the end, the Rules Committee voted 10 to 4 to move McCulloch's amendment to the House floor for debate. This issue was not a minor one. McCulloch's view that the Supreme Court was overstepping its bounds had considerable support. Writing in *The New York Times* on August 16, Anthony Lewis stated, "At the American Bar Association meeting here last week, a man who has been a close Washington observer of the Supreme Court for more than 20 years remarked soberly that he had never sensed so much hostility at the nine men in their marble palace across the lawn."

On September 15, McCulloch's office issued a press release prompted by a circuit court decision in Michigan that invalidated the apportionment used by the Kent [Michigan] County Board of Supervisors. McCulloch stated:

I have warned that the effect of the Supreme Court's decisions would be to cast doubt on the composition of not only State legislatures, and the Congress, but on the composition of each and every political subdivision of every State throughout the nation, including flood control, irrigation, and reclamation and drainage districts.

In consequence, he said, the courts will "dictate either directly or indirectly" the composition of elected legislatures, and administrative and judicial offices on every level of state and local government. This, he said, could jeopardize "the future, if not the past, financial obligations, the judicial decisions and the peoples' trust in all the legislative, judicial and other structures of most States in the Union."

Walter Lippmann, widely regarded as the nation's leading pundit, saw merit to both sides. He, on balance, favored the court decision. But he saw the potential change as momentous and, therefore, not as something to be driven solely by the federal judiciary without the states having some say in the matter. The real need, he said, was to find a means whereby a given state's upper house could, as Madison intended, temper the actions of its lower house. He did not see the issue as analogous to civil rights. In civil rights, he said, great and obvious wrongs were being committed every day; action was imperative. He did not think malapportionment, if it existed, operated at the same level of wrong, and he saw no reason that the Dirksen proposal, allowing states a chance to vote on the matter, should not pass. He imagined an outcome in which states had fewer but better-paid senators, with perforce a larger and more varied constituency, a broader view, and perhaps even "a sense of responsibility."

Lippmann's somewhat oracular views aside, McCulloch's argument lost out to simple clarity. McCulloch could dismiss "One man; One vote" as little more than a slogan. The reality is that slogans are powerful. Consider "Equal pay for equal work." Consider "Remember the Alamo." Slogans, by providing a nutshell summation of a complex matter, greatly influence how individuals think, act, and vote. Beyond that was the simple fact that the moving finger, having writ, passes on. As *The New York Times* commented, "Despite the widespread opposition to the Supreme Court ruling, there is considerable doubt on Capitol Hill that once reapportionment is completed or under way, many states will want to undo it, or that Congress will accommodate them if they should want to." Such proved to be the case. McCulloch's proposed constitutional amendment did not so much die as fade away.

McCulloch continued to press the matter. On December 23, 1964, he returned to the Ohio legislature he had once gaveled to order as Speaker to urge that both House and Senate adopt resolutions favoring a constitutional convention to address the issue. For McCulloch, the Ohio legislature was friendly turf, and the resolutions soon passed.

Skipping ahead, Congressman McCulloch raised the issue in a subsequent session of Congress. On April 27, 1967, he spoke to the House on behalf of the legislation, H.R. 2508, which he had introduced.

> It is nearly unbelievable when one realizes the wave of Congressional districting and redistricting that has occurred since the 1960 census, and particularly since the Supreme Court's 1964 decision in *Wesberry v. Sanders*. The latest count shows 41 states or 422 of our 435 Congressional districts may have to redistrict to satisfy the court made criteria.
>
> Mr. Chairman, I want to state clearly and without reservation that this legislation is not an attempt to nullify any decision of the Supreme Court or to unreasonably delay the impact or effect of any such decisions [but] the Supreme Court has never—I repeat never—established a precise Constitutional criteria for Congressional districting.

Nothing came of it. Civil Rights, as Republican Minority Leader Everett Dirksen had told the Senate in 1964, was "an idea whose time has come." McCulloch's campaign against the "One man; One vote" decision was an effort on his part to prevent the atomization of society into individuals grounded in nothing larger than their individuality. He was not necessarily wrong. He was, however, the advocate of an idea whose time had passed.

CHAPTER 16

Guaranteeing the Vote

During the hot summer struggle that came before passage of the 1964 Civil Rights Act, Congressman McCulloch received a letter from a constituent who wrote that *Progressive* magazine had reported that McCulloch "faced political troubles in your district because of your support for the civil rights bill." The writer, a recent graduate of Bluffton, a college located in McCulloch's district, said his *alma mater's* faculty and students were strong in support of civil rights. The writer urged McCulloch, if need be, to call upon them for help.

McCulloch might have been feeling the need. By 1964, McCulloch had become accustomed to winning reelection by safe margins, generally 65 to 35 percent. Measured in vote totals, this translated into margins of 50,000 votes in presidential elections, 35,000 in mid-terms. In 1964, however, he had doubts that his return to office would be easily secured. First, he anticipated losing some votes to those who opposed his leadership on civil rights. Second, he anticipated losing some votes of Republicans who were sufficiently put off by the candidacy of Barry Goldwater that they would vote Johnson for president and Democratic down the line. Indeed, one correspondent threatened that while he had "always voted Republican," he would cast "a straight Democrat ticket if Barry Goldwater was the Republican standard bearer." McCulloch's opponent, Democrat Roger Milbaugh of Lima, was a political neophyte. Still, he emerged as a hard-charging candidate who had once roomed at Notre Dame with a cousin of the Kennedy family, from whom he seemed to have caught the political bug. McCulloch confided to a reporter that he would be pleased to win by 10,000 votes.

McCulloch did receive outside support—notably from NAACP lobbyist Clarence Mitchell. Speaking on September 19 to the state NAACP convention in Toledo, Mitchell said, "There are two of your Congressmen who have such great influence and hold such important committee posts that it is no exaggeration to say that this bill (1964 Civil Rights Act) would not have become law without them." Mitchell then named

Ohio Congressmen William McCulloch and Clarence Brown, ranking members of the Judiciary and Rules Committees. He added, "Long before many others had decided that they would support the bill, Mr. McCulloch and Mr. Brown were pledged to see it become the law." On September 21, 1964, Mitchell wrote McCulloch that, having obtained "the volunteer services of six young women who wanted to do something constructive in the current election," he had directed them to stuffing envelopes on behalf of the McCulloch campaign.

McCulloch's own view of Barry Goldwater is unknown. As a delegate to the 1964 Republican Convention that had nominated the Arizona senator, McCulloch was pledged to the "favorite son" candidacy of Ohio Governor James A. Rhodes. This was convenient. He received dozens of letters from backers of Michigan Governor George Romney, Pennsylvania Governor William Scranton, Senator Goldwater, and others, all urging him to declare in favor of their respective champion. McCulloch was able to reply honestly that he was "spoken for." However, he invariably added that if Governor Rhodes released the Ohio delegation, he would fully consider whichever candidate the particular letter writer happened to favor.

Still, it is difficult to imagine that McCulloch, as the party's congressional spokesman on civil rights, did not feel bitter disappointment—if not outright betrayal—by Goldwater's vote against the 1964 Civil Rights Act, a vote that undercut the public view that civil rights had been a bipartisan accomplishment. At the same time, McCulloch was a party Republican, with no political or personal fondness for Lyndon Johnson. A review of press clippings suggests that McCulloch did little active campaigning for the Republican nominee. His stock reply to constituent mail was, "If every Goldwater supporter would see that one person voted who did not vote in 1960, victory would be ours,"a reply somewhat less invigorating than the call to battle spoken by Shakespeare's Henry V. On election morning, McCulloch emerged from his congressional office to announce to his staff, "I never told you I thought Goldwater would win." Indeed, Lyndon Johnson swamped the Arizona conservative by a historic margin. William McCulloch returned to office with the greatly reduced margin of 16,537 votes. Ironically, the election underscored McCulloch's contention that he had no self-interest in his support of civil rights. While his district was overwhelmingly white, it had a handful of precincts with black majorities. In none of these did McCulloch—despite his leadership on civil rights and despite the NAACP endorsement—receive more than 14 percent of the vote.

The Eighty-Ninth Congress

The Congress that assembled in January 1965 would undertake a historic round of legislation: Medicare; the Housing and Urban Development Act (Model Cities); the Elementary and Secondary Education Act; the Appalachian Regional Development Act (War on Poverty); and much else. But the emotional core of the session was the issue of voting rights for black Americans.

On January 20, 1965, President Lyndon Johnson delivered his State of the Union address. The principal aim of his administration, he said, was to "eliminate every remaining obstacle to the right and opportunity to vote." Comprehensive federal action, Johnson said, was required. Johnson called for legislation that would "overcome the crippling legacy of bigotry and injustice." He closed with the phrase most associated with the civil rights movement, "We shall overcome."

The status of black voting in the South was more varied than generally imagined. Across the region as a whole, about 20 percent of legally eligible African Americans were registered. There was, however, considerable variation from state to state, as the figures on black registration from the 1964 election given below show:
- Tennessee – 69.5 percent
- Florida – 51.2 percent
- Louisiana – 31.6 percent
- Alabama – 19.3 percent
- Mississippi – 7.6 percent

Many white Mississippians made no bones about their intentions. One member of the White Citizens' Council said in the early 1960s:

I was born in Mississippi and the United States, and I'm the product of my heredity and education and the society in which I was raised, and I have a vested interest in that society, and I along with a million other white Mississippians will do everything in our power to protect that vested interest. It's primarily a struggle for power, and I think we would be stupid indeed if we failed to see where the consequences of a supine surrender on our part would lead.

In the face of such attitudes, the Mississippi Freedom Democratic Party (MFDP)—a grassroots black political organization—challenged the seating of all Mississippi congressmen elected in 1964; they challenged that seating on the grounds that their elections had come in contests that reeked of racial discrimination. The challenge failed. But it was a remarkable thing that in a body with as high a regard of its membership, and as loathe to reject a fellow member however elected, 143 congressmen voted to deny the Mississippians their seats. The MFDP's greater impact came later—as the tens of thousands of pages of testimony and statistics gathered provided the grounding data for the forthcoming debate on voting rights.

Congressman McCulloch would play a central role in that debate. On February 28, he was appointed chairman of the Republican Task

Force on Voting Rights. Within the week, McCulloch announced his task force would include Governors John Love of Colorado and Daniel Evans of Washington and state attorney general Edward Brooke of Massachusetts. Brooke was that rarity: a black Republican office holder. A former Judiciary Committee staff attorney, Thomas Mooney, assessed the importance of McCulloch's role and concluded, "The GOP followed McCulloch in on civil rights; they looked to him for leadership."

Selma

Nations respond less to facts on the page than to the faces in front of them. In early 1964, those faces were front and center in Selma, Alabama. Selma was the seat of Dallas County, in which only 130 of the 15,000 blacks old enough to vote were registered. In launching a voter registration drive there in early January, Dr. Martin Luther King, Jr. said, "We are going to plague the conscience of Dallas County, non-violently and creatively."

On Sunday, March 7, 500 marchers departed Selma heading east, led by John Lewis—then of the Student Nonviolent Coordinating Committee (SNCC) and a future congressman—and the Rev. Hosea Williams of the Southern Christian Leadership Conference (SCLC). Their intention was to march on the state capital of Birmingham, fifty miles distant. That morning, Dallas County sheriff Jim Clark had called all white males in the county to step forth to be deputized. When the marchers reached the Edmund Pettus Bridge, they were confronted by a solid rank of Alabama state troopers blocking the exit on the other side. The commander on the scene directed the throng to disperse and to return home. When the marchers held their ground, the state troopers advanced—deputies fired tear gas and beat marchers with nightsticks; troopers on horseback charged the crowd. The rampage spread into some of Selma's black neighborhoods. Seventeen marchers were hospitalized. For once—due to the presence of television cameras—the whole world was indeed watching.

Tuesday, two days later, the Rev. Martin Luther King, Jr. and others organized a repeat march. They did so in the face of a restraining order issued by Judge Frank Johnson of the U.S. District Court—one of the few southern judges sympathetic to civil rights. The order forbade the marchers to cross the bridge. Judge Johnson said the restraining order would stand until he held further hearings into the matter. Civil rights leaders compromised. Dr. King led an estimated 2,500 marchers onto the Edmund Pettus Bridge, held a brief prayer service, and then in compliance with the court order they turned around. That night, unidentified individuals attacked three northern white ministers who came to Selma to join the march. One of them, the Rev. James Reeb, died of his injuries. His death might have been prevented if Selma's public hospital had been willing to treat him. Turned away by that facility, the Rev. Reeb was without medical attention until completing the two-hour drive to Birmingham.

The following morning, the two Republican congressmen most strongly associated with civil rights—William McCulloch of Piqua and John Lindsay of Manhattan—chastized President Johnson for inaction. McCulloch, *The New York Times* reported on March 10, stated that prompt presidential action "could have prevented" the situation from arising. He added that the president "has the right to act when citizens are prevented from petitioning for a redress of grievances." Lindsay said, "Johnson should have had federal troops or marshals on hand in Selma to deal with the situation before last Sunday, when the beatings by state troopers and sheriff's posse took place."

The pace was quickening. On March 15, six days before the third march began, President Lyndon Johnson spoke to the nation from the rostrum of Congress. In a speech which *The New York Times* termed "the most eloquent, many thought, of his career," Johnson said he was speaking for "the dignity of man and the destiny of democracy."

There is no cause for pride in what has happened in Selma. There is no cause for self-satisfaction in the long denial of equal rights of millions of Americans. . . . There is no Negro problem. There is no Southern problem. There is no Northern problem. There is only an American problem. And we are met here tonight as Americans—not as Democrats or Republicans—we are met here as Americans to solve that problem.

Those words are a promise to every citizen that he shall share in the dignity of man. This dignity cannot be found in a man's possessions; it cannot be found in his power, or in his position. It really rests on his right to be treated as a man equal in opportunity to all others. It says that he shall share in freedom, he shall choose his leaders, educate his children, and provide for his family according to his ability and his merits as a human being.

Yet the harsh fact is that, in many places in this country, men and women are kept from voting simply because they are Negroes. Every device of which human ingenuity is capable has been used to deny this right. The Negro citizen may go to register only to be told that the day is wrong, or the hour is late, or the official in charge is absent. And if he persists, and if he manages to present himself to the registrar, he may be disqualified because he did not spell out his middle name or because he abbreviated a word on the application. For the fact is that the only way to pass these barriers is to show a white skin.

President Johnson noted that in two days he would send to Congress a law "designed to eliminate illegal barriers to the right to vote." The heart of the law was that, in much of the South, voter registration would be federalized—that is, the authority to register voters would be taken from counties and states and transferred to federal representatives. He said any community that wished to avoid the application of this law had only to "open your polling places to all your people." He noted that passage of his proposal would not mark an end to any struggle: "Because it is not just Negroes, but really it is all of us, who must overcome the crippling legacy of bigotry and injustice. And we shall overcome."

President Johnson said he had come to address Congress directly at the suggestion of four members—among them, William McCulloch of Ohio. Civil rights activist C. T. Vivian watched the broadcast of the president's speech in company with Dr. King. When the president had finished, Vivian recalled, "I looked over . . . and Martin was very quietly sitting in the chair, and a tear ran down his cheek."

On March 17, 1965, President Johnson presented to Congress a draft of what he had privately described as "the goddamnedest, toughest voting rights bill" that could be drafted. The major points of the administration bill were:

• First, all qualification tests would be outlawed in any state in which less than half of those of voting age voted in the 1964 election;

• Second, if complaints are brought forth in other states, the attorney general may appoint federal examiners to investigate;

• Third, a federal court may hold up the results of an election in which it can be demonstrated that any voter was wrongfully denied the right to vote.

The bill carried a double triggering mechanism. It would apply to any state in which both of the following existed: 50 percent of the voting-age black population was not registered and the state had a literacy requirement for registering to vote. In those states, registration would become the task of the federal government. The consequence was that the bill would apply only to six southern states and a portion of North Carolina.

The focus of drama shifted from Washington to Alabama. Dr. King announced his intention to lead a fifty-mile march from Selma to the state capitol of Montgomery. Here, Judge Johnson was exercising the full powers of his office. First, he contacted Attorney General Nicholas Katzenbach to determine, if he waived his injunction against further marches, would the federal government undertake to protect those marchers en route. Katzenbach gave Judge Johnson his word. Johnson said he didn't want the word of the attorney general; he wanted the word of Lyndon Johnson. That word was forthcoming. Second, Johnson met with lawyers for the marchers. The plan was to cross fifty miles of territory in five days. Had the planners made arrangements for where marchers would stay overnight? For how they would be fed? For how any medical emergency might be handled? The word of the president and the plans of the marchers in hand, Judge Johnson lifted his injunction. On March 17, Judge Johnson stated that, while a fifty-mile march might push constitutional rights to the "outer limits," he was withdrawing his injunction because "in this case the wrongs are enormous." Judge Johnson ordered Governor George Wallace of Alabama to provide continuous protection to the throng. When Wallace announced that Alabama could not afford the $360,000 cost this would entail, President Johnson immediately federalized the National Guard.

On Sunday, March 21, 8,000 people gathered at the Brown Chapel in Selma. In the march's final two days, the throng swelled so that on Thursday, March 25, a crowd of 25,000 persons marched up Dexter Avenue to the Alabama State Capitol. The sidewalks on either side were crammed with jeering crowds. Nearly 2,000 federalized National Guardsmen stood between those marching to protest and those protesting the march. To Nicholas Katzenbach's fury, the guardsmen were facing the marchers, as if they were there to protect the local crowd. Katzenbach ordered the guard commander to about-face his men. The commander refused. Shortly, Assistant Secretary of Defense Cyrus Vance was reached by telephone. The local commander was put on the line and heard that order repeated. This time, it was obeyed and the federalized guard conducted an abrupt about-face. Standing before the state capitol, Dr. King delivered a speech, "How Long; Not Long." In this, he said in part, "The end we seek is a society at peace with itself, a society that can live with its conscience."

The events in Selma brought a surge in constituent mail to Congressman McCulloch's office. Most—but hardly all—argued for action on voting rights. The return addresses read like a sampling of the small-town America McCulloch represented: Lima, Alliance, Conover, Delphos, Kinsman, and a dozen others. An accountant from Lima wrote, "To permit the present situation in Selma, Alabama to continue will certainly brand us before the world as the outstanding oppressors of minorities." A minister from Alliance wrote, "For more than 100 years we, the citizens of the United States have failed to enact a law which would enable and protect the right of every citizen to register and to vote in all elections" and urged McCulloch's support in doing so. A married couple from Delphos wrote wishing "to add our names to the growing list of people who have written in support of the right-to-vote legislation, which will ensure our qualified Negro citizens to exercise their right to vote." A Kinsman resident wrote simply, "I shall appreciate whatever you can do to make our land a country where there is truly liberty and justice for all."

Nearly one-third wrote in opposition. Thus, a long-time McCulloch supporter from Allen County wrote, "I have no objection to any legal citizen of the United States casting a vote, if he has sufficient intelligence to understand what he has voted for. However, the new bill that is being presented to Congress, in my opinion, is one of the most dangerous pieces of legislation presented in years." The writer added that it "pains me no end" that McCulloch, for whom he had routinely voted, was supping with Democrats. An Allen County chiropractor wrote that he regarded the bill as an unconstitutional *ex post facto* measure, as it inflicted punishment for deeds done prior to its intended passage. Similarly, a married couple from Delphos also declared the law to be an *ex post facto* exercise, in that "it makes it a crime today to have done some act yesterday." Two days after that letter came in, McCulloch replied, "The right to vote and have the vote honestly counted is the most important cornerstone of a representative republic. Don't you agree?"

The Congressional Debate

As noted, Lyndon Johnson sent the administration's voting rights bill to the House on March 17, 1965. It was formally introduced by Emanuel Celler and referred to the Judiciary Committee the following day. When hearings began, the administration's lead witness was Attorney General Nicholas Katzenbach. William McCulloch termed Katzenbach's presentation "one of the best statements I have heard in my 17 years in the House." In his memoirs, Katzenbach admits with some embarrassment that while he welcomed McCulloch's comment, the praise rightly might have gone to those Justice Department staffers who had written his remarks. As drawn, the bill would apply to Mississippi, Louisiana, Alabama, South Carolina, Georgia, Virginia, (curiously) Alaska, and twenty-four counties in North Carolina. Tennessee and Florida were not covered because in those two states over half of the eligible blacks were registered. Texas and Arkansas would not be covered because neither state had a literacy requirement for voting, the second condition of the "trigger." A Gallup poll showed widespread support for the president's proposal—nationally, 76 percent approved; 49 percent did so in the South.

Those approving of the Johnson proposal did not include Ohio's Fourth District congressman. As reported in *The New York Times* on March 25, 1965, NAACP executive secretary Roy Wilkins—when questioned by McCulloch—termed the administration proposal "a good bill" but "not enough." What he wanted, he said, was a bill that was tied to voter discrimination, wherever it occurred, and "not to geography" as the administration proposal did. When McCulloch's asked if Wilkins favored a rewritten bill that reached the "festering pockets of discrimination" in Texas, Tennessee, Florida, Arkansas, and even New York, Wilkins replied, "Yes." *The Times* noted that in twenty-two counties in Arkansas, five in Florida, and eleven in Texas, less than one-fourth of eligible blacks were registered. Nonetheless, these areas were not covered by the bill as these states did not impose literacy tests.

Long-time Washington reporter Andrew Glass told the author that McCulloch was simply "outside the political sphere—in the sense that he was indifferent to how something might affect his political standings." Leading *New York Times* commentator James Reston—in a piece titled "A Responsible Republican Opposition"—noted that House Republicans Gerald Ford, John Lindsay, and William McCulloch were "leading a campaign to strengthen the voting rights bill." They were doing so, he stated, even though "there is no evidence that the Republican Party stands to gain, at least in the short run, by a vast increase in Negro voting. On the contrary, all indications are that the new Negro voters will side overwhelmingly with the Democratic party."

On April 5, 1965, McCulloch introduced the GOP alternative to the administration proposal, H.R. 7125, which came to be known as the Ford-McCulloch bill. He began:

Mr. Speaker, this proposal is offered to dramatize the serious deficiencies in the original administration voting rights bill. The Republican bill will correct voting discrimination wherever it occurs throughout the length and breadth of this great land. It respects the traditional and constitutional rights of the States and sets reasonable and non-discriminatory standards for voting.

McCulloch defined the goals of his proposal:
• To effectively and speedily end the unconstitutional denial of the right to vote anywhere in the United States;
• To terminate unreasonable standards for registration and voting without interfering with the reasonable requirements established by the States;
• To terminate any discriminatory application of any registration requirement;
• To avoid penalizing areas that are not guilty of discrimination.

Voter registration, he noted, was generally carried on at the county, not the state, level. The Republican alternative, he said, "does not penalize the innocent"—the significant number of counties where there was no particular evidence of discrimination. At the same time, it would be applied to the entire country, not just seven targeted states. Further, it was not tied to an "arbitrary percentage formula" which suggested that a black voter registration level of 49 percent was illegal, but a level of 51 percent was acceptable.

The Ford-McCulloch bill would be implemented as follows: If, in any of the nation's 3,107 counties, twenty-five individuals signed statements that they had been denied the right to register due to race or color, a federal hearing officer would investigate. If the federal examiner determined that the complaints had merit, this would establish a "pattern of discrimination." County officials could challenge the alleged discrimination, but could do so only on the same basis as a white applicant might be challenged, e.g., that the applicant was not old enough to vote, or did not in fact reside in the county in question. Once a "pattern of discrimination" was established, then all would-be black voters from the county in question would be automatically registered without needing to demonstrate that they had been personally discriminated against.

McCulloch noted that Article I, Section 2 of the Constitution reserved to the states the right to set voter qualifications. Such tests, however, were subjective—in consequence, would-be black voters who were college graduates were often declared illiterate by white registration boards. While, McCulloch said, Congress lacked the power to overrule the authority granted to states to set voter qualifications, it could act against their "capricious" use. Therefore, for the purposes of voter registration, anyone who had completed the sixth grade would be deemed sufficiently literate to vote. A state, however, could require a sixth-grade education of prospective black voters only if it applied the same standard to whites. Other titles of the Ford-McCulloch bill outlined civil and/or criminal penalties for anyone who attempted through coercion or intimidation to dissuade an individual from registering.

McCulloch would stress a further point as the House debated his substitute bill. The administration bill presumed seven states guilty based on a mathematical formula that would always be outdated because it was based on the national census, taken only once a decade. The state's only recourse was to appeal the decision to the same federal agency that had declared it guilty in the first place. McCulloch further objected to the administration plan because it required the seven affected states to seek prior Department of Justice approval of any law proposed in that state that might in any way influence voting.

Assessing the Ford-McCulloch proposal, political scientist Geoffrey Kabaservice commented, "The Ford-McCulloch bill was distinctively Republican in its preference for a more limited federal role and the preservation of certain states' rights, its application to a wide range of corrupt voting practices, and its concern that the South be judged on the same standard in all regions of the country." In all, the Judiciary Committee heard a wealth of witnesses before voting to approve the bill on May 12, 1965.

In the Senate, the great battle of the previous year appeared to have drained southern senators of much of their powers of resistance. Following a rather abortive filibuster, the Senate on May 21 voted 70 to 30 to invoke cloture, thus ending debate. Five days later, the Senate gave formal passage by a 77 to 19 vote. Three southerners voted in its favor: Albert Gore, Sr., and Ross Bass of Tennessee, and Ralph Yarborough of Texas. With that, the bill moved on to the House.

House Debate

House debate began on July 6, 1965, when Congress returned from its Fourth of July recess. William McCulloch took the floor to make the case for the Republican alternative. He offered the Ford-McCulloch proposal as an amendment to the Senate-passed bill—in effect, seeking to substitute his bill for that of the administration. His statement to the House began, "No issue before a legislative body in a representative republic is of greater importance than legislation which would assure the right of every qualified citizen to vote and to have that vote counted."

McCulloch reviewed the provisions of the 1957 and 1960 acts, noting that the case-by-case litigation over voter discrimination that these acts had created was inadequate: "The judicial remedy takes time; it sometimes demands delay; and it calls for great resources of manpower to successfully prosecute a case which may affect only a limited area." Any further bill, he said, should solve the problem both in the short and long term. However, he added, "the expectations of many of us for fair and sound implementation . . . [was] frustrated by the initial administration bill, and our hopes and expectations continued unfulfilled throughout the committee action." Summarizing his statement, McCulloch argued:

> The Ford-McCulloch bill is a bill of uniform nationwide application, a bill that directs its remedy at Fifteenth Amendment discrimination wherever found. It is a bill that is non-discriminatory in its approach and application to the problems it is designed to solve. It is a bill completely comprehensive in scope yet uncomplicated and flexible in operation. Its provisions are understandable to the citizens it assures, unmistakable to those whose conduct it proscribes, and in the opinion of the most able lawyers clearly in accordance with the Constitution.

The bill reflected McCulloch's fundamental belief that social improvement was likelier to come from individual responsibility than from government edict. Thus, he said, the Ford-McCulloch bill "honors the rights of the States to fix and enforce nondiscriminatory voter qualifications. It enlists and encourages good faith compliance with its terms by those it affects. . . . Without penalizing areas which have done no wrong, it applies firm, considered standards to meet the critical requirements of the present situation, standards that will continue in their validity for future times when massive discrimination has ended." Criticizing the administration bill as applying to only seven states, he quoted a recent editorial, "A voting rights bill should admit the truth, that discrimination has no home locality."

As a Republican, McCulloch was at least somewhat of the belief that the Democrats had stolen the 1960 presidential election due to voter fraud in Illinois and Texas. Texas, he further noted, was exempt from the Johnson proposal. His belief was that unlike the administration bill, the Ford-McCulloch bill covered "other illegal voting practices," by extending federal jurisdiction into the redress of local corrupt practices, including tombstone voting, ballot box stuffing, and purchasing of votes. In summary, he said of the Ford-McCulloch proposal, "Upon inspection by future generations, it will reflect upon us as wise lawgivers who in the finest tradition of the Congress of the United States, in answer to a pressing, present need, met the problem with conviction, with speed, and with vision to see beyond the confines of our times."

With that, several days of brawling followed.

Siding with McCulloch, Congressman Robert McClory (R-Illinois) said the administration's percentage-based test "produces the incongruous result that the State of Alaska falls within the unlimited discretion of the Attorney General," while Texas and Arkansas do not. He noted, "Never before has any state been found guilty by the decision of a member of the executive department with the sole alternative of disproving its guilt by an original action in the District Court of the District of Columbia."

At least some southerners were prepared to acknowledge their region had been at fault. In the opening day's debate, Congressman Charles Bennett (D-Florida) stated that he had "consistently opposed such civil rights legislation as had for its purpose the compulsory intermingling of races." Still, he was aware of one county in his state whose white and black populations were equal, but which had 9,195 registered white voters and only 156 registered blacks. Bennett's own district included Jacksonville, the setting of McCulloch's conversion to civil rights advocacy. Later in the debate, Bennett pointed out that in Jacksonville, 63 percent of voting-age blacks were registered—the same percentage as voting-age whites—suggesting strongly that matters had changed considerably since McCulloch had been in residence there.

On July 8, McCulloch read into the record a recent editorial from the *Washington Evening News* that stated in part:

Representative McCulloch's measure is better than the administration plan. The administration bill, for instance, assumes arbitrarily that a state or locality is guilty of discrimination [based on 50 percent]. This may or may not be true. But it is bad legislation—if not unconstitutional—for Congress to declare it so in the absence of concrete evidence.

Congressman Robert McCrory alluded rather pointedly to alleged voter fraud in Illinois' Cook County in the 1960 election and quoted one researcher as finding that "the voting frauds were deeply rooted, that they were general throughout the area . . . a very sad commentary on election procedures in the state of Illinois and the city of Chicago." This brought an indignant response from Representative Robert Kastenmeier (D-Wisconsin), who denied any wrongdoing had occurred and characterized McClory's remarks as the "typical sour grapes speech that Republican representatives from downstate make about the city of Chicago. They cannot win elections on the basis of the issues, so they try to justify their losses on the basis of lies."

McCulloch said that under the administration bill, a person could be elected by votes subsequently judged illegal. He quoted Attorney General Katzenbach's reply to a question posed by Judiciary Chairman Emanuel Celler: could "a vote be counted even if after the election (a) the [pending voting rights] act is found to be inapplicable; or (b) the individual is found to be illegible."

Katzenbach: "Yes."

Various southerners took to the floor to declare their innocence. Thus, Congressman Edwin Willis (D-Louisiana) stated, "In my congressional district, 57 percent of all colored people of voting age are registered. Yet, under the Celler bill, my congressional district would be covered and would have no escape valve, just because other areas of the state are not according similar rights to colored people." A McCulloch ally, Representative Charles "Mac" Mathias (R-Maryland) also attacked the percentage-based aspect of the administration bill, which, he said, "robs Negroes in the fifty-first percentile of the protection given to one in the forty-ninth."

McCulloch was in a combative frame of mind, suggesting that President Lyndon Johnson's "political instincts got the better of his sense of fairness when he accused House Republicans of seeking to dilute the voting." He presented a series of question he would wish the president to answer:

• Why Texas was not covered under his original voting rights bill and is not effectively covered now?

• Why vote frauds and dishonest elections, such as have occurred in Chicago and Texas, are not covered under this proposal?

• Why would not the right to vote be protected equally in every state, not just in seven states?

• Why should any area be exempted after only 50 percent of the Negroes are permitted to vote?

• Why should challenged votes be counted and if found invalid be used, possibly to determine the outcome of an election, including the election of a president?

Interestingly enough, for a time the Ford-McCulloch amendment had a fair chance of passing. Princeton historian Eric J. Goldman, then serving as special consultant to Lyndon Johnson, wrote, "The White House was alarmed by the McCulloch bill." It had an appeal to southerners; while it was clear that in practice the bill would be principally implemented in the South, it did not explicitly define the South as the problem. For Republicans, it gave them a bill of their own, so they would not merely be riding as the caboose to Lyndon Johnson's train. Further, Goldman acknowledged, "an argument could be made that it was superior to the Administration legislation both in being less arbitrary and more comprehensive." In consequence of these various factors, Goldman added, "Southern Democrats flocked to the McCulloch version, and GOP lines were held so firm behind it that the administration could count just ten Republican votes for its own measure, considerably less than it needed for passage."

On July 8, *The Washington Post* reported that southern Democratic support for the Republican measure "began to crystalize in the House yesterday." The newspaper, however, quoted Congressman Emanuel Celler's assertion that twelve to twenty southern Democrats would withhold their support from McCulloch's measure. And McCulloch received a setback when one of his strongest Republican allies on civil rights, Charles Mathias (R-Maryland), announced support for the administration measure.

Still, the outcome was not certain. The eleven states of the former Confederacy then elected 106 congressmen—currently, they split 89 Democrats, 17 Republicans. The whole House had 140 Republicans. If one accepts the administration's statement that it could count on support from ten Republicans and adds Celler's lower estimate of a dozen votes from southern Democrats, that yields a vote of 228 to 207 for the administration bill. That outcome rested on Celler's assertion that a dozen southern congressman would vote for a bill generally viewed as stigmatizing the South.

Here, a southern congressman committed the final required self-destructive act. The representative in question was William M. Tuck (D-Virginia), who, in addition to being a former governor of Virginia, was also a wealthy tobacco grower and banker. Discretion might have suggested that those supporting Ford-McCulloch simply stand by the virtues that William McCulloch claimed for his proposal. Deciding valor was the better part of discretion, Congressman Tuck told the House, "The plain, unvarnished truth" was that a vote against the McCulloch substitute meant a vote "to foist upon your constituents this unconstitutional monstrosity" of federal intervention to guarantee Negro voting. The McCulloch bill was "milder" and therefore "far more preferable." Chairing the House, Minority Leader Gerald Ford was appalled. He quickly asserted that the Ford-McCulloch measure merited support as simply being the better bill, not because it undercut Negro voting.

The damage, however, had been done. House Speaker John McCormack stated, "It's not for me to advise my Republican friends, but I think Governor Tuck has put them in a very untenable position." Republicans deserted McCulloch by the dozen. The House rejected the Ford-McCulloch amendment by a vote of 215 to 166.

Politically, the fundamental problem with the McCulloch proposal was that, however reasonable it could be claimed to be, it was not a remedy that could be applied rapidly. In the aftermath of Selma—in light of the continuing reports of official brutality to blacks in no few parts of the South—the pressing demand was for action that would be effective *now*. Under the Senate-passed version, federal registrars could start signing up black voters within a week. Against this simple fact, the Ford-McCulloch offering was widely viewed as the weaker alternative. As Clarence Mitchell's biographer stated, in the House "Republicans backed away from a very weak substitute bill that was being pushed by McCulloch and Ford, the new minority leader —with Dirksen's support—because they did not want to appear to be supporting the southerners in defeating a stronger bill."

In *Rule and Ruin*, Geoffrey Kabaservice sounds a similar note:

McCulloch's bill lacked the automatic trigger and raised fears that blacks might be intimidated out of making the complaints that would lead to examination of a district's voting practices. For that reason, liberals and civil rights groups attacked the bill out of all proportion to its presumed drawbacks, with Martin Luther King and other civil rights leaders mounting a major publicity initiative against it.

It turned into a stampede. On July 9, 1965, the House by a 333 to 82 margin passed a bill very similar to the Senate version. The party breakdown was 221 Democrats in favor, 61 opposed. Republicans approved the measure by a 112–21 margin.

One hurdle remained. The House version included an outright ban on the poll tax, which four southern states still levied. The Senate version, milder, criticized the poll tax and authorized the attorney general to file suit on the grounds such taxes were discriminatory. In the end, House conferees settled for an opinion from Attorney General Katzenbach that he regarded poll taxes as unconstitutional and would file immediate lawsuits against the states involved. On August 3, the House then approved the conference report by a 328 to 74 margin—with 217 Democrats and 111 Republicans voting in favor, 54 Democrats and 20 Republicans opposed. Senate passage came the following day, by a vote of 79 to 18.

President Lyndon Johnson signed the bill into law on August 6, 1965, saying, "The right to vote is the most basic right without which all others are meaningless. It gives people—people as individuals—control over their destinies. . . . The vote is the most powerful instrument ever devised by man for breaking down injustice and destroying the terrible walls which imprison men because they are different from other men."

On August 25—less than twenty days later—President Johnson reported that the law had been implemented in thirteen counties. In the first three weeks, 27,385 black Americans registered to vote. In the states covered by the law, black voter registration increased from 26.8 percent to 55 percent in the next twelve months. In Dallas County, Alabama—the scene of "Bloody Sunday"—the number of blacks registered grew from fewer than 1,000 to 8,500. One of those registering in Selma was an elderly black woman, who arrived wearing a just-ironed cotton print dress. Having registered she left the courthouse, remarking, "I'm going to vote now. I'm going to vote because I haven't been able to vote in my sixty-seven years."

CHAPTER 17

Congressman McCulloch and the Great Society

Earlier in 1965, Congressman McCulloch and his office staff packed up and moved to the newly opened Rayburn House Office Building. The Rayburn is the westernmost of the three grand House office buildings that line Independence Avenue south of the Capitol. The building was designed by the Philadelphia architectural firm of Harbeson, Hough, Livingston and Larson with the instruction that it be in harmony with the classical style of the existing Capitol Hill structures. The building remains the general first choice of congressmen with sufficient seniority to have their choices honored. It has not always enjoyed an equal standing among architects; *The Washington Post*, for example, once referred to it as a mix of "Middle Mussolini, Early Ramses, and Late Nieman Marcus." Among other things, the Rayburn Building houses 169 three-room office suites for members of Congress and the meeting rooms of nine standing committees. For his final four terms in Congress, the Rayburn was at any given moment the likeliest place to find Ohio Congressman William Moore McCulloch. This, because its Room 2186 was McCulloch's congressional office, while down the corridor its Room 2141 was the permanently assigned meeting space of the House Judiciary Committee.

McCulloch, as a ranking member, had some say over which office would be his. He and his daughter Nancy toured the building while it was under construction to select his new office. Nancy McCulloch pointed out that Room 2186 offered a magnificent view of the Capitol dome. Visiting constituents have a fondness for mementos. In Room 2186, her father would need only step away from his desk for a photo of a ceremonial handshake framed by the Capitol dome. He took her advice. One staff member recalls McCulloch's own office as fairly plain—neither a stage set nor a trophy room designed to overawe the visitor—furnished with a good-sized desk, a standard congressional sofa, and a set of side chairs.

The room's distinctive feature was a series of small statues of bulldogs, annually awarded by a group called Watchdog of the Public to those congressmen who in the judgment of the group were working to restrain the federal budget. McCulloch took some pride in his collection. Believing that stringency begins at home, he was one of a handful of congressmen who routinely returned to the federal treasury a portion of the budget allotted him for office staff and operations.

Easily the most important staff member was Vera Page, who had worked for McCulloch perhaps longer than either could recall. Page had a small office of her own behind the suite's reception area, where she sat characteristically minding a two-foot pile of papers. Page was slender and a smoker, a habit the congressman apparently did not mind as he would at intervals dump her ashtray into the wastebasket while dictating his floor statements to her. McCulloch never hired a speechwriter or a press officer. By convention, congressmen had twenty-four hours in which to revise any comment they made to the House so that the remarks would appear in the *Congressional Record* in "improved" form. McCulloch never did that. He ran everything past Vera Page, for proofreading and grammar check, after which it was sent out the door. The pair's other main activity was a running dispute that carried through multiple presidential administrations over the proper way to organize office management.

The suite's remaining room was office space for staff. Most congressional staff offices have desks piled against desks; because McCulloch kept a small staff, things were somewhat roomier. And informal. In the summers of 1966 and 1967 McCulloch had a college-age aide named Jim Dicke, who for whatever reason was never told at what time the work day was to begin. Dicke recalled, "So I showed up at the office a half-hour earlier every day." McCulloch's own work day began at 7 a.m. One day, the congressman arrived to find that Dicke, having got there first, was waiting in the hallway. At that point, McCulloch clarified matters, "You know, Jim, you really don't have to come into the office until eight."

McCulloch, said Franklin G. Polk, an attorney with the Judiciary Committee, "embodied the traditional midwestern values, but with a Scot's mentality. He was a pretty cheap guy. They used to do a calendar every year, and every year that I worked for McCulloch he would hand me one of the calendars and say, 'Merry Christmas, Frank.' He used to say, if we invited him to something, 'I invite easy'—because it meant he would not have to pay." To which Nancy McCulloch added, "My father always did his own income taxes."

Robert Kimball—never a staff member, but someone who had considerable contact with the congressman during the fight over civil rights—described McCulloch as "courtly, reserved, conservative" and the originator of ornate phrases, such as "acting out of an abundance of caution" or "I'd like you to do something commensurate with your family obligations." McCulloch had a fastidious quality. Jim Dicke recalled, "On a couple occasions he would say, 'Now, Jim, I can't ask you to do this, but if you had the day off tomorrow, would you mind taking Mrs. McCulloch and some of her friends to Mt. Vernon? Would that be something that you would enjoy? It wouldn't be part of your official duties, you understand. It would be improper for me to ask you to do it, but you could have the day off tomorrow if you want. I can't pay you or anything, but is it something you would enjoy?'" And Dicke would reply he would enjoy that very much.

Without identifiable exception, those who served on McCulloch's office staff were enormously fond of him. And somewhat protective, an attitude that in part may have derived from the circumstance—as one staff member told Vera Page—that whenever a fresh congressional scandal broke they had no need to worry about their congressman being involved. By seven o'clock, William McCulloch was always at home, where he and Mabel would be watching the news.

The Washington in which William McCulloch served was greatly less partisan than it has since become, evidenced by the varying mix of political views of those McCulloch esteemed. McCulloch rarely agreed with President Truman, but was pleased that they shared a farm background. He had great respect for President Eisenhower as the wartime leader and McCulloch's own one-time commander in chief. Beyond that, he was not overawed by presidents. In 1960, one associate described him as a Nixon supporter, "but not a Nixon man." Nor was he close to either President Kennedy or Johnson.

Among congressional associates, McCulloch was extremely fond of the liberal Manhattan Congressman John Lindsay; indeed, one former McCulloch staffer suggests that McCulloch hoped to see Lindsay in the White House. He held Gerald and Betty Ford in highest esteem: Congressman Ford frequently visited McCulloch's office to consult on whatever matter, while McCulloch thought Betty Ford was simply one of the finest people he had ever known. Among government officials, McCulloch somewhat surprisingly thought most highly of the very liberal attorney general, Nicholas Katzenbach. Katzenbach once stated, "Bill McCulloch gave me the best compliment I ever had. He told me, 'You always kept your word.'" Asked why he regarded this as a considerable compliment, Katzenbach replied, "Because so did he."

The McCullochs had by this time changed residence in Piqua. Once their daughters were through college and securely launched into the world, the McCullochs sold their home on Caldwell Street. For a time, they rented the Marten House (known for its bird population) at 515 Downing Street. Then, they became long-term tenants of the apartment attached to the large home owned by Charles Upton at 424 Downing Street. The home had a local history. Originally modest, it had been acquired by Maurice Wolfe, who in 1914 founded what became known as the Meteor Motor Car Company, a somewhat unusual name for a firm that specialized in building hearses. Wolfe expanded the house into one of the most splendid in Piqua, wrapping the property with a cast iron picket fence, which had a separate entrance for the apartment. Maurice and his wife, Irene, were travelers and art collectors and the house showed off their holdings of European art. Following Maurice Wolfe's death, his widow married Charles Upton, who had been a major shareholder in Meteor. Upton was an example of a local boy who made good. As a young man, he joined the local French Oil Mill Machinery Company and despite a lack of formal education became its general manager in 1925 and, later, the first non-family member to serve as chairman of the board. He, like McCulloch, was community minded—an early city commissioner, chairman of the Piqua National Bank, and founding chairman of the local Dettmer Hospital. Irene was a principal figure in Piqua's Westminster Presbyterian Church, to which both the Uptons and McCullochs belonged. The two couples became close in time, and the McCullochs maintained the apartment as their Piqua residence throughout the balance of his congressional career.

None of which should obscure the fact that McCulloch was a man of considerable ambition. And here, he suffered two disappointments. One unrequited wish was to be chairman of the House Judiciary Committee, which could come to pass only if the Republican Party took control of the House of Representatives. When, following the special election of 1947, McCulloch was first sworn into office, Republicans were in control of the House. They were likewise in the majority in the 1953–1954 session, following Eisenhower's first election. Other than that, McCulloch's entire career was spent in the minority. His second unreached ambition was the governorship of Ohio. McCulloch, the reader may recall, was in the early 1950s bruited about as a gubernatorial candidate in the event that sitting Governor John Bricker resigned to take the never-offered post of commissioner of major league baseball. McCulloch, who had spent six terms in the state legislature, had a clear interest in being the state's chief executive. But, as he told one aide, "If I was going to run for governor, it would take a million dollars. How can I go raise a million dollars, because the people who could give me that kind of money are going to want something in return."

McCulloch's was a circumscribed world. It was an easy stroll from McCulloch's office in Room 2186 to the House Judiciary Committee in Room 2141. The 40-by-48-foot, high-ceilinged room was entered through a pair of matched wood-paneled double-doors, bearing a five-pointed star in their center panel. Across an expanse of deep blue carpet, Chairman Emanuel Celler sat in a raised-back chair near the center of the first of two rows of tiered seats. As ranking member, McCulloch sat on Celler's left. Chairman and ranking member were flanked by the committee's lead majority and minority counsel. (In 1967, McCulloch chose as Republicans' lead counsel a young attorney named John Dean, of whom more was to be heard later.) Committee members sat in the tiered seats behind a continuous table that carried a nameplate for each member. The rear wall featured a twelve-foot bas-relief of the Official Symbol of the United States, a bald eagle with the golden olive branch of peace in its left claw and golden arrows of war in its right. If need be, the room could accommodate one hundred spectators, in addition to whoever was testifying.

Physically, Room 2141 looks today very much like it did when Celler and McCulloch were its focus of attention. The meeting process, however, has changed considerably. Political writer Andrew Glass commented, "In those days, seniority was never breached. Congressmen like McCulloch or others were assigned to a committee and would slowly move up the seniority ladder, learning as they went and eventually becoming the ranking member." Washington attorney Benjamin Zelenko—then an attorney for the committee's minority—recalled, "The reality of the committee at the time was that nothing controversial could pass without GOP votes, which in practice meant without McCulloch's support. So there was nothing to be gained by picking a fight with McCulloch." A second attorney for the Republican minority, Thomas Mooney, recalled, "McCulloch was smart; crafty." After Mooney presented him with a brief on some matter, McCulloch would read it over and usually would make changes. "He would say, 'Tom, when I present this thing, if I convey the sense that I know the matter better than anybody else then there won't be any unnecessary challenges.' It would work. Congressmen didn't have the time to be experts on everything they might deal with."

The biggest difference, though, was that in McCulloch's day, the Judiciary Committee met in closed session. Minority counsel Franklin Polk noted, "When you have closed meetings, you needed one-third the staff that you have today." In closed meetings, he added, members "would talk frankly with each other about what their bottom line was. You didn't need formal speech in closed meetings. Today, with everything on the record, everyone has staff members present writing their statements."

The Judiciary Committee lawyers who worked with McCulloch had somewhat more mixed views of the congressman than did his office staff. Many congressional committee staffers were not attorneys; all judiciary staff members were. Some wished McCulloch to be more conservative, more assertive, and less deferential to Celler. Some detected a tension between McCulloch and Richard Poff (R-Virginia), perhaps rooted in the general view that, among committee Republicans, Poff had the more acute legal intellect. (Curiously, both Celler and McCulloch later signed a telegram recommending that then-President Richard Nixon appoint

Poff to the U.S. Supreme Court. This may have been in deference to mutual regard for Poff's legal skill, to a mutual desire to get him off the committee, or both.) The committee staff did not always believe they received the same level of consideration extended to office staff. One complained that McCulloch—who generally left Washington for Piqua on Friday mornings—would call the committee staff office at 5:30 p.m. to make sure people were still working. And more than one resented the expectation that they come in on weekends to stamp "From the Office of Congressman William McCulloch" on the mounds of *Congressional Record* reprints that the office sent out. On the whole, however, minority staffers seemed resigned to the notion that whoever had invented the job of congressional committee attorney had not been particularly concerned that it be a happy one.

Standing in Opposition

Nineteen-sixty-five is not best remembered as the year 169 congressmen moved their offices into the new Rayburn era. Rather, it was the opening session of the Eighty-Ninth Congress that, in terms of landmark legislation, was unmatched by nothing since the Depression-era "Hundred Days" Congress presided over by Franklin Roosevelt.

Commonly, liberals in Congress saw civil rights as a matter that headed a list of kindred, though perhaps lesser, initiatives. They were kindred in that what civil rights and the various measures that came to be associated with the "Great Society" had in common was an expanded view of the federal government acting to advance the general well-being. The civil rights movement was, at least by its supporters, held to be analogous to the antiwar, women's, and environmental movements, which adopted many of the civil rights movement's tactics and its general claim to moral sanction.

Bill McCulloch wasn't having it. Not the expansion of government. Not the analogy to other issues. For the congressman from Ohio's Fourth Congressional District, the movements for racial equality and for free and unfettered access to the ballot box stood apart from all other matters. Stood apart constitutionally. Stood apart morally. Stood apart in the consequences the civil rights movement carried for the American experiment.

That view placed Bill McCulloch apart from the general outlook of the Eighty-Ninth Congress, which convened on January 3, 1965, two months after Lyndon Johnson's epic trouncing of Barry Goldwater. The Johnson landslide had created with it overwhelming Democratic majorities—a 295–140 margin in the House, a 68–32 margin in the Senate—numbers that reduced the Republicans to the gray horizons of irrelevance. Further, in Lyndon Johnson, the country had a president as gifted in the arts of legislating as any since Franklin Roosevelt and likely more so. This Congress and that president came together at a time when public faith in the efficacy of federal power stood at its zenith.

In the liberal imagination, three books played peculiarly important roles in building the framework for expanding federal power. These, in turn, were *The Affluent Society* (1958), in which economist John Kenneth Galbraith contrasted what he saw as the private opulence and public squalor of American life; *The Other America* (1962), in which Michael Harrington grimly detailed how short of universal that affluence was; and *Silent Spring* (1962), by Rachel Carson, the founding volume of the environmental movement. What all three shared was the view that, within the general satisfaction of American success, vast problems existed, problems that could be effectively addressed only by an active and energized federal government. The public was broadly receptive. (An annual Gallup poll has long asked whether people are more concerned with "Big Government," "Big Business," or "Big Labor." In 2013, 72 percent of respondents named "Big Government"; in 1965, only 35 percent said so.) It was a unique moment of national self-confidence. America had defeated Nazism; had held back the Soviet tide; had, with the Marshall Plan, done much to rebuild Western Europe; and had conquered polio and others diseases. Standards of living were rising.

The mood of the times was aptly captured by G. Calvin Mackenzie and Robert Weisbrot in their book, *The Liberal Hour.*

> This was a liberal hour—a time in which government was in good favor with the American people, when Americans in unusually large numbers trusted the government in Washington to act responsibly on their behalf, when government seemed the proper repository for the nation's hopes, even its dreams.
>
> There appeared to be no limits. Lyndon Johnson told Congress, "For the first time in our history, it is possible to conquer poverty."

In rough, and taking a page from Mackenzie and Weisbrot, the core of the extensive legislative program Lyndon Johnson would present was a faith in "bureaucratic experts." In this, they resembled the "top-down" reformers of the Progressive Era in the early twentieth century, who put their faith in expert knowledge, in science, and in social sciences that were not perhaps all that scientific.

With the exception of race, most of these issues had not been inspired or energized by heavy citizen pressure on government. Robert Lampman, one of the creators of the federal anti-poverty proposals, noted: "The initiatives for a poverty program came from inside government. . . . They certainly did not come from well-organized pressure groups. . . . It was an elite group inside the Kennedy administration that started talking about this."

This, the authors add, became the model:

And so it was with more of the issues that came to define the policy corpus in the 1960s: The federal government was acting not as the agent of the American people responding to their demands, but as an independent force seeking to solve problems that its experts had identified and to which they had applied the tools of modern analysis.

Intellectually distant from this perspective was William McCulloch, who was deeply skeptical of what federal power could accomplish. One is reminded of McCulloch's words on the passage of the 1964 Civil Rights Act, when he stated that life was not changed by laws alone, but by how persons lived within those laws: "How do you tear hatred and suspicion out of the heart of a man? No statutory law can completely end discrimination. Intelligent work and vigilance by members of all races will be required for many years before discrimination completely disappears."

McCulloch, in the tradition of men like England's Edmund Burke and Ohio's Robert Taft, held that he who governed locally governed best. Speaking on voting rights, McCulloch told Congress that he believed "in the effective separation of powers and in a workable federal system." He did not believe in federal usurpation of state and local prerogatives. However, "when authorities fail to shoulder their obligations, and only stress their rights, it is the duty of the Congress to correct that wrong." This was so, he added, because under the Constitution the national government carried the responsibility to see that all citizens were treated equally. In a sense, McCulloch's position begged the issue. One could always argue on any question that state authorities were failing to meet some responsibility and that federal intervention was therefore justified. Indeed, this argument was commonly put forth to justify federal initiatives. For McCulloch, however—the one-time Jacksonville, Florida, attorney—race was different. The reality was not that local authorities were failing "to shoulder their obligations." The reality was that states and localities were using their authority to carry out a continuing criminal conspiracy whose sole object was to deny black Americans access to both the "pursuit of happiness" and the ballot box.

A sampling of votes makes clear Congressman McCulloch's doubts about the "Great Society."

On March 3, 1965, McCulloch cast a "no" vote on the Johnson-proposed Appalachian Regional Development Act. The act would provide $1.1 billion for infrastructure and other improvements in the eleven-state Appalachian region. The bill passed by a 257 to 165 margin.

On March 26, he voted against the Elementary and Secondary Education Act, the first major federal legislation to provide funds to K-12 schools. The bill passed 263 to 153.

On June 16, he voted against creation of a cabinet-level Department of Housing and Urban Development. The measure passed 217 to 184.

On July 28, 1965, he voted against a measure dear to the hearts of organized labor, that is, repeal of Section 14B of the Taft-Hartley Act, which authorized states to forbid union membership as a requirement for employment. Repeal passed anyway, by a 221 to 203 margin.

On September 15, 1965, he voted to kill a bill to create a National Foundation on the Arts and Humanities. The bill eventually passed.

On September 29, 1965, he voted against authorizing self-government for the District of Columbia. Here, too, he was with the minority, as the bill passed 227 to 174.

On October 7, 1965, he voted against authorizing $325 million to remove billboards from federal highways, a particular interest of Lady Bird Johnson. The measure passed easily, 245 to 138.

Indeed, on only one significant issue did McCulloch end up in the "Great Society" majority. That issue was how the nation was to respond, if at all, to the growing burden of health care on the elderly. Increasing medical capability and improving general standards of health led to increased lifespan. The cost of the health care that stemmed from and undergirded those increases consistently rose at a rate well above that of general inflation. The fear that a single major illness could decimate a family's life savings came to haunt the lives of many who were elderly.

Morris Udall, then an Arizona congressman, clearly stated the breadth of the problem in a March 31, 1965, newsletter to constituents. First, he reported, half of the 18 million Americans then over age sixty-five had annual incomes of less than $1,000 (all figures in 1965 dollars). The average for elderly couples was $2,530. Second, half of Americans over age sixty-five had assets of $1,000 or less. Yet, if a husband or wife was hospitalized, they could expect a medical bill exceeding $800. Third, persons over age sixty-five were three times as likely to be hospitalized. Further, their hospitalizations were likely to last twice as long. Fourth, hospitalization costs were rising—since 1950, the basic daily rate for an in-patient stay had increased 154 percent.

The Johnson landslide and the Democratic congressional majorities all but ensured that Congress would enact major legislation on health care, a Democratic Party agenda item at least since the presidency of Harry Truman. The basic Democratic Party approach grew out of a 1961 proposal, the Health Insurance Benefits Act (H.R. 4222), introduced by Representative Cecil R. King (D-California). This bill proposed amending the Social Security law to include federal payment for inpatient hospital services, skilled nursing home services, home health services, and outpatient hospital diagnostic services to anyone sixty-five or older who was covered by that law or under the Railroad Retirement Act. The bill carried a "prohibition against interference by any Federal official with the practice of medicine or in the selection, tenure, or compensation of any provider of services."

That disclaimer did little to allay the concerns of the politically

powerful American Medical Association (AMA). At the time, the AMA
trashed the proposal. If enacted, the bill would undercut community
support for health care facilities; discourage medical research; usurp the
"magnificent role" that fraternal and religious groups played in providing
indigent care; and cover millions of elderly who did not face financial
need, while not covering millions of younger people who did. Waxing
eloquent, the *Journal of the America Medical Association* stated:

Independence and self-reliance have been traditional traits of Americans. We [AMA] are
convinced that this is still true, and, accordingly we believe that personal health care is
primarily the responsibility of the individual. When he is unable to provide this care for
himself, the responsibility properly passes to his family, then to the community, then to
the state, and—when all these fail—to the federal government. It is now proposed that
we reverse this chain of responsibility, giving the Federal government first priority and the
individual last priority.

The AMA, however, was in something of a bind. Traditionally, that
body held the view that "one of the strongest holds of the profession on
public approbation and support has been the age-old professional ideal
of medical service to all, whether able to pay or not. The ideal is basic in
our ethics." By 1965, however, the AMA had accepted the basic political
premise that "you can't beat someone with no one." To avoid being cast
solely in a negative role, the AMA needed a program of its own to advocate. That proposal became known as "Elder Care." The federal role
was largely limited to providing matching funds to states to underwrite
the costs of providing private health insurance to the elderly. Individual
participation was to be voluntary. Those participating would be means
tested, with a sliding scale of support ranging up to full underwriting.
Program administration would be administered by individual states.

The proposal bore a fair appeal to McCulloch. The federal role was
largely as an underwriter. Expenditures were limited to those in legitimate need. Need would be met by subsidizing private health insurance.
Initially, McCulloch favored the Elder Care alternative, as did most of
his constituents who wrote to weigh in on the issue. A Lima voter wrote
to say she feared that the administration-backed Medicare proposal
would "not cover our needs and might even wreck Social Security as
it now stands." An Allen County Republican added, "We have plenty
of private medical insurance plans if an individual is willing to pay the
premiums. So why do we need a more inefficient plan operated by the
government." Another McCulloch constituent wrote, "The more I learn
about the Medicare Bill the more I am against it." While acknowledging that "medical, surgical and hospital care have become so costly that
many Senior Citizens are utterly unable to provide for it themselves and
most young people have so many obligations that it is increasingly difficult to help their parents," a young woman from Spencerville said she

"much preferred the Republican alternative." Indeed, on few issues was McCulloch's mail so one-sided.

The key vote came on April 8, 1965, with a proposal to substitute Elder Care for the administration proposal. While Elder Care drew the support of most Republicans and nearly three score Democrats, the effort to recommit the administration bill, thereby likely killing the measure, fell short, 236-191. With that defeat, McCulloch decided to back the administration's broader Medicare measure. Medicare was a "layered" bill that incorporated the basic framework of the 1961 bill described above; added Medicare B as a voluntary plan to cover physician services; and—reflecting the AMA's stated concern for the non-elderly indigent—added what became Medicaid. Better than one-third of Elder Care's supporters joined McCulloch in voting for the administration bill, which passed the House by a heavy 307 to 116 margin on July 27. Following Senate passage by a 70 to 24 vote, President Johnson signed the bill into law on July 30, 1965.

McCulloch caught a little hell for his vote. The legislative chairman of the Miami County chapter of the AMA wrote, "I have really been put on the spot in Miami County since it was made public that you voted in favor of the Medicare package. There have been some very bitter comments not only among the professional people, but from many of the patients regarding this particular legislation." He added that McCulloch would have been wiser to have announced in advance his intended vote and his reasons for it.

Congressman McCulloch did explain his vote in a letter to a constituent in Piqua, the week after Congress had acted.

I would like to say that my first and only important vote came to recommit the Administration's Medicare bill and to substitute the Republican bill therefore. I voted for that motion and we had some sixty or more Democrats join with us. We were outvoted and then the vote came on the bill. When I cast my vote the bill had more than enough votes to pass, and since the bill had some good provisions which I felt outweighed the bad provisions, I voted for it.

McCulloch's "yes, but" endorsement of Medicare stood as the major exception to his general opposition to "Great Society" legislation. Ironically, given his opposition to expanding the federal role, Medicare/Medicaid would in time become the most expensive federal entitlement program.

Whatever the controversy McCulloch's vote on Medicare may have prompted, it was nothing compared to the controversy he was about to enter. In 1966, Congress would tackle the question of open housing, the first civil rights initiative that was not targeted only at southern states. As North Carolina Senator Sam Ervin may have felt some satisfaction in observing, "For the first time, we have a bill which proposed that other than Southern oxen are to be gored."

CHAPTER 18

Open Housing, 1966

In his book *The American Presidency*, the British political theorist Harold Laski quotes John Stuart Mill on what a popularly elected legislature can and cannot accomplish. A legislature, Mill wrote, can criticize, can ventilate, can investigate, and can "provide a process of public education which is pivotal to democratic government." Still, Mill added, a legislature is too large a body with too many crosscutting concerns "to devise an original and unified approach to the problem of the time." A legislature, he added, could not "take a continuous initiative." A continuous or concerted initiative must come from a chief executive.

Lyndon Johnson was not a small figure, and is not likely to be judged a man of only small faults. But he was one thing. Johnson, despite declining popularity and the distraction of the Vietnam War, was and remained steadfast in his belief that the nation would continue to move forward toward a racially more just society. He did so even as those about him doubted the wisdom or practicality of the course. When Congress convened in January 1966, political scientist Steven F. Lawson wrote, "The president's aides held a generally gloomy outlook for legislative success in the coming year." Lawson noted that Henry Wilson, Johnson's legislative liaison, and Attorney General Nicholas Katzenbach both thought congressional support for civil rights was in decline. Of the various civil rights measures under discussion, the one that seemed likeliest of passage would make attacks upon civil rights workers a federal crime. Least likely of passage was broadly applied open housing legislation. Despite that lack of enthusiasm, when Lyndon Johnson delivered his State of the Union address on January 12, 1966, he stated he would press Congress to make it a federal crime to "murder, attack or intimidate either civil rights workers or others exercising their constitutional rights." Of larger consequence, Johnson added he would seek congressional action on open housing.

The issue of open housing fundamentally changed the civil rights equation. First, it moved the locus of conflict from the South to the

North. Northern states had not restricted the voting rights of blacks as Mississippi, Alabama, and other states had routinely done. But where housing was concerned, Chicago, Washington, D.C., and a great many other places were just as segregated as any southern city. Second, the change in direction was not simply geographic. The general thrust of civil rights legislation directed at the South was to ensure access to public functions—to the voting booth, to the jury box, to accommodations operated for the use of the general public. Many people, North and South, saw housing less as a public right than as a private domain. In the words of British Prime Minister William Pitt the Elder:

The poorest man may in his cottage bid defiance to all the force of the Crown. It may be frail; its roof may shake; the wind may blow through it; the storms may enter, and rain may enter—but the King of England may not enter; all his forces dare not cross the threshold of the ruined tenement.

In short, a man's home was his castle, to live in as he wished and to sell to whomever he chose. Among those holding this view were an easy majority of William McCulloch's constituents. The voters of Ohio's Fourth District had not necessarily supported their congressman in his civil rights activism of 1964 and 1965, but to a good extent they had respected it or at least tolerated it. Now, however, the prospect of the "king" attempting to cross the threshold of their "castles" brought a different response.

A Lima, Ohio, resident wrote in "to express my sincere and strenuous opposition" to the pending civil rights legislation. He added, "I am opposed to the trend towards liberalism and trust you will do all within your power to defeat the above resolution."

A "school librarian and landlord" from Kenton, Ohio, wrote, "If I choose not to rent to a Jew, a Catholic or a blue-eyed blond, that's my business. But if I refuse a Negro . . . it's a FEDERAL CASE and I'd have to prove that RACE was not the issue? WHY?"

A "citizen-homeowner" from Dayton wrote that the terms "fair or open housing" were a high-sounding but intentional mislabeling of the law's intent, which was "to single out all real estate owners for the sole purpose of discriminating against them by trespassing on their civil right to completely own real property."

A farmer from Conover reported that, for some years, he had been developing a substantial property near McCulloch's hometown of Piqua. In doing so, he said, "We have tried to be selective" of the persons to whom lots have been sold, an approach, he added, that had "helped to develop a high grade community. If the above mentioned becomes law, I would be forced to sell to anyone regardless, or withdraw this area from sales altogether."

But against these assertions there weighed one undeniable fact. In the words of NAACP Executive Secretary Roy Wilkins, "Residential segregation means segregation in schools, playgrounds, health facilities, and all other aspects of our daily lives."

Housing and Race

In his book on federal attempts to integrate the suburbs, Christopher Bonastia quotes an employee of the Federal Housing Administration (FHA) as stating in 1965: "Who are we kidding when we say—on the one hand—that minority groups 'prefer to live together'—and then proceed to utilize every device available in the market place to dictate that they do so?" Segregated housing was not simply the consequence of personal preference or individual racism; it was written into organizational standards and federal, state, and local law in dozens of ways. Segregated housing was a matter of local ordinance: Beginning in 1910, Baltimore designated all-white and all-black blocks. Virginia permitted local jurisdictions to do likewise; Richmond made it illegal for anyone to move onto a street where "the majority of residences on such streets are occupied by persons with whom said person is forbidden to marry." Since Virginia law did not permit interracial marriage, this meant in practice that no black person could move into a white-majority neighborhood. Other states followed.

Segregated housing was the policy of professional organizations, notably, of the nation's realtors. For example, in 1921 the Chicago Real Estate Board voted that any member who sold a home to a black family in a white neighborhood would be booted out of the organization.

Segregated housing was blessed by the Supreme Court. In 1926 in *Corrigan v. Buckley* the High Court unanimously held that racially restrictive covenants—that is, statements in housing deeds that placed racial restrictions on to whom the house could be sold—were constitutional. While the court granted "the constitutional right of the Negro to acquire, own and occupy property," it argued that that right did not provide any particular black persons with the constitutional power "to compel sale and conveyance to him of any particular property." In short, while blacks had the right to buy, whites had the right not to sell.

Segregated housing was reinforced by the nation's lenders. Commonly, neighborhoods were divided into four classes, designated by color on maps. Persons in the highest rated neighborhood had the easiest time gaining financing; those in the lowest rated had the most difficulty. On maps, the unattractive areas—which tended to be those in which any great number of black people lived—were colored red, a fact that led to the term "redlining." Segregated housing was unchallenged by the federal government. Bonastia states that the FHA closely linked itself with the developers, builders, banking, and real estate interests that institutionally created American housing. Such ties, he states, "also led the federal government to accept without objection the segregationist practices of the private sector."

So when the 1966 civil rights bill containing an open housing provision began its legislative journey before Subcommittee No. 5 of the House Judiciary Committee on Tuesday, May 3, 1966, passage of open housing was very much in doubt. Initially, the measure bore five parts:

• Title I and II combined to ban racial discrimination in selecting federal juries;

• Title III established new federal powers to enforce desegregation orders;

• Title IV made it a federal offense to discriminate in the sale or rental of housing;

• Title V made attacks upon civil rights workers a federal crime.

Passage of Title V was all but assured by one more self-defeating outrage from the South. On June 4, 1966, James Meredith, the first African American to attend the University of Mississippi, departed Memphis on a 200-mile March Against Fear to Jackson, Mississippi. His further purpose was to encourage voter registration. Twenty-eight miles into his pilgrimage, Meredith was shot in an ambush. His wounds were not serious, and Meredith was able to complete his journey to Jackson. His efforts were credited with prompting 4,000 African Americans to register to vote.

Controversy focused most strongly on Title IV, discrimination in the sale or rental of housing. In the second day of subcommittee hearings, Congressman William Cramer (R-Florida) pointed out to Attorney General Nicholas Katzenbach that the public accommodations section of the 1964 Civil Rights Act had excluded tourist homes and boarding houses—in what had become known as the "Mrs. Murphy's boarding house" exemption. Congressman Cramer sought a similar exclusion in the pending bill. Katzenbach said he had no objection to maintaining the exclusion. Chairman Emanuel Celler nodded his agreement. A perhaps more sharp-eyed reporter for *The New York Times* wrote, "If the five-room formula is incorporated into the fair housing law, it would exempt many duplex apartments and other units typical of the white suburbs that the law is designed to reach."

William McCulloch likewise had matters to raise with the attorney general, but his related to the proposed changes in jury selection. The proposal, McCulloch noted, would eliminate in federal courts the "blue ribbon" juries often assembled to hear cases involving antitrust, patent, financial, or other complex matters. The consequence McCulloch saw was that federal juries would become less qualified. Katzenbach brushed aside McCulloch's concern, saying he did not see how anyone could be harmed by having his case heard by "a fair cross-section of the community."

By the following Tuesday, Emanuel Celler had decided that Mrs.

Murphy might not be so benign a creature after all. He noted that if "Mrs. Murphy's" five-boarder rooming house was to be exempt, then a five-tenant apartment house had just as good a case for exclusion. Celler told one reporter, "If we are to strike down ghettos and raze slums, we cannot do it with half-hearted measures. In principle a five-tenant apartment house is not different [from] a five-boarder rooming house. Mrs. Murphy's boarding house must go if it involves discrimination." Several days later, Celler drew support from NAACP executive secretary Roy Wilkins, whose race might make him an unwelcome guest at Mrs. Murphy's. Wilkins stated, "Once Congress has recognized that housing bias worked harm to the national interest that it has power to prevent, it should do the job that needs to be done."

In the end, Subcommittee No. 5 recommended Titles I, II, III, and V to the full Judiciary Committee, but declined to take a position on Title IV, sale and rental of housing. This step—which William McCulloch termed "unusual and rare"—offended the Ohio congressman's procedural sensibilities, and he urged the subcommittee to take a position.

To the two hurdles noted above—that the 1966 bill would target North as well as South and that in addressing housing it was moving from the public to what many regarded as the private arena—a third obstacle must be added. That obstacle was the shrewd and garrulous senator from Illinois, Republican Minority Leader Everett Dirksen. The 1964 Civil Rights Act and the 1965 Voting Rights Act had secured the crucial, if belated, support of Senator Dirksen. It was taken as a given that no filibuster could be broken without Dirksen's backing.

On June 15, Dirksen emerged from a ninety-minute session with Attorney General Katzenbach to announce that nothing Katzenbach had said "alters my feeling that [the open housing section of the bill] can't be sold in the Senate." William McCulloch, attending the same session, was no more optimistic. The bill as drafted, he said, faced "real difficulty" in the House. Writing in *The New York Times*, E. W. Kenworthy quoted one Republican as saying that congressmen from both parties were "resistant to 'walking the plank' for the open housing provision if it were almost certain to be killed in the Senate." That plank was being greased by an aggressive lobbying campaign undertaken by the National Association of Real Estate Brokers (NAREB), which used its 83,000 members to bring to flood level the wave of anti-housing letters pouring in on congressmen.

McCulloch was getting coverage closer to home. On June 18, the *Dayton Daily News* drew a line between Dirksen's and McCulloch's reservations. The Ohio newspaper quoted the Piqua congressman that, unlike Dirksen, McCulloch saw nothing unconstitutional about the pending legislation. McCulloch said, "I do not and have not questioned the constitutionality. I think under current decisions and reasonings of the Supreme Court it would be constitutional."

Hearings continued before the full Judiciary Committee. Southerners won a small victory on June 27 when the full committee, by an 18 to 16 vote, adopted an amendment offered by George Grider (D-Tennessee) that civil rights workers would receive federal protection only if they were engaged in "lawful" activities. The following day, by an equally close margin, the committee voted 17 to 15 to retain the open housing provision of the bill. In 1964, committee moderates had narrowly staved off an alliance of strong liberals and committed conservatives, who wished to "strengthen" the then-pending bill to the point that moderates believed it would be impossible to pass. Now, a near reversal occurred. Liberal Democrats and conservative southerners joined to defeat a series of amendments the bill's moderate supporters felt were required if the measure was to pass the full House. One such temporizing amendment met with committee approval. Coming from William McCulloch, it exempted from the housing provisions of the law retirement homes operated by churches or fraternal organizations specifically for members of their own faith or organization. At day's end, Chairman Celler expressed something less than unbridled faith in the bill's prospects. The Brooklyn Democrat said he "was personally glad to see the bill intact but feared for its future in the present form."

That "present form," however, had less than twenty-four hours to live. Congressman Charles Mathias (R-Maryland)—a leading civil rights supporter and a close ally of McCulloch—concluded that the housing section as written stood no chance whatsoever of passage in the Senate. Mathias believed this view, widely shared in the House, would in and of itself lead to the bill's defeat in the lower chamber. Therefore, he huddled with Celler and McCulloch, chairman and ranking member, to devise a "softening" amendment to the bill.

The amendment Mathias offered softened things considerably. It reserved to the individual homeowner the right to sell his property to whomever he pleased and, further, allowed that homeowner to instruct his real estate agent as to the racial preference sought in a buyer. The amendment did not extend to "Mrs. Murphy's" boarding house or five-unit apartment complexes. Businesses—property developers, builders, and financial institutions—would still be covered. By general estimate, the proposal would exempt 40 percent of the existing homes in the country and a considerably higher proportion of white-owned, suburban, single-family homes.

According to Clarence Mitchell's biographer, Mathias sought the acquiescence of the NAACP's chief lobbyist.

Mathias knew the proposition was tough for Mitchell to accept because, after a long, dry century, the civil rights forces had experienced repeated victories. No one was in the mood to compromise much. To Mathias's relief, "Clarence looked at this proposal and realized, with his experience—a long familiarity with the way the Hill worked—that by adopting it we could get the bill passed and move it from the House to the Senate. That is exactly what we did."

Explaining his position, Mitchell said the opposition to any fair housing legislation was dividing the country by race and class. The "softened" version might not accomplish a great deal, but its defeat would only benefit those who had contempt for law and order.

The full Judiciary Committee endorsed the Mathias amendment by a 21 to 13 margin. Following a few incidental changes, the full bill cleared the Judiciary Committee by a 24 to 9 vote. The bill then moved to the House Rules Committee. With the House leadership applying the "three-week rule," the Rules Committee had until July 25, 1966, to report the bill to the full House floor for debate.

On July 15, William McCulloch formally announced his support for the amended bill. *The Washington Post* quoted McCulloch and Mathias as believing that the housing section "manifests a national moral standard, making it clear that the basic and continuing aim of the Republic—to secure the rights of all individuals—will be pursued in every essential element of American life." In phrases that sounded very like William McCulloch, the pair termed the pending bill "necessary but restrained, practical though moderate."

When, however, on July 26 McCulloch stood on the House floor to argue for the bill, he found himself standing on the defensive. Congressman John Dowdy (D-Texas) asked if McCulloch realized that "every bill we have passed on this question has increased the riots, the demonstrations, and looting which concern me just as much as they do my esteemed friend?" McCulloch responded that such behavior, if it continued, would undermine the very society that was the *sine qua non* of rights and equality. Congressman Joseph Waggonner (D-Louisiana) asked how McCulloch would explain the recent use of the National Guard in response to violence in Cleveland. Had National Guardsmen been needed, Waggonner asked, "because of discrimination in Ohio? Or is it because no progress has been made?" McCulloch responded that "among other things" unrest in Cleveland reflected "the three hundred years of the planned second-rate citizenship of great bodies of our people—not planned by people of goodwill but by those who would maintain the status quo forever."

McCulloch then outlined the bill, saying he would start "about midway" in the bill in describing its titles:

• Title V applied "effective criminal sanctions to all federally protected activities" described in the 1965 Voting Rights Act; in short, it would extend federal protection to those engaged in voter registration;

• Title VI—added to the original bill—would "facilitate the desegregation of public schools" through various forms of advice and financial support;

• Title I modernized the federal jury selection process;

• Title II provided "flexible remedies" to eliminating discriminatory jury selection in state courts;

• Title III—which McCulloch inexplicably skipped in his presentation; and

• Title IV represented "a new step to open many areas of our great and bountiful housing market to minority groups."

McCulloch was clear that he had saved for last the most controversial aspect of the bill. In arguing his case, McCulloch stated, "I believe that any fair-minded American would strongly uphold an equal right of any other American to purchase, lease, or occupy a home for his family." McCulloch quoted from the 1949 National Housing Act: "The Congress declares that the general welfare and security of the nation . . . require . . . the realization as soon as feasible of the goal of a decent home and a suitable living environment for every American family." He cited President Kennedy's Executive Order 11063, which aimed at the elimination of discrimination in federally financed housing.

McCulloch then asked rhetorically, what had caused the storm over Title IV in the pending civil rights bill. He believed public education about the bill had been biased and incomplete. He believed there had been an aura of secrecy about the bill's final submitted version, and this had added to unease. Finally, he believed the administration's submission of a bill that allowed no exemptions and its "subsequent unyielding position on [that] unrealistic proposal" had deepened public concern. This, he said, had complicated the task of reaching consensus on the more reasonable Mathias compromise. The current Title IV, he noted:

• Allowed the individual homeowner to sell his home twice in any six months, without penalty;

• Exempted owner-occupied buildings of up to four separate accommodations; and

• Exempted religious groups and fraternal organizations that provided housing exclusively for their members.

McCulloch noted that Ohio and nineteen other states had already enacted open housing laws. Many of these, he noted, allowed fewer exemptions than existed in the legislation now before the House.

Representative Basil Whitener (D-North Carolina) presented the argument for personal freedom. He quoted Supreme Court Justice John Marshall Harlan: "Freedom of the individual to choose his associates or his neighbors, to use and dispose of this property as he sees fit, and to be irrational, arbitrary, capricious, even unjust in his personal relations are things all entitled to a large measure of protection from government interference."

McCulloch sought support from a recent statement by James M. Rouse, one of the country's largest real estate developers. Rouse asserted

that most developers and homebuilders wished to operate in a nondiscriminatory market, "but are unwilling to do so for fear their particular
projects will be subjected to the abnormal pressure of a distorted market." He believed the preponderance of real estate developers and homebuilders would prefer to operate in a fully open market, but they "fear the
results of going it alone." McCulloch was immediately challenged in this
by Congressman Robert Ashmore (D-North Carolina) who said that the
views of "a few mammoth builders" like Rouse did not represent "the
will of the majority of the people who deal in real estate and who own or
sell homes or other real property in this country."

Among the few welcome words were those from Charles Joelson (D-
New Jersey), who welcomed the jury amendment provision of the bill.
Joelson stated, "We have only too often witnessed mockery of justice
when defendants charged with crimes against Negroes . . . have gone
unpunished in spite of overwhelming evidence against them."

The following day, Texas Congressman John Dowdy rose to repeat
his view that each successive civil rights bill had done less to solve the
problems than to exacerbate them. "Looking at recent history," he said,
"instead of bringing relief, the passage of each bill has only stepped up
such outrageous conduct, and in this instance the so-called civil rights
organizations have served notice—that this bill will not bring law and
order."

Meanwhile, the Mathias amendment, intended to create a defensible
middle ground, was causing instead a series of rifts. On the evening of
the just-cited House session, NAACP leader Roy Wilkins argued that
compromise "would exempt so many single-family suburbs that the suburbs would remain virtually lily-white and the center city ghettos would
become poorer, blacker, and more desperate than at present." The bill,
he said, ignored the realities by which bank mortgage-lending policies,
restrictive covenants, simple prejudice, and other factors "sidestep[ped]
the plain fact that twenty million Americans are cooped up and robbed
of their money and their manhood through iron-clad, profit-encrusted
real estate practices."

Nor were McCulloch and Mathias getting any help from their own
leadership. On August 1, the twenty-seven-member House Republican
Policy Committee—of which neither Mathias nor McCulloch was a
member—denounced the housing title as "politically motivated and unrealistic." Chairman John J. Rhodes (R-Arizona) stated, "Fair housing
solutions must be developed and carried out locally. Federal legislation
in this area should encourage and promote appropriate fair housing programs at the community level."

The nation's major unions were split. The United Auto Workers and
the United Steelworkers, the strongest union advocates of civil rights, attacked the amendment. The numerically far larger AFL-CIO endorsed it.

Even the House's small contingent of black congressmen was at odds. Robert Nix of Philadelphia, William Dawson of Chicago, and Charles Diggs of Detroit voted with Mathias. John Conyers of Detroit and Augustus Hawkins of Los Angeles County voted against.

Meanwhile, the National Association of Real Estate Brokers informed its membership that their efforts in opposition to the bill "had inspired a deluge of mail against Title IV in greater volume than any other issue in the memory of many senior members of Congress."

A member of McCulloch's staff at the time remembers the mail on open housing as heavy and almost universally opposed. Few shared the views of a resident of Dayton's integrated Dayton View neighborhood, "I know that the psychological impact of this on the middle class Negro family will strengthen their faith in America."

On August 8, Arch Moore (R-West Virginia) moved to recommit the entire 1966 civil rights bill to committee. Such a move would effectively kill the bill. Moore's motion was defeated by a margin of 222 to 190. McCulloch and Mathias were able to hold only 50 of the 136 Republican votes cast. Democrats split along regional lines: northerners opposed killing the bill by 160 to 24; southerners favored its demise by an 80 to 12 margin. Clarence Mitchell believed the Mathias amendment had salvaged the much-reduced bill. He estimated the amendment brought eighteen congressmen, sixteen of them Republicans, to oppose Moore's motion. Without those votes, the bill would have died by a 208 to 204 margin.

On August 9, the House overwhelmingly added—by 389 to 25—an "anti-riot" amendment that would make it a federal crime to cross an interstate boundary with the intention of fomenting riot or civil disturbance. That done, the House gave its approval to the full measure.

The bill, which had had an extended life in the House, survived only briefly in the Senate. Majority Leader Mike Mansfield (D-Montana) announced that Senate debate would commence on September 6. The filibuster began immediately. Soon thereafter, two attempts at cloture failed to draw the support of Minority Leader Everett Dirksen. While both attempts drew majorities, they fell well short of the two-thirds required. The votes were 54 to 42 on September 14, and 52 to 41 on September 19.

Coming on the heels of the great successes of 1964 and 1965, the defeat was a bitter pill. Some attributed it to northern whites' fear of open housing. Others cited the declining support for Lyndon Johnson as an individual and for the social engineering with which he was associated. Denton Watson, Clarence Mitchell's biographer, blamed the "fear of crime largely associated with urban ghettos and a breakdown of 'law and order'—all of which spelled *riots*." Mitchell himself offered a contrary view. The 1966 civil rights bill failed, he said, because the bill's advocates had not worked as hard for it as they had in the past.

With the end of the legislative battle, Congressman McCulloch found himself with fences to mend in Ohio. One unhappy Fourth District voter wrote in, "Republicans were dismayed that you sponsored the 1964 Civil Rights bill, which did seem to translate as more of a punitive measure against the states which voted for Goldwater than as a constitutional Civil Rights bill." It remained, the writer added, "INCOMPREHENSIBLE" to many Ohio Republicans that any representative of their party had voted for the 1966 bill.

A constituent from Troy, Ohio, wrote McCulloch that measures like open housing were destroying the nation's federal system by seeking to transfer power to Washington. Increasingly, the writer stated, the national government was "poking into our personal daily lives and dominating every aspect of government. This is wrong and you only have to look to those countries where central government is the strongest to see the chaos and misapplication of authority which can result."

Three days later, McCulloch wrote back to say that he believed "the federal government should not move into any field where there is authority for the state to act, *if the state did act.*" States had not acted to protect voting rights, so federal action was needed. Equating access to housing with access to voting, McCulloch noted, "some 18 to 20 states have passed legislation in this field [open housing] and if each one of the 50 states would as well, there would have been no need for any federal law."

Other voters failed to see civil rights and open housing as parallel concerns. A management consultant from Lima wrote to say, "Your leadership in Civil Rights was a commendable accomplishment. You have now lost your sense of fair play. Even though I am a Republican, my time and money will be contributed to your defeat in the next election."

That time and money was presumably directed at election day, 1966. That fall Fourth District voters would have a clear choice, though one that was something of an anomoly. The Democrat running against McCulloch, among the more conservative of Republicans, was challenging the incumbent from the right, attacking McCulloch for his support of civil rights and Medicare. Roger Milbaugh—who had lost to McCulloch in 1964 by 16,537 votes, the incumbent's closest race since 1948—was making a second attempt to defeat him. A Lima, Ohio, attorney, Milbaugh started early; beginning in March, he was making ten speeches a week. From the platform Milbaugh "assails Mr. McCulloch's leadership in the field of civil rights at every turn." Milbaugh charged that the civil rights law passed by Congress had been "unnecessary concessions to the rioters" and that the open housing provision for which McCulloch had fought was "evil [and] unconstitutional."

McCulloch was bidding for his eleventh term. His prominence in Congress cut both ways. A *New York Times* reporter noted that while many in the district took pride in McCulloch's national standing, others felt his focus on civil rights and other matters had detracted from the attention he paid his district. Likely, McCulloch was unruffled by the challenge. He attended his usual seven county fairs, spoke to his usual scores of civic clubs, and offered a willing ear to just about anybody willing to carry the conversation. More generally, the tide was flowing McCulloch's way. On November 8, 1966, Republicans gained forty-seven seats in the House of Representatives. When the enlarged cohort of 187 House Republicans assembled in January 1967, McCulloch remained amongst them.

Barely two weeks after the election, on November 23, McCulloch added a new constituent—his daughter Ann McCulloch Carver presented Bill and Mabel with their first grandchild. Named Elizabeth Wright Carver, she was born in Barnes Hospital in St. Louis. Congressman McCulloch was in Washington when his daughter gave birth and rerouted his travel to St. Louis to see the new addition and to ply the nursing staff with boxes of chocolates to ensure that mother and newborn would be well attended. Mabel McCulloch, who disliked flying, remained in Piqua. Four weeks later, however, both McCullochs and elder daughter, Nancy, went to share Christmas with the new family member.

CHAPTER 19

Riots, Report, and Open Housing

Shortly before 4 a.m. on Sunday, July 23, 1967, Detroit police raided an unlicensed club above a printing shop at Clairmount Street and 12th Street in the city's predominately black near west side. Rather than the smattering of late-hour drinkers they had anticipated, the officers walked in on a party for two men recently returned from service in Vietnam that had drawn eighty celebrants. For reasons not readily apparent, the police decided to take all those present into custody. During the time this took, a crowd gathered, a bottle was flung at a policeman and from this spark erupted America's largest civil disturbance in over a century. By late the following Monday, 483 fires were reported; 1,800 persons had been arrested.

Governor George Romney ordered in the Michigan National Guard and appealed to President Lyndon Johnson for federal troops. By Tuesday, 8,000 guardsmen and the first of an eventual total of 4,700 officers and men of the 82nd Airborne Division were in the city. The rioters were in no mood to be intimidated. Formal and informal authority had both broken down. For example, when Detroit Congressman John Conyers drove along 12th Street asking people to return their homes, his vehicle was pelted with rocks and bottles. Five days passed before the last of the military units were withdrawn. In all, 43 persons—33 black, 10 white— were killed, with 467 persons—including 250 Detroit police officers and firefighters—injured. Over 7,000 individuals were arrested and 2,000 stores looted or burned, with property damage estimated at between forty and eighty million in then-current dollars.

Detroit's was not the first major urban riot of the decade. In 1965, thirty-four people were killed during six days of disturbances in the Watts neighborhood of Los Angeles. Less than two weeks earlier, twenty-six persons had died in rioting in Newark, New Jersey. Dozens of lesser outpourings occurred. Detroit, however, was more startling, both for the great level of its violence and for what many felt was the improbability of that violence. Sidney Fine's book on the city and its riot carried the title *Violence in the Model City*. It was an encomium many felt well deserved. *The New York Times* reported that the city had "more going for it than any other major city in the north." Detroit had a substantial and prospering black middle class; it had elected two of the nation's four African American congressmen and twelve black representatives to the state legislature. Detroit had been a major recipient of "Great Society" funds, and its redevelopment efforts drew the sustained support of the United Auto Workers, the city's principal union, led by long-time civil rights activist Walter Reuther. The U. S. Department of Justice had identified Detroit as a "model for police-community relations." Just weeks prior to the riots, Detroit Mayor Jerome Cavanagh, the elected head of the national Conference of Mayors, had stated that his city's residents did not "need to throw a brick to communicate with City Hall." All this apparent success, however, had not succeeded.

President Lyndon Johnson spoke to the nation twice. He did so on July 24, the same day he ordered federal troops to Detroit. President Johnson said his action had been prompted by "proof of [Governor Romney's] inability to restore order in Michigan." Johnson had no wish to spare local authorities; at the time, it was generally known that Romney was considered a fairly likely opponent in Johnson's then-anticipated 1968 re-election effort. Beyond that, Johnson's remarks were predictable. Looting, murder, and arson would not advance the cause of civil rights. Lawlessness would not be tolerated. Detroit residents of all races were shocked by the criminality. Rioters should return to their homes. Only then, he said, could attention "be turned to the great and urgent problems of repairing the damage that has been done."

Even as the rioting continued, Lyndon Johnson turned his attention to that task. On July 27, 1967, he announced the formation of a special Advisory Commission on Civil Disorders. It would be chaired by Illinois governor Otto Kerner (and would be commonly referred to as the Kerner Commission), with New York mayor John Lindsay as vice-chair. The commission included five from outside the federal government: I. W. Abel, the strongly pro-civil rights president of United Steelworkers of American; Charles B. Thornton, chairman of the board of Litton Industries; Roy Wilkins, executive director of the NAACP; Katherine Graham Peden, the commissioner of commerce of the state of Kentucky; and Herbert Jenkins, the chief of police of Atlanta, Georgia. To these, Johnson added four members of Congress: Senators Fred Harris (D-Oklahoma) and Edward Brooke (R-Massachusetts), and Congressmen James Corman (D-California) and William McCulloch (R-Ohio). The body would reach a rough consensus on what ailed America; at the same time, it would paper over the gap between what most liberals and William McCulloch thought needed to be done.

To his commission, President Johnson directed three broad questions and a longer list of more specific ones. The broad questions were:

What happened?

Why did it happen?

What can be done to prevent it from happening again?

The president was not the only one asking questions or seeking answers. On January 11, 1968, Dr. Martin Luther King, Jr. spoke at Ohio Northern University in William McCulloch's own Fourth District. Located in Ada, Ohio, the university boasted the only school of law in McCulloch's district. The congressman was a regular visitor to campus, either to address its law students or to make use of its law library.

Speaking to a large gathering, Dr. King affirmed his belief that nonviolence remained the most potent weapon in efforts to combat racism. At the same time, he said, one should not ignore the legitimacy of the anger that led to rioting. A riot, he said, was "the language of the unheard."

[America] has failed to hear that the plight of the Negro poor has worsened over the last ten or twelve years. It has failed to hear that the promises of freedom and justice have not been met. It has failed to hear that large segments of white society are more concerned with tranquility and the status quo than about justice, equality, and humanity.

Dr. King closed his 5,000-word speech to the assembled students, faculty, and guests by quoting the words of James Russell Lowell, "Truth forever on the scaffold, wrong forever on the throne, yet the scaffold sways the future."

Violence v. nonviolence was part of the backdrop against which the Kerner Commission would work in preparing its report due in March 1968. The committee members travelled in pairs to sites of rioting and other inner cities; McCulloch teamed with California congressman James Corman. In a later interview, McCulloch told one Ohio newspaper, "I would say that while I have been generally familiar with some of the cities, I was shocked to see conditions in one or two that I visited. I mean that. I was shocked. I am now convinced it is the most difficult, deep-seated problem of the century so far."

The Kerner Commission established advisory panels, commissioned studies, assembled a staff of over one hundred, and heard witnesses ranging from FBI director J. Edgar Hoover to Dr. Martin Luther King. The charge was open-ended; so, apparently, were the funds to carry out whatever was recommended. On December 19, 1967, *The New York Times* reported that the Kerner Commission had decided "to recommend measures that it deems essential to racial peace and justice without reference to their cost impact on other political and economic demands on the nation's resources."

The Kerner Commission issued its report on February 29, 1968.

Of its 426 pages, one rather arguable statement became by far the most quoted: "Our nation is moving toward two societies, one black, one white—separate and unequal." Clearly, public schools and residential neighborhoods were nearly as segregated as they had ever been. But just as clearly, in the preceding five years the percentage of African Americans registered to vote in the South had doubled; the public accommodations aspects of the 1964 Civil Rights Act were broadly respected; the number of young black men and women enrolled in colleges, including previously segregated ones, had greatly increased. A more reflective statement might have suggested that America and Americans were rather fumblingly and with mixed intentions attempting to address the issue of race.

That well-known statement had the character of an indictment. Of whom, it soon became clear when *The New York Times* headlined a leaked copy of the report, "Johnson Unit Assails Whites in Negro Riots." The summary that followed was equally blunt: the commission had found no evidence that the riots were anything other than unplanned spontaneous outbursts—a point with which McCulloch fully agreed. What the commission had found, *The Times* continued, was that "the primary cause of last summer's riots was a massive failure of the white majority, through prejudice and neglect, to deal justly with the Negro minority." The second page of the commission's report phrased the matter somewhat more cogently: "What white Americans have never fully understood—but what the Negro can never forget—is that white society is deeply implicated in the ghetto. White institutions created it, white institutions maintain it, and white society condones it."

The eleven commissioners broadly agreed on the nature of grievances that were common to ghetto dwellers: lack of jobs, inferior education, and insufficient and often decrepit housing. Those were corporal grievances. Next were psychological ones. The frustrations of perceived powerlessness; the contempt with which largely white police forces treated ghetto dwellers in even the most routine of contacts; impatience, particularly among the young, that the civil rights movement had not yet borne greater fruit. Finally, there was the demographic underpinning. As whites left cities for suburbs, the urban tax bases upon which all municipal services depended went into decline, and the services with them.

The published report suggested the commission was unanimous about the needed response. Though named for the Illinois governor, it was New York Mayor John Lindsay who was the driving force behind its recommendations. For Lindsay, the problems of race and the ghetto could be addressed successfully only through the massive intervention of the federal government and federal resources, a "Great Society" approach but on a considerably larger scale. This included tripling the rate of construction of public housing; two million new jobs targeted at the inner city un- and underemployed; tax relief to finance job training;

re-training of urban police forces to make them more responsive to those they were sworn to protect and serve; and considerably more. One observer suggested the proposals implied a price tag of $30 billion a year for the foreseeable future.

It was quite a list and mostly a wish. Lyndon Johnson and his "Great Society" had passed their peak. As recorded by the Gallup organization, Johnson's personal approval rating had fallen from 70 percent in June 1965 to 46 percent two years later. A fair portion of the drop may be attributed to the Vietnam War, which had the secondary consequence of absorbing the federal revenues the Kerner Commission wished to earmark for urban redemption. Second, public attitudes were changing. Hardening. According to Gallup, in 1964 the number of Americans who traced an individual's poverty to circumstances outside his control was about equal to the number who blamed lack of initiative on the part of the individual. By June 1967, only 19 percent said circumstances were the cause; 42 percent cited lack of effort. Third, whatever the justice of the indictment of white society, whites as individuals were unwilling to admit, with Pogo, "We have met the enemy, and he is us." This was made glaringly clear in a 1967 poll conducted for the Republican National Committee. Asked if most blacks were law-abiding, a very high share—84 percent—agreed, or strongly agreed, against only 13 percent who dissented. But 52 percent agreed that riots were started primarily as an excuse to loot. Only 33 percent viewed riots as a form of "protest against the unequal opportunities of most Negroes." Most glaringly—given that evidence of maltreatment was overwhelming—only 11 percent agreed that the police "use too much force and brutality in handling Negroes."

The broad agreement reported by the commission covered a deeper and unpublicized divide that lay within. In rough terms, the commission included six "liberals": Governor Kerner, Mayor Lindsay, Senators Brooke and Harris, the NAACP's Roy Wilkins, and Atlanta police chief Herbert Jenkins. Ranged against them were five "conservatives": United Steelworkers president I. W. Abel, Charles Thornton of Litton Industries, Kentucky commerce commissioner Katherine Graham Peden, and Congressmen Corman of California and McCulloch of Ohio.

A *New York Times* article published after the report was issued touched on the divide. On the one hand, the liberal faction had intended to push for a "guaranteed annual income," but had backed off when faced with conservative opposition. For their part, when the conservatives "began to read the full text, and see the breadth and scope of what they we're saying, they began to worry whether they could sign the report." Reporter Steven Roberts added, "In general, the commission decided to recommend what should be done, rather than what the members thought could be done under political circumstances, but the problem of money was never far away."

Implemented or not, the Kerner Report stood for decades as the quasi-official view of liberal Americans. The report was not without its critics. As Geoffrey Kabaservice noted:

Robert W. Gordon, reviewing the report in the Ripon Forum, felt that its aim was to establish a consensus for massive urban investment by forcing white people to guiltily confront their own racism. Gordon criticized this tactic on the ground that many whites would resent being labeled as racists, and felt that the report emphasized the gulf between whites and blacks instead of trying to close it.

McCulloch in no way disputed the severity of the problem. Interviewed by the *Cincinnati Enquirer* days after the report's release, McCulloch said he had become convinced that America's racial troubles would not be settled "in a month or in five years or in a decade. . . It's going to be with your grandchildren." He called particular attention to the sense of isolation within which the inner city poor lived: "There is a notorious lack of communication in nearly every city. It is almost impossible when you're living deep in the heart of the ghetto to get your grievances heard by responsible public officials." And he shared the view that white society was culpable: "There is white racism probably to some extent in every sector of America."

But McCulloch, as ever, was doubtful of the efficacy of massive federal undertakings. Indeed, he likely shared the view stated by Mackenzie and Weisbrot in *The Liberal Hour*, "In his rush to sell a long list of legislative goods to the American people, Lyndon Johnson had over-promised. He would end poverty in his time, conquer bigotry, heal the sick, teach all the young, provide for the aged, and so on." In some measure, the Great Society had raised expectations government could not fulfill. By another measure, it had acted with an unearned confidence in its own wisdom. As noted, the Kerner Report called for a great increase in the construction of public housing units. Much such construction—like Pruitt-Igoe in St. Louis, and Cabrini Green and the Robert Taylor Homes in Chicago—was of high-rise apartment complexes physically disengaged from the surrounding city, fatherless compounds supported by welfare checks and visited principally by caseworkers. Eventually, these three projects, 43,000 individual housing units in all, were dynamited to the ground as unlivable.

In an apparently unpublished essay written soon after the issuance of the Kerner Report, McCulloch begins by acknowledging:

Police forces routinely harass citizens while ignoring flagrant housing code violations. . . .

Mass joblessness in inner cities co-existing with a national shortage of skilled personnel. . . .

Inadequate municipal services, while the "welter of state and federal programs" intended to aid cities are bound up in "needless and frustrating jurisdictional wrangling. . . .

McCulloch at length restated his view that anyone believing that violence would bring a more just society was simply destroying the basis of
any society that could make good on a promise of justice. Still, he accepted as the riot's root cause "the continued unwillingness of too many
white Americans to admit the Negro citizen to full citizenship."

Let us admit to ourselves that, until relatively recently, we tolerated or ignored racial in-
sults, almost as a matter of routine. It was not so many years ago, for example, that white
and Negro witnesses in the courts of several states took their oaths on separate copies of
the Holy Bible.

McCulloch described the need for better education, better housing, better policing, but added, "What is often overlooked is the fact that
many of the vital steps toward more peaceful and prosperous cities do not
involve spending more money." Such steps, he said, as fair representation
of minorities in elected and advisory bodies; an honest effort at addressing citizens' grievances against the police; easier communication between
those who feel discarded and those who seemed to hold the cards—none
required major outlays of funds for success; indeed, in McCulloch's view,
the reliance on major outlays made success far less likely.

McCulloch noted, regarding police-community relations, that the
Kerner Commission had founded far less evidence of direct brutality than of continuing contempt. He wrote: "It is a paradox that this
problem—which is apparently so common—is one that should be easiest
to eliminate. In 1968, it should not be difficult to convince police officers that Negroes should not be addressed differently than whites when
stopped on the street."

The task, he asserted, was not one for government alone—but for
private enterprises, churches, labor unions, foundations, universities, and
all other institutions of society. He closed, "Only the determined will of
the most powerful and wealthy and most resourceful nation in history can
assume the wholehearted and sustained commitment that will be needed
to preserve the peace of our cities and shape their future in accordance
with the best traditions of America." Whatever its ambiguities, the Kerner Commission would have at least one influence on Congress. While the
commission was meeting, discussing and writing its report, Congress was
tackling again the bristly subject of open housing.

During Johnson's State of the Union address given on January 17,
1968, Congress fell largely silent when he mentioned his civil rights agenda, although meeting the needs of riot control garnered hearty applause.
Despite the absence of congressional enthusiasm for his civil rights proposals, the president persisted. Then, in his January 24 civil rights message to Congress, he argued for a fair housing bill because such legislation
"is decent and right." He also argued that "the criminal conduct of some

must not weaken our resolve to deal with the real grievances of all those suffering discrimination."

No particular reason existed for believing open housing would find easier sledding in 1968 than it had in 1966. For one thing, the civil rights coalition that had worked so effectively in earlier years was splintering. In April 1967, Dr. Martin Luther King, Jr., dramatically declared his opposition to the war in Vietnam in a speech entitled "A Time to Break Silence," delivered at Riverside Church in New York City. Based on his opposition to the war, it became King's stated intention to oppose Lyndon Johnson's reelection as president. Among younger cohorts, leadership of the Student Nonviolent Coordinating Committee went from John Lewis, pledged to nonviolence, to the far more militant Stokely Carmichael in 1966 and H. Rap Brown the following year. NAACP lobbyist Clarence Mitchell—essentially the man in the middle—thought King was monstrously misguided in attacking the best president black Americans had had in a century and thought the militants to the left were self-indulgent posturers for the media. And, of hardly lesser importance, Lyndon Johnson's powers as president grew weaker by the day.

Action in Congress

Two matters require clarification. Legislatively, the 1968 civil rights effort began with the Senate taking up H.R. 2516—the bill to provide protection to civil rights workers, which was passed the previous fall by the House but not by the Senate. Majority Leader Mike Mansfield announced that H.R. 2516 would be the upper chamber's first order of business once it convened in 1968, to be acted upon by the Senate Judiciary Committee. Concurrently, the Senate Housing and Urban Affairs Subcommittee held hearings on a prospective open housing provision that might be added to the House-passed measure. On January 25, 1968, Judiciary Committee member Sam Ervin (D-North Carolina) moved to strike the phrase "race, religion, color or national origin" from H.R. 2516. In effect, Senator Ervin's amendment, by protecting "everyone from everything" rather than the civil rights workers the bill intended to defend, would have left the bill meaning not much of anything. With surprising ease, the Senate tabled the Erwin motion by a 54 to 29 vote.

Civil rights supporters believed that, as any civil rights bill faced a southern filibuster, one might as well fill a single bill with everything one wanted. Open housing was by far the most important possible provision. With that in mind, Senators Edward Brooke (R-Massachusetts) and Walter Mondale (D-Minnesota) then moved to attach the open housing provision they had been preparing. Their proposal, though it excluded from coverage 5.5 million owner-occupied "Mrs. Murphy" units of up to four units, was considerably broader than the bill that had failed to pass in

1966. The case for open housing was underscored by testimony, presented to the Senate hearings, that between 1960 and 1965, one-half to two-thirds of all new homes and factories in the nation (excluding the South) had been built in the suburbs. In short, housing and jobs were moving to the suburbs; segregation prevented black citizens from following them.

When Majority Leader Mansfield moved to adopt the Brooke-Mondale amendment, a filibuster ensued. On February 20, the Senate voted 55 to 37 to end debate, a strong majority but not the necessary two-thirds. What is striking, as Jean Eberhart Dubofsky noted in a law review article, was that in 1966 there had been only 52 votes for cloture on a bill that would apply to just 40 percent of the nation's housing. Now, there were 55 for a bill that applied to 97 percent. Interesting, too, is that Republican senators in 1966, Minority Leader Everett Dirksen among them, had opposed cloture by a 20 to 10 vote. Now, they supported it by 19 to 17—a fact that left their leader, Dirksen, somewhat uncomfortably in the minority of his own party. At which point, Senator Dirksen changed his mind, telling the Senate:

It will be an exercise in futility for anyone to dig up the speech I made in September 1966 with respect to fair housing in which I took the firm, steadfast position [that it fell within state rather than federal jurisdiction]. One would be a strange creature indeed in this world of mutation if in the face of reality he did not change his mind. . . .

Dirksen added, "I simply state that I believe this proposal constitutes a very important step forward in the cause of human brotherhood." Dirksen spoke on February 28, 1968. That same day in the House, William McCulloch rose to announce the pending delivery of the report of the Kerner Commission, whose members, he added, "fervently hope . . . will bring closer to reality the pledge of social justice and domestic tranquility that are the essence of our democracy."

Dirksen, as ever, had an amendment. But the one he offered was far more limited than civil rights supporters had feared. Under his amendment, the only homes not to be covered by the legislation would be single-family dwellings that were offered for sale "by owner," without the employment of a realtor. This, and the Mrs. Murphy exclusion described above, meant that 80 percent of the nation's housing would still be covered. On March 4, by the narrowest of margins—65 Ayes, 32 Nays—the Senate voted to end debate of an open housing amendment. Such bipartisan support had been spurred in part by the release of the Kerner Commission Report on Civil Disorders, which cited housing discrimination as an underlying cause of racial unrest in the nation's cities.

On March 11, the Senate approved the full bill by a decisive 71 to 20 margin. As passed, the bill called for a phased implementation:

• Effective immediately, racial discrimination in rental or sale was banned in federal housing or multi-unit housing that had received federal funds;

• Beginning December 31, 1968, discrimination was banned in multi-unit housing and housing developments, but not in owner-occupied dwellings of four units or less;

• Starting on January 1, 1970, discrimination was banned in all single-family homes represented for sale by a realtor. Persons selling their own home could continue to discriminate, but could not advertise that fact.

Action in the House

The House of Representatives now found itself in a somewhat peculiar position. The previous fall, it had passed and sent to the Senate a relatively modest bill extending the protection of the federal government to civil rights workers. Now, the Senate had returned the bill—having added a groundbreaking open housing provision and lesser provisions.

Judiciary chairman Emanuel Celler, wholly in sympathy with the Senate's actions, sought the unanimous consent of the House to accept the Senate amendments in toto. Southern members were not in an assenting frame of mind, so the bill was steered to the House Rules Committee, which began hearings on March 28.

Then, lightning struck. Twice.

First, on March 31, 1968, President Lyndon Johnson told a largely astonished nation that he would not be a candidate for reelection that fall.

Second, on April 4, a bullet from a high-powered rifle tore through the face of Dr. Martin Luther King, Jr., as King stood on a motel balcony in Memphis, Tennessee, where he had gone to lend support to a strike by local sanitation workers. Almost immediately, one hundred American cities experienced outbreaks of riot, arson, and looting; one of those most strongly affected was Washington, D.C.

The following day, twenty-one congressional Republicans—including Ohio's William McCulloch, Robert Taft, Jr., and Charles Whalen—sent their colleagues a letter urging immediate adoption of the unamended version.

Events moved with considerable speed. On April 8 in the House, Minority Leader Gerald Ford pledged to NAACP lobbyist Clarence Mitchell that while he, personally, would not support the Senate-passed bill, he would not ask any fellow Republicans to join him in opposition. Ford was being pressured by New York governor Nelson Rockefeller and Richard Nixon—the two likeliest Republican candidates for president that fall—to accept the Senate version as written. Nixon, though he came to support open housing, regarded the matter as secondary. In his view, 95 percent of the nation's black population would not benefit from the law as they lacked the financial means to purchase homes in the suburbs. He thought focusing on the economic progress of minorities would clearly pay greater dividends.

On April 9, the Rules Committee, acting with uncommon haste, voted 8 to 7 to send the bill to the House floor, *with* the recommendation that the Senate amendments be accepted. The deciding vote was cast by Robert Anderson (R-Illinois), a previous opponent of the measure. That vote came just as Dr. King was being laid to rest.

When House debate opened on April 10, opponents of the bill, though much subdued, were not yet giving up. John Ashbrook (R-Ohio), the only member of the Ohio delegation to have voted against the 1964 civil rights bill, decried what he termed "the Reichstag-type rubberstamp process" and concluded, "The whole concept of freedom and private property are at stake here." One Louisiana congressman asserted:

I have more Negro friends than all of you put together and the truth is the vast majority of Negroes in this country are decent law-abiding citizens. But what is happening here today? We are ignoring that the 90 percent of the white people and the Negro people who are decent, law-abiding citizens, and we of this Congress, you and I, are being black-mailed by the minority of 10 percent.

But the tenor of the day belonged to the recent convert, John Anderson, and to long-time mainstay, William McCulloch. Congressman Anderson, responding to that comment, stated, "It is unfortunate that the idea has gained currency that in acting today on civil rights the House is doing so in a miasma of fear and unreasoning haste. . . . In voting for this bill I seek rather to reward and encourage the millions of decent, hard-working, loyal, black Americans who do not riot and burn." Anderson's young daughter, listening from the gallery, told a reporter, "That man's not my daddy. That man's angry."

William McCulloch, the representative from the Fourth District of Ohio, spoke at length. He quoted extensive passages from the recently released Kerner Report, and added:

Discrimination prevents access to many non-slum areas, particularly in the suburbs, where the good housing stock exists. In addition, by creating a "back pressure" in the racial ghettos, it makes it possible for landlords to break up apartments for denser occupancy, and keep prices and rents of deteriorated ghetto housing higher than they would be in a truly free market.

Man can be imprisoned outside of jails. The ghetto dweller knows that. The Negro knows that he is caged, that society really gives him no place else to go. Of course, the bill would not buy, for the prisoner, a fine home in the suburbs. But it would offer the prisoner the hope that if he tried to climb the economic ladder, society would not be forever stamping on his hands.

McCulloch added:

> If the prisoner were given access to a better home, he would then have access to a better education for his children. Then his better-educated children would have access to better jobs. And then, like all other minority groups, the Negro would have won his equality through economic power. The great American dream would, for him, in part come true.

He added that he did not regard the Senate-passed version as perfect, but thought that any effort to improve upon it now was likelier to delay action than to produce a better result.

Before any vote was taken, William McCulloch received a rare tribute from Representative Fred Schwengel (R-Iowa). Representative Schwengel began by noting that since 1865, Congressional leadership on civil rights had come from the Judiciary Committee. While, he added, "due tribute" had been paid to that committee's chairman, Emanuel Celler, he wished to call attention to "the magnificent record of the minority leadership, Mr. William M. McCulloch." He praised McCulloch as not only a great lawyer, devoted to law and one whose counsel was freely sought, but as "one of the greatest legislators of all time."

> Often marble monuments are built to our great men . . . but the most important monuments as stated so well by Sandburg when he spoke of Lincoln, "are built in the hearts and minds of Americans who are the beneficiaries of human rights legislation and from this legislation we again learn that whenever you give rights, opportunities and advantages to people that are not enjoyed by all the people, not only do the disadvantaged people benefit, but the Nation benefits and the great ideals that we espouse become even greater."

Undeterred by McCulloch's admonition against delay or Representative Schwengel's praise of McCulloch, Minority Leader Gerald Ford now moved to send the bill to a House-Senate conference, thereby delaying and possibly foreclosing action. Congressman Ray Madden (D-Indiana) offered a substitute motion that the House accept the Senate version as amended. A roar went up from the galleries as his motion was approved by a 229 to 195 margin. The House would not countenance delay. In partisan terms, 152 Democrats and 77 Republicans opposed sending the bill to conference; 108 Republicans and 87 Democrats supported the move. Ironically or not, the House voted in a building physically surrounded by troops rushed to the city the previous week to help quell the disorders following Dr. King's assassination. The Madden motion was the deciding vote. Final passage came by a margin of 250 to 172, with 23 Republicans who had voted for a conference committee reversing themselves to support the final bill.

The Fair Housing Act (formally, Titles VIII and IX of the 1968 Civil Rights Act) prohibited discrimination in the sale, rental, financing, or advertising of homes (with the exception of homes sold directly by their owner-occupier). Integration, however—particularly of residential suburban housing—proceeded slowly. First, as noted, relatively few black families had in 1968 the financial resources to purchase homes in the middle-class and affluent suburbs. Second, the Fair Housing Act itself lacked clarity. As Marcus D. Pohlmann and Linda Vallar Whisenhunt wrote in their guide to civil rights legislation, "Although the law prohibited a number of discriminatory practices, including blockbusting, it failed to specify its aim, whether to attack bias or to integrate white suburbs. The 1968 act provided little in the way of enforcement, aside of litigation by the Justice Department." They further noted, "Individuals had to file suit themselves and then had the burden of proof, even though such discrimination is often subtle and hard to pinpoint."

CHAPTER 20

The Electoral College

Author's note: In 1969, William McCulloch occupied himself with two major tasks. The first was to seek a constitutional amendment to eliminate the Electoral College. The second was to extend the term of the 1965 Voting Rights Act, set to expire in 1970. While these efforts crisscrossed in time, they did not interact with or materially affect each other. For clarity's sake, they are presented here in separate chapters.

The April passage of the 1968 Open Housing Act completed a trio of landmark bills. It stood with the Civil Rights Act of 1964 and the Voting Rights Act of 1965 as heralds of a better day for all Americans, black and white alike. Passage of the Open Housing Act should by rights have stood as a high point in America's public history, but that seminal event was soon lost in the national summer of discontent.

Of the causes, two stood out. The first was the continuing conflict in Vietnam—an aching frustration for Americans; a frustration that was felt both by those who did not understand why America could not push through to victory and by those who believed the war was a catastrophic misuse of American power. The second was a newly seething anger in the ghettos of America's major cities, where the promises encased in the civil rights acts appeared to be promises unkept. If the April assassination of Dr. Martin Luther King, Jr., was emblematic of the second, the June assassination of presidential aspirant Senator Robert Kennedy was emblematic of the first.

The divide widened: on Vietnam, it was between those who supported American policy in Vietnam, and those who were appalled by it. On race, it was between those who believed "blacks were moving too fast" and blacks who felt hardly any movement at all. The Democratic Party split over the war in Vietnam, and for that and other reasons emerged the potent third-party candidacy of Alabama governor George Wallace. Wallace, often viewed simply as an entrepreneurial racist, represented both those who felt their ways of life, their jobs, and neighborhoods were being sacrificed by white liberals to black progress, and those who felt the federal government had become an instrument less "of" the people than one used against them. Of 1968, columnist David Broder, one of the most moderate of men, later said, "It was the first time I ever thought the country might actually be coming off the rails."

For the Democrats, matters came to a head at the August 1968 Democratic National Convention in Chicago, where police battled protesters in the streets and over 1,000 were injured. Among those at that scene was Thomas Pew. Pew was then the twenty-nine-year-old editor of the *Troy [Ohio] Daily News*, published for a readership far more conservative than he was. He had taken a tour of Vietnam, writing feature stories about the young local men serving there. He concluded the war was "not only wrong; it was hopeless." Post-convention, Pew wrote a series of editorials broadly condemning the tactics used by the Chicago police. The account advanced by Chicago Mayor Richard J. Daley, he wrote, was "a total lie."

Soon thereafter, Pew attended a town hall meeting in Troy. Congressman William McCulloch was also attending. One pro-war audience member led Pew over to the congressman to ask rhetorically, "Have you read what this guy wrote about Chicago? What do you think of that being published?" McCulloch, in a crowd that was short on sympathy with editor Pew, replied, "I have read it; I think it was 100 percent accurate." Pew's reaction was, "I had just this huge respect for McCulloch"—who, Pew noted, had nothing to gain with most in the crowd by coming to the defense of the anti-war editor.

The conflict, of course, had reverberations far beyond Troy. Coming out of the convention, eventual Democratic nominee Hubert Humphrey faced a divided party and donors whose arms were not long enough to reach their checkbooks. Four weeks before the voting, a *New York Times* survey reported that Republican nominee Richard Nixon was leading in thirty-four states, George Wallace in seven, and Humphrey in just four, with five undecided. And this brought on a new fear—all but universally among political commentators and even among many private citizens. To gain election, a candidate must receive a majority of the 538 electoral votes whose casting would be determined by Election Day. If no candidate achieved a majority, the choice of president would fall to the House of Representatives. In that body, each state would cast a single vote, with a majority of state votes required for election. States with an even number of representatives —like Connecticut with four, Maryland with eight, and Missouri with ten—might find their delegations evenly split and thus unable to cast a vote. Consequently, it was possible that no candidate would receive the required state majority. Governor Wallace was not shy in suggesting that at this point some interesting political discussions might be held.

As Election Day neared, the central question was whether any candidate would receive the required 270 votes. This possibility dimmed as a pro-Humphrey surge in the campaign's final month flipped a number of states to his candidacy, narrowing the prospective electoral margin. In the end, those who feared an election determined in the House breathed a sigh of relief. Richard Nixon's total of 301 electoral votes was 31 more than the minimum required. Humphrey ended with 191, Wallace with 46. Still, Nixon carried Ohio and Missouri by a combined 111,000 votes out of 5.8 million cast. Had the Humphrey surge been only slightly stronger, Nixon's total might have dropped to 263 and the outcome would have been anybody's guess.

All of which explains why, when the Ninety-First Congress convened in the New Year, the highest item on the agendas of both judiciary chairman Emanuel Celler and ranking minority member William McCulloch was the reform of the electoral college.

Electoral College Reform Hearings

Six weeks after Richard Nixon's election, William McCulloch wrote Bryce Harlow, a senior Nixon advisor, a six-page letter on matters the new administration needed to address. McCulloch called for reform of the nation's bail bond system; judges, he wrote, routinely set high bond requirements that constituted a *de facto* punishment of persons not yet found guilty of any wrongdoing. He noted that while federal judges guilty of misconduct could be impeached, this rarely occurred. What was needed, he said, was some sanction short of impeachment to be employed when judicial misbehavior—serious but not of an impeachable nature—occurred. He urged creation of a commission to determine whether existing antitrust law was indeed effective at countering the over-concentration of economic power. The highest item on McCulloch's list, however, was the need to reform the Electoral College.

That issue came to dominate McCulloch's efforts in the opening months of the 1969 session of Congress. In this, he acted broadly in tandem with judiciary chairman Emanuel Celler. On February 5, 1969, Celler opened the congressional hearing on reform of the Electoral College by acknowledging that those seeking change "bore the burden of overturning a longstanding tradition." This, he said, was less important than the fact a possible "vacancy of uncertain duration in the principal office in this Government poses a substantial danger."

To initiate debate, Celler had introduced two resolutions:
• House Joint Resolution 179, which would abolish the Electoral College and replace it with a single national election, decided by popular vote;
• House Joint Resolution 181, which would retain the Electoral

College, but in the event an election was thrown into the House of Representatives, voting would be done not by individual state but by every U.S. representative. This, he noted, was the procedure recommended by President Johnson.

Beyond his own proposals, Celler acknowledged that a number of others had come forth. These, broadly, fell into four categories. The most common simply called for the election of the president by direct popular vote. Others called for eliminating the office of electors, but assigning one electoral vote to the winner of each congressional district, with the statewide winner getting two "bonus" votes for the senators counted in each state's electoral total. Another called for recalibrating the electoral votes to match the percentage vote each party candidate had received. Finally, there were advocates of holding national political party primary elections, followed by an election between the candidates those primaries designated. In the event of a three-way run, a candidate must gain 40 percent of the vote to be the winner. Otherwise, a runoff between the top two candidates would be held.

Celler posed a series of questions. Should Congress play a role in eliminating voter fraud and intimidation? What plans would cause small or large states to gain or lose power? Would direct popular election give too much power to the news media in determining the outcome? Would a national election require national voter laws that would invade state prerogatives? If run-off elections were established, would voters be encourage to cast "protest" votes for minor candidates on the assumption that they would have another opportunity to make their vote "count"? Might the district plan promote "gerrymandering" of districts to gain electoral advantage? Celler concluded, "I have not yet determined which electoral method or what type of reform is suitable or appropriate."

McCulloch had. He was an advocate of the direct popular vote election of the president. For purposes of debate, McCulloch introduced three proposals: one that assigned electoral votes by congressional district; one that assigned electoral votes in proportion to the popular vote in each state; and one that called for election by direct popular vote. McCulloch stated that whatever plan was adopted should address the seven inadequacies he had identified in the current system.

• First, the current system allowed a candidate with fewer popular votes than another candidate to win. This had happened with Adams beating Jackson in 1824, Tilden beating Hayes in 1876, and Harrison beating Cleveland in 1888. (And, more recently, with Bush defeating Gore in 2000.)

• Second, the electors served no useful function. McCulloch noted that as long ago as 1826, Senator Thomas Hart Benton observed that the electors "have degenerated into mere agents, in a case which requires no agency."

• Third, having the House vote by state was inherently undemocratic.

• Fourth, the Electoral College turned each state into a "winner-take-all" contest. This, McCulloch argued, promoted voter fraud in states with a near-equal partisan balance; left minority party voters in "one party" states without any influence; and in "safe" states detracted from the public's interest in taking part.

• Fifth, less populous states were able to cast disproportionately more votes than more populous ones.

• Sixth, as the Tilden-Hayes election of 1876 had demonstrated, the present system had no "fail safe" device.

• Seventh, under the current system, the election was not determined until the Electoral College met in December. No provision existed as to what would happen if the presumptive president died in the interim between the November election and the December Electoral College meeting. In closing, McCulloch asserted, "The seven failings indicate that reform is necessary. The disease is clear; the remedy is not." His intent, he added, was to formulate a plan that will last for centuries.

That striving received no particular support from the executive branch. On February 24, President Richard Nixon wrote the committee, "I have not abandoned my personal feeling . . . that the candidate who wins the most popular votes should become President." However, he said, "practicality demands" recognition that the current system is well rooted in American history. Many smaller states believed that the system for awarding electoral votes, which being stated in the Constitution, had been a condition under which those states had accepted union. President Nixon strongly doubted that any proposal to eliminate existing arrangements "could win the required approval of three-quarters of the fifty states." He did assert that one needed step was to "clarify the situation presented by the death of a candidate for President or vice president prior to the November general election."

From this starting point, the hearings settled down into three weeks of private testimony, from members of Congress, constitutional experts, historians, and others. Those others included a statement from AFL-CIO president George Meany that it was the standing policy of his organization that "the President and Vice President of the United States should be elected by direct popular vote. The electoral college system has outlived its usefulness, and should be abolished."

The issue resurfaced in the nation's press that April, when the Electoral College commission approved the wording, "The President and the Vice President shall be elected by the people of the several states," that is, by direct popular vote. Congressman McCulloch's formal endorsement of the wording, *The New York Times* reported, "is expected to prove instrumental in attracting Republican votes on the House floor. The Ohio Congressman has considerable influence over party conservatives, some of whom are wary of the plan." A wrinkle remained: McCulloch wished to amend the measure by declaring that it would not become effective until two years after ratification, which, as a practical matter, would mean it would not apply to the 1972 election in which incumbent Richard Nixon was expected to seek re-election. McCulloch denied any such machination on his part, stating, "I never discussed the matter with Nixon or any of his subordinates, directly or indirectly."

McCulloch got almost what he sought. On April 29, the full Judiciary Committee adopted a McCulloch amendment that postponed the effective date of the measure until 1976, unless the necessary ratification by thirty-eight states occurred prior to January 20, 1971—feasible, but remotely. *Washington Post* political writer David Broder said McCulloch was "instrumental in swinging GOP support behind the measure, as the author of the ratification amendment."

Full committee approval came by a lopsided 28 to 6 margin, with sixteen Democrats and twelve Republicans in favor, and three members of each party opposed. This vote all but assured future passage of the amendment by the House, an action that committee chairman Emanuel Celler predicted would come in May. McCulloch issued a statement saying the adopted proposal "eliminated both of the competing inequities in the present system—the unit rule which favors large states and the bonus rule which favors small states." He noted that endorsements had come from the American Bar Association and the U.S. Chamber of Commerce; further, fully 81 percent of respondents to a Gallup poll backed the approach. McCulloch closed by asserting that the proposal was "molded by the principles of representative government, a plan not simply for the next few elections, but a plan designed for the life of our republic."

Action by the Senate was less certain. There, Senator Birch Bayh (R-Indiana) reported that only three of the eleven members of the Senate subcommittee with jurisdiction over the matter currently favored direct election. Broder added that Bayh was "'hopeful' a way can be found to advance the alternative proposals to the full Judiciary Committee," where he believed the popular vote plan would receive majority support.

Broder, however, was not through with the subject. In a May 6 *Washington Post* column, "Political Image Is Deceiving When It Comes To Achievements," Broder contrasted the performance of the recent Republican Governors Conference held in Lexington, Kentucky, with that of the House Judiciary Committee leaders, Emanuel Celler and William McCulloch. Outwardly, he wrote, the Republican governors—"young, vigorous and tuned into the contemporary problems of the kind they find in running 30 states"—might be the people to whom one would turn for guidance on the issues facing the nation. Outwardly, he added, the 80-year-old Emanuel Celler of Brooklyn and 67-year-old Rep. William McCulloch of Ohio might seem "a pair of fusty fuddy-duddy symbols of the well-known decadence of the Congressional seniority system. Where the Governors tend to speak in well-modulated tones, Celler and McCulloch tend to mumble."

In Broder's view, however, the governors' conference was "the pinnacle of political irrelevance," with not a single statement of substance made. In contrast, he said, "The two old men [Celler and McCulloch], devoid of the struttings of ambition," showed what the committee system could accomplish when, through the use of "expert testimony, reasoned argument and careful weighing of evidence," a considered conclusion as to how the nation should select its president was reached.

There, the matter rested, until mid-September, when the full House took up debate on the measure. Meanwhile, the *Congressional Record* took note of two events. On June 16, William McCulloch's *alma mater*, the College of Wooster, bestowed the congressman with an honorary doctor of laws degree. On July 20, American astronauts Neil Armstrong and Buzz Aldrin became the first of their species to set foot on the moon.

Full House Debate

Shortly before the House took up the measure, direct election of the president received support from an unexpected quarter. On September 3, Senator Robert P. Griffin (D-Washington) reported the results of a survey of legislators in twenty-seven states—states whose ratification would be needed to enact the proposed amendment. Griffin's survey had been skewed to the smaller states, including Alaska, Delaware, Hawaii, Idaho, Maine, Montana, New Hampshire, North Dakota, Rhode Island, South Dakota, Utah, Vermont, and Wyoming, which many considered most likely to oppose the measure. Despite this, the survey showed that legislators in all but two states favored direct election as the best alternative under discussion. When asked their personal views, 64 percent of the 3,943 state legislators responding supported direct election, with 34 percent opposed. By a 50 to 41 percent margin, these same legislators said they believed such a measure would meet with the approval of the legislatures in which they served.

Full House debate opened on September 10 with Judiciary Committee Chairman Emanuel Celler striking a historic note. This, he said, marked the "first time since 1826 that the House had conducted a full-scale debate on revising the system whereby Americans elect their president." He noted that under this plan, if no candidate received 40 percent of the vote, a runoff election would be held between the top two finishers. He then applied a rich mix of adjectives to the current system, calling it "barbarous, unsporting, dangerous and downright uncivilized." Following Celler, William McCulloch told the House the current proposal was "the only realistic chance—the only chance—at reform that we have."

He then outlined his reasons for support of House Joint Resolution 681, the measure's formal name. The question, he said, turned on the answers to four questions:

• Should the people of the United States elect their president?

• Should every vote be counted in ultimately determining who is president?

• Should each voter be given an equal voice in determining who is president?

• Should the candidate with the most votes be declared the winner?

For himself, McCulloch said, "I answer those questions in the affirmative."

He then critiqued the plans to assign electoral votes to congressional district winners or to assign votes in proportion to the popular outcome. The problem, he said, is that "each of these plans holds that geographical territories—not people—elect the President." Under the district plan—because the state winner would get a "two vote" bonus—an individual's vote would count for more if he came from a less populous state. In each alternative, he said, it remained possible that "the winner should be the loser and the loser should be the winner."

Under the present system, he noted, an election thrown into the House of Representatives would be determined by the "one state, one vote" rule. This, he dismissed as "anachronistic, undemocratic, and mischievous." Further, the "unit rule"—whether the unit in question was a state or a congressional district—promoted fraud, since the corrupt theft of 10,000 votes in a "swing" state could alter the result of an election. The unit rule gave populous states excessive influence; further, it discouraged as effectively meaningless voter participation in "one-party" states. He responded to the claim that smaller states, fearing loss of influence, would reject the amendment by citing Senator Griffin's survey, described above. He noted that when the full Judiciary Committee began its hearings, a majority of committee Republicans had opposed direct election. Once full arguments—pro and con—had been heard, twelve of the fifteen Republicans on the committee voted in its favor.

Full House debate began a week later. Alton Lennon (D-North Carolina) said he believed the general public had three principal desires: to abolish the Electoral College, to abolish the "winner-take-all" rule, and to abolish the "one state, one vote" provision in the event the election was thrown into the House of Representatives. Congressman Richard Poff (R-Virginia) proposed a modified version of the district vote plan. The Poff district plan, he said, accomplished all three. David Dennis (R-Indiana) expressed the fear that direct election was contrary to the intentions of those who had written the U.S. Constitution. If, he said, the district-based bill failed and the direct approach was adopted, "we will have taken one more long step away from the federal-representative Republic of our fathers and toward a unitary democracy in which government will be conducted by blocs, pressure groups, and organized measures."

To this, William McCulloch responded rhetorically, asking if the district plan would eliminate the possibility that winners may lose and the losers may win. Answering his own question, he said, "The proponents of the district plan candidly admit that the district plan will not." He did not agree that awarding a statewide winner with two electoral votes constituted an extension of federalism, as some had argued. "To me, federalism is a form of government designed to allow the popular will to be more precisely expressed and effectuated by all allocation of responsibility to various levels of government. Just what federalism has to do with the way we count votes, I don't know." To this, Emanuel Celler added that the direct vote "provides that the individual voter shall vote directly for president—and his vote shall be counted without any intermediary. The voter needs no agent."

Defending his proposal, Congressman Poff suggested that—in order to increase their share of the total national vote—states might engage in a "race to the bottom" regarding voter registration requirements. That is, some states might lower their voting age to eighteen in order to gain influence in the result. Clark McGregor (D-Minnesota) termed the Poff approach as "less a compromise between than an amalgamation of multiple proposals." He commended Congressman Poff for "trying to build bridges" between the advocates of the proportional, the direct, and the district plans. Still, the Poff proposal had what he regarded as two glaring defects. First, it "did violence" to the broadly accepted doctrine that all votes cast should count equally; second, it devalued the voters of Minnesota, his own state, which typically had very high voter turnouts.

Congressman Lawrence Coughlin (R-Pennsylvania) offered an amendment to replace the projected runoff election with a presidential choice made by the Congress. To this, McCulloch replied that such a proposal asked the public to place greater faith in government at a time when it appeared clear public faith in government was in decline. Joseph Waggonner (D-Louisiana) read into the record an answer given in 1956 by then-Senator John Kennedy when asked if he objected to the direct election of president and vice-president. "Mr. Kennedy, in response replied, simply and directly, 'I do.'" Waggonner quoted Senator Kennedy further:

The small states have an unmerited influence over the passage of constitutional amendments. On theoretical grounds, it seems to me, it would be a breach of the agreement made with the States when they came into the union. At the same time, it was understood that they would have the same number of electoral votes as they had Senators and Representatives.

When this and all other comment was completed, the full House voted. The "district plan" received a convincing rejection. Next, House Joint Resolution 681—the plan developed and backed by both Celler and McCulloch—was considered. It carried easily, by a 338 to 70 margin— 184 Democrats and 154 Republicans were in its favor; 44 Democrats and 26 Republicans were opposed. For the first time in the nation's history, a body of Congress had voted to eliminate the Electoral College. In consequence, no intermediary would stand between the individual voter and the selection of president. Representative Carl Albert (D-Oklahoma) offered his praise for Celler and McCulloch, noting that the bill had passed without the support of the Nixon Administration: "It was the members of this committee, Democrats and Republicans alike, with no help from downtown, which formulated this historic proposal."

On September 30, McCulloch told the House that President Nixon had that morning endorsed the House action and had called upon the Senate to follow suit. McCulloch stated, "I agree with the President that the choice is direct election or nothing. I agree that for those who want reform, 'contrary views are a luxury.'"

Whatever may have been McCulloch's satisfaction over his victory, contrary views were not only a luxury. They also proved victorious. House passage was not sufficiently decisive to bring forth prompt action from Mississippi Senator James Eastland, chair of the Senate Judiciary Committee to which the Electoral College reform bill was assigned. The plan did not advance from the committee chamber to the Senate floor until August 1970, nearly a year after its passage by the House. Debate began the following month. This being an election year, the Senate had settled firmly on a mid-October adjournment. The press of time all but invited a filibuster by those opposed. Two efforts were made in late September to gather the two-thirds votes required to invoke cloture. Both failed, by votes of 54–36 and 53–34. Those opposing cloture were a mix of conservatives, southerners, and senators from small states who feared they would lose weight in presidential elections. (Some senators fit into all three categories.) The attempt to determine the selection of a president by straight popular vote had failed. Three decades would pass before the question would again be deeply pertinent, in the 2000 election between Republican George Bush and Democrat Al Gore.

On the Road

William and Mabel McCulloch were not great travelers. McCulloch, on general principle, avoided participating in most Congressional "fact-finding" missions, which were often mere excuses to fly somewhere sunny at taxpayers' expense. The couple did occasionally travel to Bermuda for a winter break. Travel, for them, chiefly meant travel to visit family. Following the 1969 session of Congress, the McCullochs went to St. Louis to visit their daughter's family, husband David Carver and young daughter Elizabeth.

Her family, Elizabeth recalls, "Loved a good fire in the fireplace." During her grandparents' visit, she added, "He was sitting in the chair next to the fireplace and taught me how to make a fire. You roll and twist some newspaper until it's like little logs and twist them very tight so they burn longer. He showed me how to sweep the hearth and how to set the kindling for maximum air flow so it burns perfectly and how to set the logs on the kindling and to make sure you have enough open space for good air flow so the fire really catches well." She added, "To this day I am the world's best fire maker."

CHAPTER 21

Voting Rights Sustained

Congressman McCulloch's failed attempt to abolish the Electoral College had been motivated in fair measure by his desire to see that all votes counted equally. During the same term of Congress in which he pushed that agenda, he pursued a second course that also turned on the right to vote.

On January 30, 1969, Congressman William McCulloch introduced legislation to extend the Voting Rights Act of 1965 for a further five years. Key aspects of that act were due to expire on August 6, 1970: the "triggering" mechanism, whereby low voter enrollments among African Americans led automatically to the appointment of federal registrars, and the mandated Department of Justice review of proposed state voting laws that might have a racial impact on voting.

Congressman McCulloch freely acknowledged that great progress had occurred. He read into the *Congressional Record* the fact that black registration in Alabama had increased from 19.3 percent to 56.7 percent between the 1964 and 1968 elections. In Georgia, the increase was from 27.4 percent to 56.1 percent. In Virginia, it increased from 38.3 percent to 58.4 percent. Similar results were reported by other states. McCulloch stated, "When I voted for the Voting Rights Act of 1965, I hoped that five years would be ample time." But, he said, he had been mistaken. For even as the proportion of African Americans registered to vote had notably increased, many southern states had taken steps to dilute, vitiate, or otherwise dissipate the impact of black voters.

McCulloch gave a list of examples. More tellingly, perhaps, one might look to the state of Mississippi where in his work *Black Votes Count,* author Frank R. Parker noted the steps the Magnolia State took in innovating ways to deny blacks the vote or to reduce the consequences of those votes. If, say, a state representative district had a black majority, then redistricting could create multiple districts with white majorities. If, say, a given office was traditionally filled by election, then offices in black majority areas could be filled by gubernatorial appointment. If a city had election wards with black majorities, then the city could abolish ward-based elections in exchange for citywide ones in which every candidate was elected by the white majority. Since Mississippians continued to vote largely Democratic in local elections, victory in the Democratic primary was tantamount to election in November. To strengthen this advantage, Mississippi raised the requirements on independent candidacies, making it more difficult to challenge the primary victor in the general election.

A good deal of legalism went into this effort. Parker noted that the Mississippi state legislature empowered itself to override the state constitution in creating electoral districts if special circumstances applied. Such circumstance included:

> Any county of the first class lying wholly within a levee district and within which there is situated a city of more than forty thousand . . .
>
> In any county created since 1916 through which the Yazoo River flows . . .
>
> In any county bordering on the Gulf of Mexico or Mississippi Sound and having therein a facility operated by the National Aeronautics and Space Administration.

Frank Parker acknowledged there were other problems. One was that having been excluded from the exercise of political power since Reconstruction, many blacks in Mississippi—and, by extension, other southern blacks—simply had no interest or faith in electoral politics. Parker stated, "With the overt legal barriers destroyed, lack of political consciousness remained a major obstacle on the road toward enfranchisement."

In introducing his bill, McCulloch cited many of the factors listed above. To this, he added the simple fact that threats of physical violence or economic intimidation kept many potential voters from taking advantage of the protections offered by the 1965 Voting Rights Act. The one-time Ohio farm boy closed his remarks by stating, "Black power is voting power. The cry of a nonvoter in a representative government is a silent cry. Let the black voices be heard."

The bill was assigned to the Judiciary Committee. The Nixon Administration was expected to put forth a bill significantly at odds with what McCulloch proposed. Prior to the release of President Nixon's proposals, Judiciary Subcommittee No. 5 began holding hearings in which those who favored McCulloch's approach strove to build support for the simple extension of the act. Not all witnesses agreed. Mississippi Attorney General A. F. Summer took particular objection to Section V of the law, which required southern states to pre-clear with the Department of Justice any law that might affect voting. That section, he said, "created an island of provinces which, if continued, will find the chief law officer of these provinces on his knees, begging and groveling for favors from the omnipotent Justice Department, or in the alternative, the Federal District Court of Washington, D.C." McCulloch's position was unyielding. On

June 20, 1969, *The Washington Post* quoted McCulloch telling those testifying before Subcommittee No. 5 "he saw no reason to budge from his position that the Act must be simply extended for another five years beyond
1970 with no complicating changes."

On June 26, Attorney General John Mitchell presented the Nixon
Administration's proposals. The attorney general asserted, "Voting rights
is not a regional issue. It is a nationwide concern for every American,
which must be tested on a nationwide basis." Further, he wanted "to encourage our Negro citizens to take out their alienation at the ballot box,
and not elsewhere."

As presented by Mitchell, the administration proposal consisted of
five sections:

• Section I—All literacy tests were to be banned until January 1, 1974.
(At this time, fourteen northern states maintained literacy tests, though it
had not been established that these discriminated against would-be black
voters.)

• Section II—State residency requirements for voting were retracted
in presidential elections.

• Section III—The attorney general was authorized to send voting
examiners and registrars anywhere in the country.

• Section IV—The Department of Justice would lose its authority to
"pre-clear" proposed state laws that might affect voting, but would retain
the right to bring suit against such laws that it believed created racially
biased results.

• Section V—A commission to study both discrimination and fraud
in voting was to be formed.

Two matters were crucial to civil rights advocates. First, Mitchell
would end the "triggering" device whereby any state with less than half
its voting-age black population registered would have that registration
done by the federal government. Second was the elimination of "pre-
clearance." Given the imaginativeness some states showed in lessening
the consequences of black voting, civil rights advocates did not want the
burden of proof shifted from the individual states to the Department of
Justice. Previously, such cases had been heard in federal district court in
Washington; under Mitchell's proposal, the cases would likely be tried in
southern courts.

The following day, *The New York Times* reported that the plan had
received "a generally chilly reception on Capitol Hill." Mitchell stressed
that his proposals were nationwide in application. He added, "I cannot
support what amounts to regional legislation. While Congress may have
had sufficient reason in the 1965 act, I do not believe that this justification
exists any longer."

In his book *Nixon's Civil Rights*, Dean J. Kotlowski termed Mitchell's
bill "a classic example of the artless compromise," adding, "This hydra-

headed bill gave each interest group a reason to slay it." (On one matter, Kotlowski points out, the attorney general was probably correct. Northern states had maintained that their literary tests were not racially biased. The broader truth was that many blacks now living in the North had been raised in the South, where they had received inferior educations. In 1970, the Civil Rights Commission reported that northern states with literacy tests had lower voter participation rates among blacks than did northern states that had no literacy tests. At the time, neither Emanuel Celler nor William McCulloch was opposed to abolishing literacy tests; their concern was that debate on the matter might push renewal of the bill past its August 1970 expiration date.)

The response from pro-voting rights groups was prompt and heated. Father Theodore Hesburgh, long-time chairman of the U.S. Commission on Civil Rights, immediately wrote Mitchell to state that his proposals were "an open invitation to those States which denied the vote to minority citizens in the past to resume doing so in the future, through insertion of disingenuous technicalities and changes in the election laws." Calling attention to Mitchell's Section V—to form a committee to investigate discrimination in voting—Father Hesburgh asked if the attorney general was aware that this was something the Commission on Civil Rights had been doing for years.

NAACP chief lobbyist Clarence Mitchell accused the attorney general of throwing "the apple of discord" into the voting rights discussion. "I am not deceived. This is a sophisticated, calculated, incredible effort on the part of the chief lawyer of the United States government to make it impossible to continue on the constructive efforts we have made."

Judiciary Committee Chairman Emanuel Celler, expressing the view that the administration proposals would slow progress toward equal rights, was moved to quote William Earnest Healy's poem "Invictus": "Along the street of by and by, we come to the house of never." Judiciary Committee attorney Franklin G. Polk noted, "On Voting Rights renewal, it's hard to say if one person changed things. Another Ohio member, Charles Whalen was for changing it, as was John Anderson (R-Illinois). McCulloch was not alone, though he certainly was the first person to take that position."

On July 1, *The New York Times* headlined the hearings, "Nixon Rights Bill Appears Doomed by GOP Attack." Mitchell's proposals, Warren Weaver, Jr., wrote, "ran into such uniform and intense opposition on Capitol Hill today that it was regarded as all but dead." Weaver speculated that the Nixon Administration believed enough Republicans would vote against their party's leader that the Mitchell proposals would never pass. This, he added, led some to believe that the administration did not particularly wish its proposal to pass; rather, it hoped defeat would increase the Republican Party's popularity in the South. As rather glaring evidence, the Nixon Administration was unable to find a single northern Republican willing to sponsor the bill. By default, the Minority Leader Gerald Ford (R-Michigan) put his name to the measure. But in questioning John Mitchell, it was Ohio Fourth District Congressman William McCulloch who brought out the heavy artillery. Writing in the *Detroit Free Press*, Jerald F. terHorst (later, press secretary of President Gerald Ford) found the telling metaphor:

> Napoleon had his Waterloo, but for Attorney General John N. Mitchell and Senator Strom Thurmond you have to spell it William McCulloch.
>
> More than anyone in Congress, the elderly little Scotsman from Piqua, Ohio bears the responsibility—or deserves the credit—for shooting down the Nixon Administration's new voting rights program. He did it in broad daylight, too.

McCulloch, terHorst added, "fell on Mitchell as though he had proposed a return to slavery." What kind of civil rights bill was Mitchell proposing, McCulloch asked. While the attorney general "stared glumly," McCulloch provided his own answer: "It creates a remedy for which there is no wrong and leaves grievous wrongs without adequate remedy." McCulloch acknowledged that some enforcement problems had existed with the 1965 act, but added, "I would have hoped that the party of civil rights, the party of human rights, the party that voted 82 percent in the Senate and 94 percent in the House for the 1965 act would not have thrown up its hands in surrender." TerHorst's account concluded: "Then, looking Mitchell straight in the eye, McCulloch told the attorney general: 'That's not the way to promote law and order.'"

On July 17, 1969, the full House Judiciary Committee rejected the substance of the Nixon Administration provisions. A motion to ban the literacy test was defeated by a 28 to 7 margin. The motion to end the residency requirements in presidential voting was defeated by exactly the same vote. The bill urging a simple five-year extension of the existing law passed by a voice vote. Of note, McCulloch had carried ten of the fourteen remaining GOP committee members with him.

The bill's next step was the House Rules Committee, whose chairman, William Colmer (D-Mississippi) was in adamant opposition. Congressman Colmer could stall, and he gained a significant victory in doing so. Two northern Democratic members of the Rules Committee—James Delaney (D-New York) and B. F. Fisk (D-California)—backed a voting measure that would apply equally across all states. The Rules Committee adopted the provision. In consequence, when on November 18 the committee voted to send the bill to the House floor, it meant that any amendment offered to nationalize the bill would be "germane" under House rules.

House debate opened on December 11, with William McCulloch speaking for thirty minutes on behalf of the bill. He detailed the efforts to dilute the black vote. He argued for the "pre-clearance" provision, in part because it meant that all such cases were heard in Washington, D.C., which promoted prompt and consistent decisions.

McCulloch was challenged by his fellow Judiciary Committee colleague, Richard H. Poff (R-Virginia), who argued that requiring states to receive federal approval before enacting law set a dangerous precedent. He added, "Virginians are proud—they are independent—and we are shamed by the status unfairly thrust upon us by a federal law which presumes us to be guilty when all of the evidence is to the contrary." He noted that no proposed election law reform put forward by Virginia had been overturned on Department of Justice review.

The Virginia Republicans were out in force. Joel Broyhill (R-Virginia) termed the bill a "perfect example of a practice we have seen all too frequently during the last decade, of attaching a glorifying name to a bad bill to disguise its true purpose." That purpose, he added, was to "force federal registrars onto southern states. . . . It arbitrarily assumes that racial discrimination exists."

Congressman Robert Eckhardt (D-Texas) furthered the assault. He was, he said, "southern with respect to geography, heritage, and vernacular." He did not believe, however, that there was such a thing as a southern orthodoxy. Congressman Eckhardt identified two faults in this bill that he thought common to legislation. The first, he said, "is that it too frequently shoots at old and infirm inequities when new and virulent ones are emerging." In this, Eckhardt advanced the general claim of southern conservatives that the 1965 Voting Rights Act had created a sufficient momentum that it need not be extended. The second flaw, he said, is that it applied the law "a case at a time." By analogy, he said, "The wolf is caught, flayed, its hide turned in, bounty collected, while whole herds of sheep are being devoured." Nor were all Democrats in favor of extending the act. Charles Wiggins (D-California) said what was crucial about the Nixon administration bill was that "it does not treat the rest of the Nation like the South, it treats the South like the rest of the nation." On the floor of the House, the tide was clearly moving against McCulloch. Almost the last speaker to address the floor, New York's black Congresswoman Shirley Chisholm, attempted to reorient debate:

In many instances those of us who have been the beneficiaries of the status quo find it most difficult to realize that, in this day and in this age, certain voices in America are now saying that we are through with gradualism and we are through with tokenism and we want our full share of the American dream that everyone so unequivocally speaks about.

William McCulloch read into the record a second letter received from Father Theodore Hesburgh, president of Notre Dame University and for twelve years the chair of the U.S. Commission on Civil Rights: "I think I can say that there has been no more effective piece of civil rights legislation than the Voting Rights Act of 1965." Father Hesburgh argued, "We cannot retreat on this front. If we do, we run the risk of endangering the faith of many of our people in the ability of our government to meet the legitimate expectations of its citizens."

Still, most observers expected the Voting Rights Act extension to pass. *The New York Times* reported, "The administration applied some last-minute pressure on House Republicans today in an apparently futile attempt to block a five-year extension of the 1965 Voting Rights Act." *The Washington Post*, less certain, reported that "the issue is considered in doubt." House Speaker John McCormack (D-Massachusetts) said that at least sixty House Republicans would have to break ranks with the Nixon Administration to bring passage of the five-year extension.

In effect, McCulloch needed fifty-nine votes in addition to his own. He did not get them. When the tally was completed, only forty-nine Republicans had withstood the pressure their president and party had brought to bear. By a breathtaking 208 to 203, the House voted to substitute the Nixon administration-sponsored bill for McCulloch's. The tally had its oddities. Ten northern Democrats voted for the Republican alternative. Even more noteworthy, fourteen southern Democrats had voted for the stronger McCulloch bill. Later that day, the House approved the final version of the administration bill by a margin of 234 to 179.

It had been the first vote, however—the one substituting the administration measure for the McCulloch measure—that had been crucial. If William McCulloch needed cause for depression, he need have looked no further than his own Ohio delegation. Excluding his own vote, only four of the remaining seventeen Buckeye State Republicans followed the lead of the man generally regarded as the dean of the delegation. Indeed, William McCulloch—the quintessential midwesterner—was defeated by the Republicans of the Midwest. The combined Republican delegations of Ohio, Indiana, and Illinois voted for the administration-sponsored measure by a 28 to 12 margin.

Washington Post political columnist Joseph Alsop wrote soon after that while there may have been an argument "for altering the rather nakedly sectional character of the expiring statute," no argument existed for diluting the statute's effectiveness. In consequence, Alsop added, "This is mighty unpalatable medicine for old-fashioned Americans, who still believe in every citizen's right to cast his vote and say his say, without regard to race, creed or color." Alsop closed with a tribute to "the doughty McCulloch . . . whose contributions to the cause of equal rights and equal opportunities have put all thinking Americans in his debt."

It had been for a considerable time the generally accepted view that on civil rights, the House was more liberal than the Senate—if only because the Senate had the power to filibuster a civil rights bill to death. Now, two liberal Democrats in the Senate sought to restore the original

House handiwork on voting rights. The pair was Philip Hart (D-Michigan) and Hugh Scott (R-Pennsylvania). They drafted a bill that extended the Voting Rights Act for five years, but added two measures from the House-passed administration version: first, the abolition of literacy tests; and, second, the ending of residency requirements in presidential voting.

The measure brought surprising support. On March 5, the Senate voted 47 to 32 against tabling (killing) the measure. There was a further wrinkle. Senator Edward Kennedy (D-Massachusetts) wanted to add to the bill a section lowering the voting age to eighteen. Some liberals feared this would simply complicate the life of the bill and make its passage by August less likely. Surprisingly, the eighteen-year-old vote amendment sailed through the Senate by a 64 to 17 margin. On March 13, 1970, the Scott-Hart bill passed the Senate by a striking 64 to 12 margin.

Three days later, Congressman Robert McCrory (R-Illinois) told the House that the Senate had "restored the measure substantially to the form as recommended by the overwhelming majority of the House Judiciary Committee." The issue of the eighteen-year-old vote, he believed, could be reconciled between the two Houses.

On June 17, the House took up full discussion of the measure. William McCulloch spoke frankly:

If H.R. 914 is not adopted today, the most effective civil rights law in our nation's history will have been emasculated. If the key provisions are not renewed, this day will go down in history as a day of infamy, a day as tragic as that day in 1894 when the Congress repealed all Federal laws prohibiting racial discrimination in voting.

At issue was whether the House would vote simply to approve the Senate version, as amended, or to seek a House-Senate conference committee to resolve the differences. Congressman John Anderson (R-Illinois) stated the matter succinctly: "The heart of the matter before us today is whether we will accept the Senate amendments which include a provision for lowering the voting age. To do so is to avoid a conference and subsequent votes in both Houses on a conference report with the delays that would attend such a decision." Congressman John Conyers (D-Michigan) spoke for the Senate version: "All black Americans ought to be able to fully participate in the political process as well as those who have the legal responsibility to bear arms in the name of their country." And, adding his own endorsement, Emanuel Celler demonstrated that William McCulloch was not the only member of the Judiciary Committee who could quote poetry. He did not, as was McCulloch's wont, quote "the bard of old." Instead, he quoted Norwegian playwright Henrik Ibsen, "I believe that man is right who is most in league with the future."

The proof, of course, was in the voting. On the key procedural vote, sixteen Republicans who had voted for the admnistration version now returned their allegiance to McCulloch. Twenty-two Democrats did likewise. Most remarkably, in the December 1969 vote, fourteen southern Democrats had voted for the "stronger" bill, the bill that most southerners felt stigmatized their region. On the June revote, twenty-seven southern Democrats did so. The McCulloch version passed the procedural test by an almost comfortable 224 to 183 margin. The final vote on the bill itself was clearer. The tally was 272 to 132.

On June 22, 1970, President Richard Nixon signed the 1970 Voting Rights Act into law. He did so, he said, despite his belief that it was unconstitutional for the Congress to lower the national voting age, when that age was stated in the Constitution. (In this, President Nixon was correct. The Twenty-Sixth Amendment to the U.S. Constitution, extending the right to vote to persons eighteen and older, was approved by Congress and the requisite three-quarters of the states in 1971.) The president noted,

The Voting Rights Act of 1965 has opened participation in the political process. Although this bill does not include all of the administration's recommendations, it does incorporate improvements which extend its reach still further, suspending literacy tests nationwide and also putting an end to the present welter of State residency requirements for voting for President and Vice President. Now, for the first time, citizens who move between elections may vote without long residency requirements.

President Nixon noted that, in the years since the 1965 Voting Rights Act had been enacted, nearly one million black citizens had registered to vote; more than four hundred Negro officials had been elected to local and state offices. "These are more than election statistics," the president said. "They are statistics of hope and dramatic evidence that the American system works. They stand as an answer to those who claim that there is no recourse except to the streets."

CHAPTER 22

Owes You His Judgement

As Washington journalist Andrew Glass, quoted earlier, said of William McCulloch, "He was totally outside the political sphere, in the sense that he was indifferent to how something might afffect his political standings." Congressman McCulloch was a steady reader of political history; unsurprisingly, his favorite American presidents were Washington and Lincoln. But McCulloch was not, in any real sense, a political philosopher—he did not dwell on the thoughts of David Hume, or Alexis de Tocqueville, or Adam Smith. There was, however, one statement of political philosophy McCulloch was likely to endorse. It came from British parliamentarian Edmund Burke, telling his constituents wherein his strongest responsibility to them lay:

Certainly, Gentlemen, it ought to be the happiness and glory of a representative to live in the strictest union, the closest correspondence, and the most unreserved communication with his constituents. Their wishes ought to have great weight with him; their opinions high respect; their business unremitted attention. . . . But his unbiased opinion, his mature judgement, his enlightened conscience, he ought not to sacrifice to you, to any man, or to any set of men living. . . . Your representative owes you, not his industry only, but his judgement; and he betrays, instead of serving you, if he sacrifices it to your opinions.

That McCulloch shared this view is underscored by looking at his handling of three matters in his final 1971–1972 term in Congress. They are what in politics are often called "hot button" issues— specifically, the proposed equal rights amendment, prayer in school, and the busing of schoolchildren for the purpose of achieving desegregation. Bearing in mind the distinct rightward tilt of his congressional district, on these matters McCulloch at least twice placed his own views above the likely majority view of his constituents.

The Equal Rights Amendment

Agitation on behalf of equal rights for women was not something new. As long ago as 1923, an equal rights amendment (ERA) written by feminist Alice Paul was introduced into Congress. Congressional, particlarly *male* congressional, sensibilities did not leap to its support. In 1964, so liberal a Democrat as Nicholas Katzenbach thought that the effort by Rules Committee Chairman Howard Smith to add a ban on sexual discrimination to the 1964 civil rights bill would lead to that measure's defeat. So liberal a Democrat as Emanuel Celler consistently used his chairmanship of the Judiciary Committee to block consideration of such proposals for equal rights for women as were introduced. Celler's committee took no action on House Joint Resolution 264, an equal rights amendment introduced early in 1969 by Congresswoman Martha Griffiths (D-Michigan). After better than a year of inaction, Congresswoman Griffiths initiated the rarely successful device of seeking a Discharge Petition to force her resolution out of the Judiciary Committee. In this instance, success was hers. By June 20, 1970, she had obtained the 218 signatures neccesary to force the measure from the committee. Celler had attempted to head off the move by announcing several days previously that the Judiciary Committee would commence hearings on H.J.R. 264 on September 16. Celler's announcement was rendered null by the success of the Discharge Petition.

House floor debate on the proposed equal rights amendment began August 10, 1970. Discussion was brief. The major opponents proved to be the chairman and ranking member of the committee that had just been sidestepped, that is, Emanuel Celler and William McCulloch. McCulloch argued, first, that the proposed amendment was unnecessary. For example, under the Civil Rights Act of 1964 and the equal protection clause of the Fourteenth Amendment, it was already illegal for employers to engage in gender-based hiring. What was needed was not an amendment, but enforcement of standing law. Second, he said, the amendment abolished any legal distinction between the sexes. He observed that a whole body of law—from workplace protection to custody rights and survivor benefits—would be affected. A policewoman, he asserted, would be unable to pass the sergeant's exam unless she could demonstrate the physical strength required of men. Adopting the ERA without "adequate hearings and debate would raise more questions than it would answer." Congress, he believed, was acting on "a wave of emotion." In sum, he said, "Never since I have been a member of the Congresss has a proposal to amend the Constitution been treated so cavalierly."

McCulloch was backed by Celler. The Judicairy chairman said that in preparation for the hearings he had intended, the American Law Division of the Library of Congress had provided a summary of state laws relating to child support, custody, legal separation, and alimony, "which could be abrogated for good or ill by the adoption of this amendment." In submitting its report, the law division stated, "So far as we can ascertain, no definite legal analysis has ever been undertaken which purports to examine in detail any of the ramifications of these problems . . . no court precedents exist." How, Celler asked the House, could members discharge their responsibilities without even knowing "which [state] laws would be abrogated, voided or changed?"

McCulloch moved that House Joint Resolution 264 be recommitted to the Judiciary Committee. Celler agreed. And the pair was crushed. On August 10, the same day debate had opened, the House voted 332 to 32 to approve the Discharge; and then, it voted 334 to 26 to approve the amendment itself.

The Senate hearings began soon after, with the proposed amendment reaching the floor of the Upper Chamber in early October. That body adjourned, however, on October 14 without taking any action.

When Congress convened in 1971, Congresswoman Griffiths tried again, introducing the equal rights amendment as House Joint Resolution 208. This time, Celler held hearings. The Judiciary Committee voted out the measure on July 14, but attached to it amendments exempting women from the draft and allowing sexual differentials in labor standards. Both amendments were unacceptable to the measure's supporters.

In support of her position, Congresswoman Griffiths distributed a 114-page *Yale Law Journal* article to her colleagues. Again, McCulloch and Celler led the opposition. On October 9, they co-signed a response noting the law school article had defined "equality" as "absolute sameness, identical treatment in all cases." Celler and McCulloch asserted that the law review article acknowledged the breakdown of family values and that the ERA would "expedite" that process. They noted that such things as "the widow's allowance or family allowance, homestead and litigation on gifts to charity or other devices to protect a surviving spouse [usually female] against complete disinheritance" would be invalidated.

Speaking on the House floor on October 12, McCulloch referred to the long fight for racial rights. He added:

Race is not the only area, however, where group discrimination exists. There is another class of human beings who have been dicriminated against since the inception of our species, that is, women. From the outset she was denied rights and privileges shared amongst most men. This we all know. However, these injustices are today closer to being abolished than ever before in the history of the human race. I am of the opinion that the statutory approach rather than the constitutional amendent approach would be more meaningful and less mischievous.

McCulloch added that if the measure were to pass, he regarded it as essential that the amendments attached by the Judiciary Committee remain. McCulloch's fellow members heartily disagreed. On October 12, 1971, they approved the unamended version of the proposed equal rights amendment by a 350 to 15 margin.

The Senate Judiciary Committee voted out a parallel measure on March 14. Debate began three days later. President Richard Nixon released a letter affirming his own support for the amendment. In the subsequent debate, Senator Sam Ervin (D-North Carolina) offered amendments similar to those voted down in the House. They were likewise voted down in the Senate. On March 22, the Senate added its own overwhelming 84 to 8 approval. The measure now went to the states, three-quarters of which were required to approve the proposed amendment before it would be added to the Constitution.

The 1971–1972 Congress would be the last for both William McCulloch and Emanuel Celler. McCulloch retired due to illness. Celler, after winning twenty-five terms, was defeated in the Democratic primary by a thirty-one-year-old challenger, Elizabeth Holtzman, who had not even been born until Celler's eighteenth year in Congress. Holtzman's challenge turned on opposition to Celler's position on the ERA. In a light turnout, she defeated the astonished forty-nine-year incumbent by 15,596 to 14,987. One consequence was that the following year, when the House Judiciary Committee considered articles of impeachment against President Nixon, the committee was chaired not by Celler but by Peter Rodino (D-New Jersey).

The second point is that, though passed by both Houses of Congress, the ERA failed to achieve adoption by the required number of states. In the end, to the extent to which equality for women was advanced, it did so not by Constitutional amendment but via the statutory route urged by William McCulloch.

School Prayer

Efforts to amend the Constitutution to permit prayer in school were made in almost every session of Congress subsequent to the 1962 Supreme Court decisions banning the practice. Those favoring prayer believed, among other things, that if prayer was unconstitutional, then it was the Constitution, and not the word of God, that was in need of altering. Without question, prayer in school was the majority preference of the Fourth District of Ohio. One newspaper photograph showed McCulloch and a school prayer advocate examining a pro-prayer petition that bore the names of 35,000 of his constituents.

Initially, McCulloch shared this view. As reported, at the time of the Court's major decisions on school prayer, McCulloch praised Justice Potter Stewart's dissent. As he and others noted, the phrase "In God We Trust" appeared on all American coinage; the Pledge of Allegiance included the phrase "under God." McCulloch noted the irony that the court that held prayer inadmissible had opened its day with the cry, "God bless the United States and this Honorable Court."

In time, McCulloch began to back away from this view. He was, at the same time, a bit anxious not to thrust his change of heart directly into the face of his constituency. On subjects that drew considerable constituent mail, McCulloch—as did other congressmen—limited his reply to a form letter. Consider the ambiguity of the following:

Dear Friend,

Thanks, much, for your letter in support of Bible reading and prayers in our public schools.

The House Committee on the Judiciary held extensive meetings and hearings on the subject several years ago, but we just did not have sufficient supporting votes to favorably report the proposal to the floor for debate and vote. However, I am of the opinion that new proposals to amend the U.S. Constitution in that regard will again be considered in this session of Congress, both in the House and in the Senate. Conditions for favorable action appear better this year.

This letter certainly gives the impression that McCulloch favored prayer in school, though it does not note what action, if any, the Ohio congressman took as a member of the House Judiciary Committee to advance its passage.

A proposed Constitutional amendment on school prayer reached the floor of the House in November 1971. Speaking to the House on November 8, McCulloch provided historical backdrop to the issue. The conflict between public school prayer and the First Amendment had not existed when the nation was formed, he said. At that time, "public" schools did not exist. Such schools as did exist were organized by churches and had the unquestioned right—as parochial schools have today—to mix biblical and educational texts. McCulloch reported that in 1869, the Cincinnati Board of Education banned prayer in school following extensive complaints from that city's considerable Catholic population that only Protestant prayers were used.

McCulloch now took a clear stand. The proposed amendment, he told the House, was "not good law. It is not good theology. The force of law is not necessary to call forth meaningful, voluntary prayer. If you and I know that, do you not think God knows that, too?" The First Amendment, as it stood, he said, protected religious liberty and "wisely" directed that the government stay out of religion. McCulloch, he said, did not believe the government should undertake to write prayer or to "act as our priest, minister, or rabbi."

His conclusion was simple: "The first amendment needs no amendment."

Later that same day, the House voted. A two-thirds vote was required for passage. A clear majority was in favor, but the actual vote of 240 to 162 fell 28 votes shy of the supermajority required. The issue raised a clear partisan split. Democrats opposed the "prayer in school" amendment by 136 to 102; Republicans favored it by 138 to 26. McCulloch's position was shared by less than one-sixth of his fellow Republicans.

School Busing

In the years following the Supreme Court's *Brown* decision banning segregated public schools, school districts north and south generally moved with something slower than the "all deliberate speed" the High Court had directed. The argument for integration was strengthened by an influential 1966 report, "Equality of Educational Oppportunity," a 600-page Department of Health, Education, and Welfare study directed by Dr. James Coleman. The study, involving 150,000 students, offered several main conclusions. The first was that southern schools for black children were not significantly underfunded relative to schools for white. The differences in education outcomes, the study asserted, stemmed from the "social disadvantages" of growing up black and, often, poor. The conclusion was that black students learned better when taught in a mixed-race environment. Given that housing remained segregated, the only apparent way to create mixed-race classrooms was by busing students of one race to schools previously attended principally by another.

Many districts tried to sidestep the issue. Some offered "freedom of choice" plans, which in theory allowed any student to attend any school in a given district, but in practice enrolled almost all students in their previous school. Some districts created "magnet schools" offering specialized curricula and open to any student in the district. Again, the actual amount of desegregation that occurred was small. More commonly, school districts intiated programs to bus students to schools with a preponderance of students of another race.

Congressman McCulloch was from the start prepared to support school busing if the evidence that it promoted improved educational outcomes was pursuasive. On October 3, 1968, McCulloch voted to table a provision offered by Congressman Jamie Whitten (D-Mississippi) that would have prevented HEW from withholding funds from districts employing "freedom of choice" as a desegregation strategy. HEW's position was that "freedom of choice" simply did not prompt desegregation. The Whitten provision was set aside by a narrow 167 to 156 vote.

On April 20, 1971, the Supreme Court ruled that the "freedom of choice" desegregation plan employed by the Charlotte-Mecklenburg (North Carolina) Board of Education failed to meet the standard set in *Brown* that school integration occur "with all deliberate speed." The High Court ordered the North Carolina district to initiate large-scale busing of students. Evidence was growing that only school busing to achieve racial integration would meet the judicial standard.

Busing for desegregation was deeply unpopular. One Gallup poll showed that only 4 percent of white adults and 9 percent of black adults supported it. While busing advocates were inclined to attribute opposition to racism, a 1978 study by the RAND Corporation concluded that opponents believed busing undercut neighborhood cohesion and involved spending on transportation funds that would be better spent in the classroom. Opposition was not limited to words. In Boston, near-riots occurred as white parents attempted to block the transport of students. In Dayton, Ohio, the city school district's desegregation planner was shot to death by an irate parent.

The issue spilled into the political arena. Congressman Norman Lent (R-New York) introduced a proposed constitutional amendment, House Joint Resolution 646, to ban busing for purposes of desegregation. The proposed amendment read, "No public school student shall, because of his race, creed, or color, be assigned to or be required to attend a particular school." Interviewed on the NBC network's *Newslight* program, Congressman Celler stated, "The Constitution is a group of principles that are to guide government, not mere gimmicks to help local situations. It would be horrendous—I use the word with all the emphasis within me—to have a Constitutional amendment passed with reference to busing. I would do everything in my power to prevent it."

Anti-busing advocates pursued a second front, through a pending education bill. The House adopted by a 235 to 125 margin an amendment to the education bill that no future court-ordered busing would take place until the case had been argued all the way to the Supreme Court. A second amendment prohibited using any funds from any federal source to pay any of the costs, including gasoline, of busing for desegregation. This would force thousands of school districts that used federal funds to support busing to pay for that program through cuts in other budget lines. The same day Celler appeared on NBC, Congressman Lent announced that 145 members had signed a Discharge Petition to force the proposed amendment out of the Judiciary Committee.

With that pressure mounting, Celler commenced hearings before Judiciary Subcommittee No. 5 that ran from late February until the end of May. During that time, the Discharge Petition never reached the number of signatures needed to force it from the committee. Indeed, most of its signers were long-term opponents of civil rights. One study showed that signers had voted 102 to 14 against the 1970 extension of the Voting Rights Act. Legal expert Gary Orfield wrote, "Although a large number of members were prepared to press for an amendment, the proposal never convinced the moderates who opposed busing." In short, while there was strong legislative opposition to busing, that support fell short of amending the Constitutuion.

The subcommittee heard seventy-two witnesses, including many members of Congress. Most testified in favor of the proposed amendment. Congressman William Minshall (R-Ohio) stated, "I have voted for every civil rights bill they have sent to the floor of the House. I reject the idea that racism is involved in objections to school busing." Liberal Congressman John Dingell (D-Michigan) stated, "Time unnecessarily spent riding a bus does not contribute to a child's education" but only denies "children an opportunity to enjoy high quality educational opportunities by diverting funds from the classrooms."

On March 16, 1972, President Nixon disavowed the anti-busing amendment, stating that amending the constitution has "a fatal flaw—it takes too long." Instead, Nixon introduced H.R. 13916, a bill that would limit the power of federal judges to order school desegregation in any instance in which the busing of schoolchildren would be the means to achieve it. Further, the bill sought a moratorium while existing school busing programs were reviewed.

For procedural reasons, as ranking member of the Judiciary Committee, it fell to William Moore McCulloch to introduce the administration bill. And having done so, he launched a broadside against it. Congress, he noted, enjoyed the right to limit the actions of the federal courts, "but Congress does not have the power to eliminate *constitutional* rights."

On April 12, when Attorney General Richard Kleindienst appeared before the Judiciary Committee, McCulloch addressed him directly:

It is with the deepest regret that I sit here today to listen to a spokesman for a Republican Administration asking the Congress to prostitute the courts by obligating them to suspend the equal protection clause for a time so that Congress may debate the merits of further slowing down and perhaps even rolling back desegregation in public schools.

McCulloch said it was also "with deepest regret" that he listened to a debate that suggested "the moral and constitututional rights of countless human beings were somehow negotiable." The measure was before Congress only because "some prominent politicians have fueled false fears and raised false hopes."

Wasn't it only yesterday when we in Congress told our deprived citizens to press their claims not in the streets but in the courts? Now, when some of them have taken their case to the courts and under the laws of the land have won victories, it is suggested that it is time to change the rules. What message are we sending to our black people? Is this any way to govern a country? Is this any way to bring peace to a troubled land?

McCulloch's statement received support back home in the form of an April 14, 1972, editorial in the *Dayton Daily News*, which accused President Nixon of "forcing a gratuitous constitutional crisis." The newspaper added, "Nixon probably doesn't much care one way or the other. If the courts knuckle under, he will be a hero to the antibusing mobs. If the courts hold firm, they will be the villains. Either way, Mr. Nixon will gain politically."

A lengthy assessment published May 18, 1972, in the *Washington Evening Star* depicted the issue as the final battle between "three old lions": Congressmen McCulloch, Celler, and William M. Colmer, a Mississippi Democrat now in his fortieth year in the House. Colmer took no little satisfaction in observing that where civil rights enforcement was concerned, "The chickens have come home to roost in the North." The issue mattered further because of President Nixon's expressed oppositon to school busing. For this, the *Evening Star* wrote, "Colmer gave Nixon major credit, McCulloch grumbled about it and Celler condemned the President's position."

Celler and McCulloch succeeded for some time in keeping the proposed anti-busing constitutional amendment bottled up in the Judiciary Committee. Then Colmer, as chairman of the Rules Committee, forced the bill from the Judiciary Committee to the House floor. Celler and McCulloch urged rejection of the measure. As the *Evening Star* reported, "When they lost the procedural test by a whopping 318 to 71, they knew they were beaten on final passage." McCulloch, for once, was not terribly optimistic, telling a reporter, "The flood tide of civil rights legislation has been slowed materially. I don't know if the current has been reversed. I hope not."

Here, the Senate intervened. Briefly summarized, the Senate stepped away from any direct confrontation with the federal judiciary. Instead, they framed a compromise that sounded strongly anti-busing—thereby giving members an opportunity to take the popular stand—but in practice was much more moderate than the House-passed measure. Legal scholar Gary Orfield said it "gave the conservatives some rhetorical satisfaction while attempting to protect most of the momentum of racial change." Considerable back and forth ensued in the House-Senate conference committee. In the end, the Senate accepted much of the House language in the expectation that it would be declared unconstitutional (as it was). The amendment to ban use of federal funds for busing fell by the wayside. The truncated bill passed the Senate by 63 to 16 on May 24, 1972. House approval came June 10 by a narrower 218 to 180 margin.

President Nixon was clearly unhappy with the result. In his June 23 signing statement, he noted a few good aspects of the bill, among them the creation of the National Institute of Education. On busing, he said: "We asked the Congress to draw up new uniform national desegregation standards for all school districts—South, North, East, and West. The Congress determined to allow the existing inequities and injustices to remain." Congress had been asked for a moratorium on further court-odered busing until national standards were established; it had declined to act. Congress had been asked to limit busing of sixth-grade or younger students; it had declined to act. Congress, he said, "has not given us the answer we requested; it has given us rhetoric . . . it has provided a clever political evasion. The relief it provides is illusory."

In sum, the action of Congress was hardly a victory for civil rights; rather, it was the avoidance of a sweeping defeat. William McCulloch had feared that progress on civil rights might be reversed. At worst, however, it was treading water.

In these matters—school prayer, the equal rights amendment, and school busing— McCulloch could hardly be said with any certainty to be representing the wishes of his constituents. His behavior takes one back to a second statement Edmund Burke made in 1774 to his constituents in Bristol: "You choose a member indeed, but when you have chosen him, he is not a member of Bristol, but he is a Member of Parliament."

CHAPTER 23

Retirement and Death

The year 1971 was not a happy time for William McCulloch. Several years earlier, the McCullochs had moved again, this time to the Cathedral West Apartments at 4100 Cathredal Avenue NW, where they lived in a somewhat smaller but still elegant quarters, Apartment 703. Their daughter Nancy lived one floor down in Apartment 605. The building, she said, gave her a great sense of security because it was generally believed to be the residence of the head of the Central Intelligence Agency. That sense of security vanished when a friend suggested that a fair number of people might be out to kill the CIA director.

Whatever hazard the putative CIA director might have faced, Apartment 703 was ill-omened for William McCulloch. The apartment faced south onto the city's Rock Creek Park. Sometime in November 1970, McCulloch attempted to open the window that faced onto the park. It resisted, he slipped, hitting his head on the sill and giving his skull a severe jolt. He was briefly hospitalized. At first the injury appeared relatively minor. By the first of the year, however, McCulloch was admitted to Johns Hopkins Hospital because the injury had revealed itself to be a dangerous subdural hematoma. On January 6, Mabel McCulloch wrote a friend, "I have spent a great deal of time with Bill at the hospital. We are thankful that at last the doctors are very encouraging about Bill's condition."

The encouragement proved illusory. Congressman McCulloch worsened and fell into a coma. The *1971 Congressional Quarterly Almanac* recorded McCulloch as missing the first eight of the fourteen "selected votes" it identified as of prime importance during that year. These included the March 31 vote when McCulloch's close colleague, Charles Whalen (R-Ohio), failed by a 198 to 200 margin to reduce the extension of the military draft, through the October 14, 1971 vote when Congress broadened the authority of the Consumer Protection Agency. During this time, McCulloch's congressional office managed as best it could. Routine tasks continued. Requests for interviews or for the congressman's position on a given issue were handled by office manager Vera Page. An example was her reply to a July 19 request from *Louisville Times* reporter Mike Wines, "Mr. McCulloch underwent surgery earlier this year and has not yet returned to the office." Thomas Mooney, then a Judiciary Committee attorney, recalls, "After his fall, I would go out to his house. Mabel was always fussing over him. They were a very close couple. Even in older age, she was beautiful."

With no particular basis for optimism about the congressman's prognosis, Mabel McCulloch began discussions with Mooney about what needed to be done. Mooney recalled, "Mabel said it was time to think about retiring." The McCulloch daughters were consulted. Mooney added, "I helped Mabel draft the press release. She announced his retirement without his knowledge."

The announcement drew forth a ream of tributes. Among them was one from *The Washington Post*, which reported the "sad but not surprising news" that for reasons of health William McCulloch would not be a candidate for reelection. *The Post* editorial was practically a eulogy:

Quiet, direct, hardworking conservative in taste and stubborn in principle, Mr. McColluch has been the kind of representative who shows up at 7 a.m. to begin the day's business. This may have worked some hardship on his staff, but it also worked to the enormous advantage of the country. For the fact is that no man can claim a larger role in the passage of the landmark civil rights legislation of the past 14 years than Mr. McCulloch. The subject had become his quiet passion. What put his commitment beyond challenge was the fact that there was nothing in his background to suggest that it proceeded from fashion, social pressure or political urgencies.

All but instantly, the news of McCulloch's retirement brought a three-page personal letter of thanks from Jacqueline Kennedy Onassis, who recounted the importance of McCulloch's loyalty on the issue of civil rights. The former First Lady wrote in part, "You made a personal commitment to President Kennedy in October 1963. . . . You held to that commitment despite enormous pressure and political temptations not to do so. There were so many opportunities to sabotage the bill, without appearing to do so, but you never took them. On the contrary, you brought everyone along with you."

Having been praised, however, the Ohio Congressman was not quite ready to be buried. Indeed, when he regained consciousness, committee counsel Thomas Mooney stated, William Moore McCulloch was furious to learn that he was foregoing reelection. The Congressman had no intention of going gently into that retirement. On September 28, 1971, his office issued a press release, "McCulloch Back in Action," noting that while his doctors had advised him to take it easy for a few weeks, he intended to be back on the House floor soon. And he was—voting October 19, 1971, in favor of the defense appropriations bill. On October 27, his hometown newspaper, the *Piqua Daily Call*, reported that McCulloch was reconsidering retirement. The newspaper quoted him, "I have said heretofore that if I continued to improve, I certainly would be a candidate. I have continued to improve." His spirits may have been bouyed by the November 9 birth of his second grandchild, Sarah, whose parents were then living in Washington, D.C.

On January 7, 1972, he made it official when his office issued a press release announcing that he would be a candidate for a thirteenth term. The announcement, however, did not prove as welcome as McCulloch might have hoped. He was informed that he should expect—for the first time in two decades—a serious challenger in the Republican primary. He was further informed that his eight months' absence from Congress had led many of even his long-term supporters to question whether McCulloch, now seventy, had the stamina to remain in public life. This decided him. In a January 18, 1972, press release, he abruptly reversed himself, stating, "At the end of this year, I will have completed 36 years of publc service in the Ohio House of Representatives and in the United States House of Representatives and I now wish to enjoy a more quiet life with my family and my friends."

Though working a reduced load, Congressman McCulloch remained diligent about his duties for the balance of the 1972 session, present for more than three-quarters of the votes taken in the House. He remained a maverick within Republican ranks. One of the last votes he cast came on August 16 when he voted against sustaining Republican President Richard Nixon's veto of funding for the Departments of Labor and Health, Education and Welfare. His last year in office included two characteristic gestures, one personal, one professional. McCulloch believed in thrift. When his five-year-old granddaughter Elizabeth was visiting Piqua with her family, William and Mabel McCulloch talked to her about the importance of saving one's money and then took her to the Piqua National Bank. Elizabeth recalled: "I remember going to the bank and they had a red carpet rolled out with the red roping that led up to the teller's window. They had placed a small little set of stairs so I could see over the teller's desk and we made my first deposit." The second was the attention he continued to pay to the appointments he made to the nation's service academies. One of his final appointees was a young man from Piqua, James P. Wisecup, who recalled, "I remember my interview with him very well; he was so down to earth and unassuming. He put you at ease immediately." James Wisecup, now Rear Admiral Wisecup, served as president of the Naval War College before his 2011 appointment as Naval Inspector General.

William McCulloch took formal leave from Ohio politics at a gathering of nearly one thousand Republicans at the Allen County Fairgrounds on October 5, 1972. Those present included three former Republican governors—James Rhodes, C. William O'Neill, and John Bricker—and a host of lesser state officials.

McCulloch's departure from the national scene was noted by a series of tributes appearing in the *Congressional Record*. One particularly eloquent statement came from Father Theodore Hesburgh, president of the University of Notre Dame and longtime head of the U.S. Civil Rights Commission. He stated in part,

> To the growing number of Americans who declare that they are losing faith in our system, the rebuttal is the civil rights stand of Congressman McCulloch. . . . Your reward was simply the reward of doing the right thing. We would have far less cynicism about American politics if we had more politicians like Bill McCulloch.

There was also, in a sense, a negative tribute to William McCulloch. Facing the electorate in 1948, McCulloch had declared, "If you expect to measure your congressman's ability by what he can get from Congress, I would rather not be returned." Typically, particularly when a long-term member is involved, a congressman's retirement is marked by naming for the departing member some federal facility he had helped his district acquire. In McCulloch's case, those charged with the task came up empty handed. In a quarter-century in Congress, McCulloch had never once used his influence to gain for the Fourth Congressional District of Ohio a single bit of federal largesse.

Many who come to Washington to serve in Congress—even those whose terms of service were brief—find the nation's capital a difficult place to leave. For the McCullochs, retirement meant a return to the Piqua apartment they rented from Charles Upton. To lighten the burden of moving, Mabel McCulloch told the *Piqua Daily Call*, "I let my daughters choose any furnishings they wanted. There wasn't a stick left to pack—which I consider complimentry and very sly of me."

Back in Piqua, William McCulloch continued his practice of law. He continued his civic involvements, and was named chairman of the Piqua National Bank on whose board he had served since 1964. He traveled, though not often, as when he accepted an invitation from the Yale School of Law to take part in an April 7, 1973, conference whose attendees were to include Nicholas Katzenbach, Burke Marshall, and Emanuel Celler.

Piqua, as the McCullochs' home for forty-five years, was a place of great comfort to him. But it was not a place of sufficient expertise. He never fully recovered from his accident; his health worsened, and in time he needed better medical care than Piqua could offer. So the McCullochs returned to the nation's capital. The couple took an apartment at 5420 Connecticut Avenue NW, but the former congressman was hospitalized much of the time.

A series of brain operations brought no improvement. Eventually, he moved to the Washington Home, which, located near Wisconsin Avenue, was a residence for the permanently invalid. It was, his doctors assured the family, the place he could get the best of care.

That thought was lost on Elizabeth Carver, thirteen and a visiting granddaughter.

I remember he looked frail but still had that bright smile and gleam in his eyes. That comforting and loving smile and aura he had even during his last days. I remember the pajamas, the wheelchair, and the plastic tube running out from under his pant leg. I was uneasy. He opened his hands out to me and looking up at me with that loving smile he said, as he patted his hand on his knee, "Why don't you come over here and sit on your old granddad's lap."

This, with some difficulty given the wheelchair, she did. "I sat for the last time on my granddaddy's lap. I think I kind of knew that somehow this was it."

Twenty-five-year Ohio congressman William Moore McCulloch died at the Washington Home of a heart attack suffered February 22, 1980. An unobtrusive man, McCulloch was overshadowed even in death. The day's headlines were captured by the "miracle" victory of the American Olympic hockey team over their Soviet rivals at the Lake Placid Winter Games. The obituaries largely recounted McCulloch's contributions to the field of civil rights. The one in *The Washington Post* carried the perhaps unintentional reminder of the small-town boy he had once been. Among the survivors were listed Mildred Lecky, Elva Zehnder, and Stella Hoffman, all still of Holmesville, Ohio.

The funeral service was set for the following Saturday at the Church of the Presbyterian Congregation in Georgetown at 3115 P Street, NW, of which the McCullochs had been long-time members. When he read the news, Robert Kimball—who had helped broker the saving compromise of the 1964 civil rights bill—telephoned McCulloch's onetime colleague and former New York City mayor John Lindsay; the pair immediately decided to fly down to Washington for the service. Airborne, Kimball looked over at Lindsay to discover that the latter's eyes were, like his own, filled with tears. The two were nearly on the same flight as former McCulloch congressional staffer Joseph Metz, who awakened himself early enough to catch the 7 a.m. shuttle from New York's LaGuardia Airport to Washington National.

The church at which three score or so of mourners gathered is not a showy structure, but in its refined understatement was well suited to the nature of the man being buried. Mabel McCulloch helped select the hymns, which included Johan Sibelius' "Be Still My Soul." At the urging of McCulloch's daughter Nancy, the eulogy was delivered by the former congressman's close associate, Senator Charles Mathias of Maryland. From there, McCulloch was taken by motorcade to Arlington National Cemetery for burial. The pallbearers included former judiciary attorney Thomas Mooney, former congressional office staffer Joseph Metz, and other family and friends. His granddaughter Sarah, then eight, recalled:

I will never forget driving into Arlington National Cemetery in the long motorcade in the limo with grandmommy. She was dressed in a black lace dress. She seemed proud that granddaddy would be laid to rest. It was a windy late February day. I remember the servicemen had trouble folding the flag, but they finally got it right and gave it to grandmommy. Then the twenty-one-gun salute. It was so official. I remember thinking: who was he that all this was going on? All these people saying sorry for your loss and that the country had lost a great man. To me he was just my granddaddy.

William McCulloch was buried in Arlington National Cemetery's section 11, gravesite 584-2, which is now shared by Mabel McCulloch, who died October 3, 1990.

Any person is various people to others. To eight-year-old Sarah, William McCulloch was a loving grandfather. To NAACP chief lobbyist Clarence Mitchell, he was something rarer. In a tribute published shortly after McCulloch's death, Mitchell wrote:

After viewing the flag-draped coffin of William McCulloch last week in the Church of the Presbyterian Congregation in Georgetown, I thought of the Grecian helmet on display in the Truman Library in Independence, Missouri, a helmet worn by a warrior who died with Leonidas and his 300 Spartans defending Western civilization at Thermopylae.

Bravery is important on the battlefield, but through the centuries it has been necessary for courageous people to protect freedom in governmental institutions as well.

Mitchell noted that from the end of Reconstruction to the middle of the twentieth century, "few were willing to stand up in Congress and attack injustice based on race." This, he wrote, was because the power to reward or to punish anyone who did so rested largely with those who vigorously advocated segregation. He counted William McCulloch among those few. He cited McCulloch's 1964 advocacy of civil rights; his 1969 insistence on the extension of voting rights. Mitchell added, "It was during the long sessions in committee and on the floor of the House that, like the Spartans of old, Congressman McCulloch's courage and moral commitment became most evident."

Beyond the question of how various others see one, there is the question of how one sees oneself and one's task. On October 12, 1971, late in his Congressional career, William McCulloch described to the House in which he served the task he set for himself.

We are a nation of many people and many views. In such a Nation, the prime purpose of a legislator, from wherever he may come, is to accommodate the interests, desires, wants, and needs of all our citizens. To alienate some in order to satisfy others is not only a disservice to those we alienate, but a violation of the principles of our Republic. Lawmaking is the reconciliation of divergent views. In a democratic society like ours, the purpose of representative government is to soften tension—reduce strife—while enabling groups and individuals to more nearly obtain the kind of life they wish to live.

The function of Congress is not to convert the will of the majority of the people into law, rather its function is to hammer out on the anvil of public debate a compromise between positions acceptable to the majority. In a democracy, the people themselves vote "yes" or "no" on the issues and there is less opportunity for compromise. When a referendum is taken, no amendments are allowed; there is quite clearly a losing side. In a republic, representatives vote for the people. There is discussion and debate. There are amendments. There is opportunity for compromise. It is less clear that there is a losing side.

CHAPTER 24

Delta Queen

People have pet peeves; members of Congress have pet projects—self-selected acts of advocacy unlikely ever to make the slightest difference to their electoral success. For William McCulloch, that advocacy was of the *Delta Queen*, which by the time McCulloch took an interest in the matter was the last paddlewheel steamer plying the inland waters of the Mississippi, the Ohio, the Cumberland, and the Tennessee Rivers.

The 285-foot-long *Delta Queen* was built by the William Denny & Brothers shipyard on Scotland's River Clyde. Shipped in pieces to Stockton, California, in 1926, she was assembled and provided transit between San Francisco and Sacramento. During the Second World War, the *Delta Queen* did military service in San Francisco Bay. Post-war, she was purchased by the Greene Line, Cincinnati, Ohio, and placed into service as a cruise ship on the nation's inland waterways. The *Delta Queen* accommodated 192 passengers, generally on three-day cruises, and carried a crew of seventy-five. Her hull was steel, but her superstructure was a blend of mahogany, ironwood, and walnut, including a curved mahogany staircase trimmed with brass. A rare feature was the *Delta Queen's* steam calliope that thundered out her arrival into port.

The ship's fine wooden accoutrements were almost the end of her. On November 15, 1965, the *S. S. Yarmouth Castle*—with a similar wooden superstructure—caught fire while en route from Miami to Nassau. Ninety persons died sixty miles short of their intended destination. The result was the 1966 passage of the Safety at Sea Act, which required all ships flying a United States flag to be constructed of steel. The *Delta Queen* managed to obtain two two-year extensions to bring itself up to code. The second extension expired November 2, 1970.

On April 23, 1970, William McCulloch and several other legislators, including Ohio's U.S. Senators William Saxbe and Robert Taft, introduced legislation to grant the *Delta Queen* an exemption. Granting the exemption, McCulloch told the House, would "preserve the last page of America's 160-year-old riverboat history." McCulloch added:

The law that would retire the *Delta Queen* was enacted in 1966 to rid the seas of unsafe ships. . . . Inadvertently, it seems, this legislation was made broad enough to encompass passenger vessels carrying overnight passengers operating in our inland waters. For the purpose of safety standards, the *Queen* was placed in the same category as deep-draft vessels traveling on the high seas.

McCulloch asserted the safety risk was nil. The *Queen* never traveled in water deeper than her middle deck; even if she hit bottom, she would remain largely above water. The bill was referred to the Merchant Marine and Fisheries Committee, which took no action. Indeed, the Merchant Marine and Fisheries Committee never held a single hearing on any of the twenty separate bills introduced on the *Queen's* behalf. The committee was chaired by Edward Garmatz (D-Maryland).

At one point, McCulloch dispatched judiciary staff attorney Thomas Mooney to see if some solution could be had. To Mooney's "great surprise," Congressman Garmatz suggested that a $5,000 contribution to Garmatz's campaign fund might ease the wheels. When Mooney reported this solicitation to McCulloch, the Ohio congressman uttered what in his native Holmesville, Ohio would be known as a "barnyard epithet." McCulloch, Mooney recalled, quickly added, "Don't you dare suggest that to anyone."

In a seemingly unrelated move, the House of Representatives on October 8, 1970, passed H.R. 6114 to reimburse a federal employee, one Elmer M. Grade, the $900 he had spent on realtor's fees when he sold his Denver home after his transfer to Washington, D.C. Grade was due the money, as by regulation when the federal government relocates an employee, the government picks up the tab for any realtor's fee involved.

As the November 2, 1970, deadline approached, the *Delta Queen* became a *cause célèbre*. Thirteen governors weighed in on the *Queen's* behalf. Two hundred newspapers in thirty-one states editorialized in favor of the extension. President Nixon received 1,500 letters on the subject. Others wrote to McCulloch, including an eighth-grader from Versailles, Ohio, who—apparently unaware that he was addressing a sixty-eight-year-old member of Congress—wrote, "I don't want that ship torn apart just because some old men don't like it." The deadline passed, and the *Delta Queen* appeared to be docked for good. On November 23, 1970, Indiana Senator Vance Hartke stated, "The quality of American life in the future will depend in large measure on how wisely we deal with our heritage from the past." For the moment, this appeared to be the story's epitaph.

Congress, as noted, can be a highly imaginative place. Recall how in 1960 Majority Leader Lyndon Johnson and Minority Leader Everett Dirksen contrived to amend a most incidental measure—the leasing of an unused Army facility to a school district in need—by adding to it the entire text of the 1960 civil rights bill. The Senate now amended the bill reimbursing Mr. Grade for his realtor's expense by adding a rider to grant the *Queen* a further three-year extension. This carried the matter over to the pending post-election lame-duck session. On November 29, United Press International reported that, due to a surprise move it attributed to Congressman McCulloch and Senators Marlow Cook (R-Kentucky) and William Saxbe (R-Ohio), Congress would have one more chance to save the *Delta Queen*. The wire service reported, "Everyone except those in on the secret thought the bill only involved a $900 reimbursement from the government to Elmer M. Grade, Arlington, Virginia, for moving expenses as a government employee."

Because the House-passed version of the 1970 merchant marine bill carried an extension for the *Delta Queen* and the Senate-passed version deleted the extension, a conference committee was required. However, since the sponsor of the rider, Senator Cook, was a member of the Senate Judiciary Committee, the conference was of members of the respective House and Senate Judiciary Committees, thereby smoothly bypassing the recalcitrant Merchant Marine and Fisheries Committee. Since the issue was a riverboat, McCulloch shuffled the cards and stacked the deck. The House conferees were himself, Emanuel Celler (whom McCulloch had recruited to the cause), and a pro-*Delta* Congressman Harold Donahue (D-Massachusetts). Not surprisingly, the conference committee recommended an extension for the *Delta Queen*, somewhat imaginatively trying to draw the National Aeronautics and Space Administration into the equation. The formal wording was:

Permitting the DELTA QUEEN to operate until November 1, 1973, will give the Congress time to hear and to decide how to assist in saving the last symbol of a bygone era. Furthermore, the conferees recommend early and expedited hearings on the feasibility of applying recent NASA technological developments to the vessel's wooden superstructure to determine their effect in reducing the combustability and flame-spread characteristics of these surfaces.

The House debated the committee report on December 15, 1970. Celler, who had never been on a riverboat in his life, was nonetheless a great fan of Broadway. This brought forth the observation that were it not for America's riverboats, Oscar Hammerstein II and Jerome Kern would never have written *Showboat* and Americans would never had heard "Old Man River" and "The Man I Love." The eighty-two-year-old congressman added, "Life without a bit of romance is listless and lacks luster." More prosaically, various congressmen whose districts bordered on the Mississippi River argued for the economic contribution the *Delta Queen* made.

The opposition was led by Congressman Garmatz. The Maryland representative was furious that his Merchant Marine and Fisheries Committee had been bypassed. He stated his opposition bluntly. The *Delta*

Queen, he told the House, "is a firetrap. It is made largely of wood. Wood burns." He noted that the U.S. Coast Guard, which held responsibility for maritime safety, opposed continued operation of the boat. He distributed a statement that read in part, "I hope the *Delta Queen* never burns, but if it does, the blood will be on Congress." Underscoring that point, the *Louisville Times* noted, "The paragraph begun by that sentence was indented, and hand-drawn skulls and crossbones were placed on either side."

The House was undaunted by the warning. On December 15, it voted by a one-sided 295 to 74 margin to give the *Delta Queen* its extension. Soon thereafter, the operators of the *Delta Queen* announced a 1971 season of forty-one three-day cruises. McCulloch was from the Midwest, a place of land and rivers. When one traveled between the cities at which the *Queen* made port, one caught a glimpse of an earlier America, riverbanks not greatly different from those viewed by Mark Twain over a century earlier. McCulloch was emblematic. He had instigated great changes in America motivated largely by applying the best of the nation's enduring traits. Nothing is quite like the Mississippi River, McCulloch told the House, reading the words of Mark Twain into the *Congressional Record*:

One cannot see too many summer sunrises on the Mississippi. They are enchanting. First, there is the eloquence of silence; for a deep hush broods everywhere. Next there is the haunting sense of loneliness, isolation, remoteness from the worry and hustle of the world. . . . And all this stretch of river is a mirror, and you have the shadowy reflections of the leafage and the curving shores and receding capes pictured in it. Well, that is all beautiful; soft, rich and beautiful; and . . . you grant that you have seen something that is worth remembering.

Notes

Chapter One: Mr. Marshall to Piqua

1   Marshall meeting with Carver: Interview, David Carver, October 17, 2012;
        Whalens, page 11
    "Cool his heels": Whalens, page 11
    "A perfect gentleman": Interview, David Carver, October 17, 2012
    "I have to buy": Interview, David Carver
2   "The Congressman's office": Whalens, page 12
    Physical description to McCulloch: Ibid
    "Both were lawyers": Interview, Andrew Glass, December 18, 2012
    McCulloch presents GOP views on 1957 and 1960: Whalens, page 13
3   McCulloch's conditions: Whalens, page 13

Chapter Two: An Ohio Farm

4   "An individual interested": Interview, David Stallman
    McCullochs settling in Holmes County: Stallman, pages 3, 11
    Underground railroad: Stallman, page 19
5   Twenty escaping slaves: Stallman, page 21
    Penalties for aiding slaves: Stallman, page 19
    "During the Civil War": Library of Congress, "Chronicling America," on-line
        description of Holmes County Newspapers, www.chroniclingamerica.loc.gov/
        lccn/sn84028822]
    "Lincoln and Liberty": Ibid
    The more extreme language: Lehman and Nolt, pages 112-113
    "Daddy was the fair-haired": Interview, Nancy McCulloch, November 12, 2012
    "My father's father kept": Interview, Ann McCulloch Carver, October 19, 2012
6   "Did unlawfully fail" and lawsuits following: Stallman, pages 46-47
    Louisville sluggers: Ibid, page 19
    The town boasted three saloons: Ibid, page 144
    Church services: Interview, Nancy McCulloch, November 12, 2012
    "Why, none of them": Interview, Lester Blanke, March 12, 1987
    High school graduation: Stallman, page 129
7   McCulloch's sisters: Interview, Nancy McCulloch, August 7, 2013
    Short pants: *Ohio State Journal*, December 2, 1938, page 6

Chapter Three: An Ohio Education

8   McCulloch likely to listen: Interview, Nancy McCulloch, November 12, 2012

Description, College of Wooster: Notestein, pages 131, 134

$250,000 challenge grant; Ibid, 212

Football success: *The Index* [Wooster yearbook], 1922 edition

McCulloch's entering class: Notestein, page 235

9   Kaiser Wilhelm beheaded: Ibid, page 169

Student and staff enlistment: Ibid, page 177

"Our country needs": Ibid, page 235

Professor Chancellor controversy: Ibid, pages 226-228 [The question of Harding's ancestry is best handled in The Shadow of Blooming Grove, by Francis Russell, McGraw-Hill, 1968]

10   African American graduates: Notestein, page 226

"The price, the purpose": Ibid, page 188

Visit by Jubilee singer: *The Wooster Voice* [campus newspaper], May 3, 1922

"Negro colony": Notestein, 227

"It would be wise": *The Index*, 1922 edition

"Sweet and smiling" though "Shades of Socrates": *The Index*, 1921 edition, page 99

"Having completed two full years": Ohio State University Bulletin, January 15, 1925; School of Law, 1925-1926, page 7

11   "The purpose of the College": OSU Bulletin, 1925; School of Law, 1925-1926, page 6

Description of campus and law school facilities: OSU Bulletin, 1925; School of Law, 1925-1926, pages 5-6

Costs of attendance: OSU Bulletin, 1925; School of Law, 1925-1926, page 15

McCulloch's fraternity life: 1924 *Makio* [school yearbook], page 480

Tertulia council: *Ohio State Lantern* [student newspaper], May 16, 1922, page 3

"Forbid all favors" and subsequent quotes: *Ohio State Lantern*, January 8, 1925, page 4

12   McCulloch graduates: 1925 *Makio*, page 171

Chapter Four: Jacksonville

13   "The financial wizard": *New York Times*, November 8, 1925, page E2

"His purpose in coming to Florida": Ibid

Ponzi arrested: *New York Times*, February 9, 1926, page 3

"A New Season's Rush": *New York Times*, November 8, 1925, page XXI

14   Real estate expert advice: *New York Times*, November 11, 1925, page RE1

Davis Shores development: *Florida Times-Union*, November 15, 1925

Tallest buildings in Jacksonville: http://en.wikiipedia.org/wiki/List_of_tallest_buildings_in_Jacksonville

Jacksonsville population: Davis, page 500

Construction and bank clearings: *Florida Times-Union*, January 1, 1926, page 1

"No matter how 'good'": Ibid, page 4

15   "I am generous": *Congressional Record*, January 31, 1964, page 1544

"I lived in one": *Congressional Record*, June 14, 1957, Page 9217

16   Charles Brantley case: *Florida Times-Union*, January 7, 1926

"In those days": Interview, Colleen McMurray, January 9, 2013

"Obsession to maintain": Sokol, page 54

"If they did notice it": Ibid, page 61

James Weldon Johnson bio note:www.biography.com/people/ja,es-weldon-john-
son-9356013

17 "Streets were sandy": Johnson, page 430

[Note: All "Johnson" references in this chapter are to James Weldon Johnson]

"Yes, when I was in Jacksonville": Ibid, page 488

"It is a struggle": Ibid, page 430

"The South today": Ibid, pages 433-434

"And yet in this respect": Ibid, pages 487-488

"These men conform": Ibid, page 436

"Assaulted a white woman": *Florida Times-Union*, January 2, 1926

18 "A negro truck driver": *Florida Times-Union*, January 10, 1926

"Negro armed with pitchfork": Ibid

Negro desperado": Ibid

White youth near death: *Florida Times-Union*, January 22, 1925, page 32

J. Edgar Hoover quote: King, page 134

19 Florida lynchings: King, page 108

"It was the virtually angelic": Ibid, page 3

Marshall escapes lynching: Ibid, pages 14-20

McCulloch's residence and employers: Jacksonville genealogist Yvonne Johnson

20 Fleming law firm: www.jaxbar.org/about-us/past-presidents/

Francis Philip Fleming Sr. bio: en.wikipedia.org/wiki/Francis_P._Fleming

"She thought he was the one." Interview, Ann McCulloch Carver; Friday, October
19, 2012

Mabel McCulloch characteristics: Interviews, including Nancy McCulloch,
November 12, 2012; Ann McCulloch Carver, October 19, 2012; Joseph Metz,
December 27, 2012

21 Elopement: Interview, Ann McCulloch Carver, October 19, 2012

Oak Street Residence: Jacksonville genealogist Yvonne Johnson

State controller indicted: *New York Times*, September 22, 1926, page 31

Forty-two indictments: *New York Tmes*, August 8, 1926, page 1

$2 million in cash: *New York Times*, March 9, 1927, page 1

"Florida has never been": *New York Times*, May 8, 1927, page 24

"Served to clear Florida": Ibid

Chapter Five: Piqua

22 McCullochs relocate to Piqua: Interviews, David and Ann McCulloch Carver,
October 19, 2012

McCullochs as Presbyterians: Hill, page 163

Founding of Piqua: Interview, James Oda, August 3, 2012

Early Piqua industry: Oda [Transportation], pages 16-21

23 Randolph slaves: Interview, James Oda, August 3, 2012

Flaxseed industry: Oda [Industry], page 11

Underwear industry: Interview, James Oda, August 3, 2012

Piqua politics: Interview, James Oda, August 3, 2012

Johnny Weissmuller: Oda [Transportation], page 26

24. "Their insigificant other": Interview, James Oda, August 3, 2012

Description of McCulloch home: Interview, Nancy McCulloch, November 12, 2012

Death of Ida Moore McCulloch: *The Holmes County Farmer's Hub*, February 26, 1931
"You have something": Letter from George Berry to William McCulloch, February 19, 1931, McCulloch Papers, Ohio Congressional Archives. Series 1: Personal/ Political, Box 2; folder 3

Chapter Six: Depression Era Legislator

25   "Are you sure?" and "Abundance of Caution": Interview, Robert Kimball, December 28, 2012
"Somewhat audaciously": *Ohio State Journal*, January 17, 1939, page 4
"Miami county citizens": *Piqua Daily Call*, November 8, 1932, page 4
26   "He was born": *Piqua Daily Call*, November 4, 1932, page 11
McCulloch victory margin: *Piqua Daily Call*, November 9, 1932, page 1
Ohio Statehouse: Gold, page 92
James Thurber quote: Gold, pages 318-319
27   Effect of "free silver": Fenton, page 122
German-American voters: Ibid, page 123
1928 Ohio election returns: Dave Leip's Atlas of U.S. Presidential Elections, http://uselectionatlas.org/
"Sixty-four counties": Gold, page 423
"You are meeting": [Ohio] House [of Representatives] Journal, January 2, 1933, page 8; *hereinafter: House Journal*
Unpaid schoolteachers: *New York Times*, January 12, 1933, page 23
"Removing" bidder: *Washington Post*, January 27, 1933, page 15
"No bank holiday": *New York Times*, February 26, 1933, page N9
28   McCulloch bills: *House Journal*, February 7, 1933, page 263 [Bill signed May 19, 1933]
"Both Ohio and Indiana": *Washington Post*, February 7, 1933, page 6
Sales tax introduced: *House Journal*, February 8, 1933, page 280
Shortening the work week: *House Journal*, February 20, 1933, pages 364-365
"In space of 38 minutes": *New York Times*, February 28, 1933, page 8
McCulloch votes: *House Journal*, February 27, 1933, pages 421, 423
Pari-mutuel betting: *New York Times*, April 8, 1933, page 17
29   "Made further efforts": *Washington Post*, July 22, 1933, page 6
"We are considering" and further remarks: *House Journal*, April 16, 1933, pages 7-10
"Ohio House of Representatives": *New York Times*, March 23, 1934, page 39
Dismissal of muncipal workers: Ibid
30   "The 90th General Assembly": *House Journal*, November 20, 1934, pages 472-476
Ohio sales tax: Ohio Retail Sales Tax of 1935, www.ohiohistorycentral.org/w/ Ohio_Retail_Sales_Tax_Law of 1935
$47.8 million: Ibid
McCulloch victory margin: *Piqua Daily Call*, November 7, 1934, page 4
"In William McCulloch": *Piqua Daily Call*, November 1, 1934, page 4
31   "Gov. George White": *Gongwer*, January 14, 1935, page 1
"Faced the possibility": *Washington Post*, March 18, 1935, page 1
"Incontrovertible evidence": Ibid
"Criminal libel": *Washington Post*, March 19, 1935, page 1
Football players on payroll: *Washington Post*, October 12, 1935, page 1

32   "For the purpose of creating": *House Journal,* February 20, 1935, page 249

    "Revolution in public school": *New York Times,* April 21, 1935, page E6

    McCulloch vote: *House Journal,* May 16, 1935, page 1076

    Free textbooks: *House Journal,* February 27, 1935, page 57

    Chicken v. fox: *House Journal,* February 27, 1935, page 54

    McCulloch bills on debt, jury service and cemetery trustee compensation: *Gongwer,* May 31, 1935, page 2; *Gongwer,* June 3, 1935, page 1; *Gongwer,* June 3, 1935, page 2

    Gessaman chosen Columbus mayor: en.wikipedia.org/wiki/List_of_Mayors_of_Columbus,_Ohio

    Composition of legislature: Gold, page 274

    Women legislators: Ibid, page 275

    James Rhodes appointment: Ibid, page 388

33   McCulloch reelection figures: *Piqua Daily Call,* November 4, 1936, page 1

    "Seldom in the history": *Piqua Daily Call,* October 24, 1936, page 4

    Election of speaker: *House Journal,* January 4, 1937, page 8

    Birth of daughter: Interview, Ann McCulloch Carver, October 17, 2012

    "Two fervent hopes": *Gongwer,* January 6, 1937, page 1

34   "Assembly which veteran": *Washington Post,* June 27, 1937, page 29

    "Subjected to the worst": *House Journal,* January 3, 1938, page 168

    Senators named: *House Journal,* January 4, 1938, pages 169-171

    "The spark that drove": *Ohio State Journal,* December 2, 1938, page 4

    "The House sometimes": *Ohio State Journal,* January 17, 1939, page 4

Chapter Seven: Mr. Speaker

35   McCulloch elected speaker: *House Journal,* January 2, 1939, page 8

    "I believe members": Ibid, page 9

    Ceremonial Dinner program: McCulloch Papers, Ohio Congressional Archives. Series 1: Personal/Political Box 1, Folder 13

36   "Once a state accepts": *House Journal,* January 2, 1939, page 33

    "Common honesty," "stringent economies": Davies, page 53

    State employee layoffs: Ibid, page 52

    $3 million budget cut: *Gongwer,* January 9, 1939, page 1

    "The world has seen": Ibid

    "We shall defend": Ibid

    "McCulloch has gotten off": *Gongwer,* January 12, 1939, page 1

    "House Speaker McCulloch": *Ohio State Journal,* February 5, 1939, page 1

37   "McCulloch and his majority leader": Ibid

    Tie vote: *Columbus Journal,* March 15, 1939, page 3

    "The Republican party believes": Ibid

    "Would not prevent injustices": Ibid

    "The Republican leadership in direct opposition": Ibid

    "An absolute total waste": Interview, James Dicke, October 18, 2012

    "Considered the same" and "Had the bill": *Piqua Daily Call,* May 31, 1939

38   "The chair trusts": *Ibid.*

    "For more than five months": Ibid

    "As speaker of the House": Ibid

    Cut in WPA jobs: Davies, page 59

"The time to resume relief": [Cleveland] *Plain Dealer*, November 21, 1939, page 1

"Feared the results": *Washington Post*, December 7, 1939, page 19

"Proudest achievement as governor": Ibid

"How to run our state": *Washington Post*, December 12, 1939, page 4

Sufficient funds: Ibid

39   "Lies with the rural": Gold, page 430

"Blamed Depression-era problems": Ibid

1940 election results: Davies, page 70

"There were no question": *Gongwer*, December 3, 1940, page 1

"The [outgoing] Legislature;" *Ohio State Journal*, December 5, 1940, page 4

"McCulloch's ability": Ibid

McCulloch elected speaker: *House Journal*, January 6, 1941, page 6

"To fairly and impartially preside": Ibid

40   "Not one single charge": Davies, page 69

"Today state employees are doing": Ibid, page 70

"A few days ago": *Ohio Republican News*, April 3, 1941, page 4

"The Republican majority members": Ibid

1941 areas of contention; "the long-drawn-out": *Ohio State Journal*, May 19, 1941, page 3

Willow Grove and Nelms mining disasters: www.remarkableohio.org/Historical Marker.aspx?historicalMarkerId=525

41   "But it is probably a safe bet": *Piqua Daily Call*, May 31, 1939

"Might fairly have been called": Gold, page 302

"Public utility lobbyists wining and dining": Gold, page 408

"Another Ohio legislative session": *Ohio State Journal*, May 19, 1941, page 3

"A feat which is exceptional": Ibid

Chapter Eight: War and Thereafter

43   McCulloch reelected as Speaker: *House Journal*, January 4, 1943, page 7

"Ohio… war production": *House Journal*, January 11, 1943, page 1195

Industrial figures: Davies, page 75

44   "He repeatedly preached": Davies, page 74

$111.5 million surplus: *House Journal*, January 14, 1943, page 38

"James McCulloch had been": *House Journal*, February 18, 1943, page 276

"Was a lifelong Republican": Ibid

Dominic Gentile heroics: *Dayton Daily News*, January 31, 1951, page 1

45   "Commending the Negro race": *House Journal*, February 10, 1943, page 233

Career of Mills Brothers: http://en.wikipedia.org/wiki/Mills_Brothers

Gave birthplace as Bellefontaine: Interview, James Oda, August 3, 2012

46   McCulloch friendship with Emerson and Viola Clemens: Interview, Colleen Clemens McMurray, January 9, 2013

"Mr. McCulloch would visit in the daytime": Ibid

"He was a listener": Ibid

"Did what he thought was right": Interview, Joseph Metz, December 27, 2012

47   "McCulloch is to have a captain's": *Cincinnati Enquirer*, October 24, 1943

"I am of the opinion": McCulloch letter to Mabel McCulloch, March 28, 1944

"It can be said of McCulloch": *Cincinnati Enquirer*, October 24, 1943

McCulloch induction physical: "Report of Physical Examination, William M.

McCulloch, Patterson Field, Fairfield, Ohio, December 20, 1943, Official
  Records, War-Navy Departments, Washington DC. Records supplied by
  McCulloch family.
McCulloch's departure: Interview, Ann McCulloch Carver, October 19, 2012
"We really swung": McCulloch letter to Mabel McCulloch, January 10, 1944
"I had two T-bone steaks": Ibid
Test on "Legal Aspects": McCulloch letter to Mabel McCulloch, January 11, 1944
48 "I noticed not only": Interview, Ann McCulloch, October 19, 2012
McCulloch crosses the Atlantic: *Piqua Daily Call*, November 6, 1945, page 4
Shrivenham "had served as housing": Johnson, page 28
Description of conditions: Ziemke, page 65
McCulloch visit to London: McCulloch letter to Mabel McCulloch, March 25,
  1944
49 McCulloch describes his fellow soldiers: McCulloch letter to Mabel McCulloch,
  April 4, 1944
"All but three or four": Ibid
"To the student officers": Ziemke, pages 65-66
"They have a very proud father": McCulloch letter to Mabel McCulloch, April 11,
  1944
"I'm not sorry that I went": McCulloch letter to Mabel McCulloch, May 3, 1944
Eisenhower visit and "more or less well executed": Ziemke, page 66
50 "Now a word about what you are doing": Ibid
"If the children wish": McCulloch letter to Mabel McCulloch, June 3, 1944
"A few moments ago": Ibid
"When the broadcast was complete": Ibid
"Our trip" and "We were greeted": McCulloch letter to Mabel McCulloch, July 1,
  1945
McCulloch quarters in Paris: McCulloch letter to Mabel McCulloch, September
  24, 1944
"We had a theatre party": McCulloch letter to Mabel McCulloch, November 18,
  1944
51 "The still unsettled estate": Quoted letter from probate judge in letter to Mabel
  McCulloch, April 6, 1945
"I trust you may work out": Ibid
"I really sweat for an hour": McCulloch letter to Mabel McCulloch, April 15, 1945
"Hardly a building": McCulloch letter to Mabel McCulloch, May 13, 1945
"The Germans . . . cast furtive": Ibid
52 "War, to me, will always be damage": Ibid
"The pressure is really on": McCulloch letter to Mabel McCulloch, July 26, 1945
"Mr Berry is simply swamped": Letter from Emmett P. Brush, July 27, 1945. Mc-
  Culloch Papers, Ohio Congressional Archives, Series 1: Personal/Political: Box
  1; folder 9
"I heard someone say": Interview, Colleen Clemens McMurray, February 3, 2014
"We went in and sat everywhere": Ibid
"They should be allowed to sit": Ibid
Partner "has a large number": McCulloch Papers, Ohio Congressional Archives,
  Series 1: Personal/Political: Box 1; folder 9
53 "I might add that I have donned": McCulloch letter to Cong. Robert F. Jones,

October 20, 1945. ; McCulloch Papers, Ohio Congressional Archives, Series 1: Personal/Political: Box 1; folder 9

"My teacher sent me": Interview, Ann McCulloch Carver, October 19, 2012

Chapter Nine: Junior Congressman

54   1947 special election: *Ohio Republican News*, October 10, 1947, page 1

"Always run scared": Interview, Paul Gutmann, August 3, 2012

Battered brown felt hat: *Piqua Daily Call*, November 11, 1947 [unpaginated]; McCulloch Papers, Ohio Congressional Archives, Series 3: Media Relations, Box 12; folder 1 [scrapbook]

55   McCulloch 1947 primary victory: *Piqua Daily Call*, October 8, 1947, page 2

"We feel that with McCulloch's": *Stillwater* [Ohio] *Valley News*, October 2, 1947, page 4

McCulloch's 1947 victory margin: *Ohio Republican News*, November 6, 1947, page 1

McCulloch's swearing in: *Congressional Record*, November 17, 1947, page 10597

McCulloch appointed to Judiciary: *Congressional Record*, November 18, 1947, page 11666

Truman's speech to Congress: www.gordonskene/president-truman-addresses-special-ses

"I am a private in the rear rank": *Troy Daily News*, November 20, 1947, [unpaginated]; McCulloch Papers, Ohio Congressional Archives, Series 3: Media Relations, Box 12; folder 1 [scrapbook]

"Old home week": *Piqua Daily Call*, December 8, 1947, page 4

56   "The sandy-moustached McCulloch": *Washington Post*, November 30, 1947, page A6

"Drastic proposal": *Celina* [Ohio] *Daily*, July 11, 1948, [unpaginated]; McCulloch Papers, Ohio Congressional Archives, Series 3: Media Relations, Box 12; folder 1 [scrapbook]

McCulloch maiden speech: *Dayton Daily News*, April 13, 1948, page 4

Congressman McCulloch listened": *Lima* [Ohio] *News*, August 19, 1948, page 4

57   *Ohio Republican News* poll: *Ohio Republican News*, March 6, 1948, page 5

"Red menace in both": *Stillwater* [Ohio] *Valley News*, October 14, 1948, page 3

"If you expect to measure": *Dayton Daily News*, October 20, 1948, page 1

58   "I would like to advise": *Congressional Record*, 1950, page 6825

1948 victory margin: *Piqua Daily Call*, November 3, 1948, page 1

"Some of the friends": *Washington Post*, November 30, 1947, page 6

59   "I learned my most important": Ibid

"My mother's career": Interview, Nancy McCulloch, December 17, 2013

"So we rode to school": Interview, Ann McCulloch Carver, February 1, 2014

"I'll try for summer stock": *Piqua Daily Call*, February 5, 1949, [unpaginated]; McCulloch Papers, Ohio Congressional Archives, Series 3: Media Relations, Box 12; folder 1 [scrapbook]

"The town only had": Interview, Nancy McCulloch, November 12, 2012

"Smelled of sour milk": Ibid

60   "A game of uncertain rules": Interview, Ann McCulloch Carver, October 19, 2012

Pumpkin pie doused with turkey gravy: Ibid

The world's "best cherry pie": Ibid

Shopping at Ulbrich's market: Interview, Ann McCulloch Carver, May 8, 2013

"Drove like a bat out of hell": Interview, David Carver, May 8, 2013

61   "I would like to suggest": Interview, David Carver, October 19, 2012

"And when Rob Barkley": Ibid

"In times of prosperity": *Congressional Record,* May 24, 1949, page A3200

Rights of "insane": *Congressional Record,* August 25, 1949, page 12270

"Continue to advocate economy": *Piqua Daily News,* January 18, 1950 [unpaginated clipping] McCulloch Papers, Ohio Congressional Archives. Series 3: Media Relations: Box 12; folder 2 [scrapbook]

"Not nearly as good": *Piqua Daily Call,* July 29, 1950. Page 1

62   "If you hire me": *Piqua Daily Call,* September 29, 1950, page 1

"Because too many of us": *Piqua Daily Call,* October 11, 1950

"America's progress": *Piqua Daily Call,* November 5, 1951

McCulloch's 1950 reelection": *Piqua Daily Call,* November 8, 1950, page 1

"Long before the election": *Piqua Daily Call,* November 10, 1950, page 6

Vote against aid to Yugoslavia: *Piqua Daily Call,* December 21, 1950, [unpaginated]; McCulloch Papers, Ohio Congressional Archives, Series 3: Media Relations, Box 11; folder 3

McCulloch "a likely prospect": *Troy Daily News,* August 27, 1951, page 3

63   Republican caucus: *Wapakoneta* [Ohio] *Daily News,* January 15, 1952, page 1

Alphonso Taft as founding Republican: Ross, pages 23, 61, 69

64   "A high class man": Halberstam, page 205

"Eat less": Wunderlin, page 127

"If Democracy is to be preserved": Clayton, page 324

"Might I conclude": *Congressional Record,* May 28, 1950; page 6190

"A disillusioned skeptic": Ross, page 314

"it is based on theory": Halberstam, page 207

Taft as liberal on race: Kabaservice, page 103

65   1952 primaries: en.wikipedia.org/.../Republican_Party_presidential_primaries_ 1952]

Taft's early lead: Halberstam, page 212

66   "Terrible with everything battered": *Wapakonata Daily News,* September 23, 1952

McCulloch's 1952 reelection: *Piqua Daily Call,* November 8, 1952, page 1

"We have lost a great": *Congressional Record,* August 4, 1953, page 10879

"Have begun talking up": [Dayton] *Journal Herald,* August 29, 1953, [unpaginated]; McCulloch Papers, Ohio Congressional Archives, Series 3: Media Relations, Box 11; folder 4

"a Worthy Successor": *Troy Daily News,* December 12, 1953, page 4

67   "Sizeable savings": *Sidney Daily News,* November 24, 1953,

McCulloch 1956 reelection: *Piqua Daily Call,* December 3, 1956, page 1

52-year mailbox effort: *Piqua Daily Call, August 25, 1954,* [unpaginated]; McCulloch Papers, Ohio Congressional Archives, Series 3: Media Relations, Box 11; folder 4

Assists Chinese couple: *Sidney Daily News,* March 7, 1956, page 12

"While the financial remuneration": Louis G. Peffer, President, Third Savings and Loan, letter to William McCulloch, January 6, 1954, OCA Series I: Box 2; folder 47

"My father felt he belonged," Interview, Ann McCulloch Carver, May 8, 2013

Ann McCulloch graduates: *Piqua Daily Call,* June 3, 1955, page 9

"The essential thing": *Congressional Record,* March 6, 1957, pages 3231-3232

68   "We in Congress": *Congressional Record*, March 6, 1957, pages 3232
     Introduces small business bills: [Dayton] *Journal Herald*, July 9, 1957, [unpaginated].
        McCulloch Papers, Ohio Congressional Archives, Series 3: Media Relations, Box
        11, Folder 6

Chapter Ten: First Attempt
69   "Something difficult to settle": Myrdal/introduction xiv
     "A believer in and a defender": Myrdal/introduction xvi
     "The glory of the nation": Myrdal/Ibid
     "To a great majority": Myrdal/introduction xiv
     "Togther with all of the confusion": Myrdal/Ibid
     "The moral struggles goes on": Mrydal/introduction xviii
70   *Smith v. Allwright*: Watson, page 148
     California Supreme Court decision: Watson, page 140-141
     Shelly v. Kramer, Watson, page 27
71   *Brown v. the Topeka [Kansas] Board of Education*, Watson, page 23
     Murder of Emmett Till: Anderson, page 2-3
72   "A mad dog": Caro [Power], page 784
     "Senate liberals had almost a tradition": Anderson, 102
73   Rayburn: "I knew Howard Smith": Berman, page 22
     Discharge Petition background: Anderson, page 63
     Cloture background: Whalens, page 126
     Murders of voting rights organizers: Anderson, pages 2-3
     Racial views of Hebert Brownell: Caro [Master], page 780
     Eisenhower orders DC school integration: Anderson, page 2
74   Eisenhower: "It is disturbing": Anderson, page 5
     Blacks registration in various counties: Emanuel Celler, quoting U.S. Civil Rights
        Commission, *Congressional Record*, March 11, 1956; page 5347
     Brownell's four-part bill: Anderson, pages 15-16
     Eisenhower limits support: Anderson, page 39
     Brownell informs Keating: Caro [Master], page 781
     "In his astonishingly bold tactic": Anderson, page 43
     Alsop: "If the Eisenhower administration": Anderson, page 46
75   Eisenhower reverses position: Anderson, page 135
     Powell endorses Eisenhower: Anderson, page 133
     Stevenson opposes Powell amendment: Anderson, page 23
     "Slavering for it": Caro [Master], page 790
     Rules Committee to House Floor: Bolling, page 199
     House approves bill, 279-126: Caro [Master], page 792
     Both sides got what they wanted: Anderson, page 139
76   Eisenhower endorses bill; Brownell resubmits: Caro [Master], page 873
     TIME: "The tiny band of southerners": Caro [Master], page 873
     "Johnson's office quietly let it be known": Watson, page 359
     Hennings sees no need for hearings: Caro [Master], page 874
76   "If the U.S. Supreme Court": Watson, page 369
     "[Black] progress has been accomplished": Anderson, page 84
77   Smith: "With the stated intent" and subsequent comments: *Congressional Record*,
        June 10, 1957: page 8649

McCulloch: "Defendant was ordered": *Congressional Record*, June 10, 1957, page 8667

Ashmore: "Correct, sir": Ibid

78 McCulloch: "I want to say": *Congressional Record*, June 10, 1957, page 8670

Rivers: "We are not talking": Ibid

Colmer: "When all is said": *Congressional Record*, June 10, 1957. Page 8671

Hoffman: "The answer that": *Congressional Record*, June 17, 1957, page 9377

Hoffman: "Persecutions": Ibid

McCulloch: "It will have served": Ibid

McCulloch: "Does not have": *Congressional Record*, June 17, 1959, page 9381

79 McCulloch: "One of the great Southern states": *Congressional Record*, June 17, 1957, page 9217

McCulloch: "I hope that": Ibid

McCulloch: "I do not think": Ibid

"The American Negro problem": Myrdal/introduction, page xvii

"The moral struggle goes on": Myrdal/introduction, page xviii

House vote on civil rights bill: Anderson, 99

Mitschell: "Why this normally urbane": Caro [Master], page 917

80 Russell: "Conscious hate" through "bring to bear": Caro [Master] page 916

Russell: "Great sadness" through "Long established law": Ibid

Johnson: Once you break": Caro [Master], page 793

81 Mitchell: "The restraining hand": Watson, page 390

Senate drops Part III: Watson, page 389

"If a federal judge tried": Pohlmann and Whisenhunt, page 166

Bolling: "It seem apparent": Bolling, page 186

Black leaders oppose signing: Caro [Master], page 990

"Emboldened to continue": Caro [Master], page 1002

"Lack of will": Ibid

82 Reedy: "He felt that": Caro [Master], page 1003

"The Civil Rights Act of 1957": Caro [Master], page 1004

Russell: "The fact that we": Pohlmann and Whisenhunt, page 166

Gutmann: "Absolutely in awe": Interview, Paul Gutmann, August 3, 2012

Mabel McCulloch and Winnie-the-Pooh: Interview, Paul Gutmann, August 3, 2012

McCulloch: "There has been": *Piqua Daily Call*, September 18, 1958 [unpaginated clipping] McCulloch Papers, Ohio Congressional Archives. Series 3: Media Relations: Box 13; folder 1 [scrapbook]

83 Small business bill enacted: [Dayton] *Journal Herald*, July 22, 1958, page 4

Service academy appointments: Interview, Nancy McCulloch, November 12, 2012

"Miss Chick": *Palladium-Item & Sun-Telegram*, Richmond [Indiana], June 13, 1958 [unpaginated clipping] McCulloch Papers, Ohio Congressional Archives. Series 3: Media Relations: Box 13; folder 1 [scrapbook]

McCulloch reports to Rotary Club: *Troy Daily News*, September 17, 1958 [unpaginated clipping] McCulloch Papers, Ohio Congressional Archives. Series 3: Media Relations: Box 13; folder 1 [scrapbook]

"Few congressman have voted": [Dayton] *Journal Herald*, 1958 [undated clipping] McCulloch Papers, Ohio Congressional Archives. Series 3: Media Relations: Box 13; folder 1 [scrapbook]

84 "Some of the dignity": *Piqua Daily Call*, September 18, 1958. [unpaginated clipping]

McCulloch Papers, Ohio Congressional Archives. Series 3: Media Relations: Box 13;
    folder 1 [scrapbook]
McCulloch in line for judiciary post: [Dayton] *Journal Herald*, August 27, 1958 [unpagi-
    nated clipping] McCulloch Papers, Ohio Congressional Archives. Series 3:
    Media Relations: Box 13; folder 1 [scrapbook]
McCulloch 1958 reelection: *Piqua Daily News*, November 5, 1958, page 1

Chapter Eleven: Four Perspectives

86 Celler's grandparent's harbor meeting: Celler, page 27
    Celler passes bar; marries: Celler, page 49
    Celler elected to Congress: Celler, page 62
    Celler's causes: Celler, pages 93-112
    "Deliberately and calculatedly": Celler, 172
87 "An arrogant old man": O'Neill, page 249
    "I know of no man who": Celler, page 179
    "While making a reputation": Berman, page 12
    "We aren't going to give": Interview, Thomas Mooney, January 15, 2013
    "Friends, but not close friends": Interview, Nancy McCulloch, July 22, 2013
    "You and I have performed": Letter from Celler to McCullloch, August 25, 1960;
        McCulloch Papers, Ohio Congressional Archives, Series I: Box 1, Folder 15
    "Generally recognized as feeble-minded": Watson, page 32
88 "A cursory glance": Watson, page 32
    "Upsouth Baltimore": Watson, page 81
    1911 Baltimore ordnance: Watson, page 81
    "The system of justice": Watson, page 84
    Mitchell's marriage: Watson, page 113
89 "Amidst such turmoil": Pohlmann and Whisenhunt, page 163
    "Being Clarence's fellow traveler": Watson, page 18
    Increase in registered voters: Watson, page 348
    Rejection of Congressman Powell's proposal: Watson, page 314
    "I remember Mr. Mitchell": Interview, James Dicke, October 18, 2012
90 Eisenhower 1956 vote total: Anderson, page 139
    "Mitchell was impressed": Watson, page 415
    "We hold these truths": Laird, page 227
91 "There shall be neither slavery": Laird, page 228
    "Merely words of unfilled promise": Laird, page 229
    Amendment abolishing slavery fails: Laird, page 230
    "Unwise, impolitic, cruel, and unworthy": McPherson, page 839
    Amendment abolishing slavery passes: Ibid
    "That all persons born": Laird, page 230
    "The right of citizens": Laird, page 231
    "Ku Klux Klan Act": Laird, page 232
92 "A comprehensive program": Laird, page 232
    "The sudden revolution in the Negro status": Laird, page 233
    "Repealed no less than 39": Laird, page 233
93 "As you well know": Sokol, page 44
    "The white man of the Delta": Sokol, page 57
    Methodist ministers leave Mississippi: Sokol, page 104

"Never shook hands with": Sokol, page 109
"To the many fine": Sokol, page 99
94   "Up until thirty years ago": Sokol, page 110

Chapter Twelve: McCulloch Steps Forth

95   Alsop: "In August 1959": *Washington Post/Times Herald*, July 17, 1959, page A15
     "Moderate, practical, sound": *Congressional Record*, February 12, 1959, page 2276
     Civil Rights Titles: *Congressional Record*, February 12, 1959, pages 2276-2277
96   "We must consider the image"; Berman, page 3
     "I am convinced that this bill": *Congressional Record*, February 12, page 2277
     "We cannot leave to the young child": [Dayton] *Journal Herald*, March 6, 1959, page 1
     "We have been 'hanged, drawn and quartered'": Berman, page 13
97   Bill rejected, 18-13: [Dayton] *Journal Herald*, July 29, 1959, page 4
     "Had been eliminated": *Piqua Daily Call*, August 6, 1959
     "First, last and always": Berman, page 12
     Olin Johnson talk: Berman, page 30
     Renewal of Civil Rights Commission: Berman, page 32
     "I serve notice on all members": Berman, page 32
98   McCulloch designated for GOP post: *Washington Post*, January 1, 1960, A2
     Simpson's successor eventually": *Piqua Daily Call*, January 8, 1960, page 3
     "Openly and ardently": Ibid
99   "A great deal of pressure": *Washington Post*, January 22, 1960, page A1
     "An apparently close race": Ibid
     "A bill to provide": *Congressional Record*, January 28, 1960, page 1575
     "We cannot afford": McCulloch press release, January 28, 1960. McCulloch
       Papers, Ohio Congressional Archives, Series 2: Legislative, Box 6, folder 7
100 "Any individual could": Berman, page 36
     Eisenhower's "referee" plan: Berman, pages 44-45
     "Says that Negroes shall appear": *New York Times*, February 19, 1960
     "After the appointment": *Congressional Record*, March 14, 1960, page 5484
     Adversary proceedings": *Congressional Record*, March 16, 1960, page 5778
101 "At the same time, I am": *Congressional Record*, February 23, 1960, page 3293
     Because it presented virtually limitless": Berman, page 99
102 Johnson introduces Stella, Missouri measure: Berman, pages 52-53
     "High time our northern brothers": Berman, page 34 [note]
103 Rayburn appoints Walker: Berman, page 81
     "To speak in support': *Congressional Record*, March 10, 1960, page 5206
     "The United States had a vital stake": Ibid, page 5207
     Title I-VII: Ibid, pages 5207-5209
     "Mr. Chairman, I am in an enviable": *Congressional Record*, March 15, 1956, page 5656
104 "That legislation might raise": *Congressional Record*, March 10, 1960, page 5343
     Celler: "We see, therefore, that in each title": *Congressional Record*, March 14, 1960, page 5478
     McCulloch": With regard to the question": Ibid, 5479
     Celler defeated 157-67: Berman, page 84
     Next amendment "not germane": Berman, page 85

"We all have known": *Congressional Record,* March 14, 1960, page 5441
105 "One of my good friends": *Congressional Record,* March 16, 1960, page 5774
   [Following Reconstruction] we were": *Congressional Record,* March 15, 1960, page 5659
   Forrester: "The civil rights issues": *Congressional Record,* March 10, 1960, page 5211
   Winstead: "If I did not know": *Congressional Record,* March 14, 1960, page 5420
   Alexander: "The liberal Democrats": Ibid, page 5471
106 Rivers: "It won't be long": *Congressional Record,* March 15, 1960, page 5650
106 McCulloch, Lindsay, Kastenmeier amendments: Berman, page 89
   "The rare combination": [Dayton] *Journal Herald,* March 16, 1960, page 1
   Kastenmeier defeated: Berman, pages 89-91
   Russell Baker comments: *New York Times,* March 16, 1960, page 1
   McCulloch's substitute amendment: Berman, page 90
   Came within three votes – 137-134: Berman, page 90
   Final House passage: *New York Times,* March 24, 1960, page 1
   Provisions of bill: Berman, page 95
107 "He was perhaps a bit": *Washington Evening Star,* March 24, 1960, [unpaginated]
   McCulloch Papers, Ohio Congressional Srchives, Series 3: Media Relations, Box 11, folder 8
   "Congressional Republicans": Ibid
   "The Southern opponents": Ibid
   "Turned the trick": *Columbus Dispatch,* March 27, 1960, [unpaginated] McCulloch Papers, Ohio Congressional Archives, Series 3: Media Relations, Box 11, folder 8
   "McCulloch is not a forceful": Ibid
   Votes on Part III and Javits amendment: Berman, 105
108 Clark: "Surely in this battle": Berman, page 107
   Celler: "Sometimes a small key": Berman, page 112
   Marshall: "Isn't worth the paper": Berman, page 117
   "Finally, after months of bitter debate": *Lima News,* May 8, 1960, page 4
   Woolworth's sit-in: en.Wikipedia.org/wiki/Greensboro_sit-ins
109 Marshall: "The young people": Watson, page 450
   "The 1950's civil rights legislation": Stern, page
   Katzenbach: "Legal suits took": Stern, page 57
   Kennedy 'Southern strategy': Stern, page 14
   Wilkins: "Not once were the responsible": Stern, page 53
   King: "I am different from my father": Stern, page 61
110 "I do remain of the strong opinion": McCulloch to constituent, June 1, 1968.
   McCulloch Papers, Ohio Congressional Archive, Series 2: Legislative, Box 7, folder 31
   "Less interested in the dusty legislative process": Berman, page 122
   "It was easier for the liberals": Berman, page 119
111 Lippmann: "The cause of desegregation": Stern, page 86

Chapter Thirteen: The Battle Is Joined
112 Possible wedding data conflict: Interview, David Carver, October 12, 2012
   Ann McCulloch and Dave Carver meet: Ibid
113 "It was assumed": Ibid
   "I would like to marry": Ibid

"I knew he disapproved to that": Ibid

"Escorted by her father": *Piqua Daily Call,* January 22, 1960, page 9

"When we got married one": Interview, David Carver, October 12, 2012

"When we were back in Piqua": Ibid

114 ADA voting record: "House Voting Record, 1959" [unpaginated], McCulloch
    Papers, Ohio Congressional Archives, Series 2: Legislative – Voting Record, Box
    7

    CIO voting record: *Washington Post,* October 3, 1956 [unpaginated] McCulloch
    Papers, Ohio Congresional Archives, Series 2: Legislative–Voting Record, Box 7

    ACA Distinguished Service Award: Americans for Constitutional Action press
    release, May 23, 1961; McCulloch Papers, Ohio Congresional Archives, Series 2:
    Legislative – Voting Record, Box 7

    Reappointed to Small Business Committee: *Congressional Record,* February 17, 1961,
    page 2271

    "The time has therefore come": *Congressional Record,* June 13, 1962, page 10418

    "God bless the United States": *Congressional Record,* March 25, 1962, page 11755

    "I realize that the pressures": *Congressional Record,* May 4, 1961, page 7376

    "I am reminded": *Congressional Record,* July 16, 1962, page 13695

115 "It was bourbon and branch water": Interview, Thomas Mooney, January 15, 2013

    "It was such a time": Interview, Andrew Glass, December 18, 2012

116 Truman: "Are used as a cloak": *Congressional Record,* July 22, 1962, page 14343

    "Revenue of $7 billion": Ibid

    "The good that has resulted therefrom": Ibid

    "We have trial lawyers": *Congressional Record,* August 29, 1961, page 17405

    "There was no consideration of civil rights": *Congressional Record,* September 26,
    1961, page 21702

    "The decision to delay": Stern, page 42

117 Jackie Robinson endorses Nixon: Kahn, page 397

    "He [Kennedy] was perfectly happy": Stern, page 43

    Prince George County lawsuit: Watson, 462

    President "has let it be known": Stern, page 73

    "The anti-poll tax measure:" *Washington Post,* March 16, 1962, page A5

    "With the possible exception": *Congressional Record,* August 27, 1962, page 17657

    "Do we really believe": Ibid

118 Constituent letters: Random sampling, McCulloch Papers, Ohio Congressional
    Archives; Series 4: Box 21, District Affairs, Correspondence

    "Hundreds of thousands of pages": McCulloch Papers, Ohio Congressional Ar-
    chives, Series 4: Box 21; File 7

    "A sad commentary on our times": Ibid

119 "The street" v. "the Senate": Interview, Adam Clymer, December 17, 2012

    "The bill that passed the House": Ibid

    McCulloch introduces civil rights bill: *Congressional Record,* January 31, 1963, pages
    1560-1561

120 "Not nearly as broad in scope": *Congressional Record,* February 28, 1963, page 3264

    "I am further disturbed": Ibid, page 3265

    "I wonder if poor Abe Lincoln": Ibid

    "Rather than take the hint": Watson, page 543

    "Asking for the moon": *New York Times,* March 15, 1963, page 1

Lincoln would fail literacy requirement: Ibid

Greenfield; beginning: "I seemed to have": Kabaservice, page 66-67

121 "No one would suggest": *Washington Post*, May 9, 1963, page A15

"Here, then, is a comprehensive bill": Ibid

122 McGill: "One of the persistent": Sokol, page 62

"Are any of you disturbed?": Sokol, page 76

Warren: "The white southerner": Sokol, page 112

Katzenbach: "We arrived down there": Nicholas Katzenbach Oral History Interview, JFK 2#, November 29, 1964, page 98. John F. Kennedy Oral History Collection, National Archives and Records Administration (NARA), Office of Presidential Libraries [Hereafter: John F. Kenndy Oral History Collection (NARA)]

123 "General, you put this into a pay phone and dial NA 8-1414, collect." Nicholas Katzenbach Oral History Interview – JFK#2, November 29, 1964, page 107. John F. Kennedy Oral History Collection (NARA)

"Kennedy, responding to the Birmingham crisis": Watson, page 547

Celler: "barbaric": *Washington Post*, May 9, 1963, page A15

Keating: "a glaring gap": Ibid

Glass: "At this time": Interview, December 18, 2012

Kennedy address: "The heart of the question": Address on Civil Rights (June 11, 1963), John Fitzgerald Kennedy; en.wikipedia/org/wiki/Civil_Rights_Address

124 Broder comment: Interview, David Broder, April 27, 2009

125 Kennedy had not read bill: Whalens, page 6

Lewis: "unnecessarily insulting": *New York Times*, October 31, 1963, page 22

Lindsay: "The rumor is all over": Whalens, page 6

RFK: "I don't think": Whalens, page 7

Lindsay: "Do you think I was too hard": Whalens, page 6

McCulloch: "You and I may never": Interview, Robert Kimball, October 29, 2012

126 Katzenbach: "I think initially we thought": Nicholas Katzenbach Oral History Interview, JFK 2#, November 29, 1964, page 132; John F. Kennedy Oral History Collection (NARA)

"However principled on McCulloch's part": Katzenbach, page 121

"Wanted an unequivocal assurance:" Nicholas Katzenbach Oral History Interview, JFK 2#, November 29, 1964, page 131. John F. Kennedy Oral History Collection (NARA)

"At which point we began": Nicholas Katzenbach Oral History Interview, JFK 2#, November 29, 1964, page 133. John F. Kennedy Oral History Collection (NARA) Presidential Library

"I remember a large meeting": Katzenbach, page 123

127 "Finally, the most experienced and thoughtful": Katzenbach, page 123

"Very early in the game": Nicholas Katzenbach Oral History Interview, JFK 2#, November 29, 1964, page 131; John F. Kennedy Oral History Collection (NARA)

Lippmann: "The cause of desegregation": Stern, page 86

"Was very concerned": Stern, page 93

"Looked into this matter": Ibid

Possible Pentagon countermeasures: Interview, William Geoghegan, September 19, 2012

128 "They are not going to bluff": Whalens, page 24
      "While the administration": Katzenbach, page 125
      "For the most part": Stern, page 104
129 Birmingham church bombing: Stern, page 106
      "Believed Celler was losing," Whalens, page 30
      Reuther belittles Katzenbach: Katzenbach, page 126
      Katzenbach: "Well, Manny": Nicholas Katzenbach Oral History Interview, JFK
          2#, November 29, 1964, page 151. John F. Kennedy Oral History Collection
          (NARA)
      "Despite seniority based on": Bolling, page 99
130 "Despite an earlier pledge," Stern, page 107
      "Stomped Manny": Whalens, page 36
      "Would allow Celler to score points": Whalens, page 31
      "So severe they threaten": Whalens, page 35
      "A pile of garbage": Whalens, page 39
      "The subcomittee strenghtened": Bolling, page 99
131 Lewis: "Nearly everyone by now": *New York Times*, June 10, 1964, page 21
      Libonati presents amendments: Whalens, page 48
      "Had the unpleasant task": Katzenbach, page 124
132 "No reason for this type of sellout": Watson, page 573
      "There are few, if any": Stern, 111
      Lindsay foresees passage: *Washington Post*, October 18, 1963, Page A1
      Celler's motives: Interview, Robert Kimball, October 8, 2013
      Libonati: "So then I'm sitting down": Bolling, page 101
      Libonati withdraws motion to accept amendments: Whalens, page 48
      Moore's motion would have passed: Interview, Robert Kimball, October 8, 2013
133 McCulloch: "Certainly I can't vote": Whalens, page 51
      Halleck: "Goddammit, Mr. President," Ibid
      "And can I interrupt there, Charlie": Ibid
      Brown: "We cannot cut it back": Interview, Robert Kimball, October 29, 2012
      "President Kennedy pointed out that": Whalens, page 39
134 "This got him upset": Interivew: Robert Kimball, October 29, 2012
      "The whole thing would fall": Ibid
      "We have been screwed": Ibid
      "Stricken eagle good looks": Mailer, page 57
      "My impression": Interview, Robert Kimball, October 29, 2012
      "Not that we don't want a bill": Whalens, page 54
      Alsop: "The vital civil rights bill": Whalens, page 56
135 "And throughout, Kimball played": Whalens, Ibid
      Creation of consensus bill: Interview, Robert Kimball, October 29, 2012
      Biemiller: "There is no FEPC": Watson, page 548
      "Was one of the people who": Nicholas Katzenbach Oral History Interview, JFK
          2#, November 29, 1964, page 157. John F. Kennedy Oral History Collection
          (NARA)
136 "Made earnest and emotional": Katzenbach, page 127
      "It could go either way": Interview, Robert Kimball, January 6, 2014
      Judiciary Committee series of votes: Ibid.
      Congressman Libonati, for reasons unknown: Whalens, page 65

"After 30 years of fine service": Interview, Adam Clymer, December 17, 2012

Chapter Fourteen: The Battle Is Won

137 "He just thought it was a terrible thing": Interview, Nancy McCulloch, October 22, 2013

"No memorial oration or eulogy": Whalens, page 79

138 "Very damaging to the bipartisan": Whalens, page 81

"I know something about the facts of life": Whalens, page 86

139 "I spent hours": Interview, Robert Kimball

"'You guys are going to have to": Whalens, page 91

"He was a natural leader": Interview, Robert Kimball, October 28, 2013

"stretched the commerce clause" and Mann Act: *New York Times*, January 10, 1964, page 1

"Because of my receding red hair": Whalens, page 93

"Comprehensive in scope": Ibid

McCulloch: "There is a considerable": *Congressional Record*, January 31, 1964, page 1529

140 "In the effective separation": Ibid

"No one would suggest": Ibid

"They do strange things in Ohio": *New York Times*, January 16, 1964, page 16

"Mr. McCulloch waited for dramatic effect": Ibid

"Under the somewhat aggressive questioning": Ibid

"That for hundreds of years": Ibid

"Head was still bloody": Watson, page 592

"The key guys to watch": Whalens, page 94

141 "If they were unable": Ibid

Watson: "Let me say": *Congressional Record*, February 1, 1964, page 1546

McCulloch's 20,000 word statement: Iibid, pages 1654-1663

"I admit the parentage": *Congressional Record*, February 3, 1964, page 1682

Smith: "Or in part": *New York Times*, February 4, 1964

McCulloch: "Aims at the very heart": Ibid

142 McCulloch: "Scot though I am": Ibid

McCulloch: "Home of a great university": Whalens, page 111

Meader amendment defeated 153 to 68: Ibid

Harris: "Shall be interpreted": *New York Times*, February 8, 1964, page 1

"The House was immediately in an uproar": Ibid

143 "His face white": Ibid

"Look! Bill's face is red": Whalens, page 115

" A voice of barely controlled anger" *New York Times*, February 8, 1964, page 1

McCulloch: "I regret to say": Ibid

Case: "Singlehandedly, I believe": *Congressional Record* [Senate], February 11, 1964, page 6777

Smith: "Or sex": Whalens, page 115

Smith: "Will help an important minority": Ibid

Five Democratic congresswomen; amendment passes: Whalens, page 117

144 "The bill did not have an easy passage": Bolling, page 193

"The bill that passed the House": Interview, Adam Clymer, December 17, 2012

Greenfield: "Was struck by how much": Kabaservice, page 100

"As Congressman McCulloch had been key": Katzenbach, page 140

"If it takes until September": Lion, page 599

145 Russell proposes redistributing black population: Whalens, page 145

"Once a filibuster commences": Katzenbach, page 142

146 "CBS Reports": "CBS Reports: Filibuster – Birth Struggle of a Law (March 18, 1964) CBS New Archives, Division of CBS Inc.

"Had a nice demeanor": Interview, Joseph Metz, December 27, 2012

"Keep up the good work": Ibid

"Go to the men's room door": Ibid

"I went to a Judiciary": Ibid

"To some annoyed with McCulloch's": Whalens, page 181

Coordinating for Fundamental American Freedoms: Whalens, page 145

"A man's home is his castle": Interview, Andrew Glass, December 18, 2012

147 McCulloch clarifies bill's intent: *Washington Post*, April 26, 1964, page A15

"When the day comes that picketing": Whalens, page 133

148 "Dirksen demanded and got": Interview, Adam Clymer, December 17, 2012

House approves bill, 289 to 126: Whalens, page 226

The air of grand occasion": *New York Times*, July 3, 1964, page 1

Johnson: "It does not restrict": en.wikipedpia.org/wiki/Civil_Rights_Act_of_1964

149 "Goldwater and his legal advisors": Kabaservice, page 103

"A number of political scientists": Kabaservice, page 104

"Couldn't understand that": Whalens, page 54

"How do you tear hatred": Whalens, page 228

150 "There was widespread": Stern, page 185

In Albany, Georgia" and examples following: *Piqua Daily Call*, July 3, 1964, page 1

Chapter Fifteen: Reapportionment

152 *Nation's Cities*, July 1964, page 11

"Legislatures represent people, not trees": Ibid

"Section I: Nothing in the Constitution": *Congressional Record*, June 24, 1964, page 14929

Mencken "said in the 1920s": *New York Times*, August 16, 1964, page E3

153 "Factors other than population": *New York Times*, June 25, 1964, page 21

"Without federal Constitutional significance": Ibid

Table on disproportionate representations: *New York Times*, June 17, 1964, page 29

Georgia representation: *Washington Post*, August 9, 1964, page A4

154 "It has appeared to a rapidly increasing": *Congressional Record*, June 24, 1964, page 14929

Lincoln: *Congressional Record*, June 24, 1964, page 14930-14931

"Legislatures represent people, not trees": Ibid

McCulloch's views on organic society: *Congressional Record*, June 24, 1964, page 14930

"The opportunities for graft": *Salinas* [Kansas] *Journal*, June 16, 1964, page 4

155 "This pronouncement finds no support": *Dodge City* [Kansas] *Globe*, July 17, 1964, page 4

Indianapolis Star: "The [Supreme] Court" [undated editorial from McCulloch Papers, Ohio Congressional Archives. Series 3: Media Relations, Box 15; folder 1 [clippings scrapbook]

Richmond News Leader: "Constituencies...": Ibid

"Could wind up rendering the court": *Washington Post*, August 6, page A4

"Word got out early": *New York Times*, August 14, 1964, page 1

156 "At the American Bar Association": *New York Times*, August 16, 1964, page E3

"I have warned that the effect": McCulloch press release, September 15, 1964, McCulloch Papers, Ohio Congressional Archives, Series 2: Legislative, Box 10; folder 4

"Dictate either directly or indirectly": Ibid

"The future, if not the past:" Ibid

Lippmann on reapportionment: Quoted in Congressional Record, August 18, 1964, page 20151

"Despite the widespread opposition": *New York Times*, December 12, 1964, page A2

157 McCulloch address Ohio Legislature: *Washington Post*, December 23, 1964, page A2

"It is nearly unbelievable": *Congressional Record*, April 27, 1967, page 11075

Chapter Sixteen: Guaranteeing the Vote

158 "Faced political troubles": Constituent correspondence, McCulloch Paper, Ohio Congressional Archives, Series 4: District Affairs, Box 26; folder 24.

"Always voted Republican": Ibid

Mitchell: "There are two of your Congressmen": Letter from Clarence Mitchell to William McCulloch, September 21, 1964. McCulloch Papers, Ohio Congressional Archives, Series 2: Legislative, Box 6; folder 12

159 "Long before many others": Ibid

"The volunteer services of six": Letter from Clarence Mitchell to William McCulloch, September 24, 1964. McCulloch Papers, Ohio Congressional Archives, Series 2: Legislative, Box 6; folder 12

"If every Goldwater supporter": McCulloch Papers, Ohio Congressional Archive, Series I: Personal/Political Box 5; folder 22

"I never told you I thought": Interview, Joseph Metz, December 27, 2012

160 "Eliminate every remaining obstacle": Pohlmann and Whistenhunt, page 235 [For full text, see

Speech Before Congress on Voting Rights: millercenter.org/presidents/speeches/.../338

"Overcome the crippling legacy": Ibid

Black registration in southern states: Parker, page 23

"I was born in Mississippi": Parker, page 6

McCulloch appointed chair of task force: Press release, Committee on Planning and Research Republican Conference, February 28, 1965. McCulloch Papers, Ohio Congressional Archives, Series 2: Legislative, Box 7,

161 "The GOP followed McCulloch": Interview, Thomas Mooney, January 15, 2013

King: "We are going to plaque": en.wikipedia.org/wiki/Selma_to_Montgomery_Marches

"Bloody Sunday": Katzenbach, page 163

Death of Rev. Reeb: en.wikipedia.org/wiki/Selma_to_Montgomery_Marches

162 McCulloch: "Could have prevented": *New York Times*, March 10, 1965, page 23

"Has the right to act": Ibid

Lindsay: "Johnson should have had federal troops": Ibid

"The most eloquent, many thought": *New York Times*, March 21, 1965, Section 4, page 1

"The dignity of men and the destiny of democracy": Ibid

"There is no cause" and succeeding paragraphs: Ibid

"Designed to eliminate" through "We shall overcome": Ibid

163 "I looked over… and Martin": en.wikipedia.org/wiki/Selma_to_Montgomery_ Marches

Voting rights bill contents: Pohlmann and Whisenhunt, page 236

Judge Johnson establishes march criteria: May, pages 127-128

164 Katzenbach orders guard to about-face: Katzenbach, page 170

King: "The end we seek is a society": en.wikipedia.org/wiki/Selma_to_Montgom-ery_Marches

Constituent letters: McCulloch Papers, Ohio Congressional Archive, Sampling of constituent mail: Series 4: District Affairs, Box 26; folders 20-22

165 McCulloch reply: "The right to vote": Ibid, folder 21

McCulloch: "One of the best statements": *New York Times*, March 21, 1965, Section 4, page 1

Gallup poll results: Pohlmann and Whisenhunt, page 236

"A good bill" [but] "not enough": *New York Times*, March 25, 1965, page 20

"Festering pockets of discrimination": Ibid

"Outside the political sphere": Interview, Andrew Glass, December 18, 2012

Reston: "leading a campaign": *New York Times*, March 26, 1965, page 34

166 "There is no evidence": Ibid

McCulloch: "Mr. Speaker, this proposal is offered": *Congressional Record*, April 5, 1965, pages 6891-6893

McCulloch explains his bill: Ibid, page 6892

"Does not penalize the innocent": Ibid

"Arbitrary percentage formula": Ibid, page 6893

"Pattern of discrimination": Ibid

167 "The Ford-McCulloch proposal": Kabaservice, page 141

Senate vote cloture: Stern, page 227

168 McCulloch: "No issue before a legislative body": *Congressional Record*, July 6, 1965, page 15652

"The judicial remedy takes time": Ibid, page 15653

"The expectation of many of us": Ibid

The Ford-McCulloch bill: Ibid

"Honors the rights of the states": Ibid

"A voting rights bill should admit the truth": Ibid

"Upon inspection by future": *Congressional Record*, July 6, 1965, page

169 McClory: "produces the incongruous result": Iibid, page 15661

"Never before has any state": Ibid

Bennett: "Consistently opposed": Ibid, page 15664

Editorial: "Representative McCulloch's measure": *Congressional Record*, July 8, 1965, page 16055

McClory: "The voting frauds": *Congressional Record*, July 9, 1965, page 16247

Kastenmeier: "Typical sour grapes": Ibid

McCulloch: "A vote could be counted": Ibid, page 16251

170 Katzenbach: "Yes": Ibid

Willis: "In my congressional": Ibid, page 16254

Mathias: "Robs Negroes": Ibid

McCulloch: "political instincts" and questions following: Iibid, page 16401

"The White House was alarmed": Goldman, page 329

"An argument could be made": Ibid, pages 329-330

"Southern Democrats flocked": Ibid, page 330

171 "Began to crystalize": *Washington Post*, July 8, 1965, page A2

Tuck: "The plain, unvarnished truth" and subsequent comments: May, page 165

McCormack: "It's not for me to advise": Goldman, page 330

"Republicans backed away from": Watson, page 656

172 "McCulloch's bill lacked the automatic trigger": Kabaservice, page 141

House vote on bill: Pohlmann and Whisenhunt, page 236

House vote on conference report: Ibid, page 237

Johnson: "The right to vote": Remarks on the Signing of the Voting Rights Act
    (August 6, 1965; millercenter.org/presidents/speeches/.../403

In the first three weeks: Stern, page 228

"I'm going to vote now": Goldman, page 332

Chapter Seventeen: Congressman McCulloch and the Great Society

173 "Middle Mussolini, Early Ramses, and Late Niemen-Marcus": www.Capitol.
    gov/html/VGN_2010061423534l.html

Choosing an office: Interview, Nancy McCulloch, January 22, 2014

Returned portion of office allowance: Interview, James Dicke, October 18, 2012

174 Vera Page's office: Interview, Joseph Metz, December 17, 2012

Vera Page description: Interview, James Dicke, October 18, 2012

"So I showed up at the office": Ibid

"You know, Jim, you really don't": Ibid

"'Merry Christmas, Frank'": Interview, Franklin Polk, December 20, 2012

"My father always did his own": Interview, Nancy McCulloch, November 12, 2012

"Courtly, reserved, conservative": Interview, Robert Kimball, October 29, 2012

McCulloch phrases: Ibid

175 "On a couple of occasions": Interview, James Dicke, October 18, 2012

No concern McCulloch would stray: Interview, Joseph Metz, December 27, 2012

"But not a Nixon man": Interview, James Dicke, October 18, 2012

Persons McCulloch admired: Interviews, Nancy McCulloch, November 12, 2012;
    James Dicke, October 18, 2012

Katzenbach: "Bill McCulloch gave me": Private communication to author

176 Charles Upton background: James Oda, August 3, 2012

McCulloch's ambitions: Interview, James Dicke, October 18, 2012

"If I was going to run for governor: Ibid

Description of Judiciary Committee meeting room: Site visit by author

177 "In those days, seniority was never": Interview, Andrew Glass, December 18, 2012

"The reality of the committee": Interview, Benjamin Zelenko, December 18, 2012

"McCulloch was crafty": Interview, Thomas Mooney, January 15, 2013

"He would say, 'Tom'": Ibid

"When you have closed meetings": Interview, Franklin Polk, December 20, 2012

178 McCulloch and Celler recommend Poff: Interview, Benjamin Zelenko, December
    18, 2012

179 Gallup poll on government: www.gallup.com/poll/.../americans-belief-gov-power-

ful-record-level.aspx

"This was a liberal hour": Mackenzie & Weisbrot, page 5

"For the first time in our history": Ibid, page 104

"With the exception of race": Ibid, page 97

180 "And so it was with more of the issues": Ibid

"How do you tear hatred": Whalens, page 228

"In the effective separation of powers": *Congressional Record*, January 31, 1964, page 1529

"When authorities fail to shoulder: *New York Times*, January 16, 1964, page 16

"No" vote on Appalachian Regional Development Act: 1965 *Congressional Quarterly Almanac*, page 88

"No" vote on Elementary and Secondary Education Act: Ibid

"No" vote on Department of Housing and Urban Development: 1965 *Congressional Quarterly Almanac*, page 91

181 "No" vote on Section 14B: Ibid

"No" vote on National Foundation on the Arts and Humanities: Ibid, page 93

"No" vote on D.C. home rule: Ibid

"No" vote on highway beautification: Ibid

Udall background on health of elderly: Congressman's Report, Morris Udall, 2nd District, Arizona; March 31, 1965, Vol. IV, no. 2

"Prohibition against interference": The AMA and Medicare and Medicaid, 1965, Prepared by Ololade Olakanmi, For the Writing Group on the History of African Americans and the Medical Profession

182 "Independence and self-reliance": *Journal of the American Medical Association* 177 (1961: 368-370)

"One of the strongest holds": The AMA and Medicare and Medicaid, 1965, Prepared by Ololade Olakanmi, For the Writing Group on the History of African Americans and the Medical Profession (HOD Proceedings, June 11-15, 1934: 29)

"Not cover our needs" and letters following: McCulloch Papers, Ohio Congressional Archive, Series 4: District Affairs, Correspondence, Box 28, folders 1-4

183 Eldercare defeated, 236-191: Iric Nathanson, www.minnpost.com/politics/policy/2010/03/when-another-landmark-health-bill-passed-in-1965-it-was-less-drama

Johnson signs Medicare: www.trumanlibrary.org/anniversaries/medicarebill.htm

McCulloch: "I would like to say": McCulloch Papers, Ohio Congressional Archive, Series 4: District Affairs, Correspondence, Box 28, folder 4

Ervin: "For the first time": Watson, page 672

Chapter Eighteen: Open Housing

184 "Provide a process of public education": Bolling, page 29

"The president's aides held": Lawson, page 69

"Murder, attack or intimidate": Lawson, page 66

185 "The poorest man may": *Congressional Record*, July 26, 1966, page 17112

Constituent letters: McCulloch Papers, Ohio Congressional Archives: Series 4: District Affairs, Correspondence: Box 26; folders 23-26

186 "Residential segregation means": Watson, page 670

"Who are we kidding": Bonasitsa, page 57

"The majority of residents": Ibid, page 59

Chicago Real Estate Board: Bonasitsa, page 60
"The constitutuonal right": Ibid
187 "Also led to the federal government": Bonasitsa, page 57
"Mrs. Murphy's boarding house": *New York Times*, May 6, 1966, page 1
"If the five-room formula": Ibid
"A fair cross-section of the community": Ibid
"Once Congress has recognized": Watson, 671
188 "If we are to strike down": *Washington Post*, May 11, 1966, page A5
"Unusual and rare": *Dayton Daily News*, June 18, 1966, page 1
"Alters my feeling": *Washington Post*, June 16, 1966, page A1
"Resistant to 'walking the plank'": *New York Times*, June 16, 1966, page 21
"I do not and have not questioned": *Dayton Daily News*, June 18, 1966, page 1
"Lawful activities": Lawson, pages 70-71
189 Judiciary retains open housing: *New York Times*, June 29, 1966, page 1
"Was personally glad to see": Ibid
Mathias "softening" amendment: *New York Times*, June 30, 1966, page 1
"Mathias knew the proposition": Watson, page 673
190 Judiciary adopts Mathias amendment: Ibid, page 675
"Manifest a moral standard": *Washington Post*, July 16, 1966, page A4
"Necessary but restained": Ibid
Dowdy: "Every bill we have passed": *Congressional Record*, July 26, 1966, page 17111
Waggonner: "Because of discrimination in Ohio?": Ibid
McCulloch: "Among other things": Ibid
McCulloch outlines bill: Ibid, page 17112
191 McCulloch: "I believe that any fair-minded": Ibid
"The Congress declares that the general welfare": Ibid
McCulloch: "Subsequent unyielding position": Ibid
McCulloch presents open housing title: Ibid
192 "But are unwilling to do so": Ibid, quoted from "From the Work Bench," Clarence
Mitchell, Jr., [Baltimore] *Afro-American Newspaper*, May 24, 1966
Ashmore: The will of the majority: *Congressional Record*, July 27, 1966, page 17183
Joelson: "We have only too often": *Congressional Record*, July 26, 1966, page 17114
Dowdy: "Looking at recent history": *Congressional Record*, July 27, page 17222
Wilkins: "Would exempt so many": *New York Times*, July 27, 1966, page 1
"Sidestep[ped] the plain fact: Ibid
House Policy Committee: "politically motivated": *New York Times*, August 1, 1966,
page 1
Rhodes: "Fair housing solutions": Ibid
193 Union and black congressmen's position: Watson, page 675
"Had inspired a deluge of mail": Ibid
"I know that the psychological imact": McCulloch Papers, Ohio Congressional
Archives: Series 4: District Affairs, Correspondence: Box 26; folder 25
Mitchell on effect of Mathias amendment: Watson, page 676
Anti-riot measure added: Ibid
"Fear of crime largely associated": Ibid
Mitchell: advocates had not worked hard enough: Watson, page 680
194 "Republicans were dismayed" and other constituent letters: McCulloch Papers,
Ohio Congressional Archives: Series 4: District Affairs, Correspondence: Box 26;

folders 23-26

McCulloch: "The federal government should not": McCulloch Papers, Ohio Congressional Archives: Series 4: District Affairs, Correspondence: Box 26; folder 26

"Some 18 to 20 states have passed legislation": Ibid

"Assails Mr. McCulloch's leadership": *New York Times*, September 24, 1966, page

195 McCulloch's granddaughter born: Interview, Ann McCulloch Carver, February 3, 2014

Chapter Nineteen: Riots, Report, and Open Housing

196 Detroit riot: en.wikipedia.org/wiki/1967_Detroit_riot

197 "More going for it than any other city": Fine, page 32

"need to throw of brick to communicate": Ibid, page 31

"Proof of [Governor Romney's] inability": millercenter.org/president/speeches/.../403

"To be turned to the great and urgent": Ibid

Johnson established advisory panel: *New York Times*, July 29, 1967, page 1

198 Johnson poses three questions: Ibid

King: "the language of the unheard": Dr. Martin Luther King Jr.'s Presentation, January 11, 1964, Ohio Northern University, Ada, Ohio, University Archives, located in Heterick Library, http://www.onu.edu/node/28509]

King: "America" has failed to hear": Ibid, page 4

King quoting Lowell: "Truth forever on the scaffold": Ibid, page 6

"I would say that while": *New York Times*, December 19, 1967, page 37

"To recommend measures that it deems": Ibid

199 "Our nation is moving": Kerner, page 1

"The primary cause of last summer's riots:" *New York Times*, February 25, 1968, page 1

"What white Americans have never": Kerner, page 2

200 Gallup Poll results: "Republican Research Report," Republican National Committee, October 19, 1967, page 4

Circumstance v. lack of effort: Ibid, page 16

"Protest again the unequal opportunities: Ibid, page 18

Split within Kerner commision: *New York Times*, March 3, 1968, page 1

"Began to read the full text": Ibid

"In general the commission decided": Ibid

201 Robert W. Gordon: Kabaservice, page 233

McCulloch: "in a month or in five years:" *Cincinnati Enquirer*, April 3, 1968, page 1

"There is a notorious lack": Ibid

"There is white racism to some extent": Ibid

"In his rush to sell": Mackenzie and Weisbrot, page 328

"Police forces routinely harass citizens": McCulloch Paper, Ohio Congressional Archive. Apparently unpublished/untitled/undated 14-page document, Box 6; folder: Legislative: Bills, Crime, Advisory Commission on Civil Disorders (Kerner Commission), 1967-1968, page 1

"Mass joblessness": Ibid

202 "Inadequate municipal services": Ibid

"The continued willingness": Ibid, page 5

"Let us admit": Ibid, page 6

"What is often overlooked: Ibid, page 10

"It is a paradox that this problem": Ibid, page 12

"Only the determined": Ibid, page 16

203 Johnson 1968 State of the Union: Bonasista, page 77

King speech: "A Time to Break Silence": en.wikipedia.org/..../ Beyond_Vietnam:
_A_Time_To_Break_Silence

Ervin motion, tabled: Watson, page 689

Brooke/Mondale attach open housing provision: Watson, page 690

204 Comment on cloture attempt: Dubofsky, "Fair Housing: A Legislative History and
Perspective," *Washburn Law Journal*, 1969, page 155

Dirksen in minority within party: Watson, page 691

"It will be an exercise in futility": quoted in Debofsky, op cit, page 157

McCulloch: "fervently hope": *Congressional Record*, February 28, 1968, page 4411

Senate passes bill, 71-20: Dubofsky, op cit, page 159

205 Johnson announces withdrawal: Watson, page 698

Dr. King assassinated: Ibid

McCulloch and others urge adoption: *New York Times*, April 6, 1968, page 1

Nixon questioned value of open housing: Kotlowski, page 46

206 Ashbrook: "the Reichstag-type": Pohlmann and Whisenhunt, page 264

"The whole concept of freedom": Ibid

"I have more Negro friends": Ibid

Anderson: "It is unfortunate that": *Congressional Record*, April 10, 1968, page 9557

"That man's not my daddy": Kabaservice, page 235

McCulloch: Discrimination prevents access": *Congressional Record*, April 10, page
9558

McCulloch: "Man can be imprisoned": Ibid

207 McCulloch: If the prisoner were given": Ibid

Schwengel tribute to McCulloch: *Congressional Record*, April 10, 1966, page 9592

"Often marble monments are built": Ibid

Open Housing bill passes House: *New York Times*, April 11, 1968, page 1

208 "Although the law prohibited": Pohlmann & Whisenhunt, page 264

"Individuals had to file suit": Ibid

Chapter 20: Electoral College

210 "It was the first time I ever": Interview, David Broder, April 27, 2009

"Not only wrong, it was hopeless": Interview, Thomas Pew, September 29, 2012

"A total lie": Ibid

Pew's encounter with McCulloch: Ibid

211 State election survey: New York Times, October 6, 1968, page 1

Ohio and Missouri vote: David Leip's Atlas of U.S. Presidential Elections,
www.uselectionatlas.org]

McCulloch on priority of Electoral College reform: Correspondence from William
McCulloch to Bryce Harlow, December 17, 1968; McCulloch Papers, Ohio
Congressional Archives, Series I: Personel/Political, Box 5; folder 47

Celler: "Bore the burden": Opening Remarks of Emanuel Celler at the Electoral
College

Reform Hearings, February 5, 1969. McCulloch Papers, Ohio Congressional
Archives: Series II: Legislative – Bills, Electoral College Reform, Box 6

"Vacancy of uncertain duration": Ibid

212 Celler describes alternatives and poses questions: Ibid

"I have not yet determined": Ibid

213 McCulloch's "seven failings": *Congressional Record,* February 6, 1969, page 3030-3031

Nixon: "I have not abandoned": February 24, 1969 McCulloch Papers, Ohio Congressional Archives: Series II: Legislative – Bills, Electoral College Reform, Box 6

"Could win the required approval": Ibid

"Clarify the situation presented": Ibid

"The President and Vice President": Statement by George Meany, March 20, 1969. McCulloch Papers, Ohio Congressional Archives, Series II: Legislative – Bills, Electoral College Reform, Box 6

"The President and the Vice President": *New York Times,* April 18, 1969, page 1

McCulloch "is expected to prove instrumental": Ibid

214 "I have never discussed": *New York Times,* April 23, 1969

"Instrumental in swinging GOP support": Washington Post, April 30, 1969, page A1

Judiciary approves direct vote: *New York Times,* April 30, 1969, page 1

"Eliminated both of the competing": McCulloch's statement, July 15, 1969

"Molded by the principles": Ibid

"'Hopeful' a way can be found": *Washington Post,* April 30, 1969, A1

215 Broder column: "Political Image Is Deceiving": May 6, 1969, A19

McCulloch receives degree: *Congressional Record,* June 16, 1969, page 15823

Men walk on moon: New York Times, July 21, 1969, page 1

Griffin survey: *Congressional Record,* September 3, 1969, page S9452

"First time since 1826": *New York Times,* September 11, 1969, page 1

"Barbarous, unsporting, dangerous": Ibid

"The only realistic chance": Ibid

216 "I answer those questions in the affirmative": Ibid, page 2

"The winner should be the loser": Ibid

"Anachronistic, undemocratic and mischievous": Ibid

Poff: modified district plan: *Congressional Record,* September 17, page 25819

Lennon: three public desires: Ibid, page 25820

Dennis: "We have taken a long step": Ibid

217 McCulloch: "The proponents of the district plan": Ibid, page 25821

McCulloch: "To me federalism is a form": Ibid

Celler: "Provides that the individual voter": Ibid

Poff: "Race to the bottom": Ibid, 25831

McGregor: "Less a compromise between": Ibid

Coughlin offers runoff amendment: *Congressional Record,* September 18, 1969, pages 25982

Waggonner: "Mr Kennedy, in response": Ibid, page 25982

Kennedy, quoted: "The small states": Ibid

218 House approves direct vote amendment: IIbid, page 26008

Albert: "It was the members": Ibid

McCulloch: "I agree with the President": *Congressional Record,* September 30, 1969, page 27668

Efforts to end filibuster fail: Longley and Braun, page 171-172
219 "Loved a good fire": Communication, Elizabeth Carver, February 18, 2014

Chapter Twenty-One: Voting Rights Sustained

220 "When I voted for the Voting Rights Act": McCulloch press release, January 30, 1969, page 1. McCulloch Papers, Ohio Congressional Archive, Series 3: Media Relations, Box 8

Description of voting law obstacles: Parker, page 3

221 Examples of constitutional exceptions in Mississippi: Parker, page 57-58

"With the overy legal barrier": Parker, page 7

McCulloch: "Black power is voting power": McCulloch press release, January 30, 1969, page 4. McCulloch Papers, Ohio Congressional Archive, Series 3: Media Relations, Box 8

"Created an island of provinces": Lawson, page 136

222 McCulloch: "saw no reason to budge": *Washington Post,* June 20, 1969, A6

Mitchell: "Voting rights is not a regional": Lawson, page 136

"To encourage our Negro citizens": Ibid

"Triggering" and "pre-clearance":

"A generally chilly reception": *New York Times,* June 27, 1969, page 1

Mitchell: "I cannot support": Ibid

"A classic examle of the artless compromise": Kotlowski, page 81

Civil Rights Commission position on literacy tests: Ibid, page 84-85

223 Hesburgh: "an open invitation to those States": Letter from Father Theodore Hesburgh to Attorney General John Mitchell, June 28, 1969. McCulloch Papers, Ohio Congressional Archives, Series 2: Legislative. Box 7; folder 11

Mitchell: "I am not deceived": Lawson, page 138

Celler: "Along the street of by and by": *New York Times,* June 27, 1969, page 1

"On Voting Rights renewal": Interview, Franklin Polk, December 20, 2012

"Ran into such uniform and intense": *New York Times,* July 1, 1969, page 1

224 "Napoleon had his Waterloo": *Detroit Free Press,* July 2, 1969: McCulloch Papers, Ohio Congressional Archives, Series 3: Box 11; folder 14

Ohio Congressional Archive, Series 2: Legislative. Box 7; folder 14

"Fell on Mitchell as though" through "That's not the way to promote law": Ibid

McCulloch backs pre-clearance: *Congressional Record,* December 11, 1969, page 38486

225 Poff: "Virginians are proud": Ibid, page 38490

Broyhill: "Perfect example of a practice": Ibid, page 38495

"Force federal registrars onto southern states": Ibid

Eckhardt: "Southern with respect to geography": Ibid, page 38496

"Is that it too frequently shoots": Ibid

"The wolf is caught, flayed,": Ibid, pages 38497

Wiggins: "Does not treat the rest of the nation": Ibid, page 38501

Chisholm: "In many instances": Ibid, page 38503

Hesburgh quoted: "I think I can say": Ibid, page 39526

226 "We cannot retreat on this front": Ibid

"The administration applied": *New York Times,* December 11, 1969, page 1

"The issue is still in doubt": *Washington Post,* December 11, 1969, page A1

House votes 208 to 203 for administration bill: 1969 CQ [Congressional Quarterly] Almanac, "Key Votes," pages 104-105

Alsop: "For altering the rather nakedly": *Washington Post,* December 15, 1969, page A21

Effort to table Scott-Hart fails: Lawson, page 149

Scott-Hart passes Senate: Kotlowski, page 88

McClory: "restored the measure": *Congressional Record,* March 16, 1970, page 7417

McCulloch: "If H.R. 914 is not adopted": *Congressional Record,* June 17, 1970, pages 20162-20163

Anderson: "The heart of the matter": Ibid, page 20163

Conyers: "All black Americans": Ibid

Celler quotes Ibsen: "I believe that man": Ibid

McCulloch version passes procedural test: Lawson, page 154

McCulloch version receives final passage: Ibid

Nixon signing statement: Lawson, page 155

Chapter Twenty-two: Owes You His Judgement

229 "He was totally outside": Interview, Andrew Glass, December 18, 2012

"Certainly, Gentlemen, it ought": Bolling, 46

230 Celler's committee took no action: Congressional Research Service Report, "The Proposed Equal Rights Amendment: Contemporary Ratification Issues," by Thomas H. Neale, Specialist in American National Government, May 9, 2013, page 6

Griffin Discharge Petition succeeds: Neale, op cit, page 6

Celler attempted to head off hearings: Ibid

McCulloch: "adequate hearings and debate": *Congressional Record,* August 10, 1970, page 28006

"Never since I have been a member of Congress": Ibid

Celler: "Which could be abrogated for good or ill": Ibid, page 28000

231 Celler: "So far as we can ascertain": Ibid

House approves proposed ERA: Ibid, page 28011

Celler/McCulloch letter of October 9, 1971: McCulloch Papers, Ohio Congressional Archives, Series 2: Legislative: Box 8; folder 17

McCulloch: "Race is not the only": McCulloch floor statement of October 12, 1971. McCulloch Papers, Ohio Congressional Archives, Series 2: Legislative. Box 8; folder 17

House passes ERA: *New York Times,* October 13, 1971, page 1

232 Celler fails of renomination: Peter Samson [Celler researcher], November 15, 2013

"God bless the United States": *Congressional Record,* June 26, 1963, page 11755

233 "Dear Friend: Thanks much": McCulloch Papers, Ohio Congressional Archive, Series 2: Legislative Box 9, folder 14

McCulloch provides history on school prayer: *Congressional Record,* November 8, 1971, page 10596

McCulloch: "Not good law. It is not good theology": Ibid

"The first amendment needs no amendment": Ibid

School prayer amendment defeated: *Washington Post,* November 9, 1971, Page A1

234 McCulloch votes to table: 1968 CQ [Congressional Quarterly] Almanac, Key Votes, pages 4-5

Supreme Court ruling in Charlotte-Mecklenburg: en.wikipedia.org/wiki/Desegre-

gation_Busing
235 Gallup poll on unpopularity: Ibid
   RAND Corporation study: Ibid
   Lent: "No public school student shall": library.cqpress.com/cqalmanac/document.
      phd?id=cqal72-1251640
   Celler: "The Constitution is a group of principles": Celler Papers, Library of Con-
      gress, Box 351: National Broadcasting Company [appearance on February 27,
      1972]
   "Although a large number of members": Gary Orfield, "Congress, the Press and
      Anti-Busing Legislation, 1966-1974," Journal of Law and Education, Volume 4,
      No. 1, page 81. Publishd by the Louis D. Brandeis School of Law, University of
      Louisville
236 Minshall: "I have voted for": March 6, 1972 statement to Judiciary Committee.
      McCulloch Papers, Ohio Congressional Archives, Series 2: Legislative. Box 9;
      folder 23
   Dingell: "Time unnecessarily spent": March 6, 1972 statement; Ibid
   McCulloch: "It is with deepest regret": McCulloch floor statement, April 12, 1972.
      McCulloch Papers, Ohio Congressional Archives, Series 2: Legislative. Box 9;
      folder 27
   McCulloch: "The moral and constitutional rights": Ibid
   McCulloch: "Some prominent politicians": Ibid
   McCulloch: "Wasn't it only yesterday": Ibid
   "Forcing a gratuitous constitutional": *Dayton Daily News*, April 14, 1972, page 34
   "Nixon probably doesn't much care": Ibid
237 Colmer: "Chickens have come home": *Washington Evening Star*, May 18, 1972
   "Colmer gave Nixon major credit": Ibid
   "When they lost the procedural": Ibid
   McCulloch: "The flood tide of civil rights": Ibid
   Orfield: "Gave the conservatives": op cit
   Nixon: "We asked the Congress" et al: President Nixon's signing statement, June
      23, 1972. www.presidency.ucsd.edu/wis/?/pid=3473
238 "You choose a member indeed": Bolling, page 25

Chapter Twenty-three: Retirement and Death
239 McCullochs' new residence: site visit by author
   CIA director's residence: Interview, Nancy McCulloch, February 10, 2014
   McCulloch returns to hospital: *Washington Post*, January 21, 1971, page A2
   "I have spent a great deal": Mabel McCulloch letter, January 6, 1971
   McCulloch misses votes: 1971 Congressional Quarterly "Key Votes"
   "Mr. McCulloch underwent surgery": Letter from Vera Page to Mike Wines, July
      19, 1971. McCulloch Papers, Ohio Congressional Archives, Series 3: Media
      Relations. Box 11; folder 17
   "After his fall": Interview, Thomas Mooney, January 15, 2013
   "Mabel said it was time": Ibid
   "Quiet, direct, hardworking": *Washingon Post*, June 11, 1971, page A24
   "You made a personal commitment": Letter to McCulloch from Jacqueline Ken-
      nedy Onassis, June 24, 1971. Letter courtesy of the McCulloch family.

McCulloch disavows retirement: Press Release, Congressman McCulloch's office, September 28, 1971. McCulloch Papers, Ohio Congressional Archives, Series 3: Media Relations. Box 11; folder 30

"I have said heretofore": *Piqua Daily Call,* October 27, 1971, page 1

"At the end of this year": Press release, Congressman McCulloch's Office, January 7, 1972. McCulloch Papers, Ohio Congressional Archives, Series 3: Media Relations. Box 11; folder 31

"I remember going to the bank": Communication from Elizabeth Carver, February 18, 2014

"I remember my interview with him": Communication from Rear-Admiral James P. Wisecup, February 17, 2014

Tribute at Allen County Fairgrounds: *Sidney Daily News,* October 6, 1971, page 1

"To the growing number of Americans": *Congressional Record,* October 12, 1972

"If you expect to measure": *Dayton Daily News,* October 20, 1948, page 1

"I let my daughters choose": *Piqua Daily Call,* December 9, 1972, pages 4-5

Yale conference: Letter to McCulloch from Jerry Katzman, executive director, Yale Legislative Services, March 8, 1973

"I remember he looked frail": Communication from Elizabeth Carver, February 18, 2014

Washington Post obituary: *Washington Post,* February 23, 1980, page C8

Kimball and Lindsay attend: Interview, Robert Kimball, February 15, 2014

Metz attends: Interview, Joseph Metz, February 15, 2014

"I will never forget": Communication from Sarah [Carver] Lim, February 18, 2014

"After viewing the flag-draped coffin": Clarence Mitchell, *Baltimore Sun,* March 2, 1980

"It was during the long sessions": Ibid

"We are a nation of many people and many views": McCulloch floor statement, October 12, 1971. McCulloch Papers, Ohio Congressional Archives, Series 2: Legislative. Box 8; folder 17

Chapter Twenty-four: Delta Queen

246 Description of Delta Queen and history: en.wikipedia.org/wiki/Delta_Queen
S. S. Yarmouth sinking: *Congressional Record,* December 15, 1970, page 41512

247 "The law that would": *Congressional Record,* April 23, 1970, page 12881
Contribution solicited: Interview, Thomas Mooney, January 15, 2013
"Don't you are suggest that to anyone": Ibid
Nixon receives 1,500 letters: *Congressional Record,* April 23, 1970, page 12881
"I don't want that ship": McCulloch Papers, Ohio Congressional Archives: Series 2: Legislative, Bills – Delta Queen Exemptions, Box 6
"The quality of American life": *Congressional Record,* November 23, 1970, page 38466

248 Everyone except those in on the secret": *Kansan City* [Kansas] *Kansan,* November 29, 1970. McCulloch Papers, Ohio Congressional Archives: Series 3: Media Relations, Box 17; folder 1 [Scrapbook of clippings]
Conference committee established: *Winona* [Minnesota] *Daily News,* December 16, 1970, page 13A
"Permitting the DELTA QUEEN": McCulloch statement to the House on Conference Report 91-1769, page 2. McCulloch Papers, Ohio Congressional Archives:

Series 2: Legislative, Box 8; folder 4

Celler: "Life without a bit of romance": *Congressional Record,* December 15, 1970, page 41512

249 Garmatz: "Is a firetrap": Ibid

Garmatz: "I hope the Delta Queen": Ibid

"The paragraph begun by that": *Louisville Times,* December 3. 1970. McCulloch Papers, Ohio Congressional Archives: Series 3: Media Relations, Box 17; folder 1 [Scrapbook of clippings]

House votes extension: *Congressional Record,* December 15, 1970, page 41522

McCulloch quoting Twain: *Congressional Record,* April 23, 1970, page 12881

Bibliography

BOOKS

Anderson, Elijah, and Douglas S. Massey, editors. *Problem of the Century: Racial Stratification in the United States.* Russell Sage Foundation, 2001.

Anderson, J. W. *Eisenhauerm Brownell, and the Congress: The Tangled Origins of the Civil Rights Bill of 1956-1957.* University of Alabama Press, 1964.

Bayh, Birch. *One Heartbeat Away: Presidential Disability and Succession.* Bobbs-Merrill Company, 1968.

Berman, David M. *A Bill Becomes a Law: The Civil Rights Act of 1960.* The Macmillan Company, 1962.

Bernstein, Mark. *John J. Gilligan: The Politics of Principle.* Kent State University Press, 2013.

Bonastia, Christopher. Knocking on the Door: Federal Government Attempt to Desegregate the Suburbs. Princeton University Press, 2006.

Bolling, Richard. *House Out of Order.* E. P. Duttton, 1965

Branch, Taylor. *Parting the Waters: America in the King Years, 1954-1963.* Simon & Schuster, 1988.

Caro, Robert A. *The Years of Lyndon Johnson: Maaster of the Senate.* Alfred Knopf, 2002.

_____. *The Years of Lyndon Johnson: Passage of Power.* Alfred Knopf, 2013.

Cash, W. J. *The Mind of the South.* Vintage, 1941.

Celler, Emanuel. *Your Never Leave Brooklyn: The Autobiography of Emanuel Celler.* John Day Company, 1953.

Clayton, Andrew R. L. Ohio: The History of a People. Ohio State University Press, 2002.

Davies, Richard O. *Ddfender of the Old Guard: John Bricker and American Politics.* Ohio State University Press, 1993.

Davis, T. Frederick *History of Jacksonville, Florida, and Vicinity.* Reprinted San Marco Bookstore, Jacksonville, 1990.

Fenton, John H. *Midwest Politics.* Uiversity of Massachusetts Press, 1966.

Fine, Sidney. *Violence in the Model City: The Cavanagh Administration, Race Relations, and the Detroit Riot of 1967.* Michigan State University Press, 2007.

Gold, David M. *Democracy in Session: A History of the Ohio General Assembly.* Ohio University Press, 2009.

Goldman, Eric F. *The Tragedy of Lyndon Johnson.* Alfred A. Knopf, 1969

Halberstam, David. *The Fiftoes.* Villard Books, 1993.

Hill, Leonard U. *A History of Our Church: Piqua Presbyterian Church.* Magee Brothers, 1962.

Hurston, Zora Neale. *Their Eyes Were Watching God.* Harper Perennial, 2006.

Johnson, Howard Wesley. *Holding the Center: Memoir of a life in Higher Education.* MIT Press, 1999.

Johnson, James Weldon. *The Autobiography of an Ex-Colored Man.* From: *Three Negro Classic.* Avon Books, 1965.

Kabaservice, Geoffrey. *Rule and Run: The Downfall of Moderation and the Destruction of the Republican Party, from Eisenhower to the Tea Party.* Oxford University Press, 2012.

Kaplan, Fred. *1959: The Year Everything Changed.* John Wiley & Sons, 200

Katzenbach, Nicholas deB. *Some of It Was Fun: Working With RFK and LBJ.* Norton, 2008.

King, Gilbert. *Devil in the Grove: Thurgood Marshall, the Groveland Boys, and the Dawn of a New America.* Harper, 2012.

Knepper, George. *Ohio and Its People.* Kent State University Press, 2003.

Kotlowski, Dean J. *Nixon's Civil Rights: Politics, Principle, and Policy.* Harvard University Press, 2001.

Laird, Melvin, editor. *Republican Papers.* Anchor Books, 1968. [Contains William McCulloch essay: *"Man Was Born to be Free."*]

Lamis, Alexander P. and Brian Usher. *Ohio Politics.* Kent State University Press, 2007.

Lawson, Steven F. *In Pursuit of Power: Southern Blacks and Electoral Politics, 1965–1982.* Columbia University Press.

Lehman, James O., and Steven M. Nolt. *Mennonites, Amish, and the American Civil War.* Johns Hopkins Press, 2007.

Longley, Lawrence D., and Alan G. Braun. *The Politics of Elecotral College Reform.* Yale University Press, 1972.

Mackenzie, G. Calvin, and Robert Weisbrot. *The Libeeral Hour: Washington and the Politics of Change in the 1960s.* Penguin Press, 2008.

Myrdal, Gunnar. *An American Dilemma: The Negro Problem And Modern Democracy.* Harper & Brothers, 1944.

Notestein, Lucy Lilian. *Wooster of the Middle West.* Kent State University Press, date?

Oda, James. *A History of Piqua: The Impact of Transportation.* Flesh Public Library [Piqua, Ohio] 1998.

_____. *Piqua Industry: 1800–1900.* Piqua Historical Society, 1985.

Parker, Frank R. *Black Vutes Count: Political Empowerment in Mississippi after 1965.* The University of North Carlina Press, 1990.

Peirce, Neal R. *The Megastates of America.* W.W. Norton, 1972.

_____ and Lawrence D. Longley. *The People's President: The Electoral College in American History and the Direct Vote Alternatives.* Yale University Press, 1981.

Pohlmann, Marcus D., and Linda Vallar Whistenhunt. *Student's Guide to Landmark Congressional Laws on Civil Rights.* Greenwood Press, 2002.

Ross, Ishbel. *An American Family: The Tafts: 1678–1964.* World Publishing Company, 1964.

Russell, Francis. *The Shadow of Blooming Grove.* McGraw Hill, 1968.

Sokol, Jason. *There Goes My Everything: White Southerners in the Age of Civil Rights, 1945–1975.* Vintage Books, 2007.

Stallman, David A. *Holmesville, Ohio—Our Home Town.* Carlisle Printing, 2001.

Stern, Mark. *Calculating Visions: Kennedy, Johnson and Civil Rights.* Rutgers Univiersity Press, 1992

Watson, Denton L. *Lion in the Lobby.* William Moore & Company, 1990.

Whalen, Charles and Barbara. *The Longest Debate: A Legislative History of the 1964 Civil Rights Act.* Seven Locks Press, 1985.

Wunderlin, Clarence E. *Robert A. Taft: Ideas, Tradition, and Party in U.S. Foreign Policy.* Rowman & Littlefield, 2005

Ziemke, Earl F. *ARMY HISTORICAL SERIES: The U.S. Army in the Occupation of Germany 1944–1946.* Center of Military History, United States Army, 1990.

REPORTS AND PROCEEDINGS

The Kerner Report: 1968 Report of the National Commission on Civil Disorders. Pantheon Books, 1968.

Congressional Record, 1947–1972

[Ohio] *House Journal,* 1933–1943

Index